Hilary Johnson, Lawrence Nigay and
Chris Roast (Eds)

People and Computers XIII

Proceedings of HCI '98

Published in collaboration
with the British Computer Society

 Springer

Hilary Johnson, BSc, PhD
Queen Mary and Westfield College, Mile End Road, London, E1 4NS

Laurence Nigay, PhD
CLIPS-IMAG, Bat. B Bureau 204, BP 53-38-41 Grenoble cedex 9, France

Christopher Roast, BSc, MA, PhD
School of Computing and Management Services,
Shefffield Hallam University, Sheffield, S1 1WB

ISBN 3-540-76261-2 Springer-Verlag Berlin Heidelberg New York

British Library Cataloguing in Publication Data
A catalogue record for this book is available from the British Library

© Springer-Verlag London Limited 1998
Printed in Great Britain

Typeset by *Winder.&*
Printed and bound at the Athenæum Press Ltd., Gateshead, Tyne and Wear
34/3830-543210 Printed on acid-free paper

People and Computers XIII

Springer

London
Berlin
Heidelberg
New York
Barcelona
Budapest
Hong Kong
Milan
Paris
Santa Clara
Singapore
Tokyo

Contents

Preface: Diversity of Avenues

These proceedings contain the refereed full technical papers presented at the HCI'98 conference. HCI is the annual conference of the British HCI Group and in 1998 was hosted by Sheffield Hallam University.

1 Paper Selection

The papers selected for presentation at the conference and published here constitute a quarter of those submitted and reviewed by an international panel of reviewers, overseen by the technical chairs. The accepted papers come from many different countries, with half of the papers from European countries and half from USA, Japan, Australia and New Zealand, reflecting the truly international nature of the conference.

This volume shows the diversity of subject matter and concerns that are familiar to the conference. In particular, the work reported reflects a variety of research backgrounds including psychology, ergonomics, computer science and design. Additionally, we are pleased to see a significant amount of HCI research being conducted by practitioners within industrial settings.

2 Paper Content

This collection illustrates both the exciting and developing nature of the field of HCI. The diversity of studies in HCI today is characteristic of a subject area which is rapidly growing and broadening both in terms of theoretical underpinning, process and product. The holistic perspective, which is often necessary in effective user interface design, requires this diversity.

Progress in the understanding of underlying concepts has supported developments in: the scope of methods, techniques and tools appropriate for the improved design and usability of interactive systems; the technologies now being employed by designers and users; and the experience of applying the established design and evaluation techniques within context.

3   Proceedings Structure

The papers are categorized into four sections:

1. Usability testing: methods and empirical studies.

2. Design: process, task analysis, requirements and specification.

3. Visual interfaces.

4. Innovative user interfaces: multimedia and multi-modal user interfaces, wearable computing, virtual reality.

The first section examines usability and empirical studies. These crucial topics have been the focus of attention for many years. The papers here include the critical assessment of usability criteria and empirical studies. The examination of usability illustrates the potential value of linking differing HCI perspectives. The second section concerns design and includes the process of modelling, representing and re-using user requirements. In addition, the appropriateness of task and requirements representations are assessed. The two last sections address the design of innovative interaction devices and techniques, including visualization techniques, multi-modal interaction techniques and wearable computing. The advances reported in these two sections reveal a variety of challenges for software engineering and the need to develop HCI theories, techniques and tools for the future.

4   Enjoy the Book

The book provides a valuable source of information for researchers and practitioners in HCI. The work reported indicates the directions in which HCI as a field is currently progressing. In doing so it serves a number of purposes assisting the development process and underpinning as well as broadening the skills on which effective interface design depends.

The editors are indebted to many individuals for the quality of this year's conference and associated proceedings. Specifically we would like to acknowledge the considerable efforts of the conference chair and committee. In addition, our thanks go to the authors and review panel for ensuring the high quality of accepted papers.

Chris Roast
Hilary Johnson
Laurence Nigay

June 1998

The Conference Committee

Conference Chair	Bob Steele (*Sheffield Hallam University, UK*)
Technical Programme	Chris Roast (*Sheffield Hallam University, UK*)
	Laurence Nigay (*CLIPS-IMAG of Grenoble, France*)
	Hilary Johnson (*QMW, University of London, UK*)
Demonstrations	Andrew Stratton (*Stratton & English Software Ltd, UK*)
	Atif Waraich (*Liverpool Hope University College, UK*)
Doctoral Consortium	Stephen Brewster (*University of Glasgow, UK*)
Industry Day	Tony Rose (*Canon Research Centre, UK*)
	Peter Windsor (*Usability Ltd, UK*)
Organizational Overviews	Nick Rousseau (*Employment Service, UK*)
Panels	Andrew Monk (*University of York, UK*)
Posters	Julie Wilkinson (*Sheffield Hallam University, UK*)
Short Papers	Jon May (*University of Sheffield, UK*)
	Jawed Siddiqi (*Sheffield Hallam University, UK*)
Tutorials	Sandra Foubister (*Napier University, UK*)
Videos	Chuck Elliot (*Sheffield Hallam University, UK*)
Exhibition	Richard Wilson (*University of Glasgow, UK*)
Local Coordinator	Grace Roberts (*Sheffield Hallam University, UK*)
Proceedings	Russel Winder (*King's College London, UK*)
Publicity	Andy Dearden (*University of York, UK*)
Website	Jill Laing (*Sheffield Hallam University, UK*)
Site Visits	David Jennings (*David Jennings Associates, UK*)
Social Programme	Sue Morton (*Sheffield Hallam University, UK*)
	Thomas Green (*University of Leeds, UK*)
Technical Coordinator	Chuck Elliot (*Sheffield Hallam University, UK*)
Treasurer	Pauline Smith (*Nottingham Trent University, UK*)
BCS-HCI Liaison	Gilbert Cockton (*Sunderland University, UK*)
European Liaison	Philippe Palanque (*University of Toulouse, France*)
Pacific Basin Liaison	Richard Thomas (*University of Western Australia, Australia*)
Publisher Liaison	Dan Diaper (*Bournemouth University, UK*)
USA Liaison	Jenny Preece (*Maryland Baltimore, USA*)

The Reviewers

G Al-Qaimari (*Royal Melbourne Institute of Technology, Australia*)
R Anderson (*Rank Xerox Research Laboratory, UK*)
T J Anderson (*University of Ulster, UK*)
A K Attipoe (*EURISCO, France*)
S Balbo (*CSIRO/MIS, Australia*)
D Benyon (*Napier University, UK*)
N Bevan (*National Physical Laboratory, UK*)
A Blandford (*Middlesex University, UK*)
S Brewster (*University of Glasgow, UK*)
J-M Burkhardt (*Ergonomic Psychology Group, INRIA, France*)
L Calvi (*University of Antwerp, Belgium*)
C Chen (*Brunel University, UK*)
A Crerar (*Napier University, UK*)
M Czerwinski (*Microsoft Corporation, USA*)
O Daly-Jones (*National Physical Laboratory, UK*)
D Day (*Towson University, USA*)
A Dearden (*University of York, UK*)
M Dooner (*University of Hull, UK*)
C Dormann (*Technical University of Denmark, Denmark*)
R Fields (*University of York, UK*)
J Finlay (*University of Huddersfield, UK*)
I Franklin (*Occupational Psychology Division, Employment Service, UK*)
P Gray (*University of Glasgow, UK*)
S Greenwood (*Oxford Brookes University, UK*)
D Haw (*Harlequin Ltd, UK*)
H-J Hoffmann (*Darmstadt University of Technology, Germany*)
S Howard (*Swinburne University of Technology, Australia*)
I Ismail (*University College London, UK*)
L Johnston (*University of Melbourne, Australia*)
M Jones (*Middlesex University, UK*)
A Jorgensen (*Copenhagen University, Denmark*)
C Kelly (*Defense Research Agency, UK*)
Kinshuk (*German National Research Centre for Information
        Technology, Germany*)
M A R Kirby (*University of Huddersfield, UK*)
D Lavery (*University of Glasgow, UK*)
D Bonyuet Lee (*Polytechnical University of Catalonia, Venezuela*)
Y K Leung (*Swinburne University of Technology, Australia*)
A Lewis (*BT Laboratories, UK*)
N Lompre (*National Centre for Scientific Research, France*)
P Luff (*King's College, UK*)
R Macredie (*Brunel University, UK*)
J May (*University of Sheffield, UK*)
A Monk (*University of York, UK*)
R Moyse (*Lucent Technologies, UK*)
C Nadja (*University of Bari, Italy*)
J L Nealon (*Oxford Brookes University, UK*)
D G Novick (*EURISCO, France*)

K O'Hara (*Rank Xerox Research Centre, UK*)
R Oppermann (*GMD.FIT, Germany*)
P Palanque (*LIS University Toulouse 1, France*)
C Parker (*Husat Research Institute, UK*)
U Patel (*City University, UK*)
N Prekas (*UMIST, UK*)
D Ramduny (*Staffordshire University, UK*)
N Rousseau (*Occupational Psychology Division, Employment Service, UK*)
R Ruocco (*Telematics Support Centre, UK*)
J Seton (*BT Laboratories, UK*)
B Shackel (*Loughborough University, UK*)
C Siemieniuch (*Husat Research Institute, UK*)
M Smyth (*Napier University, UK*)
R H Y So (*Hong Kong University of Science and Technology, Hong Kong*)
K Stockton (*University of Teesside, UK*)
A Stork (*University College London, UK*)
R Thomas (*The University of Western Australia, Australia*)
M Treglown (*University of Bristol, UK*)
L Tweedie (*Imperial College, UK*)
L Uden (*Staffordshire University, UK*)
D Usher (*InterAction of Bath Ltd, UK*)
J van de Ven (*The Netherlands*)
D Van Laar (*University of Portsmouth, UK*)
J Vanderdonckt (*Institut d'Informatique, Belgium*)
W Visser (*INRIA, France*)
C Warren (*British Aerospace Plc, UK*)
J Wilkinson (*Sheffield Hallam University, UK*)
M Wilson (*Rutherford Appleton Laboratory, UK*)
M Zajicek (*Oxford Brookes University, UK*)
L Zhengjie (*Dalian Maritime University, P. R. China*)

Usability Testing: Methods and Empirical Studies

Usable Software and Its Attributes: A Synthesis of Software Quality, European Community Law and Human–Computer Interaction

Ronan Fitzpatrick & Catherine Higgins

Department of Mathematics, Statistics and Computer Science, Dublin Institute of Technology, Kevin Street, Dublin 8, Ireland.

Tel: *+353 1 4024610, +353 1 4024834*

Fax: *+353 1 4024994*

EMail: *{rfitzpatrick, chiggins}@maths.kst.dit.ie*

Strategic managers and IS professionals who are responsible for specifying, acquiring and producing quality software products are not supported by the endless flow of new international standards, legislation and user requirements. In order to clarify the current situation for everybody concerned with software quality, and especially those interested in usability, there is a need for a new review and evaluation of the various strands that contribute to software quality. By way of review this paper recalls the original software quality factors which were defined twenty years ago by McCall et al. (1977) and presents a methodical analysis and synthesis of three modern strands which influence these factors. The three strands relate to software quality, statutory obligations and human–computer interaction. All three strands rely on well respected sources which include the European Council Directive on minimum safety and health requirements for work with display screen equipment (Council Directive, 1990), ISO 9241-10 (ISO, 1993) and ISO 9000-3 (ISO, 1997). This synthesis produces a new set of quality factors, and the paper provides a new perspective of software usability by showing that the external quality factors in this new set are the usability attributes of a software product. New attributes like *suitability, adaptability, functionality, installability* and *safety* are identified and other attributes like *usability* and *integrity* are clarified within the three strands.

Keywords: software quality, European law, international standards, quality factors, usability, usability models, usability attributes.

1 Introduction

Software usability is described in terms of attributes of a software product, the measures that should be measured for those attributes, and metrics (numbers) which are the results of measurement (Holcomb & Tharp, 1991; ISO, 1991b; Preece et al., 1994; ISO, 1995). So, in order to measure usability it is necessary to know what attributes must be measured, the type of measures that must be considered and what metrics to expect. The aim of this paper is to identify the attributes which should be measured. The paper begins with a review of formal definitions associated with software usability (Ravden & Johnson, 1989; ISO, 1995; McCall et al., 1977). The reason for this review is to show how computer scientists' views of usability has changed over the past twenty years and to show that there are problems associated with these definitions. The paper continues with an examination of three strands which identify the set of attributes which are used to measure software usability. The strands are the software quality strand, the statutory obligations strand and the human–computer interaction strand. Section 2 introduces some facets of usability and explains the motivation for the three strand approach. Section 3 reviews usability definitions and explains problems associated with them. Section 4 examines the three strands in detail and identifies the usability attributes of a software product.

2 Facets of Software Usability

Usability is a key component in the overall quality of a software product (Porteous et al., 1993) which is concerned with making the product easy to learn and [easy to] operate (McCall et al., 1977). Usability also has a legal dimension. There are legal obligations for employers to protect the health of employees who use software interfaces (Council Directive, 1990). Usability is also a key concept of human–computer interaction (HCI), where, in addition to being concerned with making systems easy to learn and easy to use (Preece et al., 1994), it is also concerned with supporting users during their interactions with computers (Shneiderman, 1992). So, usability is a desirable feature that threads its way into different facets (quality, legal and HCI) of computer software. Collectively, these three facets are of interest to quality assurance managers, system designers, system developers, end-users and to those with organizational responsibility for selecting and acquiring usable systems (Reiterer & Oppermann, 1993; Robson, 1994). In its simplest form, we would describe usability as the extent to which a computer system interface supports end-users. Because there are many facets to usability and in order to fully understand what usability is (so that it can be specified and measured), it is necessary to first establish a comprehensive set of attributes that make up usability. In this paper, usability is considered to be an all embracing description of software. So, the attributes that make up usability can also be termed as the attributes of a usable software product.

There are many different definitions and models which clarify the meaning of software usability (McCall et al., 1977; Ravden & Johnson, 1989; ISO, 1991b; Nielsen, 1993; Bevan & Macleod, 1994; ISO, 1995). Some of these, e.g. (ISO, 1991b; Nielsen, 1993) concentrate on the attributes that constitute usability while other definitions concentrate on how usability should be measured, e.g. (Bevan & Macleod, 1994; ISO, 1995). However, while these definitions support our understanding of software usability, there are problems associated with them. For example, the definitions that focus on attributes are weak in their support for measures and visa versa.

There is a natural relationship between usability and a quality software interface and it follows that an interface that has a high level of quality will have a high level of usability (Ince, 1994). Consequently, the attributes that influence usability can be viewed as being quality factors. This paper establishes the quality factors that influence usability by reviewing three strands, each of which contributes different quality factors. These strands are reviewed using a quality-focused philosophy and are called the software quality strand, the statutory obligations strand and the human–computer interaction strand.

The software quality strand reviews quality models (McCall et al., 1977; Boehm, 1978) and international standards (IEEE, 1989; ISO, 1991a; ISO, 1991b; ISO, 1997) which relate to software quality. The statutory obligations strand addresses the legislation enacted throughout the European Community (Council Directive, 1990) which requires that software should be easy to use and easy to adapt. This legislation also sets minimum requirements for the equipment that should be available to users and for the environment in which the users must work. The human–computer interaction strand examines current principles and practice in order to establish the usability requirements of end-users (Shneiderman, 1992).

The motivation for this three strand approach is the growing strategic need within business organizations for quality interfaces, which comply with current legislation and which support end-user employees (Reiterer & Oppermann, 1993; Robson, 1994). Only by combining the three strands is it possible to identify a comprehensive set of quality-focused attributes that influence usability. The presence or absence of these attributes is what is measured during usability measurement (Reiterer & Oppermann, 1993).

Before reviewing the three strands, it is first necessary to examine definitions and models of usability that are used in the software industry and in academia.

3 Definitions and Models of Usability

In this section, four definitions of usability are reviewed to show how computer scientists' views of usability have changed with advances in technology. Academic and commercial models are reviewed, and problems associated with these definitions and models are examined.

3.1 Definitions of Usability

Usability as a software quality factor was defined by McCall et al. (1977, pp.3–5) as "the effort required to learn, operate, prepare input and interpret output of a program".

To gain a proper understanding of McCall et al.'s perspective of usability in 1977, it is appropriate to recall the taxonomy of computers in those days. The environment consisted of mainframe and mini computers running major data processing applications. Staff were simply required to learn how to operate the system, input data, receive output and keep the system running. Software was developed for low specification monitors that used simple combinations of green and black text. Usability was perceived to be confined to operators and their learning process in this environment. The era of end-user computing was only beginning. More recently, Ravden & Johnson (1989, p.9) defined usability as "the extent to which an end-user is able to carry out required tasks successfully, and without difficulty, using the computer application system".

From this definition comes some idea of the complexity of usability, especially considering that there are many different:

- Profiles of end-users.

- Skills among end-users.

- Attitudes among end-users.

- Complexities of tasks.

- Measures for success.

- Interpretations of difficulty.

To these can be added the different equipment that users need and the different environments in which users can work (Council Directive, 1990). An important advance in Ravden & Johnson's (1989) definition is that they introduced an element of measure by using the expression 'the extent' in their definition.

The International Organization for Standardization (ISO) also define usability. In their standard (ISO, 1991b), usability is defined as "a set of attributes of software which bears on the effort needed for use on an individual assessment of such use by a stated or implied set of users".

This definition adds to our understanding of usability by considering a set of attributes of software. The standard names three attributes (which it calls sub-characteristics). These are learnability, understandability and operability.

The element of measure is also contained in a new international standard (ISO, 1995), which is currently under development. The standard is named "Ergonomic requirements for office work with visual display terminals (VDTs)" and consists of 17 parts. Part 11 (eleven) is specifically concerned with usability and defines it as "the extent to which a product can be used by specified users to achieve specified goals with effectiveness, efficiency and satisfaction in a specified context of use".

3.2   *Usability Models*

Nielsen (1993) explains usability as part of the wider aspect of system acceptability and suggests that usability is part of a much broader scene — see Figure 1.

Nielsen's approach focuses on social acceptability and practical acceptability. In his text, the concept of social acceptability is not developed to any great extent other

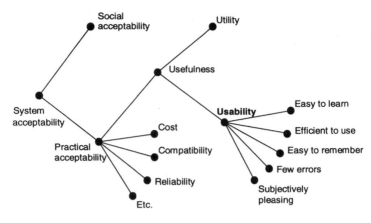

Figure 1: Nielsen's model of system acceptability.

than in the context of an example of a possible undesirable system. Systems with cultural influences or subliminal practices would be appropriate for consideration under social acceptability.

The sub-characteristics of practical acceptability of Nielsen's model are not unlike the technical or internal quality characteristics of a software product (Ghezzi et al., 1991; Ince, 1994; ISO, 1997). For example, compatibility is the same as interoperability. Perhaps, to correspond with the 'Etc.' in the model, the author intended that practical acceptability should refer to factors like efficiency, portability, testability, maintainability and reusability as these are the factors that are not mentioned elsewhere in the model. Nielsen's (1993, p.25) model sub-divides usefulness into utility and usability which are described respectively as: "the question of whether the functionality of the system in principle can do what is needed [and] the question of how well users can use that functionality". The usability dimension of the model incorporates 'easy to learn', 'efficient to use', 'easy to remember', 'fewer errors' and 'subjectively pleasing'. All of these are familiar expressions easily associated with the definitions of usability in Section 3.1. They are also similar to the external quality characteristics of a software product (Ghezzi et al., 1991; Ince, 1994; ISO, 1997). Consequently there are close connections between usability and software quality. 'Subjectively pleasing', however, is new and introduces a new view of usability where end-users' subjective evaluations of a system come into play. This approach is also considered by Kirakowski & Corbett (1993) and by Bevan & Macleod (1994).

Dr Kirakowski of the Human Factors Research Group at University College Cork has conducted extensive research in this area. His work is based on subjective user evaluations and he has developed a method for measuring software usability. This method — Software Usability Measurement Inventory (SUMI) — measures five sub-scales, i.e. efficiency, affect, helpfulness, control and learnability (Kirakowski & Corbett, 1993). The method is an attitude-measuring questionnaire that is completed by end-users.

More recently, Bevan & Macleod (1994, 136) have suggested that usability has to be viewed in different ways for different purposes, focusing on one or more of the following complementary views:

1. *The product-centred view of usability*: that the usability of a product is the attributes of the product which contribute towards the quality-of-use.

2. *The context-of-use view of usability*: that usability depends on the nature of the user, product, task and environment.

3. *The quality-of-use view of usability*: that usability is the outcome of interaction and can be measured by the effectiveness, efficiency and satisfaction with which specified users achieve specified goals in particular environments.

Another approach to understanding software usability is to consider actual practice as conducted by industrial leaders like IBM, Apple, Hewlett Packard and Microsoft. Kan (1995) reports that:

> IBM monitors the CUPRIMDSO satisfaction levels of its software products (capability [functionality], usability, performance, reliability, installability, maintainability, documentation, service and overall). Hewlett-Packard focuses on FURPS (functionality, usability, reliability, performance and serviceability).

3.3   Problems with Usability Definitions and Models

There are three problems associated with the above definitions of software usability. The first problem is that there is no consistent set of attributes of software. While ISO (1991b) and Nielsen (1993) focus on the attributes of software, their listings of the attributes are different. They are also inconsistent with commercial practice. For example, ISO (1991b) mentions usability and suggests that its sub-characteristics are learnability, understandability and operability while Nielsen (1993) considers the broader concepts of social acceptability and practical acceptability and lists, easy to learn, efficient to use, easy to remember, few errors and subjectively pleasing. Commercial organizations like IBM and Hewlett-Packard use similar listings (Kan, 1995), but, there is no consistent set. Furthermore, is it not possible to know if a composite list of these four would represents all of the attributes of a usable software product.

The second problem with usability definitions is that, while recent definitions and models concentrate on the need to measure usability and even state what the measures should be, the definitions do not support a universal set of measures. ISO (1995) and Bevan & Macleod (1994) favour effectiveness, efficiency and satisfaction as usability measures while IBM measure satisfaction only (Kan, 1995). Kirakowski's SUMI product measures efficiency, affect, helpfulness, control and learnability.

The third problem is that it is not clear whether each measure should be applied to all attributes or whether some measures only apply to a selected set.

Therefore, strategic managers who have responsibility for software products are not supported by all this confusion. What end-users want to use, and what strategic managers want to acquire are usable software products which comply with the latest legislation. Therefore, what is now required is a clear listing of the attributes of a usable software product together with the measures that should be applied to these attributes. Then, by applying the measures to the attributes it should be possible to establish a 'usability quotient' for any software product. The remainder of this paper focuses on the first of these requirements and identifies these attributes using a three strand approach.

4 Three Strands that Influence Usability

To identify the attributes of a usable software product, three specific strands are examined. The first strand is the software quality strand, which in turn identifies the statutory obligations strand, which in turn identifies the human–computer interaction strand. From these strands, software quality factors are identified and a specific set of these factors (those that directly impact on the end-user) are shown to be the usability attributes of a software product.

4.1 Software Quality Strand

The first strand to be examined is concerned with software quality. Studies in this domain began in the 1970s when desirable features for inclusion in software products were quantified by authors like McCall et al. (1977) and Boehm (1978) who both produced quality models. Later, the world-wide success of quality standards like ISO (1987), resulted in international standards for software quality (IEEE, 1989; ISO, 1991a).

4.1.1 Quality Models and Quality Factors

Software quality is defined by the Institute of Electrical and Electronics Engineers (IEEE, 1983) as "the degree to which software possesses a desired combination of attributes".

These attributes are typically referred to as quality factors or quality characteristics and models for these were suggested in the late '70s by McCall et al. (1977) and Boehm (1978). Such quality factors include software correctness, reliability, efficiency, integrity, usability, maintainability, testability, flexibility, portability, reusability and interoperability (or interface facility). For a full explanation and recent review of each of McCall et al.'s quality factors, the reader is referred to Wallmüller (1994). These factors can be conveniently categorized as external quality factors (mainly relating to HCI issues) and internal quality factors (which relate to the technical excellence of the product).

Ghezzi et al. (1991, p.18) support this view by stating that "In general, users of the software only care about the external qualities".

Because external factors affect users, we refer to these as usability factors. So, McCall et al.'s quality factors can be sub-divided into external and internal factors. A sub-division of these factors — based on Wallmüller (1994) — is set out in Table 1.

The reader's attention is drawn to the quality factor called 'usability'. McCall et al.'s definition of this factor is shown in Table 2. The focus of this paper is that the term usability is better used to describe the entire software product and that repeating the term to describe a quality factor is inappropriate. Accordingly, this quality factor

Quality Factor	Category
integrity reliability usability correctness efficiency interoperability	External quality factors (i.e. Usability factors)
maintainability testability flexibility reusability portability	Internal quality factors

Table 1: Categorized quality factors.

Source	Definition
McCall et al.	The effort required to learn, operate, prepare input and interpret output of a program.
Ravden & Johnson	The extent to which an end-user is able to carry out required tasks successfully, and without difficulty using the computer application system.
ISO/IEC 9126 1991	A set of attributes of software which bear on the effort needed for use and on the individual assessment of such use by a stated or implied set of users.
ISO/DIS 9241–11 1995	The extent to which a product can be used by specified users to achieve specified goals with effectiveness, efficiency and satisfaction in a specified context of use.

Table 2: Definitions of usability.

will be renamed as learnability and ease-of-use thereby avoiding further confusion. Ghezzi et al. (1991) and Daily (1992) suggest that it is important to prioritize these factors. These authors argue that if a software product cannot be installed, then it cannot be launched and therefore cannot be used. As a result, the other quality factors cannot be considered. Daily (1992, p.9) also addresses this issue and suggests that "once the software is usable, correct and reliable then efficiency, compatibility [interoperability] and integrity can be considered in more detail".

The concept of *installability* is new. It is favoured by IBM (Kan, 1995) and supported by Ghezzi et al. (1991) and Daily (1992). So, this is the first new quality factor which must be added to McCall et al.'s original list.

In the intervening years since 1977–8 (when quality models were first published), there has been enormous technological advances and it is necessary to rethink and revise this area accordingly. Reference to Wallmüller (1994) shows that during this time some of the quality factors have become outdated. The remainder of this paper shows that some quality factors need to be renamed to reflect modern vocabulary and understanding. It also shows that new factors need to be added to McCall et al.'s list.

4.1.2 International Quality Standards

The systems professional who has the responsibility for selecting and acquiring quality software might, with good reason, look to the international standard relating to quality as a starting point to provide guidance on the best approach to adopt. In 1991, the International Organization for Standardization published "Guidelines for the application of ISO 9001 to the development, supply and maintenance of software" (ISO, 1991a). It is reasonable to expect that this international standard would address quality factors using the same vocabulary and meaning as used by McCall et al. (1977) and by Boehm (1978). Unfortunately, this was not the case and consequently a new Draft International Standard (ISO, 1997) was introduced and approved in June 1996. This became an International Standard in 1997. This new standard (ISO, 1997) goes a long way towards resolving the deficiencies of its predecessor. For example, Section 4.4.4 (p.11) of the standard uses language which is in keeping with established quality models. It reads:

> "The requirements may include, but not be limited to the following characteristics: functionality, reliability, usability, efficiency, maintainability and portability (ISO, 1991b). Sub-characteristics, may be specified, for example security. Safety considerations and statutory obligations may also be specified.
>
> If the software product needs to interface with other software or hardware products, the interfaces between the software product to be developed and other software or hardware products should be specified ... ".

So, using familiar terminology, the standard is now recognizing six quality factors by name. A seventh factor, *interface facility* (interfaces between software products) is covered by the second paragraph. Elsewhere in the document (Clause 4.10) *testability* is mentioned. *Functionality* is a new quality factor, so, it is the second addition to McCall et al.'s list. The inclusion of *security, safety* and *statutory obligations* are welcome additions.

Security in the standard appears to relate to integrity as stated by McCall et al. (1977) and as stated by Boehm (1978). McCall et al. (1977) describe it as being concerned with putting into place controls which guard against programs and data being incorrectly altered either by accident or by design. As an external quality factor, it supports user confidence in the software. To comply with the quality focus of this paper the term *security* (as opposed to integrity) will be used.

There are two aspects to *safety*. First there is the issue of operator safety which is covered by law and will be addressed in Section 4.2 under the statutory obligations strand. The second aspect of safety is the safety of the general public. This is a special application of software for which designers and specifiers of safety-critical systems need to specify.

To reflect McCall et al.'s vocabulary, the *interface facility* as mentioned in the second paragraph of Section 4.4.4 can be renamed interoperability (Ince, 1994).

However, the most significant aspect of Clause 4.4.4 of the international standard is the inclusion of the expression 'statutory obligations'. This immediately brings into play all statutory regulations relating to health and safety issues including those relating to the minimum safety and health requirements for work with display screen equipment (Council Directive, 1990). This is the justification for the second strand in this three strand approach. This Council Directive is described in Section 4.2.

So, from this review of the software quality strand, *installability, functionality* and *safety* are new factors to be added to McCall et al.'s list. McCall et al.'s integrity needs to be renamed as *security* and interface facility (in the standard) needs to be renamed *interoperability*.

That concludes the review of the software quality strand — the first of the three strands being considered in this paper. The second strand — statutory obligations — is examined in detail in the next section to identify additional factors that influence usability.

4.2   Statutory Obligations Strand

The second strand that impacts on usability is legislation and in keeping with Clause 4.4.4 of ISO (1997), this strand is addressed as statutory obligations.

Statutory obligations are concerned with regulations which relate to health and safety issues but particularly those relating to the minimum safety and health requirements for work with display screen equipment. These obligations are outlined in a European Directive (Council Directive, 1990). National Governments also legislate for the safety and health of workers in their own countries. Both the Directive and general regulations relating to end-users health and safety are now explained.

4.2.1   European Display Screen Directive

On the 29th May 1990, the Council for the European Communities published a directive relating to minimum safety and health requirements for those working with display screens (Council Directive, 1990). This directive became fully effective from 31st December 1996.

The directive sets out the employer's obligations and the employee's entitlements in relation to matters like:

- Analysis of workstations to ensure compliance with the directive.

- Training of employees.

- Employees daily work routine.

- The need for employee consultation and participation.

- Procedures for the protection of worker's eyes and eyesight.

The definition of a workstation (given by the directive) clearly includes software, so employers, as part of their analysis, training and consultation procedures

---

3. OPERATOR/COMPUTER INTERFACE

In designing, selecting, commissioning and modifying software, and in designing tasks using display screen equipment, the employer shall take into account the following principles:

1. software must be suitable for the task;

2. software must be easy to use and, where appropriate, adaptable to the operator's level of knowledge or experience; no quantitative or qualitative checking facility may be used without the knowledge of the workers;

3. systems must provide feedback to workers on their performance;

4. systems must display information in a format and at a pace which are adapted to operators;

5. the principles of software ergonomics must be applied, in particular to human data processing.

Table 3: European Council Directive 90/270/EEC 1990 Summary of minimum safety and health requirements.

---

must take cognisance of current best practice in human–computer interaction. This is further stated in the annex of the directive which sets out the minimum requirements under the heading Operator/Computer Interface. The five principles set out in Part 3 of the Council Directive (1990) are relevant to usability and external software quality, and are set out in Table 3. Closer examination reveals that they are quality factors. 'Suitable for the task' is easily expressed as *suitability*, 'easy to use' could be usability (but to avoid adding further confusion it will be referred to here as *ease-of-use*). And the third principle, 'adaptable to the operator's level of knowledge' is *adaptability*. Feedback, format & pace and software ergonomics all correspond to the golden rules for dialogue design (Shneiderman, 1992). These rules are an essential component of human–computer interaction and are the justification for the third strand and are explained in Section 4.3.

So, from this strand three more quality factors can be added to those identified in the earlier strands. These new factors are *suitability, ease-of-use* and *adaptability* and have been derived from Council Directive (1990). The full list of new software quality factors that have been identified, so far, are *installability, functionality, safety, suitability, ease-of-use* and *adaptability*. Later, these will be combined with McCall et al.'s list to create an updated set of quality factors. At that stage, two factors (integrity and interface facility) will be renamed as *security* and *interoperability* respectively.

That concludes the examination of the second strand and in the next section the human–computer interaction strand will be examined for further quality factors.

4.3 Human–Computer Interaction Strand

Human–computer interaction is described as "the study of people, computer technology and the way these influence each other" (Dix et al., 1993). It is the third strand to be examined in this paper. Authors in this domain (Shneiderman,

1992; Dix et al., 1993; Preece et al., 1994) address these topics in three categories. These categories are human issues, technology issues and interaction issues and they are described in the following sub-sections under the headings Human dimensions in HCI, The computer's capabilities in HCI and Users interacting with systems.

4.3.1 Human Dimensions in HCI

Issues that contribute to effective human usage of computers are well defined as part of the science of human psychology. The issues involved are human behaviour, human memory, ability to learn, human knowledge acquisition, cognitive issues, human perception of the working of the system and how these workings are best conceptualized (Shneiderman, 1992). Other issues that must be considered relate to the profile of the user and include the user's physical abilities and motor skills, previous knowledge or expertise in the domain, general education and training and the overall attitude of the user towards technology — see ISO (1995) for a full listing of user considerations. Through study and understanding of these issues, HCI professionals can specify and design interfaces that support these human factors. A useful way of illustrating these issues is to review some examples of their practical implementation. For example, the Internet might support users wishing to search for books in a second-hand bookshop. Typical users will want to browse many different departments searching for items that appeal to them. The interface style (metaphor) selected to present such an application on screen might include a series of floor plans with departments like local history, early printed and antiquarian books, maps, historical documents, prints, military, nautical history and similar divisions. Simple pointing and clicking accesses the preferred department for browsing, so there is no relearning expected of the user. All of the departments use names familiar to the user. Furthermore, the software applications developed to support these users are popularly referred to as browsers. So it is easy for the non-technical user to have the impression of browsing through the familiar departments of a bookshop. The system has become transparent to the user. Another example of a practical implementation of a software interface assisting human factors might be where interface designers support coherence by grouping similar tasks together. Similar design strategies can be used to best match other human factors with modes of interaction and other computer capabilities.

4.3.2 The Computer's Capabilities in HCI

The main technological focus of HCI is concerned with devices for human interaction with computers. Generally the devices used reflect the preferred dialogue style. A dialogue style is one of a number of methods by which users interact with the system (Shneiderman, 1992). These methods have evolved from command line solutions in the early days of computing to the hands-free, voice recognition systems which are becoming available. The most common dialogue styles are, command line interaction, batch programs, form filling, menu selection, query language, voice recognition WIMPS (Widgets, Icons, Menus and Pointers) and hyperlinks. Another term, WIRPS (Wireless, Intelligent, Remote, Probes and Sensors), can be used to describe the dialogue style of hostile environments. The evolution of these styles has been driven by a desire to improve the overall usability of the interface. For example, command line interfaces normally use keyboards as the input device while voice communication requires microphones. An excellent review of input and output devices is given by Preece et al. (1994).

Achieving the objectives of HCI is enhanced by the proper alignment of the input/output devices, both with the tasks to be completed and with the skills of the users. For example, secretaries with keyboarding skills are obviously more effective using a keyboard for word processing tasks while supermarket checkout operators are obviously more effective using a barcode scanner as their input device. Voice recognition and gesture recognition also enable easier interaction by users with differing skills. Different types of devices are needed for different environments. Office, home and educational environments are generally regarded as safe environments. Workshop floor and engineering plants are described as harsh environments while underwater and radioactive environments are hazardous environments. All three environments have very different device requirements.

4.3.3   Users Interacting with Systems

There are two distinct topics of interest in this area which affect end-users and which will be used to identify further characteristics that impact on usability. These are the established good principles and guidelines for dialogue design and the equipment and environment available to the user.

4.3.4   Principles and Guidelines for Dialogue Design

Principles and guidelines for dialogue design have been suggested for interface evaluation (Ravden & Johnson, 1989; Shneiderman, 1992). Naturally these same principles and guidelines can also be used for specifying the requirements for interface design. Typically, these principles address:

- Consistency of screen presentation.

- Visual clarity on screen.

- Informative feedback to users.

- Compatibility with user conventions and expectations.

- Error prevention and correction.

- Appropriate functionality.

- User control, confidence and satisfaction.

- General user support.

Dialogue principles are addressed by the international standard for ergonomic requirements for office work with visual display terminals (ISO, 1993). The standard addresses some of the issues covered by the above list together with some familiar quality factors which were identified in earlier strands. The seven dialogue principles in the standard and how they might be expressed as quality factors are:

Suitability for task	Suitability
Self descriptiveness	Usability (Ease-of-use)
Controllability	Usability (Ease-of-use)
Conformity with user expectations	Usability (Ease-of-use)
Error tolerance	Security
Suitability for individualization	Adaptability
Suitability for learning	Learnability

Self descriptiveness is the standard's terminology for informative user feedback, controllability relates to user control/user pacing of the use of the product and conformity with user expectation addresses compatibility with user conventions. User feedback, user control/pacing and compatibility with user conventions are all part of Shneiderman's golden rules which were the issues in Section 4.2 that justified the human–computer interaction strand.

4.3.5 Equipment and Environment

User productivity, confidence and satisfaction are all supported by the proper equipment to perform the tasks and by a proper environment in which to work (Preece et al., 1994). So, HCI specialists are particularly interested in ensuring that these two issues are also addressed. The Council Directive (1990) has focused on this aspect and has set out a full schedule of minimum requirements — see Table 3.

Associated with the equipment and the environment is the health and safety of users. The research literature in the field of ergonomics shows considerable concern for a vast array of human disorders and explains how to design interaction in order to best prevent them. These include musculoskeletal disorders like Repetitive Strain Injury (RSI), Work Related Upper Limb Disorders (WRULDs), radiation emissions and facial rash (HSE, 1996).

Combining all of the above topics, it is easy to see how human–computer interaction is concerned with the broad range of issues which contribute to the development of usable systems interfaces. The proper combination of all the topics, (i.e. human issues, technology issues and interaction issues), make the computer operator's role easier to perform, less prone to error, less anxious, builds confidence and many other psychological considerations that impact on computer users (Shneiderman, 1992; Reiterer & Oppermann, 1993).

Central to these topics have been the disciplines of psychology and ergonomics, both of which have contributed to defining best practice to support those who interact with computers. The overall aim of HCI should be to devise usable interfaces that employ the most suitable metaphor and then layout the screen so that human memory, coherence, cognition, perception, learning and previous knowledge are all supported to maximum effect. Interfaces should be designed to be as adaptable as possible in order to better support all end-user skills. Finally, the environment should be made as safe and comfortable as possible using selected devices which best suit the tasks to be performed. The ultimate objective is to create interfaces that are totally transparent to the users.

Like the quality strand and the statutory obligations strand, the human–computer interaction strand also identifies quality factors. These factors include *suitability,*

Quality Factor	Category	Strand
suitability	External quality factors	Statutory obligations
installability	(i.e. Usability factors)	Quality
functionality		Quality
adaptability		Statutory obligations
ease-of-use		Statutory obligations
learnability		HCI
interoperability		Original quality factor
reliability		Original quality factor
safety		Quality
security		Renamed quality factor
correctness		Original quality factor
efficiency		Original quality factor
maintainability	Internal quality factors	All original quality
testability		factors as proposed by
flexibility		McCall et al. (1977)
reusability		
portability		

Table 4: Software quality factors table.

usability (ease-of-use), security, adaptability and *learnability. Learnability* is a new factor and must be added to McCall et al.'s list. This strand also identifies the needs of different users, particularly their needs in different environments using equipment appropriate to that environment. This in turn has given rise to the study of the context of use. Furthermore, the human–computer interaction strand provides a series of checklists and guidelines which combine current best practice for interface development.

This concludes the review of the three strands that identify quality factors. Currently, as three separate strands, their scope is very broad with considerable duplication. For the benefit of systems professionals, one composite table that combines the different strands is needed. Such a table should reflect the changing significance of the original quality factors suggested by McCall et al., the guidelines offered by ISO (1997), the statutory obligations resulting from Council Directive (1990) and HCI developments (ISO, 1993). Such a table is shown in Table 4. To prepare this table, McCall et al.'s model is used as a foundation and it is sub-divided to show external and internal quality factors. Simple priority is also incorporated in the external factors. From Table 1, *reliability, correctness* and *efficiency* are all included together with the internal quality factors. Note that usability is not included at this stage and is replaced by *ease-of-use*. From the software quality strand, *installability, functionality* and *safety* are included. Integrity is renamed as *security* in order to better reflect the wording of ISO (1997) and interface facility — in ISO (1997) — is renamed as *interoperability* to reflect McCall et al.'s vocabulary.

Attribute	McCall et al. (1977)	Comments/Source
suitability		To comply with EU law — Council Directive (1990)
installability		To reflect commercial practice. To comply with ISO (1997)
functionality		To comply with ISO (1997)
adaptability		To comply with EU law — Council Directive (1990)
ease-of-use	usability	To comply with EU law — Council Directive (1990)
learnability		To comply with ISO (1993)
interoperability	interoperability	Original quality factor
reliability	reliability	Original quality factor
safety		To comply with ISO (1997)
security	integrity	To reflect the wording of ISO (1997)
correctness	correctness	Original quality factor
efficiency	efficiency	Original quality factor

Table 5: Usability attributes of a software product.

To fulfil the ISO requirement that statutory obligations must be complied with, the items set out in sub-division Operator/Computer Interface of the Council Directive (1990) are also included in the table. These items are *suitability*, *ease-of-use* and *adaptability*. From the human–computer interaction strand, *learnability* is added.

It is now necessary to return to McCall et al.'s original definition of usability, i.e. easy to learn and operate. Both of these issues are now catered for as quality factors in their own right, i.e. *learnability* and *ease-of-use*, and, as both are included in the new list, usability from McCall et al.'s original list is obsolete and is omitted.

4.4   The Usability Attributes of a Software Product

In Section 2 usability is described as "the extent to which a computer system interface supports end-users" and in Section 4.1, it is explained that it is preferable to describe external quality factors as usability factors. To confirm that this preference is valid, it is only necessary to apply the following simple query to each quality factor. Does the individual quality factor support the end-user? If it does, then it is a usability attribute. Applying this technique, the software quality factors in Table 4 can be transposed to a list of usability attributes as set out in Table 5 and called the usability attributes of a software product (or the attributes of a usable software product).

The attributes set out in Table 5 are those that impact the end-user. They are external quality factors and include attributes which must be considered during software usability measurement and evaluation in order to comply with current ISO standards and European Community law.

5 Conclusion

The quality of user interfaces is a central part of software development, not least because of European Community Law. This paper explained how the study of software usability has advanced over the past twenty years by reviewing four formal usability definitions. This review showed that some of the definitions focus on software attributes while other definitions focus on usability measures. The paper showed that in order for management to assess usability there is a need for a consistent set of usability quality attributes.

The approach used to identify this set of attributes involves a methodical analysis of well regarded sources in order to establish academic thinking and commercial practice. The paper uses a quality-focused self-justifying synthesis of three strands and identifies a new critical set of quality factors. It is then shown that the external quality factors in this set are the 'usability attributes of a software product'.

Which of the three strands is the most important is an issue that might arise for strategic managers. Both quality and HCI issues are matters of organizational policy, which may be decided by management. But statutory obligations are part of European Community law and must be complied with.

Acknowledgements

Thanks are due to Dr. Jakob Nielsen for permission to reproduce his model of system acceptability, to Mr. Brian Abbot of the National Standards Authority of Ireland for making information regarding to ISO Standards available and to Professor Alan Dix of Staffordshire University for his support and encouragement during the preparation of this paper.

References

Bevan, N. & Macleod, M. (1994), "Usability Measurement in Context", *Behaviour & Information Technology* **13**(1-2), 132–45.

Boehm, B. (1978), *Characteristics of Software Quality*, Vol. 1 of *TRW Series on Software Technology*, North-Holland.

Council Directive (1990), "Minimum Safety and Health Requirements for Work with Display Screen Equipment", *Official journal of the European Communities* (**90/270/EEC**), L 156/14–18.

Daily, K. (1992), *Quality Management for Software*, NCC Blackwell.

Dix, A., Finlay, J., Abowd, G. & Beale, R. (1993), *Human–Computer Interaction*, Prentice–Hall.

Ghezzi, C., Jazayeri, M. & Mandrioli, D. (1991), *Fundamentals of Software Engineering*, Prentice–Hall.

Holcomb, R. & Tharp, A. (1991), "Users, a Software Usability Model and Product Evaluation", *Interacting with Computers* **3**(2), 155–66.

HSE (1996), *Working with VDUs*, Health and Safety Executive Books. Booklet No. IND(G) 36(L).

IEEE (1983), "Standard Glossary of Software Engineering Terminology", Institute of Electrical and Electronics Engineers, IEEE Std 729-1983.

IEEE (1989), "Standard for Software Quality Assurance Plans", Institute of Electrical and Electronics Engineers, IEEE Std 730-1989.

Ince, D. (1994), *ISO 9001 and Software Quality Assurance*, McGraw-Hill.

ISO (1987), "ISO 9000 International Standard. Quality Management and Quality Assurance Standards". International Organization for Standardization, Genève, Switzerland.

ISO (1991a), "ISO 9000-3 International Standard. Quality Management and Quality Assurance Standards — Part 3: Guidelines for the Application of ISO 9001 to the Development, Supply and Maintenance of Software". International Organization for Standardization, Genève, Switzerland.

ISO (1991b), "ISO/IEC 9126 International Standard. Information Technology — Software Product Evaluation — Quality Characteristics and Guidelines for their Use". International Organization for Standardization, Genève, Switzerland.

ISO (1993), "ISO/DIS 9241-10 Draft International Standard. Ergonomic Requirements for Office Work with Visual Display Terminals (VDTs). Part 10: Dialogue Principles.". International Organization for Standardization, Genève, Switzerland.

ISO (1995), "ISO/DIS 9241-11 Draft International Standard. Ergonomic Requirements for Office Work with Visual Display Terminals (VDTs). Part 11: Guidance on Usability". International Organization for Standardization, Genève, Switzerland.

ISO (1997), "ISO 9000-3 International Standard. Quality Management and Quality Assurance Standards — Part 3: Guidelines for the Application of ISO 9001:1994 to the Development, Supply, Installation and Maintenance of Computer Software". International Organization for Standardization, Genève, Switzerland.

Kan, S. (1995), *Metrics and Models in Software Quality Engineering*, Addison–Wesley.

Kirakowski, J. & Corbett, M. (1993), "SUMI: The Software Usability Measurement Inventory", *British Journal of Educational Psychology* **24**(3), 210–2.

McCall, J. A., Richards, P. K. & Walters, G. F. (1977), *Factors in Software Quality*, Vol. I-III, Rome Aid Defence Centre.

Nielsen, J. (1993), *Usability Engineering*, Academic Press.

Porteous, M., Kirakowski, J. & Corbett, M. (1993), *SUMI Users Handbook*, Human Factors Research Group, University College, Cork, Ireland.

Preece, J., Rogers, Y., Sharpe, H., Benyon, D., Holland, S. & Carey, T. (1994), *Human–Computer Interaction*, Addison–Wesley.

Ravden, S. & Johnson, G. (1989), *Evaluating Usability of Human–Computer Interfaces: A Practical Method*, Ellis Horwood.

Reiterer, H. & Oppermann, R. (1993), "Evaluation of User Interfaces: EVADIS II — A Comprehensive Evaluation Approach", *Behaviour & Information Technology* **12**(3), 137–48.

Robson, W. (1994), *Strategic Management and Information Systems: An Integrated Approach*, Pitman.

Shneiderman, B. (1992), *Designing the User Interface: Strategies for Effective Human–Computer Interaction*, second edition, Addison–Wesley.

Wallmüller, E. (1994), *Software Quality Assurance: A Quality Approach*, Prentice–Hall International.

Analysis of Problems Found in User Testing Using an Approximate Model of User Action

Wai On Lee

Microsoft Corporation, 1 Microsoft Way, Redmond, Washington 98052–6399, USA.

EMail: *waionl@microsoft.com*

This paper describes an analysis of user testing using an approximate model that separates user action into Goal Formation, Action Specification, and Action Execution. It was found that the majority of the problems found in user testing, as reported within 30 usability reports, were within the Action Specification phase of user action. In particular, problems in finding an action or object and in understanding names used were most prevalent. The implication is that user testing as carried out in an industrial setting might be beneficial to easing Action Specification whilst neglecting potential problems in other phases of user action.

Keywords: iterative design, user testing, usability reports, approximate phases of user action.

1 Introduction

Within the iterative cycles of design and evaluation, one of the most important activities is that of user testing. For example, Landauer (1995) described user testing as the "gold standard of usability engineering" (Landauer, 1995, p.281). Murdock (1996, p.13) commented that: "Without question, usability testing is one of the best ways yet devised to find out if and where a design works (software or hardware), or how and why it needs correction." From the results of a survey of European IT organizations, Dillon et al. (1993) found that over 80% of the respondents rated the importance of user testing as important, very important, or essential.

Given the importance of user testing, there is an increasing need for researchers and practitioners to clearly understand the benefits of user testing. To this end, a number of researchers have questioned various aspects of user testing. For example,

Bailey (1993) examined the effects of designer training on the iterative design process; Whitefield et al. (1991) discussed various characteristics and drawbacks of iterative design and evaluation. Much of the work on cost-justifying usability engineering also make high level assumptions about the benefits of user testing based on performance improvements from published literature (Mayhew & Mantei, 1994). Recently, there is also a plethora of studies that have used results of user testing as a baseline for comparison between inspection and walkthrough evaluation methods without examining the user test results in detail (Jefferies et al., 1991; Lee et al., 1995).

Much of the literature on examining the benefits of user testing comes from illustrative case studies. For example, (Gould et al., 1987) described how iterative user testing and redesign helped to create a successful system within a tight project schedule. Although Gould et al.'s study focused on how usability principles can be incorporated within iterative design, user testing within various stages of the design was said to have improved the design in a number of ways:

- Simplified the design by removing unimportant options and features.

- Changed the way the user manual was written.

- Changed various prompts.

- Identified a number of help messages.

In the Superbook (an information retrieval system) project, Landauer (1995) attributed the improvement of the Superbook system to the resolution of four major problems identified by user testing:

- Slow system response.

- Bias toward the use of non-optimal strategy (a method for search that would have made the users more efficient was not used).

- Non-optimal arrangement of screen (the mouse cursor had to move a long distance across the screen to select various objects).

- Difficulty noticing the results of search.

Although these case studies provided valuable information concerning the effects of user testing in a particular situation, there is also a need for systematic study of its effects across cases. Thus, to further our understanding of the benefits of user testing and what it reveals, an analysis on the results of user testing on various products within Microsoft was carried out. The aims of the analysis were:

1. To reveal the kinds of problems typically identified by formative user testing in a large software development company.

2. To reveal the kinds of solutions typically recommended for dealing with the problems identified.

2 Data Set and Background

Although the results of a user test can be communicated to designers and developers in a variety of ways, written usability reports are still one of the most popular method used in many organizations (Mack & Montaniz, 1995). The data examined in this study were the results of 30 user tests on 18 different products carried out by 22 different usability specialists. The tests were carried out over a period of about 3 years, from April, 1993 to June 1996, and the products tested were desktop applications, an operating system, as well as a number of consumer-type software. Usability Specialists all have a background in behavioural science or a related discipline. Eleven of the specialists had 3 to 6 years of experience, 7 had about 2 years of experience, 2 had about 1 year of experience, and 2 had less than 3 months of experience.

The general methodology used in these tests was formal laboratory-based user testing. These tests were carried out with the aim to improve the product being tested — so called 'formative testing', cf. (Scriven, 1967). In each test, subjects were asked to carry out a number of predetermined tasks by thinking aloud (Erricson & Simon, 1984). Typically, subjects were given very little time to learn and were simply told to carry out the task by figuring out what to do given particular prototypes. Verbal protocols and questionnaire results were collected, analysed, and written up as a report before being distributed to the team. The turn-around time in this user testing process was typically about 2 weeks. Roughly speaking, the first part of this time was spent in planning and testing and the second part spent in analysing the results and writing the report. However, there were variations in the process and the time required to do this — see (Dieli et al., 1994) for a discussion.

The organizational context in which usability specialists work, and the design process at Microsoft is similar to many large software development companies. However, in contrast to the organizational structure within which the aforementioned case studies were carried out, the usability group within our company is separate from the product groups (Cusumano & Selby, 1995) for a discussion of the organizational structure and the general design and usability process at Microsoft). The main focus of the usability group is the evaluation of various products; as such, the result of this analysis should be applicable to organizations with a similar structure and whose usability group serves a similar purpose.

3 Results

Although the usability reports contained findings which dealt with non-usability problems (e.g. characterization of subjects' behaviour, confirming that something had worked, subjects liking of certain aspects of the UI), the majority of the findings focused on usability problems with the interface being tested and how the problems should be dealt with. To better understand the nature of users' problems, a categorization scheme based on Norman's (1986) approximate theory of action is used. This scheme seems promising for this type of analysis since a number of researchers have used it similarly with some success. For example, Barnard (1987) used a similar scheme as the basis for cognitive task analysis; Carroll & Kellogg (1989) also used a similar scheme as a framework for structuring their psychological claims analysis of artifacts. Following Barnard (1987), a three-stage approximation is used to partition user action:

Goal Formation Specifying the intention and establishing the desired state by evaluating external information and using prior knowledge of possible achievable system state. In this phase, users' activities are focused on making sense of the system and determining what has to be done.

Action Specification Translating the psychological goals into a sequence of internal, mental specifications of the physical manipulations to be carried out. Users' activities in this phase are involved in determining the system actions required to achieve a given goal.

Action Execution Carrying out the physical actions according to the mental specifications and to ensure actions are appropriately carried out. In this phase, users' activities are involved in actually performing the actions specified from the previous phase and in evaluating the success of the actions carried out.

Put simply, this scheme essentially separates human computer interaction into three simple stages: deciding what to do, determining how to do it, and actually doing it. Within these three simple stages however, continuous uptake and evaluation of external information are necessary to support the cognitive activity involved in each of the stages. The emphasis in this conception of user action is that the process of information uptake, the perceiving of system state, and information evaluation are all *on-going* processes rather than separate stages in the sequence of user action as put forward by Norman (1986).

4   What Problems Were Revealed?

Table 1 shows the number of problems in each problem category and in each stage of approximate action. Fifteen problem categories were found in the data (see appendix for a detailed discussion of the problem categorization process): five were within Goal Formation, seven within Action Specification, and three within Action Execution (each category contained two or more problems; nine unique problems were found which did not belong in any of the categories, e.g. "It's odd to have Email address which is the primary label come after Email 2 and Email 3 in the drop down", "this is a bug"). Although some of the problem categories could be considered as the cause of the problem rather than the problem itself (e.g. difficulties with terminology, difficulties with reading from the screen), the specialists chose to describe them as the problems themselves rather than their causes during task performance.

5   Problems found in Goal Formation

As stated earlier, Goal Formation is not a process without the uptake and evaluation of external information. In particular, as evident in the problems found, processes involved in evaluating what the system does, determining the structure of the system, and a general making sense of the system by surveying the screen, are required before 'what to do' can be realized. Five problem types were found within this phase of

Stage	Problem Type	Examples from Reports	#
Goal Formation (Total: 35, 20.7%)	Uncertainty about when to use a particular function	e.g. "subjects did not understand when to use filters"	9
	Difficulties in understanding what a function does	e.g. "subjects had difficulties understanding what the 'back' icon does"	9
	Uncertainty about relationship or distinction between user interface elements or functions	e.g. "subjects were confused by the relationship between Find and List Maker"	8
	Difficulties in conceptualizing the system	e.g. "subjects had difficulties understanding how selecting a certain portion of the PivotTable would relate to the available functionality"	7
	Difficulties in seeing and reading off the screen in the initial survey of the screen	e.g. "subjects had difficulties reading the label"	2
Action Specification (Total: 107, 63.3%)	Cannot find action or object	e.g. "subjects were unable to find the customize command bar without hint"	47
	Difficulties with terminology	e.g. "subjects could not understand 'Concatenate'"	23
	Difficulties figuring out how to do carry out an action	e.g. "Subjects did not understand how to use the yellow sliding bar"	10
	Failure to choose a more effective function	e.g. "subjects did not use the toolbar provided to assist the task"	9
	Missed a step in the procedure	e.g. "subjects did not enter a required field"	7
	Uncertainty about system status	e.g. "subjects mistakenly launched the calendar application multiple times"	6
	Difficulties with seeing or reading off the screen	e.g. "subjects had difficulties seeing the highlighting on buttons"	5
Action Execution (Total: 27, 15.9%)	Difficulties carrying out an action	e.g. "subjects had difficulties placing a command in a toolbar or menu"	10
	Uncertainty about system status during action execution	e.g. "subjects had difficulties knowing when search was in progress"	9
	Confused by the result of an action	e.g. "subjects were not able to tell if a search had been executed because the results were not visible"	8

Table 1: The number of problems found belonging to each type within each stage of approximate stages of human action.

approximate user action. However, no problem type stood out as the most dominant in this phase. Two problem types tied for the most number of problems accrued:

- Uncertainty about when to use a particular function. Problems of this type were identified from the reports if the problem description indicated that subjects failed to carry out the required task in an 'appropriate' way (as determined by the usability specialist) or had some confusion about the appropriate situations to use particular functions. For example, "subjects did not understand when to use filters" (5.3% of the total number of problems found).

- Difficulties in understanding what a function does. Subjects were found to have difficulty in understanding the utility of a function even having seen the effects of activating the function. This problem type differs from the first type in that in the first type subjects knew and understood (or thought they did) the effects of the function whereas here subjects did not know what a function does. For example, "subjects had difficulties understanding what save would save" (5.3% of the total number of problems found).

6   Problems found in Action Specification

Problems within Action Specification are those problems subjects had in determining the system actions required to achieve a given goal. Seven types of problems were found within this stage. As shown in Table 1, two problem types stood out as being the most frequently occurring problems in this phase. Each of the problem types accounted for more than 20% of the problems within Action Specification:

- Subjects' failure to find an action or object (that exists) was the most frequent problem observed within user testing. Data from usability reports showed that subjects had difficulties finding toolbars, menu items, buttons, tabs, options within a dialogue, icons, operations (e.g. right clicking the mouse, drag and drop), etc. Forty-seven problems were found to be of this type, making it the most frequent problem found overall (27.8% of the total number of problems found). These results suggest that user testing most frequently contributes to better user interface design by revealing parts of the interface which are difficult to discover.

- Subjects' difficulty in understanding the names used was the second most frequent problem type found within Action Specification. Data from usability reports showed that subjects had difficulties in understanding the names used in menus, buttons, or labels used in the user interface. Although subjects' failure to understand a name may often lead to difficulty in finding the required function, reporting of this difficulty had typically been independent of the physical manifestation of the problem (e.g. failure to find the function). Twenty-three problems were found to be of this type, making it the second most frequent problems found overall (13.6% of the total number of problems found).

7 Problems found in Action Execution

Three problem types were found in the Action Execution phase. Similar to problem types within Goal Formation, no problem type stood out as the most dominant in this phase. The problem type that had the largest number of problems associated with it was 'difficulties carrying out an action':

- Subjects' difficulties in this area included shift-clicking, double clicking, drag & drop between UI controls, wait-click (waiting for an object to change state once it had been selected before clicking on it again), horizontal scrolling, deselecting objects (5.9% of the total number of problems found).

8 Problems within the Approximate Phases of User Action

As shown in Table 1, the majority of the problems revealed were within Action Specification. One hundred and seven problems (63.3% of all the problems reported) can be attributed to problems within Action Specification. Only 35 problems (20.7% of all the problems reported) were within Goal Formation and only 27 problems (15.9% of all the problems reported) were within Action Execution.

The high percentage of problems found within Action Specification is not surprising since it could be argued that user testing is typically *set up* to reveal problems of an Action Specification nature. That is, subjects are typically provided with a task list in which the high-level goals of the tasks are already established. Subjects' job within a user testing session is therefore often reduced to finding the necessary user interface components to carry out the task provided. Problems that users typically face in the Goal Formation phase of interacting with a user interface (e.g. forming the appropriate mental model, task formulation, intention specification) are usually by-passed in the typical user testing session.

As Table 1 shows, although about 16% of the problems were found within the Action Execution. Many of the problems were found to be in the evaluation of the system state and in physical difficulties carrying out the actions required rather than problems which are associated with highly practiced skills and long term learning. All the test reports examined users who had never seen or used the system before and since the tests typically lasted between 1–3 hours with few task repetitions, there was little opportunity for skill development. Therefore, the nature of user testing examined and the limited time subjects had to develop their skills may be two of the reasons why few problems were revealed within the Action Execution phase compared to the Action Specification phase.

9 What Recommendations Were Made?

Ten different recommendation types were found in the reports that covered all the recommendations except 12 ('Others' in Table 2).

9.1 *Recommendations for Supporting Goal Formation*

The most frequent recommendation for Goal Formation problems was 'change or add description'. Within this category, ten recommendations were to provide additional description and only two were to change existing description. This finding suggests that usability specialists have concluded that users are lacking the adequate information to resolve misunderstandings and uncertainties in determining what to do. To mitigate this problem, usability specialists typically opt for a solution of adding more text descriptions in the user interface.

9.2   Recommendations for Supporting Action Specification

As shown in Table 2, when a recommendation was made for Action Specification problems, the most frequent recommendation was 'change name'. In fact changing the name of a user interface object was the most frequent made recommendation overall. Thirty-four of all the recommendations made was to change the name of a button, a label, an icon, etc. The high percentage is partly due to the high number of terminology problems (23 in all). However, further analysis showed that only 11/34 of the recommendations were accounted for by terminology problems. In addition, a recommendation to change the name of a user interface component was made to 10 of the 15 problems found. This finding suggests that a recommendation for changing name is frequently made to deal with a variety of problems.

A recommendation to 'change name' implies a mismatch between the name the system used and one that is mentally specified by the user. Indeed, warnings concerning such a mismatch between system and real world are frequently made in guidelines and in usability inspection methods. For example, "the system should use the users' language, with words, phrases, and concepts familiar to the user rather than system- oriented terms." (Nielsen & Molich, 1990). However, the data showed little evidence that the terminology problem was mostly caused by designers using system-related terms. Rather, the data suggested that the problem was caused by the use of names which were too general or imprecise to enable users to map to their mental specification. Of the 28 recommendations that suggested alternative names, 18 suggested names that were more specific than the ones used (e.g. 'Suggests' to 'Movie suggestions', 'Find' to 'Find Zip Code'). That is, it was typically recommended for the name of the object to be added. Only 2 out of the 28 recommendations suggest the problem was caused by a mismatch due to system focus (e.g. change 'item to run' to 'software available on the network', change 'concatenate' to 'compress or condense').

9.3   Recommendations for Supporting Action Execution

The most frequent recommendation within Action Execution was 'add or change feedback'. Seventeen recommendations were of this type. Within this category, 11 were of the type 'add feedback' and 6 were 'change feedback'. Usability specialists seem to be tackling problems within action execution by suggesting the addition of feedback or the improvement of feedback already provided. The implication is that designers are still having problems with ensuring that adequate feedback is provided despite the prevalence of design principles to advise on this issue (Apple Computer Inc., 1987; Microsoft Corporation, 1995).

9.4   Local and Global Recommendations

As shown in Tables 1 & 2, the problems found and the changes recommended are typically local (focused changes to individual elements of the design, e.g. 'change

Recommendation Type	Examples from Reports	GF	AS	AE	Total
Change name	e.g. "change the name from Time to Time guide"	6	26	2	34
Add or change feedback	e.g. "make it clear that the filter had been selected"	0	10	17	27
Add or change visuals	e.g. "make the tabs to look more like arrows"	5	19	2	26
Add or change description	e.g. "add information to explain what the field is for"	12	10	3	25
Add function or object	e.g. "add a customize command in the Tools menu"	2	22	0	24
Move it	e.g. "place it under Find"	4	10	1	15
Remove	e.g. "get rid of the Next and Previous buttons"	3	6	0	9
System change	e.g. "make sure the application is loaded or that the wait cursor is up before the application window appears"	0	5	4	9
Global redesign	e.g. "redesign the launcher dialogue screens"	4	1	1	6
Change controls	e.g. "use a list box instead of a drop-down control"	0	1	1	2
No recommendation †		8	42	4	54
Others (unique recommendations)	e.g. "question the assumption that users need to select from templates first"	1	9	2	12
Total		45	161	37	243

† Analysis of the reports showed two main reasons as to why no recommendations were made. First, the problem was minor or the solution was obvious (e.g. if the text is difficult to see then make it bigger). Second, the problem is difficult and a solution was not obvious.

Table 2: The type and number of recommendations made (GF=Goal Formation, AS=Action Specification, AE=Action Execution). Multiple recommendations for a problem were split into individual recommendations for the analysis.

the name of the menu') rather than global (whole scale changes which affect more than one element of the design, e.g. "use an object-action model for structuring the menu items"). Although one should not underestimate the effect of a local change such as changing the name of a function on usability, with so many problems being dealt with via such a solution, usability specialists may be overlooking deeper and more global problems or are unable to recommend solutions of a more global nature.

Further examination of the reports showed little evidence that recommendations were relating multiple problems in the interface. Instead, the reports focused on the problems in piece-meal fashion, identifying problems subjects had, occasionally describing the cause of the problem (some provided supporting evidence in terms of what subjects did or said), and typically providing local recommendations to deal with the problems identified.

10 Summary and Discussion

Overall, the analysis shows that user testing fits well with Landauer's characterization of design and the effects of user testing in that it is " ... akin to a pile of ore containing a few gold nuggets. The whole thing is not much use until you wash away the dirt" (Landauer, 1995, p.274). However, the analysis adds to this by suggesting that the 'dirt' that is washed out tends to be in the action specification phase of user action. That is, the type of user testing examined here supports the iterative design process primarily by identifying areas where action specification is problematic and hence allows the design effort to be focused on easing this phase of user action. More specifically, the results showed that user testing most frequently reveals problems within action specification by revealing parts of the interface that are difficult for users to discover and by identifying terminology users have difficulty understanding.

Although rectifying these problems would undoubtedly improve the user interface designs, it is problematic in a number of ways. First, establishing what needs to be done is a major problem that users have to resolve in their software usage. For example, as shown by Lee & Barnard (1993), formulating a problem in a particular way has important implications on how the problem is tackled or what features are used to carry out a task. By removing a large part of this phase of activity, user testing might be unintentionally ignoring important types of usability problems. Second, the focus on initial learning and the short time subjects have to develop their skills limit the consideration of usability to the short-term usage of software. User testing of the type examined had little to say about the evolution of skill development and how to ensure that software is designed to meet the needs of users through this process (Campbell, 1990).

Further examination of the problems identified and the recommendations made also revealed that few global problems were detected. This finding raises a concern about the general claims made in the literature about the benefits of user testing. In the industry, where turn around of usability testing needs to be quick and where the time allowed for thinking about problems is often limited, there might be a danger that user testing may be reduced to 'fine-tuning' the action specification phase of human–computer interaction. In particular, usability groups that treat testing as a non- integral part of design and where the responsibility of the group is regarded as being solely in 'testing' might limit themselves to revealing local problems and hence unable, or are inappropriately positioned to make recommendations of a more global nature. As a number of authors have noted, different types of organization (Floyd, 1987), and different ways in which usability is integrated within an organization have different impact on the effectiveness of usability resource (Grudin, 1991; Scholtz, 1995). Although the value of the type of user testing examined here should not be underestimated, further research into understanding how best to reveal problems within Goal Formation and Action Specification, understanding why revealing global problems is difficult, understanding the limitations of user testing in different contexts, and how usability specialists can be best situated to make a wider range of recommendations, are important to ensure that user testing is best engineered.

Acknowledgements

Thanks to Linda Carlin, Michael Muller, and Mary Czerwinski for comments and discussions on earlier drafts of the paper. Thanks also to the three anonymous reviewers for their comments on the submission.

Appendix

Problem Categorization Process

1. What is the problem as described by the specialist? The first phase of the problem categorization process is to identify the problems found in user testing as described in the report. As described in the main text, the usability reports typically focused on subjects' problems in piece-meal fashion. Thus, this phase is typically straightforward. For example, subjects did not understand when to use filters, subjects did not understand 'concatenate', subjects had difficulties knowing when search was in progress.

2. What is the subject doing at this point? Having identified the problems, the next phase is to decide whether the problem occurred in Goal Formation, Action Specification, or Action Execution. The decision process is as follows:

   - Are subjects trying to understand the task instructions? Are they trying to relate or conceptualize the system in order to understand what they need to do? Are they exploring functions to see what they can do with it? Are they surveying the screen and trying to understand what they are seeing? In these cases, they are in carrying out Goal Formation. That is they are deciding what to do.

   - Are subjects trying to figure out how to carry out the task given they have understood what they need to do? More specifically, are they trying to find the action or object they think are required to carry out the task? Are they trying to map the terminology used in the user interface to their mental specification of what needs to be done? Are they trying to figure out the steps in the procedure for carrying out the task? In these cases, they are carrying out Action Specification.

   - Are subjects trying to physically carry out the action? Has the action been carried out and they are trying to make sense of the results? In these cases, they are carrying out Action Execution.

3. At what point in the test did the problem occur? If it is unclear from the description what subjects is doing at that point, it is possible to infer this by determine when the problem occurred based on the test script, the task that subjects is carrying out, and the way the problem is described. Typically, this provides corroborative evidence for deciding which stage of the approximate action users are having problems.

4. Consult the videotape. The last resort is to go back to the videotape of the usability test. The videotapes should enable the determination of when

the problem occurred and a clearer picture as to what subject is trying to accomplish when the problem occurred.

5. Categorize the problem type within each phase of approximate action. Once problems have been classified as GF, AS, or AE, a further categorization process is needed. Each problem is given is category name based on the way the problem is described. For example, "the terminology 'items to run' was not well understood" (difficulties with terminology), "subjects were not able to tell if a search had been executed" (confused by the result of an action).

6. Group together problems with same category name Problems with the same category name are grouped together.

References

Apple Computer Inc. (1987), *Human Interface Guide: The Apple Desktop Interface*, Addison–Wesley.

Bailey, G. (1993), Cognitive Resources and the Learning of Human–Computer Dialogues, *in* S. Ashlund, K. Mullet, A. Henderson, E. Hollnagel & T. White (eds.), *Proceedings of INTERCHI'93*, ACM Press, pp.198–215.

Barnard, P. J. (1987), Cognitive Resources and the Learning of Human–Computer Dialogues, *in* J. M. Carroll (ed.), *Interfacing Thought: Cognitive Aspects of Human–Computer Interaction*, Cambridge University Press, pp.112–158.

Campbell, R. L. (1990), Developmental Scenario Analysis of Smalltalk Programming, *in* J. C. Chew & J. Whiteside (eds.), *Proceedings of CHI'90: Human Factors in Computing Systems*, ACM Press, pp.269–276.

Carroll, J. M. & Kellogg, W. A. (1989), Artifact as Theory-nexus: Hermenutics Meets Theory-based Design, *in* K. Bice & C. H. Lewis (eds.), *Proceedings of CHI'89: Human Factors in Computing Systems*, ACM Press, pp.7–14.

Cusumano, M. A. & Selby, R. W. (1995), *Microsoft Secrets: How the Worlds' Most Powerful Software Company Creates Technology, Shapes Markets, and Manages People*, Free Press.

Dieli, M., Dye, K., McClintock, M. & Simpson, M. (1994), The Microsoft Usability Group, *in* M. E. Wiklund (ed.), *Usability in Practice: How Companies Develop User Friendly Products*, Academic Press, pp.327–358.

Dillon, A., Sweeney, M. & Maguire, M. (1993), A Survey of Usability Engineering Within the European IT Industry — Current Practice and Needs, *in* J. Alty, D. Diaper & S. Guest (eds.), *People and Computers VIII (Proceedings of HCI'93)*, Cambridge University Press, pp.81–94.

Erricson, K. A. & Simon, H. A. (1984), *Protocol Analysis*, MIT Press.

Floyd, C. (1987), Outline of a Paradigm change in Software Engineering., *in* G. Bjeknes, P. Ehn & M. Kyng (eds.), *Computers and Democracy*, Avebury Press, pp.191–210.

Gould, J. D., Boies, S. J., Levy, S., Richards, J. T. & Schonard, J. (1987), "The 1984 Olympic Message System — A Test of Behaviour Principles of System Design", *Communications of the ACM* **30**(9), 758–769.

Grudin, J. (1991), "Systematic Source of Suboptimal Design in Large Product Development Organizations", *Human–Computer Interaction* **6**(2), 147–196.

Jefferies, R., Miller, J. R., Wharton, C. & Uyeda, K. (1991), User Interface Evaluation in the Real World: A Comparison of Four Techniques, *in* S. P. Robertson, G. M. Olson & J. S. Olson (eds.), *Proceedings of CHI'91: Human Factors in Computing Systems (Reaching through Technology)*, ACM Press, pp.119–124.

Landauer, T. K. (1995), *The Trouble with Computers: Usefulness, Usability and Productivity*, MIT Press.

Lee, W. O. & Barnard, P. J. (1993), Precipitating Change in System Usage by Function Revelation and Problem Reformulation, *in* J. Alty, D. Diaper & S. Guest (eds.), *People and Computers VIII (Proceedings of HCI'93)*, Cambridge University Press, pp.35–47.

Lee, W. O., Dye, K. & Airth, D. (1995), Evaluating Design Specifications Using Heuristic Evaluation, *in* K. Nordby, P. H. Helmersen, D. J. Gilmore & S. A. Arnessen (eds.), *Human–Computer Interaction — INTERACT'95: Proceedings of the Fifth IFIP Conference on Human–Computer Interaction*, Chapman & Hall, pp.376–379.

Mack, R. L. & Montaniz, F. (1995), Observing, Predicting, and Analyzing Usability Problems, *in* J. Nielsen & R. L. Mack (eds.), *Usability Inspection Methods*, John Wiley & Sons, pp.295–340.

Mayhew, D. J. & Mantei, M. (1994), A Basic Framework for Cost-Justifying Usability Engineering, *in* R. G. Bias & D. J. Mayhew (eds.), *Cost-Justifying Usability*, Academic Press, pp.9–43.

Microsoft Corporation (1995), *The Windows Interface Design Guidelines for Software Design*, Microsoft Press.

Murdock, M. (1996), "Software Design Teams at Iomega", *Interactions* **3**(2), 11–14.

Nielsen, J. & Molich, R. (1990), Heuristic Evaluation of User Interfaces, *in* J. C. Chew & J. Whiteside (eds.), *Proceedings of CHI'90: Human Factors in Computing Systems*, ACM Press, pp.249–256.

Norman, D. A. (1986), Cognitive Engineering, *in* D. A. Norman & S. W. Draper (eds.), *User Centered Systems Design: New Perspectives on Human–Computer Interaction*, Lawrence Erlbaum Associates, pp.31–62.

Scholtz, J. (1995), Organizing Usability in the Corporation, *in* K. Nordby, P. H. Helmersen, D. J. Gilmore & S. A. Arnessen (eds.), *Human–Computer Interaction — INTERACT'95: Proceedings of the Fifth IFIP Conference on Human–Computer Interaction*, Chapman & Hall, pp.372–375.

Scriven, M. (1967), The methodology of evaluation, *in* R. Tyler, R. Gagne & M. Scriven (eds.), *Perspectives of Curriculum Evaluation*, Rand McNally, pp.39–83.

Whitefield, A., Wilson, F. & Dowell, J. (1991), "A framework for human factors evaluation.", *Behaviour & Information Technology* **10**(1), 65–79.

Software Support for Usability Measurement: An Application to Systems Engineering Data Exchange Development

James Britton, Linda Candy & Ernest Edmonds

LUTCHI Research Centre, Department Computer Studies, Loughborough University, Ashby Road, Loughborough, Leicestershire LE11 3TU, UK.

Tel: *+44 1509 222690*

Fax: *+44 1509 610815*

EMail: *L.Candy@lboro.ac.uk*

The goal of ensuring that usability measurement results can contribute to the ongoing development of a software product in a formative way is, in practice, difficult to achieve. The paper presents an innovative approach to supporting that process exemplified in SEDRES, a large European Aerospace collaborative project on developing a data exchange capability for systems engineering design tools. The main subject is the role of a software tool called NUD*IST (Non-numerical Unstructured Data Indexing Searching and Theorizing), in providing a method for longitudinal data collection and analysis and support for feedback to the project partners about the product under development. It describes the analysis techniques employed, the main features and operational use, followed by examples of results that can be obtained. The implications of the use of this tool for both the analysis process and support for formative evaluation are discussed and recommendations for improvements made.

Keywords: usability, qualitative data analysis, NUD*IST, context of use, evaluation, systems engineering, data exchange.

1 Introduction

The need for ensuring that usability measurement results can contribute to the ongoing development of a software product in a formative way is the main theme of this paper. It is recognized that acquiring, structuring, and analysing data about the actual progression of a product's development is a challenging task. Even more difficult, is the problem of making the results of any analysis of that data readily accessible to all the participants at regular intervals in the process. The paper presents an approach to supporting that process exemplified in SEDRES (Systems Engineering Data Representation and Exchange Standardization), a European Aerospace collaborative project on developing a data exchange capability for design tools. The main subject is the role of a software tool called NUD*IST (Non-numerical Unstructured Data Indexing Searching and Theorizing) (QSR, 1997), in providing support for structuring and analysing longitudinal data and for regular feedback to the project partners about the product under development.

The paper begins with an overview of the context of use, a systems engineering project involving five major companies in the European Aerospace industry. SEDRES is a three year project which started in January 1996, co-funded by an ESPRIT grant from the European Commission. The project partners comprise Aerospatiale, Alenia, British Aerospace, Daimler-Benz Aerospace, Saab and Linköping University (Sweden), the Australian Centre for Test & Evaluation (ACTE), and Loughborough University Telecommunications and Computer–Human Interaction (LUTCHI) Research Centre.

The work described addresses two issues: first, how to collate, structure and analyse large amounts of qualitative data over a sustained period of time and second, how to provide regular feedback about the software development process that informs an international collaborative development team located in different sites. It describes the analysis techniques employed using NUD*IST, the main features and operational use, followed by examples of the kind of results that can be obtained. The implications of the use of this tool for both the analysis process and the support for formative evaluation are discussed and recommendations for improvements made.

2 Context of Use

2.1 Computer Aided Systems Engineering

Systems Engineering involves the application of a wide range of skills to ensure a system product meets a set of customer requirements that are likely to evolve throughout the time in service. The 'life cycle' is defined as the set of phases through which the development and maintenance of a system passes. The development stages of a system's life cycle are supported by sets of formal methods, and Systems Engineering projects typically start with the identification of customer requirements through analysis of the customer's environment and needs. A process known as requirements engineering is then used to identify separate requirements, categorize them appropriately, and establish links between these requirements and design data. Techniques such as functional, state-based, and object-oriented analysis are used to produce and refine a design that meets the identified requirements (Johnson, 1997).

In the context of the Aerospace industry, and SEDRES, a 'system' may be defined as:

> "A set of predominantly active components, many of which are electronic components like embedded computers, sensors, displays and actuators that are interconnected via dedicated direct links or by communications busses." (SEDRES, 1998)

Modern aircraft avionics systems are made up of hundreds of interacting systems, resulting in an enormous degree of complexity. Established formal methods for the systematic development and maintenance of these complex products are applied incrementally during the entire life cycle of the system.

Many software tools are currently available which support the application of particular established Systems Engineering methods. However, single tools do not provide support for the entire system development and maintenance process. While their degree of specialization may vary, each tool tends to support a fairly narrow part of a system's life cycle. For example, one tool may support the development of the customer's requirements into an abstract preliminary design specifying high level functional aspects of the product. Each component of that preliminary design may be specified in more detail using a different tool, or in many cases, several different tools.

The development of maintenance of large, complex systems may involve contributions from a broad set of software tools. The concepts (e.g. behavioural states or functional attributes) employed by each tool will depend largely on the area and degree of specialization of that tool in the Systems Engineering process. Some concepts (for example, definitions of abstract functions) may be widely supported across the tools, while others, such as physical definitions of system components, may be outside the scope of many of the tools.

2.2 Exchanging Design Information between Sites, Teams and Tools

Each phase in the design of a system may be carried out by different groups of engineers who have specialized knowledge of particular design tools. This is becoming increasingly common in the modern global market, where co-location–same site projects are being replaced by remotely located-multiple site projects. Thus, to add to the multiplicity of design tools and the complexity of the products under development are many differences in the physical and technical environments in which the engineers are working.

Each design team and the software tools used must possess a representation an appropriate set of the design data. Such representations must be accurate (i.e. free from errors, misinterpretations, ambiguity) and consistent (i.e. all design representations must refer to the same design version). Maintaining the accuracy of design representations involves a significant amount of work when these are transferred between teams and tools. Further problems may arise out of the need to integrate changes to the emerging design into each representation whilst maintaining consistency of design information.

Current methods for the exchange of design information involve a combination of ad hoc automatic transfer mechanisms involving small groups of tools and manual transfer of designs 'on paper'. Thus, when the design engineers at one site complete a design, the transfers that take place normally include large amounts of supporting information in order that the receiving team can interpret the design fully. This takes time and effort and there is always room for error.

The successful implementation of a standard automated data exchange mechanism, widely adopted across the Systems Engineering community, will provide significant benefits to the design process (Johnson, 1997).

2.3   *The SEDRES Context: Objectives and Methods*

The long term objective of the SEDRES project is to develop a standard Data Exchange Mechanism (DEM) for the electronic exchange of design information between computer based system engineering tools). This will be based upon an existing standard for exchange of product data: STEP (ISO 10303, STandard for the Exchange of Product data). The resulting standard will be applied initially to ongoing aircraft development projects such as Eurofighter, but is intended eventually to be applicable to the system engineering industry as a whole.

At the highest level, the SEDRES project is intended to contribute to systems engineering process improvement and design re-engineering. To that end, the evaluation stream of the project aims to provide evidence that the SEDRES DEM contributes to those goals. Thus a key question to be addressed is how to identify and demonstrate the benefit to be gained from better data exchange between design tools?

The immediate short term objective is to develop a usable and efficient data exchange capability which is supported across a selection of systems engineering tools, including commercially available and maintained tools. This capability is being tested in a number of scenarios of use which exemplify real world Systems Engineering problems. The results of the analysis are fed into the development process to provide feedback to the design teams in different sites and help identify priorities for further work.

3   SEDRES Evaluation Approach

An evaluation approach was established in parallel with the Data Exchange Mechanism (DEM) work. The starting point for this was the identification of requirements, and test criteria or Measures of Effectiveness (MoE), against which the design tools, infrastructure tools and data exchange mechanisms were evaluated (Harris, 1997).

In order to demonstrate that the test criteria were being met and the requirements being satisfied, it was necessary to collect information about the operational effectiveness of the DEM during real world design exercises — the Use Scenario case studies. For that purpose, a number of methods for identifying the kinds of data needed, devising the techniques for acquiring the data, and applying appropriate analysis methods were developed. The usability framework, the context of evaluation and the methods for data collection are outlined below.

3.1   Usability Standards and Methods

Usability, as defined by the ISO Standard 9241, provided a conceptual framework for the evaluation stream of SEDRES which focused on the qualities of a software product in terms of its benefit to users, tasks and organizational goals. By addressing the design and development of software products in these terms, there is a direct link with the SEDRES business benefit goal to be realized in terms of process improvement. The aim is to improve software product development with regard to three criteria: effectiveness, efficiency and satisfaction (Harker, 1995). The 'product' is defined as an object, mechanism or method that can be shared (e.g. fully described), or passed across (e.g. bought). In this case the 'software products' being evaluated were primarily Data Exchange Mechanisms (DEM). In the light of ISO 9241, usability-specific MoEs and requirements were developed and incorporated into the SEDRES evaluation framework.

The SEDRES evaluation methods drew upon the results of two ESPRIT Projects: Project 2020, 'Front Ends for Open and Closed Systems' (FOCUS) (Candy et al., 1995), and Project 5429, 'Measuring Usability of Systems in Context' (MUSiC) (NPL, 1993-5; Thomas & Bevan, 1995). In particular, techniques for data collection for specifying product usability requirements and assessing whether the product meets these requirements were applied.

Prior to the Use Scenario case studies, which formed the central focus of the evaluation work, an analysis of the context in which the SEDRES DEM is to be used was carried out. Relevant users, their skills, attitudes, roles, and requirements were identified using the Stakeholders and Context Analysis (SACA) method set out in the FOCUS project. FOCUS Project methods were also applied to establish details of the tasks involved in exchanging design information between tools, and to break these down into identifiable sub-tasks and goals. With the addition of organizational information such as security constraints and resource availability, this work provided a complete view of the context in which the SEDRES DEM was intended to be used. It also provided details of the tasks to be performed and the organizational constraints associated with them, enabling evaluation exercises to be developed appropriately.

3.2   Evaluation Context: Tailoring Existing Methods to Industrial Constraints

The context analysis work demonstrated that some tailoring was needed to introduce a greater degree of flexibility into the data collection techniques. The scale of the case studies, requiring evaluation work to be conducted simultaneously across five countries, meant that users of the DEM (the design engineers) would be involved in the collection of a significant portion of the evaluation data. This led to the development of a flexible set of data collection techniques, based on the FOCUS and MUSiC methods, intended to provide sufficient data to assess both the usability of the DEM and its effects on the Systems Engineering process.

The entire set of evaluation data collection exercises were set out in detail in a document distributed to all those involved in the development of the DEM. The SEDRES Evaluation Manual (Britton & Candy, 1997) is a comprehensive manual for the collection of data during the design data exchange exercises. It specifies which data collection techniques are to be used, when they are to be applied, and by whom. It also provides guidelines for their implementation. These include the complete set of data collection forms. This document provides guidance to enable engineers and observers from each of the partners companies to perform the data collection activities. As a result of preliminary data collection exercises carried out by partner companies, further refinements to the checklists and forms were made. Thus the SEDRES Evaluation Manual is a 'live' document, which incorporates the results of experiences, and lessons learned.

The data collection relies primarily on observations made by the design engineer (as a participant observer) and another member of the team (as an external observer) based on site. Security constraints do not permit the use of video and audio recording as a method of data collection. During an observation session, both participant and external observers will be faced with a large amount of information, only a small proportion of which might be useful to usability evaluation. In order to focus the observations, a combination of checklists specifying categories of events to be monitored and recorded, and record forms which allow free form notes to be taken, were developed. The participant and external observers were given training in the use of the techniques.

3.3 *Nature of Data Collected*

The observation and monitoring activities taking place during the design data exchange exercises were designed to collect a variety of data. In the kind of scenario case study under evaluation in SEDRES, the gathered data ranges from the electronic data exchanges themselves to the instances of telephone calls made, faxes and emails sent, to whole design documents and reference manuals. It is evident therefore, that great deal of the raw data is qualitative and initially unstructured.

Figure 1 provides an overview of the evaluation data collection activities during a single data exchange. The scope of each data form is represented as the region of activities between the arrows either side of the form's name. The purpose of the data collected by each form is also represented.

In the early stages of the development process, the main effort is spent on eliminating problems in the tool interface software and the files that comprise the design fragments being exchanged. The type of problems encountered give rise to different kinds of observations by the participant engineers and the external observers. All this data must be monitored and recorded as it arises in the different sites over time. It is then necessary to structure it in such a way as to be able to make sense of it, recall it easily and analyse it. An important issue that should be borne in mind is that the data must at all times be accessible to the development team both its primary raw form and also in its secondary state when it has been transformed through structuring and analysis.

Given the immense difficulties that handling qualitative data poses with the additional need to make the results readily available to partners at regular intervals during the development cycles, it was important to find an effective means of structuring and analysing it. The following section describes the software tool acquired and tailored for this purpose.

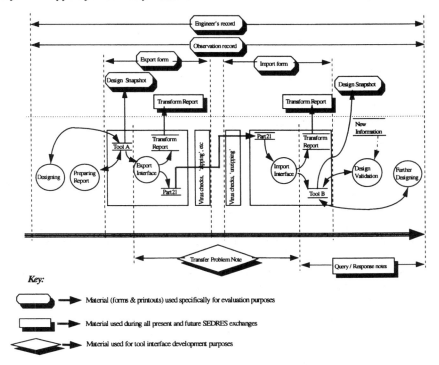

Figure 1: Overview of data collection activities within the context of a data exchange.

4 Applying NUD*IST to Qualitative Data Analysis

NUD*IST is a software package for the application of Qualitative Data Analysis (QDA) methods (Miles & Huberman, 1994). This section describes the application of NUD*ISTto support for the analysis process and also for the project development process. NUD*IST was identified as an appropriate means of representing categories of data expected, and providing means to view them as a hierarchical structure as described further by Richards & Richards (1994). NUD*ISTs features and operation are described below, followed by examples of interim results.

4.1 Overview of the NUD*IST Software

Data is stored as sets of text documents, which can include field notes, interview transcripts, communications between individuals (especially email communications), and any other form of textual data. Entire documents or sections of them can be assigned to categories or *codes* which are set up by the analyst. NUD*IST represents codes as a set of interconnected nodes in a tree structure called the *index tree*. The position of each node within that structure is defined by the user, and can be changed at any time. This enables logical relationships between ideas (such as sub-classes of codes) to be represented by their structure, and this can be altered as relationships change or new ones emerge. The contents of a single node can be viewed, and information stored at various nodes can be combined and filtered using NUD*IST's *search operators*. These provide a means of retrieving selected parts of the data set, such as all data belonging to particular combinations of categories. Contextual information surrounding text retrieved by such searches can be accessed by jumping to the source of selected text (the document from which that text was taken).

4.2   NUD*IST Support for the Analysis Process

4.2.1   Coding Data

In cases where a significant amount of structuring has been imposed on data, and/or the issues to be addressed are known in advance, a set of codes can be implemented prior to analysis. In the case of SEDRES, a set of nodes representing the requirements and each of the observation checklist items was set up prior to analysis. Further codes such as patterns or themes relating to these can be incorporated into the tree structure at any time and the structure of existing nodes can be altered as and when appropriate. Coding structures can also be implemented for 'demographic' data such as: Author, Interviewer/Interviewee, Site, Date, Information relating documents to specific tasks. Nodes contain a reference to each set of text units coded at that node (belonging to the category described by that node). This is achieved in NUD*IST simply by selecting relevant text units, either manually or using NUD*IST's text search facilities and choosing (or creating) an appropriate node. Some nodes contain references to entire documents (for example, nodes for 'document author'), and others to only relevant text (for example, all pieces of text relating to a particular requirement).

4.2.2   Analysing Data

The text coded at selected nodes can be viewed easily, allowing all data relating to that issue to be considered together. NUD*IST's index search facilities extend this by allowing the data to be filtered to include, for example, only data from specific sources.

Groups of text units retrieved by index searches can be imported directly into word processing software. Quantitative information about patterns of document coding can also be exported to spread sheet packages. This can be used to provide the analyst with graphical representations of the volume of text coded at selected nodes. Such information can be used to:

- Identify potentially important issues to direct detailed analyses of qualitative data.

- Identify potential shortcomings in data collection techniques.

- Identify areas of a project where data collection techniques are being applied inconsistently.

Most of the analysis work involves reflecting on the implications of quantitative and qualitative representations of the dataset, and contextual information surrounding such data. Emerging ideas and other notes can be recorded as *memos* attached to relevant nodes or documents. Memos can also be used to document changes to the database made as new ideas emerge. Entries can be date-stamped to provide an audit

```
*External Observation Record
*Observer: NM***
Date: 14/10/97
Start & end time: 11:26 — 12:00
Company & Engineer: ***/ GH
Task: Import Risk Reduction material from G*

%G***, %TASK/USx, %RISK_REDUCTION_MATERIAL, %IMPORT, %CHECKLIST_USED
Receiving transferred file via Internet
%EVENT TYPE? 11:26 Start %Observer: Import started at 11:26
%SNAG/PROBLEM 11:26 Wait %Observer: Waiting for Team Links to wait & see if there's a
message
%Engineer: Usually takes from 1 min to 2 hours. Don't know when sent, only when received
%HELP SOUGHT 11:27 Question %Observer: What are we importing?
%EVENT TYPE? 11:28 Comment %Observer: Email question about sending email to A***
successfully delivered / transferred %Engineer: Only A*** gives these messages supposedly.
%SNAG/PROBLEM 11:30 Email %Observer: Email problems when sending to L***to postmaster
%Engineer: Apart from this, NOT difficult to send email
%EVENT TYPE? 11:13 Reading %Observer: Reading file in email %SNAG/PROBLEM 11:33
Receiving %Observer: Received file but PCMS does not work. Tailored config. problem %Engineer:
Don't know how long it will take.
%HELP SOUGHT 11:34 Break %Observer: Ask question about what actually happened to import
file sent to himself
```

Figure 2: Example coded observation record.

trail of developing ideas. This is especially important during longitudinal studies where ideas may change considerably during the course of the analysis.

4.3 NUD*IST Support for the SEDRES Project

The section illustrates the use of NUD*IST's facilities to structure and analyse data in the context of SEDRES. The first examples are mainly of benefit to the analyst and the evaluation team. However, where participative observers are involved, having access to the structured data may also be required. The various uses to which NUD*IST may be put can have value in different ways to the analyst's ongoing tasks and be used to inform the project development team of the results of that work whenever required.

4.3.1 Storing and Structuring Data

Observers assigned events into categories using a checklist, and these categories were represented by nodes in NUD*IST's index tree. Key words were used to mark these categories. Observations not categorized were marked with the key words '%EVENT TYPE?'. This enabled such events to be grouped together and categorized by the analyst. The use of the '%' symbol enables text searches to distinguish key words from document text. Lines of text preceded by a * character are recognized by NUD*IST as headers and sub-headers.

Figure 3 illustrates the structure of a small part of the index tree established prior to, and during, analysis of SEDRES evaluation data. Each box represents a single node. Nodes implemented during the analysis process (below the dashed line in the figure) show how actions relating to 're-keying data' (and therefore the requirement

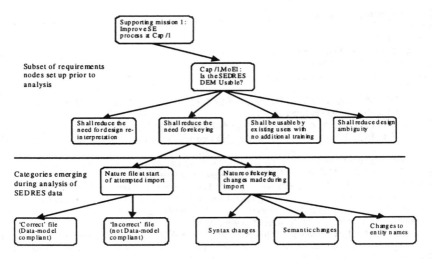

Figure 3: Part of the index tree showing some original requirements nodes and examples of subclasses of actions arising during analysis.

"Shall reduce or eliminate the need to re-key data") can be broken down into distinct sub-classes. These sub-classes have arisen during reflections on the data coded at the "Shall reduce re-keying" node, which were recorded using NUD*IST's memoing facility. In addition to this, a limited graphical representation of the tree structure is available in NUD*IST.

NUD*IST provides a facility to export the entire structure of the index tree to a software package call Inspiration, which can automatically produce a graphical representation similar to the one above (Inspiration Software Inc., 1994).

Reflections and ideas arising during analysis can be stored as memos (text files) attached to relevant nodes. The screen shot in Figure 4 contains an example of such a memo, along with NUD*IST's representation of the index tree structure.

4.3.2 Deriving Quantitative Measures from Usability Data

The following examples are taken from a set of initial results that are being used to inform the project development process. Using NUD*IST in conjunction with Microsoft Excel, it is possible to represent qualitative information as quantitative measures. The chart in Figure 5 shows the number of text units coded at each observation category node during each of the months shown.

This chart illustrates how the type of observed events changes over time. This is based on all observation data collected between October and May and can be broken down further to show, for example, observed actions for individual design tools.

4.3.3 Deriving Insights from Usability Data Analysis

Quantitative representations of qualitative information may be used as a diagnostic or monitoring tool. The changing profiles of the data over time may indicate the resolution or emergence of problems in relation to the requirements. By monitoring

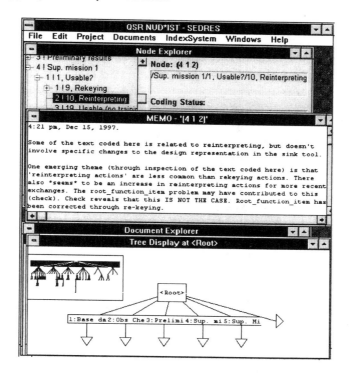

Figure 4: Screen shot with memo and tree structure.

the peaks in the data shown, it is possible to highlight specific issues that require further investigation. This can be carried out by using the browsing and reporting facilities, and going direct to the source documents and tracing the events.

Figure 5, showing the number of text units collected for each observation category during each month, suggests that significantly more interface operations were carried out in February than in other months. In light of this finding, the relevant qualitative data were re-assessed to establish reasons for this apparent inconsistency. It was found that a recurring system crash during a single observed exchange was responsible for this finding. Once this was taken into account, a relatively smooth reduction over time in the number of interface operations required to successfully import data was observed. This reflects the increasing maturity of the developing tool interfaces.

As illustrated above, quantitative measures of coding patterns provide an effective means of identifying possible issues in the data. In order for isolated quantitative results to be meaningful, coding must be carried out very rigorously to ensure the coding reflects all aspects of the data accurately. It is also important to maintain a consistent, non-biased set of data. In interpreting these quantitative data, the original sources (the text containing the relevant information) must be consulted.

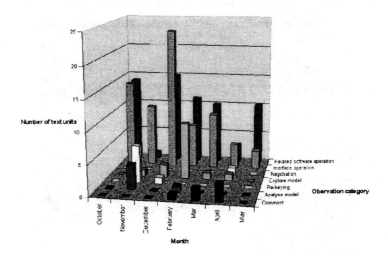

Figure 5: Number of text units referring to each observation category for each month. No exchanges were carried out in January.

Quantitative coding data as a method of identifying possible issues and avenues for further investigation has proved very useful. This technique provides a quick, effective means of directing future analysis of the large volumes of the evaluation data. In particular, it proved to be an effective way of providing interim feedback to the project developers.

5   The Role of NUD*IST: Discussion

NUD*IST supports the efficient management, structuring and manipulation of large amounts of qualitative data. This frees the analyst from tasks associated with managing such data, allowing him/her to spend more time interrogating and reflecting on the data. In addition to the obvious benefits arising due to the automation of clerical tasks (i.e. more 'reflection time' therefore more ideas and more robust interpretations), NUD*IST provides more direct support for the analysis process.

5.1   Support to Analysis Process

The flexibility of NUD*IST's index system is a key feature of the software, enabling relationships between ideas and concepts to be developed and refined as analysis proceeds. Combinations of the search operators that exploit the index system enable data to be filtered according to complex rules set by the user. This allows specific questions to be addressed. By allowing the developing ideas to be stored along side the data they relate to, NUD*IST's memoing facilities support careful recording and auditing of ideas. This helps ensure that the results of the analysis can be backed up by explanations and justifications of the steps taken to produce them.

Analysis work carried out as part of the SEDRES project has also identified a set of high level benefits to the analysis process resulting from the use of NUD*IST. These include:

Analysis and management of data from longitudinal studies: NUD*IST enables information to be incrementally incorporated into the data set, coded, and analysed. Analyses of new data can be carried out along side existing data to establish common themes and patterns, or comparisons between older and more recent information can be made. This is especially important to SEDRES due to the need to monitor and compare the effectiveness of the DEM at different stages in its development.

Targeted feedback at level of detail appropriate to audience: The level of detail available from NUD*IST for reporting to project stakeholders ranges from appropriate parts of the 'raw' data to the 'high level' results of detailed analyses. The level of detail can therefore be tailored to suit the audience. For example, the software development team in SEDRES may require access to actual passages of text, or entire documents (such as observations made during particularly problematic test exchange). At the project management level, however, only the final outcomes of the analysis (such as recommendations and models of key processes) would be of interest.

Rapid, almost continuous, feedback to specific developers questions/needs: Specific answers to questions at all levels of detail can be provided in considerably less time than with conventional qualitative data analysis techniques. Immediate feedback can be provided in addition to more detailed written reports.

Quantitative information about coding patterns: Quantitative information about coding patterns (for example, comparisons between the volume of text coded at a group of nodes) can be used to quickly identify areas where the data collection techniques are providing insufficient information to address particular issues or requirements. Comparisons can also guide the analysis towards potentially significant issues.

5.2 *Support to Project Development*

NUD*IST has been of benefit to the SEDRES project in a number of ways. These include:

- Verifying project requirements using flexible qualitative evaluation data collection techniques.

- Providing usability information without the need for data collection techniques such as video recordings, which may lead to security problems in sensitive industrial situations.

- Providing full support to longitudinal studies such as SEDRES, by allowing new data to be added to database, coded, and analysed at any time. Analyses using new data can be carried out in terms of new-old comparisons, or new and old data can be considered as a whole.

- Supporting continuous analysis of evaluation data, and producing formative results and feedback during system development.

- Generating immediate feedback to specific questions from the software development team.

- Providing targeted feedback at all levels of detail from software development to project management issues.

5.3   Proposed Enhancements to NUD*IST

There is considerable potential for multi-user access to the data and results provided by NUD*IST. Further investigations are needed into the implications of such access in respect of data fidelity and confidentiality. An enhanced system could enable continuous updates to a remotely stored NUD*IST database (i.e. same contents at each site) with rights of access by team members and the role of a system administrator defined according to the particular requirements of the context of use. Some limitations were identified and improvements proposed as follows:

User Interface: The flexibility of NUD*IST's Graphical User Interface provides the user with essential control over the information displayed. There were, however, interface limitations, which had significant effects on some parts of the analysis process: for example, the facility to allocate an entire document to a node provided a means of storing information relating to the entire document, such as its author. However, this facility requires a means to select the entire set of base data nodes in order to carry out the coding in a single operation. This would greatly reduce the time and effort required.

Document Formatting and Storage: NUD*IST divides document text into text units, marked by hard-return characters. A single text unit is the smallest amount of text that can be coded. The appropriate size for each text unit will depend on the nature of the data being analysed, but, in general, a line, sentence, or paragraph is appropriate. A text unit of a paragraph was considered to be appropriate for SEDRES, as much of the data was expected to be in note form containing short paragraphs addressing single issues. Keywords may also be added to documents to take advantage of NUD*IST's text-search facilities.

NUD*IST's document storage system requires appropriately formatted text-only documents. Inferring an appropriate text unit size, useful keywords, and meaningful document headers and sub-headers presents the analyst with a difficult task. Even after initial codings, changes to documents are carried out in a word processor package. A facility to make changes to documents without removing them from the NUD*IST data base would enable the analyst to refine document formatting without the need for extensive work.

Establishing the most appropriate headers, sub-headers, keywords, and text unit size requires a significant amount of insight into how the documents will be analysed, what they will contain, and how key words and sub-headers will aid the coding and analysis processes. Once documents have been imported into NUD*IST, making changes to text unit size is very difficult.

Index System: The flexibility of NUD*IST's index system is a key feature of the software, enabling relationships between ideas and concepts to be developed and refined. Making small changes to the structure of the index tree is a simple process, producing reliable, predictable results, aided by the memos produced automatically logging changes to the structure. Larger changes can, however, be quite difficult, partly because of the complexity of the task. It seems necessary to reassess the index structure from time to time during analysis and hence, more help for the larger changes would be valuable.

Designing the structure of codes requires some care, particularly in cases where these are implemented prior to analysis. This is because the structure of codes imposes certain restrictions on the way those categories can be combined with others during analysis. Designing effective structures requires some prior understanding about the way in which the categories represented by them are likely to be used, both by the analyst and the search operators provided by NUD*IST. Improvements to code structures can be made after their effectiveness has been established. However, it was found that careful consideration to structuring prior to analysis was more efficient due to the significant amount of work required to make large changes.

6 Conclusions

The paper has described a method for the analysis of qualitative usability data and the use of a software support tool called NUD*IST. The work is illustrated by its application in SEDRES, a Systems Engineering project for data exchange development. A number of advantages have been identified in relation to support for the analysis process and project development. Some limitations were outlined and improvements proposed to the design of the software. The method continues to be used in the context described and it is suggested that it may be applicable in other contexts where usability measurement is being carried out.

Acknowledgements

The work was partly funded by the European Commission under ESPRIT Project 20496. The authors wish to thank the SEDRES partner companies whose contribution to the evaluation data collection was invaluable. The role of ACTE, University of South Australia, in developing the evaluation framework with LUTCHI should be noted.

References

Britton, J. H. & Candy, L. (1997), *The SEDRES Evaluation Manual*, LUTCHI Research Centre, Loughborough University, UK. SEDRES Project Esprit 20496.

Candy, L., Edmonds, E. A., Heggie, S. P., Murray, B. S. & Rousseau, N. P. (1995), A Strategy and Technology for Front End System Development, *in* Y. Anzai, K. Ogawa & H. Mori (eds.), *Proceedings of the 6th International Conference on Human–Computer Interaction (HCI International '95)*, Elsevier Science, pp.103–108.

Harker, S. (1995), "The Development of Ergonomic Standards for Software", *Applied Ergonomics* **26**(4), 275–279.

Harris, D. (1997), Test and Evaluation in the SEDRES Project., *in Proceedings International T&E Association National Conference*, Australian Centre for Test and Measurement (ACTE), University of South Australia.

Inspiration Software Inc. (1994), *Inspiration Version 4*, Portland, Oregon, USA.

Johnson, J. F. E. (1997), The SEDRES Project (System Engineering and Data Representation and Exchange Standardization): Extending STEP from Structural Definition to Product Functionality, *in* H.-J. Warnecke & R. Esposito (eds.), *Proceedings 8th International Conference on CALS and Electronic Commerce in Europe*, Direct Communications GmbH, pp.92–107.

Miles, M. B. & Huberman, M. (1994), *Qualitative Data Analysis: An Expanded Source Book*, Sage Publications.

NPL (1993-5), *MUSiC Performance Measurement Handbook*. National Physical Laboratory, Teddington, UK. Crown Copyright.

QSR (1997), *NUD*IST 4 User Guide*, second edition. http://www.sagepub.co.uk.

Richards, T. & Richards, L. (1994), Creativity in Social Sciences: The Computer Enhancement of Qualitative Data Analysis, *in* T. Dartnall (ed.), *Artificial Intelligence and Creativity*, Kluwer Academic, pp.365–83.

SEDRES (1998), "SEDRES Project Home Page", http://www.ida.liu.se/projects/sedres/.

Thomas, C. & Bevan, N. (1995), *Usability Context Analysis A Practical Guide*, National Physical Laboratory, Teddington, UK. EC funded project version. Crown copyright.

The Persona Effect: How Substantial Is It?

Susanne van Mulken, Elisabeth André & Jochen Müller

*German Research Centre for Artificial Intelligence (DFKI),
Stuhlsatzenhausweg 3, D–66123 Saarbrücken, Germany.*

Tel: *+49 681 4128, +49 681 5252*
EMail: {*mulken, andre, jmueller*} *@dfki.de*

Personification of interface agents has been speculated to have several advantages, such as a positive effect on agent credibility and on the perception of learning experience. However, important questions less often addressed so far are what effect personification has on more objective measures, such as comprehension and recall, and furthermore, under what circumstances this effect (if any) occurs. We performed an empirical study with adult participants to examine the effect of the Ppp Persona not only on subjective but also on objective measures. In addition, we tested it both with technical and non-technical domain information. The results of the study indicate that the data from the subjective measures support the so called *persona effect* for the technical information but not for non-technical information. With regard to the objective measures, however, neither a positive nor a negative effect could be found. Implications for software development are discussed.

Keywords: personified interface agents, persona effect, empirical evaluation.

1 Introduction

In the past years, there has been a growing interest in the personification of intelligent interface agents. Personified agents are interface assistants that are visually present on the computer screen in the form of an animated life-like character (Ball et al., 1997; Rickel & Johnson, 1997; Rist et al., 1997). Their tasks range from merely performing the tasks delegated to them by the user (e.g. collect particular information from the World-Wide Web) to explaining and presenting information on the screen.

The main reason for personification is that it is believed to render human–computer interaction more human–human like, more social (Nass et al., 1994). This is speculated to lead to several advantages:

- The social aspect of personified agents is believed to raise the trustworthiness and believability of agents — aspects which are important if interface agents are to be authorized by the user (Lester & Stone, 1997).

- Because it makes interaction more social, it increases the user's engagement (Walker et al., 1994; Sproull et al., 1996). Furthermore, in learning environments, personification can positively affect the student's perception of his learning experience (Lester et al., 1997a).

However, personification of intelligent interface agents not only offers opportunities, it also raises questions. Many empirical evaluation studies that have been carried out so far have started from the assumption that personification should indeed be strived for, the only question to answer is how this should be done. Furthermore, most studies have concentrated on subjective measures such as acceptance and believability (Takeuchi & Naito, 1995; Koda & Maes, 1996). An exception to this forms a study by Lester et al. (1997b) who investigated the effect of different clones of an interface agent exhibiting different types of feedback behaviour on learning performance in a learning environment for children. However, the main question addressed in this study was what type of feedback the agent should exhibit and not what effect the mere presence of such an agent has on learning performance. A recent informal study by Lester and colleagues (Towns et al., 1998) concentrated on the empirical evaluation of a Persona's pointing gestures. However, the study only investigated whether the Persona's referential expressions were intelligible; it did not compare the learning effect in the Persona condition with the learning effect in a no-Persona condition.

To investigate this issue, we performed an explorative empirical study that evaluates the effect of one such agent, the Ppp Persona (Rist et al., 1997) — both on subjective and on objective measures.

The Ppp Persona is a life-like interface agent that presents multimedia material to the user following the directives of a script (André & Rist, 1996). This material is either automatically generated or retrieved from the World-Wide Web. While the user views the presentation, the Persona can among other things comment on particular parts and highlight them through pointing gestures. Currently, the repertoire of presentation gestures includes: gestures that express emotions (e.g. approval or disapproval), gestures that convey the communicative function of an utterance (e.g. to warn, to recommend, or to dissuade), gestures that support referential acts (e.g. to look at an object and point at it), gestures that regulate the interaction between the Persona and the user (e.g. to establish eye-contact with the user when talking to him or her), and gestures that indicate that the Persona is speaking*. However, the Persona's behaviour is not only determined by the directives specified in the script. Rather, the behaviour of the animated character follows the equation:

---

*In the experiment, however, these behaviours were not fully put to use.

Persona behaviour = directives + self-behaviour

Such self-behaviours are indispensable in order to increase the Persona's vividness and believability. Currently, they comprise idle-time actions, such as tapping with a foot, actions for indicating activity, such as, to turn over pages in a book, navigation acts, such as walking or jumping, and immediate reactions to external events, such as mouse gestures on the presented material. While the presentation script is created in a proactive planning phase, the Persona's self-behaviours are determined reactively taking into account the current situation at runtime.

In the experiment we performed, we were specifically interested in:

- The effect of the presence of Persona on a comprehension and recall task and its effect on subjective assessment.

- Any effect of the domain of the presented information on these measures.

We believed three possible effects on comprehension and recall to be possible:

- Persona increases comprehension/recall performance in the user, for instance, through an increase in the user's motivation;

- Persona decreases performance on comprehension and recall, for instance, because it attracts the user's attention to the Persona herself and thus away from the relevant information;

- Persona neither decreases nor increases comprehension and recall, for instance, because neither of the above mentioned effects exists or because the respective effects are equally strong and thus — acting as antagonistic factors — prevent any effects on comprehension and recall from being observable.

On the basis of related studies, we expected that, with respect to subjective assessment, presentations with Persona should be rated more positively (with respect to such issues as entertainment and interestingness) than presentations without Persona.

The exploratory study consisted of three parts: In the first two parts, we investigated the effect of Persona on the objective measures with respect to technical and non-technical information. In the last part, we were interested in the influence of Persona on subjective assessments of the presentation.

2 Method

2.1 Subjects and Design

Subjects were 15 females and 15 males, all native speakers of German, on average 28 years of age, and recruited from the Saarbrücken university campus. The subjects were paid DM 10,- for participation. The experiment was conducted in German and lasted about 45 minutes.

The independent variables were Persona (with the levels *absent* and *present*) and the Type of Information (*technical* vs. *non-technical* information). As dependent

Type of Information	Persona	
	Present	Absent
Technical	Ss 1-15	Ss 16-30
	Comprehension / Recall / Quest. A+B	Comprehension / Recall / Quest. A
Non-technical	Ss 1-15	Ss 16-30
	Comprehension / Recall / Quest. A+B	Comprehension / Recall / Quest. A

Figure 1: Schematic representation of the experimental design.

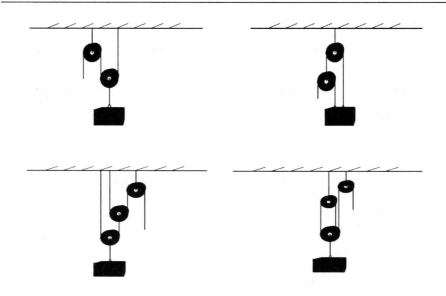

Figure 2: Pulley systems used for the technical presentations.

variables, we defined performance on comprehension and recall tests and subjective ratings on an assessment questionnaire.

The variable Persona was manipulated between-subjects, whereas the variable Type of Information was manipulated within-subjects (see Figure 1).

All subjects were assigned to the conditions randomly. Twenty-one of these subjects had no prior familiarity with the building in which the experiment was carried out. Of the nine remaining subjects, four were in the no-persona condition, five were in the persona condition.

2.2 Materials

2.2.1 Presentations

In both Persona conditions, subjects were presented with technical and non-technical material. For the technical material, we relied on the material used by Hegarty et al. (1988) and Hegarty & Just (1993) to investigate the understanding of machines from

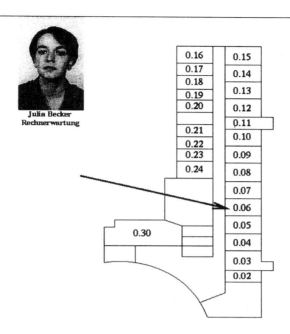

Figure 3: Example of the items used in the non-technical presentations. For privacy reasons, we here substituted the photograph with that of one of the authors.

text and diagrams. The material consisted of information about four different pulley systems (see Figure 2). The spatial information concerning each of the pulleys was presented visually through its depiction on the screen. Whereas in Hegarty & Just (1993), information about the pulley system's parts and its kinematics was presented textually, in this experiment, it was presented acoustically so as to enhance Persona's life-likeness.

For the condition with non-technical material, we designed a presentation in which ten fictitious employees of DFKI were introduced. For each employee, his or her photograph was presented. In addition, the employee was introduced by his/her name and occupation. The office which s/he worked in was pointed at in a map of the DFKI floor (see Figure 3 for example material). The occupations were kept as distinct and concrete as possible. Examples are press officer, secretary, and programmer. Moreover, so as to ease discrimination, the offices assigned to the employees were never adjacent.

2.2.2 Tests

Subjects were tested on their comprehension of the pulley system material in four test sessions, each directly following the presentations. Test questions concerned both

General Questions (Q-A)

1. Did you find the presentation difficult to understand?
2. Did you find the presentation entertaining?
3. Did you find the tests difficult?
4. Did you find the presentations interesting?
5. Did you feel overloaded by the information presented?
6. General remarks about the presentations: ...

Persona-Specific Questions (Q-B)

7. Was Persona's behaviour appropriate for the presentation?
8. Did Persona distract you from the relevant information?
9. In which of both parts did you find Persona more appropriate?
10. Did Persona help you concentrate on relevant information?
11. Did Persona motivate you to further pay attention to the presentation?
12. If in future you could choose between presentations with and without Persona (but with arrow annotations), which would you prefer?
13. Other remarks about Persona: ...

Figure 4: Questionnaires A and B. Where possible, questions were to be answered on a five-point scale, for the pulley system material and the DFKI-employee material separately.

configuration and kinematics of the pulley systems. An example of the questions about the configuration is "What objects does the red rope touch?". An example of the kinematics questions is "How does the lower pulley move if one pulls the free end of the red rope?". The former type of questions was open-ended. The latter type of questions was multiple choice: Possible answers to the kinematics questions were, for instance, "Does it move up, down, or stay in the same place", and "Does it rotate clockwise, counter-clockwise, or not rotate?". It was assumed that a prerequisite for correct answers to these questions is that the subject had built a mental model of the system, which in turn is regarded as indicative of understanding (Weidenmann, 1988).

The recall tests on the employee material followed after all employees had been introduced. On presentation of an employee's photograph and a map of the DFKI floor showing numbered rooms, subjects had to fill in the employee's name, occupation, and office number.

At the end of the experiment, the subjects were asked to fill in a questionnaire. This questionnaire consisted of two parts (Q-A and Q-B). The first part contained questions that concerned, among other things, the difficulty of the presentation and the tests, and the degree of entertainment experienced during the presentations (see Figure 4). The second part of the questionnaire (Q-B) contained questions concerning Persona. This part aimed to find out any differences in acceptance depending on the type of information presented. An example of these questions is "Did you find Persona's behaviour appropriate for the presentation?". These questions were to be answered on a five point scale for both domains. Whereas the first part, Q-A, was

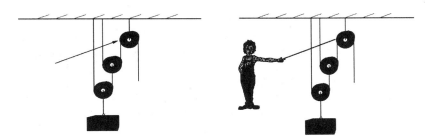

Figure 5: Example presentations for the technical domain information. Left: No-Persona condition; Right: Persona condition.

This pulley system consists of 3 pulleys (<pointing>), 2 ropes (<pointing>), and a weight (<pointing>). The upper pulley (<pointing>) is attached to the ceiling (<pointing>). The other pulleys (<pointing>) can freely move up and down. The upper rope is attached to the ceiling at one end (<pointing>), goes under the middle pulley (<pointing>), over the upper pulley (<pointing>), and is free at the other end (<pointing>). The lower rope is attached to the ceiling at one end (<pointing>). It goes under the lower pulley (<pointing>) and is attached to the middle pulley at the other end (<pointing>). The weight (<pointing>) hangs from the lower pulley.

If one pulls the free end of the upper rope (<pointing>), it moves over the upper pulley (<pointing>), under the middle pulley (<pointing>) and lifts it. The lower rope then moves under the lower pulley (<pointing>) and the weight is lifted.

Figure 6: Text spoken during the animation (translated from German).

---

given to all subjects, the second part, Q-B, was only given to the subjects in the Persona condition.

2.2.3 Operationalization of the Independent Variables

The independent variable Persona could take on two values: No-Persona, in which Persona was absent; and Persona, in which it was present. The only difference between the Persona and No-Persona conditions was that in the No-Persona condition, the specific components referred to in the acoustically presented information were annotated by arrows so as to facilitate integration of visual and acoustic information. In the Persona condition, pointing gestures had the form of Persona pointing with a pointer stick. Because we were interested in the effect of the mere presence of Persona, we had to ensure that the difference between the two conditions really concerned the presence of Persona only. Therefore, we decided to make two conditions that concerned a one to one mapping with respect to the information contents. Thus, all and only the information presented in the one condition was also presented in the other condition. Figure 5 shows screen shots of the Persona and No-Persona conditions for the technical material. Figure 6 shows the information presented acoustically.

2.2.4   Apparatus

The experiment was run on a Sun SPARCstation 5. The material was presented to the subjects on a colour monitor, in the Netscape Web-browser environment. The browsing facilities were disabled. Acoustic information was produced with a speech synthesizer developed at DFKI. The Persona animations were generated by the Ppp Persona animation generator (André et al., 1996). The animations for the No-Persona condition were implemented using Animator v1.8 (Jellinek, 1996).

2.3   Procedure

The experiment was run in one of the offices at DFKI. During each experimental session, an experimenter was present in order to answer any possible questions by the subject and to see that everything proceeded as intended.

The subjects were told that the goal of the experiment was to investigate different multimedia presentations with respect to their effects on comprehension and recall. They were informed that in the first part of the experiment, they would be presented with information about pulley systems, while in the second part they would be given information about employees of DFKI. In addition, they were told that after each of the presentations they would be tested on their knowledge of the configuration and kinematics of the respective pulley systems (in the first part) or on their knowledge of the names, occupations, and offices of the respective employees (in the second part).

After each pulley system presentation, the subjects were first asked to indicate on a five-point scale whether they found the presentation difficult. This question — forming part of questionnaire Q-A — followed directly after the presentation so as to avoid that the subjects' answer would be confounded by their impression of the difficulty of the test. Next, they were administered a test that asked questions about the constituents and kinematics of the pulley system. Subjects could take as long as necessary to complete the test.

After the test about the last pulley system, the subjects would enter the second part of the experiment. This part concerned the employee descriptions. The subjects were informed that they would be introduced to ten employees, and that for each employee they had to memorize as much information as possible. Subjects were asked to imagine starting as a new employee at DFKI, intending to get acquainted with his/her colleagues as fast as possible. They were told that in the test that followed they would be asked to give the name, the occupation, and the room number of the respective employee.

After the presentation of the ten employees, the subjects were again asked to rate the difficulty of the presentation. After this question, they entered the test. Each test item showed a picture of the employee and a map of the DFKI floor. In three entries, subjects could type in their answers to the respective questions. There were no time restrictions.

Finally, the subjects were asked to fill out a questionnaire. This questionnaire consisted among others of questions about the difficulty of the tests, the degree of entertainment experienced during the presentation, and about how interesting they found the presentation. Subjects in the No-Persona condition only received the general questions whereas those in the Persona condition additionally received the part with Persona-specific questions.

Figure 7 shows a schematic depiction of the experimental procedure.

Figure 7: Procedure of the expériment.

Type of	Persona Condition	
Information	No Persona	Persona
Technical Material	36.14	37.57
Person Descriptions	11.43	10.35

Table 1: Means for Comprehension and Recall Performance by the Conditions Persona and Type of Information.

3 Results

In the following analyses an α level of 0.05 is used[†]. Furthermore, the data of two subjects were discarded because of technical difficulties.

3.1 Comprehension and Recall

The answers to the tests were scored by the experimenter. Each correct answer was awarded one point, thus in the tests about the pulley systems leading to a maximum score of 44; in the test about the employees to a maximum score of 30.

For each subject, two scores were calculated: one for the technical domain test; one for the non-technical domain test. These data were then subjected to two-tailed t-tests. For the technical material, the t-test testing the difference between the mean of the condition No-Persona and the condition Persona showed no significant effect ($t(26) = -0.73$; $p = 0.47$).

A second t-test was done for the means on the non-technical information test. Again the data showed no significant effect ($t(26) = 0.82$; $p = 0.42$).

Thus, the analyses showed neither a positive nor a negative effect of Persona, neither for technical information, nor for non-technical information (see Table 1).

3.2 Subjective Assessment

The questionnaire data concerned ratings on a five-point scale, ranging from 0 (negative answer, i.e. indicating disagreement) to 4 (positive answer, i.e. indicating agreement).

[†]This means that in the decision as to reject or retain the null hypothesis (that there is in fact no difference between the means of the two groups) we accept a risk of 0.05 of making a false decision. Put differently, if we observe an effect with $p < 0.05$, we may conclude that the probability that the sample means would have occurred by chance if the population means are equal is less than 0.05.

	Type of Information			
	Technical Information		Person Descriptions	
	Persona Condition		**Persona Condition**	
Question	No-Persona	Persona	No-Persona	Persona
1 Presentation hard to understand	1.63	1.09	2.07	2.14
2 Presentation entertaining	1.28	2.07	1.78	2.0
3 Test difficult	2.00	1.50	2.86	2.93
4 Presentation interesting	1.71	2.21	2.0	2.28
5 Information overload	1.43	1.14	2.50	2.86

Table 2: Means for the General Questions Asked in the Questionnaire (Part A).

	Type of Information	
Question	Technical Information	Person Descriptions
7 Persona's behaviour is tuned to presentation	3.00	1.67
8 Persona distracts subject from relevant info	1.00	.93
10 Persona helps concentrate on relevant parts	2.43	1.57
11 Persona motivates to further pay attention to presentation	2.21	2.00

Table 3: Means for the Persona-Specific Questions asked in the Questionnaire (Part B).

In order to analyse the affective impact of the variable Persona, the data of Questionnaire A were subjected to t-tests. The four ratings concerning the difficulty of the pulley system presentations were averaged to produce a single mean rating for each subject. As a t-test showed, there was a significant effect of Persona ($t(26) = 2.51$; $p = 0.0186$), with subjects in the Persona condition on average giving more positive ratings than those in the No-Persona condition. For the non-technical domain, no such effect was found.

In addition, the analysis of the questions asking about the entertainment degree of the presentations showed a significant effect for the technical domain ($t(26) = -2.38$; $p = 0.0247$): Subjects in the Persona condition gave significantly more positive ratings than those in the other group. Again, no effect was found for the non-technical domain.

The difference in ratings for the question asking about the difficulty of the tests just failed to reach significance for the technical domain ($t(26) = -1.71$; $p = 0.098$). For the non-technical material, there was no such tendency.

For all other questions, the analyses showed no significant effects (see Table 2).

In order to investigate the effect of the domain on subjective assessment, the questions of questionnaire B (see Table 3), asking specifically about Persona, were submitted to t-tests with Type of Information as a repeated measure. Here, the results showed significant effects for the question asking whether the subject felt that Persona had helped her concentrate on the relevant parts of the presentation ($t(13) = 2.37$; $p = 0.033$) and for the question whether Persona's behaviour was tuned to the presentation ($t(13) = 8.027$; $p = 0.000$): With the technical presentations, subjects thought Persona to be more of an aid and found her behaviour more tuned than with non-technical presentations. Subjects did not find Persona more or less encouraging in either of the two domains ($t(13) = 1.14$; $p = 0.272$).

Finally, Questionnaire B contained two additional questions. One question asked in which domain the subject felt that Persona was more appropriate. To this question, 43% of the subjects answered that they thought Persona to be more adequate for the technical material, 57% answered that they thought Persona to be equally adequate in both domains. None of the subjects considered Persona more adequate for the employee descriptions.

The second question asked the subject to imagine that, in future, she could choose between presentations with Persona and presentations without Persona (but with arrow annotations). They were then asked which presentations they would prefer. To this question, 50% answered to prefer presentations with Persona; 43% answered that their preference depends on the material; and 7% answered to prefer presentations without Persona.

4 Discussion and Conclusions

The data did not support any positive or negative effect on comprehension and recall, neither for technical information, nor for non-technical information. The reason for this may lie in the possibility mentioned in the introduction: As motivation and distraction should act as antagonistic factors, the respective effects on comprehension and recall might be mutually outweighed so that no effect can be observed. It should be noted, however, that in this study we only examined short-term effects. It is very well possible that other effects can be found if subjects are asked to interact with personified agents on a longer term. Furthermore, except for an introductory and closing greeting and lip movements, our Persona did not exhibit any additional behaviours that might have amplified any engaging effect.

Subjects in the Persona condition rated the presentations as more entertaining than those in the No-Persona condition. Considering previous empirical studies, this was to be expected. However, we were quite surprised to find that even though the conditions No-Persona and Persona differed solely with respect to the fact that in the Persona condition pointing was done by a lifelike character, subjects who had seen presentations with Persona judged these presentations significantly less hard to understand than those who had seen presentations without Persona.

Even more surprising, although subjects did not perform better on the comprehension and recall tests, subjects in the Persona condition tendentially (significant at the 0.10 level) rated the tests as less difficult than the subjects in the No-Persona condition.

Thus, these data support a *persona effect* that plays an even larger role than so far speculated in the literature (Lester et al., 1997a). The mere presence of the character appears to influence subjects' perception of the difficulty of both the presentation itself and that of the test.

The data showed a differential effect of Type of Information on some of the acceptance questions: Both the question asking whether Persona helps to concentrate on relevant information and the one about whether its behaviour is tuned to the presentation were rated more positively for the technical information than for the non-technical information. We hypothesize therefore that Persona is accepted more readily in case of technical presentations than in case of non-technical presentations. However, from this study we cannot tell unequivocally whether it is indeed the technicality that causes the effect. Another explanation may be that the tasks in the two conditions differed to the extent that in the first, subjects were tested on their understanding — requiring not only recall but also the construction of a mental model — whereas in the second, subjects had to merely memorize as much as possible — something that not really requires the formation of a coherent mental representation. To examine this issue, further empirical studies will have to be performed.

To summarize the results of the study, we see that the presence of Persona neither has a positive nor a negative effect on comprehension and recall performance, and that the type of information does not seem to play a role in this. However, Persona does have a positive effect on the subject's impression of the presentation: Even its mere presence causes presentations to be experienced as less difficult and more entertaining. In addition, tests following presentations by Persona are experienced as less difficult.

Finally, the type of information was seen to affect the subject's impression of the help they received from Persona. In the case of technical information, Persona was perceived to be more of an aid than in the case of non-technical information.

Overall, Persona was received quite positively: 50% of the subjects in the Persona condition indicated that if they could choose, they preferred presentations with Persona, regardless of the type of presentation. 47% answered that their preference depends on the type of material.

Although the results of this study can only be generalized with caution, the findings discussed above suggest some important implications for software development.

- Firstly, because the presence of Persona does not affect objective performance measures, the inclusion of such an agent in software can be considered safe from the point of view of effective information provision.

- Secondly, the presence of Persona appears to have a positive effect on the experience of some types of presentations — even for adult users. Thus, for some applications it may be worthwhile to include such an agent. On the one hand, the effect may be useful in that it may take away the fear of failure that some students experience with regard to particular educational material — see (Salomon, 1984) with respect to the influence of medium type on perceived difficulty. On the other hand, it may be put to use in Web applications — consider, for instance, its use for commercial Web-sites.

- Users appear to have clear preferences about when to have a personified agent in the interface. Thus, it may not only be important to take into account inter-individual differences but also intra-individual differences.

Acknowledgements

This work was partially supported by the BMBF under the contracts ITW 9400 7 and 9701 0 and by European Community under the contract ERB 4061 PL 97-0808. We wish to thank Wolfgang Pöhlman for assistance with the implementation of the animations.

References

André, E. & Rist, T. (1996), Coping with Temporal Constraints in Multimedia Presentation Planning, *in Proceedings of AAAI-96*, Vol. 1, MIT Press, pp.142–7.

André, E., Müller, J. & Rist, T. (1996), The PPP Persona: A Multipurpose Animated Presentation Agent, *in* T. Catarci, M. Costabile, S. Levialdi & G. Santucci (eds.), *Advanced Visual Interfaces*, ACM Press, pp.245–7.

Ball, G., Ling, D., Kurlander, D., Miller, J., Plugh, D., Skelly, T., Stankosky, A., Thiel, D., Dantzich, M. V. & Wax, T. (1997), Lifelike Computer Characters: The Persona Project at Microsoft Research, *in* J. M. Bradshaw (ed.), *Software Agents*, MIT Press, pp.191–222.

Hegarty, M. & Just, A. (1993), "Constructing Mental Models of Machines from Text and Diagrams", *Journal of Memory and Language* **32**, 717–42.

Hegarty, M., Just, M. A. & Morrison, I. R. (1988), "Mental Models of Mechanical Systems: Individual Differences in Qualitative and Quantitative Reasoning", *Cognitive Psychology* **20**, 191–236.

Jellinek, H. (1996), Animator v1.8, Animation tool available via http://java.sun.com/applets/Animator/.

Koda, T. & Maes, P. (1996), Agents with Faces: The Effect of Personification, *in Fifth IEEE International Workshop on Robot and Human Communication (RO-MAN'96)*, IEEE Computer Society Press, pp.189–94.

Lester, J. C. & Stone, B. A. (1997), Increasing Believability in Animated Pedagogical Agents, *in Proceedings of the First International Conference on Automomous Agents*, ACM Press, pp.16–21.

Lester, J. C., Converse, S. A., Kahler, S. E., Barlow, S. T., Stone, B. A. & Bhogal, R. S. (1997a), The Persona Effect: Affective Impact of Animated Pedagogical Agents, *in* S. Pemberton (ed.), *Proceedings of CHI'97: Human Factors in Computing Systems*, ACM Press, pp.359–66.

Lester, J. C., Stone, B. A., Converse, S. A., Kahler, S. E. & Barlow, S. T. (1997b), Animated Pedagogical Agents and Problem-solving Effectiveness: A Large-Scale Empirical Investigation, *in Proceedings of the Eighth World Conference on Artificial Intelligence in Education*, IOS Press, pp.23–30.

Nass, C., Steuer, J. & Tauber, E. R. (1994), Computers are Social Actors, *in* B. Adelson, S. Dumais & J. Olson (eds.), *Proceedings of CHI'94: Human Factors in Computing Systems*, ACM Press, pp.72–7.

Rickel, J. & Johnson, W. L. (1997), Intelligent Tutoring in Virtual Reality: A Preliminary Report, *in* B. du Boulay & R. Mizoguchi (eds.), *Proceedings of the Eighth World Conference on Artificial Intelligence in Education*, IOS Press, pp.294–301.

Rist, T., André, E. & Müller, J. (1997), Adding Animated Presentation Agents to the Interface, *in* J. Moore, E. Edmonds & A. Puerta (eds.), *Proceedings of the 1997 International Conference on Intelligent User Interfaces*, ACM Press, pp.79–86.

Salomon, G. (1984), "Television is 'Easy' and Print is 'Tough': The Differential Investment of Mental Effort in Learning as a Function of Perceptions and Attribution", *British Journal of Educational Psychology* **76**(4), 647–58.

Sproull, L., Subramani, M., Kiesler, S., Walker, J. H. & Waters, K. (1996), "When the Interface is a Face", *Human–Computer Interaction* **11**, 97–124.

Takeuchi, A. & Naito, T. (1995), Situated Facial Displays: Towards Social Interaction, *in* I. Katz, R. Mack, L. Marks, M. B. Rosson & J. Nielsen (eds.), *Proceedings of CHI'95: Human Factors in Computing Systems*, ACM Press, pp.450–5.

Towns, S. G., Callaway, C. B., Voerman, J. L. & Lester, J. C. (1998), Coherent Gestures, Locomotion, and Speech in Life-like Pedagogical Agents, *in Proceedings of the 1998 International Conference on Intelligent User Interfaces*, ACM Press, pp.13–20.

Walker, J. H., Sproull, L. & Subramani, R. (1994), Using a Human Face in an Interface, *in* B. Adelson, S. Dumais & J. Olson (eds.), *Proceedings of CHI'94: Human Factors in Computing Systems*, ACM Press, pp.85–91.

Weidenmann, B. (1988), *Psychische Prozesse beim Verstehen von Bildern* (trans. *Psychological Processes in Picture Understanding*), Hans Huber.

The Influence of Target Size, Distance and Direction on the Design of Selection Strategies

Xiangshi Ren & Shinji Moriya

Department of Information and Communication Engineering, Tokyo Denki University, 2-2 Kanda-Nishikicho, Chiyoda-ku, Tokyo 101-8457, Japan.

Tel: *+81 3 5280 3335, +81 3 5280 3343*
Fax: *+81 3 5280 3335, +81 3 5280 3564*
EMail: *{ren, moriya}@c.dendai.ac.jp*

The influence of various parameters on the design of selection strategies was investigated. Our question is, do changes in the size, distance or direction to a target affect the differences in performance between selection strategies? We performed an experiment on a pen-based system to evaluate the effect of size, distance and direction on six strategies for selecting a target. Three target sizes, three pen-movement-distances, and eight pen-movement-directions were applied to all six strategies. The results show that the differences between selection strategies are affected by target size (when target size decreases below a certain size, differences between selection strategies appear; conversely, differences between selection strategies disappear when target sizes are increased beyond a certain size). The results also show that the differences between selection strategies are not affected by pen-movement-distance and pen-movement-direction. Issues relating to the merits of individual strategies will be the focus of planned future investigations.

Keywords: mobile computing, pen-based systems, pen-input interfaces, target selection strategies, small targets, variations in differences.

1   Introduction

Since the advent of mobile computing, pen-based input has been employed in many portable applications. In portable pen-based systems, target selection, e.g. selection of menus, data (one character of the text or graphic segment, etc.), and ranges etc. is more often attempted than data input. In these small pen-based systems, the target size decreases as the amount of information on the screen increases. The trade-off between the accessibility of targets and the amount of information presented is a fundamental problem in human–computer design (Ren & Moriya, 1997b; Worden et al., 1997).

In order to solve the problem, some leading studies have developed a variety of relatively efficient selection strategies. Sears & Shneiderman (1991) tested three selection devices; touch screen, touchscreen with stabilization, and mouse. The task was the selection of rectangular targets of 1, 4, 16 and 32 pixels per side. Their results showed that a stabilized touchscreen was effective for reducing the error rates when selecting a target. McClintock & Hoiem (1993) conducted a study to determine the smallest optimal size for targets in a pen-based system. Eight kinds of targets were used but the study did not report on any target-selection strategies. Zhai et al. (1994) designed the silk cursor that provided the volume/occlusion cues for target selection and showed its effectiveness. Kabbash & Buxton (1995) developed an area cursor which has a larger than normal area in order to improve target selection. Moreover, Worden et al. (1997) have provided a study of the effectiveness of two target selection strategies: area cursors and sticky icons.

Some findings concerning selection strategies have been described elsewhere (see, for example, (Potter et al., 1988; Buxton, 1990; MacKenzie et al., 1991; Sears et al., 1992). However, current target selection strategies on pen-based systems are mostly only imitations of selection techniques for mouse and touch-screen devices. Investigations which focus on differences between selection strategies on pen-based systems have not been conducted. This study focuses on the effect of target size, pen-movement-distance and pen-movement-direction on target-selection strategies for a pen-based system.

Fitts's (1954) law is commonly used to model a target selection. But Fitts' law only describes the situation for one kind of selection strategy. Our question is, when target size, distance to the target, direction to the target are changed, how are the differences among selection strategies affected?

We are not merely discussing the differences between selection strategies. We are discussing variations in the differences between selection strategies, variations in differences which are caused by changes in target size, distance and direction.

2   Tablet Structure and the Six Strategies

An electromagnetic tablet was used in the experiment. When the pen-tip is within a given height above the tablet surface (1cm), the computer can recognize the coordinates (x, y) of the pen-tip. Thus, even though the menu on the screen is 2 dimensional (2D), it can be highlighted or selected when the pen is above the tablet surface (within 1cm). This means that the menu can be expressed as a 3 dimensional (3D) target.

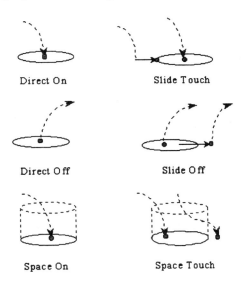

Figure 1: The six strategies used in the experiment. The arrow shows the movement of the pen-tip. A dashed line arrow means the pen-tip is above the screen and a solid line arrow shows that the pen-tip is on the screen. The point shows where the target selection is made by the pen.

The oval and the cylinder shown in Figure 1 illustrate targets on the pen-based system screen. The oval shows that the target is a 2D target. The cylinder shows that the target is a 3D target. That is, the circle with a solid line is at the bottom of the 3D target.

Some responses will take place when the pen is in the cylinder. It is important to note that although the illustration in Figure 1 shows circular targets, the shape of the target has no definitive bearing on this discussion.

The six strategies for selecting a target in the experiment are as follows:

- Direct On: the pen approaches from above. The target is selected only momentarily at the time the pen makes contact with the screen in the target area.

- Slide Touch is an extension of the Direct On strategy. Here also the target is selected when the pen touches it for the first time, but in this case the pen lands outside the target area before moving into it.

- Direct Off: the target is highlighted only while the pen is touching it. The selection is made at the moment the pen is taken off the target.

- Slide Off is an extension of the Direct Off strategy. The target is highlighted only while the pen is in contact with it, however the selection is made when the pen is removed from any point on the screen either inside or outside the target area.

- Space On: the pen approaches from above. The target is highlighted while the pen is within the 1 cm high cylinder above the target. Selection is made at the moment the pen makes contact with the target area (i.e. inside the bottom circle).

- Space Touch is an extension of the Space On strategy. The target is highlighted while the pen is within the 1cm high cylinder above the target. After highlighting, the selection is made when the pen makes contact with any point on the screen either inside or outside the target area.

The Direct On and Direct Off strategies are already in common use. The Slide Touch strategy corresponds to the first-contact strategy (Potter et al., 1988). The Slide Off, Space On and Space Touch strategies were new strategies designed for this experiment.

The main factors affecting our choice of these six strategies were the six conditions created by the pen parameters (Ren & Moriya, 1995). They are: contact with the screen, removal from the screen, contact inside the target, contact outside the target, target highlighted and target not highlighted.

Pen contact involves a movement from 3D to 2D, while removal involves a movement from 2D to 3D. These changes were considered to be suitable conditions for a subject to affect and confirm the moment of target selection. The strategies in which selection was made by contact with the screen were the Direct On, Slide Touch, Space On and Space Touch strategies. The strategies in which selection was made by removal from the screen were the Direct Off and Slide Off strategies. These conditions exist in both 2D targets and 3D targets. Here, the Direct On, Slide Touch, Direct Off and Slide Off strategies can be used for 2D target selection. The Space On and Space Touch strategies were used for 3D target selection assuming that the pen was approaching the target from above, thus 3D targets permit visual confirmation before screen contact.

We considered the movement of the pen into and out of the target (2D or 3D) from the perspective of the user's eyes and ears. When the pen moved into or out of the target, users could confirm whether or not the target was highlighted. Those strategies in which selection was made by screen contact within the target area were the Direct On, Direct Off and Space On strategies. On the other hand, those strategies in which selection was made by screen contact either inside or outside the target were the Slide Touch, Slide Off and Space Touch strategies.

Those strategies in which selection was made when the pen was removed from the surface of the target or from above the target after visual confirmation, were the Direct Off, Slide Off, Space On and Space Touch strategies. Those strategies in which visual confirmation was not possible were the Direct On and Slide Touch strategies.

3   Method

3.1   Subjects

Twenty-one subjects (17 male, 4 female; all right-handed, university students), were tested for the experiment. Their ages ranged from twenty-one to twenty-three years.

Ten had had previous experience with pen-input systems, while the others had had no experience.

3.2   Equipment

The hardware used in this experiment was: a tablet-cum-display (HD-640A, WACOM Corp.), a stylus pen (SP-200A, WACOM Corp.), and a personal computer (PC9801-DA, NEC Corp.). The space resolution of the tablet input was 0.05mm per point. The height of the liquid crystal screen was 144.0mm and the width was 230.4mm. The liquid crystal display resolution was 400 pixels high × 640 pixels wide. 1 pixel was about 0.36mm. The pen/screen contact area was 1.40mm in diameter.

3.3   Procedure

First the experiment was explained to each subject and then each of them had 20 practice trials immediately before the experiment started.

A message 'Select a target as quickly and accurately as possible using the strategy' was displayed on the screen of the experimental tool when the experiment started.

When a target was being selected using any one of the strategies, the steps were as follows:

1. Initial position: a circular initial position was displayed at the centre of the screen. The initial position was the place where the pen was pointed immediately before beginning the selection procedure. The subject had been told which strategy was to be used and how many trails had to be done.

2. Touching the initial position: the subject touched the initial position with the pen.

3. Display of a target: the target was displayed with size and position changed at random. These parameters (target size, position) were randomly selected by the computer. Targets of a particular size were never displayed in the same position twice. The distances between the initial position and the target were 39, 131 or 160 pixels, randomly selected by the computer.

4. Target selection: the subject received a message on the screen to indicate whether he/she had made a successful selection or not.

5. The subject then repeated (a) to (d) above.

6. End of test: a message indicating the end of the test was displayed when the subject had completed the task.

The strategies were not mixed. In a given trial each subject used only one strategy.

3.4   Design and Data Processing

Figure 2 shows an example of the display of a target.

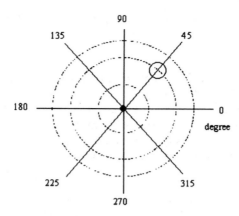

Figure 2: An example of the display of a target.The black point (centre ●) is the initial position. The small circle (○) shows one of the twenty-four possible positions for the display of a target. The dotted line shows the pen-movement-distances from the initial position to the target. The solid line indicates the pen-movement directions to the target from the initial position.

- Size of target: all the targets for the experiment were circular. Circular targets were used so that the distance between the initial position and the edge of all targets on each radius remained constant in all directions. To examine the relationship between target size and strategy, three target sizes of 3, 5 and 9 pixels (1.1 mm, 1.8 mm and 3.2 mm diameter circles) were used in all trials.

- Pen-movement-distance: the distance to the target was the radius of a circle in which the centre point was the initial position. To examine the relationship between distance and strategy, the distances of 39, 131 and 160 pixels (14.0, 47.2 and 57.6 mm) were determined by a preliminary experiment performed by ten subjects. When their wrists were in a fired condition, 39 pixels was the average radius of the arc which could be drawn by the ten subjects; 131 pixels was the average radius of the circular arc which was the maximum finger-movement-distance. The outside circle radius of 160 pixels was determined according to the size limitations (height) of the tablet screen. It was also a distance by which the wrist could be moved.

- Pen-movement-direction : eight directions were used. They were at 0, 45, 90, 135, 180, 225, 270 and 315 degrees from the initial position.

The subject had a total of 92 trials for each strategy. These consisted of 20 practice trials and 72 test trials (= 3 target sizes × 3 distances × 8 directions).

A break was taken at the end of each strategy trial. Whenever the subject felt tired he/she was allowed to take a rest. Each subject completed 432 test trials (= 6 strategies × 72). In each strategy 1512 test trials (= 21 subjects × 72) were completed. The order for the six strategies was different for each of the twenty-one subjects.

The data for each strategy was recorded automatically as follows:

1. Presence or absence of error when a target was selected. (One selection was a continuous operation from the moment the pen touched the initial position until the removal of the pen from the tablet surface.) Feedback to the subject indicated whether the selection was successful or not. In either case, the subject could not cancel the selection.

2. Position and size of the target displayed.

3. The time lapsed between display of the target and the moment when the pen contacted the screen.

4. The time lapsed between contact with the target and removal from the screen.

5. The time lapsed between contact with the screen and contact with the target.

These times were measured to an accuracy of 10ms using a special program.

Data as defined in item (3) was recorded for the Direct On, Space On and Space Touch strategies. Data as defined in item (5) above was recorded for the Slide Touch strategy. Data as defined in item (4) above was recorded for the Direct Off and Slide Off strategies.

3.5   Subject Preferences

The subjects were questioned about their preferences after they finished testing each strategy. The first question was: 'For the strategy tested just now, when selecting T, how do you rate P? Please answer on a 1-to-5 scale (1 2 3 4 5)'. Here, 1 = lowest preference, and 5 = highest preference. 'T' means large or small targets as tested in the particular trial. 'P' consisted of the six sub-questions regarding selection accuracy, selection speed, selection ease, learning ease, satisfaction and desire to use. The questions (P) were asked of both large and small target sizes in each strategy.

The second question was: 'Which positions (i.e. direction and distances) were most comfortable for selecting the targets in the strategy?'. The subject marked his/her preferences on Figure 2.

4   Results

To determine the effect of target size, pen-movement-distance and pen-movement-direction on error rate, selection time and subject preferences, in all six strategies, an ANOVA (analysis of variance) with repeated measures was performed. Error rates were determined by dividing the number of errors by the total number of selection attempts. Selection time was the time required to select the target correctly.

4.1   Selection Times

There was a significant difference between the six strategies, $F(5,120) = 10.8$ ($p < 0.0001$). From this we have concluded that the selection time was influenced by the particular strategy, i.e. selection time changed according to the strategy being applied. Figure 3 shows the average selection times for each of the six strategies. The Slide Touch strategy was the fastest among the six strategies (mean = 0.98s).

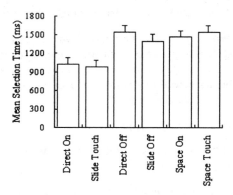

Figure 3: Means (with standard error bars) for selection time in each strategy.

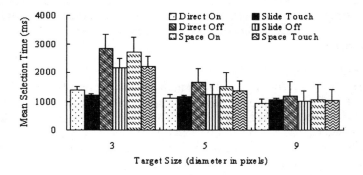

Figure 4: Mean selection time for each strategy according to target size.

Furthermore, there was a significant difference between the Slide Touch, Slide Off and Space Touch strategies, $F(2,60) = 19.8$ ($p < 0.0001$).

To investigate the reason for this, analyses were conducted to determine the significant difference between the six strategies in terms of each target size, each pen-movement-distance and each pen-movement-direction.

- Target size: There were differences between the six strategies in selection time for each target size, 3, 5 and 9 pixels, $F(5,120) = 9.75$, 6.85 ($p < 0.0001$), and 5.22 ($p < 0.001$). This means that significant differences between the six strategies in selection time did not change even when the target size was changed. Figure 4 shows the selection times for each of the six strategies according to each target size.

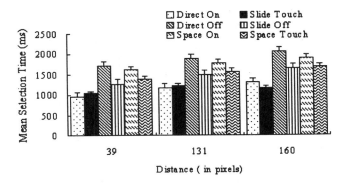

Figure 5: Mean selection time for each strategy according to distance.

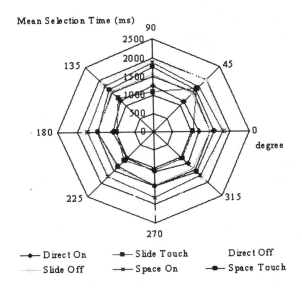

Figure 6: Mean selection time for each strategy according to direction.

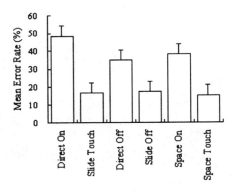

Figure 7: Means for error rate in each strategy.

- Pen-movement-distance: There were significant differences between the six strategies in selection time for each distance, 39, 131 and 160 pixels, $F(5,120) = 7.33$, 10.3 and 10.1 ($p < 0.0001$). Figure 5 shows the selection times for each of the six strategies according to each distance.

- Pen-movement-direction: Significant differences in selection time were observed between the six strategies for all directions 0, 45, 90, 135, 225, 270 degrees ($p < 0.0001$, in case of 180 degrees, $p < 0.001$). Figure 6 shows the selection times for each of the six strategies according to each direction.

4.2 Error Rates

There was a significant difference between the six strategies in error rate, $F(5,120) = 17.8$ ($p < 0.0001$). This means that the error rate was influenced by the differences between the strategies.

Figure 7 shows the mean error rates for each of the six strategies. The Slide Touch, Slide Off and Space Touch strategies show lower error rates (16.6%, 17.4% and 15.5%) than the other three (Direct On, Direct Off and Space On), however, there was no main effect between the three (the Slide Touch, Slide Off and Space Touch strategies) in error rate, $F(2,60) = 0.08$.

To investigate the reasons for this, analyses were conducted to determine the significant differences between the six strategies in error rate, in terms of each target size, each pen-movement-distance and each pen-movement-direction.

- Target size: There were significant differences between the six strategies in error rate for each of the target sizes of 3 and 5 pixels, $F(5,120) = 24.7$, 9.99 ($p < 0.0001$). On the other hand, there was no significant difference between the six strategies in error rate for the target size 9 pixels, $F(5,120) = 0.66$. Figure 8 shows the error rates for each of the six strategies according to target size.

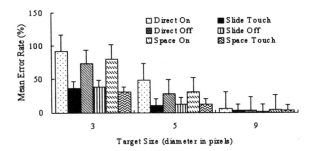

Figure 8: Mean error rate for each strategy according to target size.

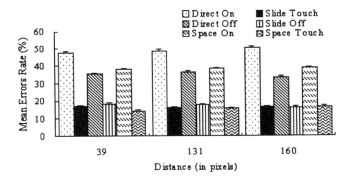

Figure 9: Mean error rate for each strategy according to distance.

- Pen-movement-distance: There were significant differences between the six strategies in error rates for each distance, 39, 131 and 160 pixels, $F(5,120) = 15.2$, 16.3, and 16.5 ($p < 0.0001$). Figure 9 shows the error rates for each of the six strategies according to distance.

- Pen-movement-direction: There were significant differences between the six strategies in error rate for all eight directions ($p < 0.0001$, in case of 180 degrees, $p < 0.001$). Figure 10 shows the error rates for each of the six strategies according to direction.

4.3   Analysis of Subject Preferences

Significant main effects were seen among the six strategies regardless of target size (large target, $F(5,30) = 14.8$, $p < 0.0001$, and small target, $F(5,30) = 58.1$, $p < 0.0001$). This was based on the average value of the answers given by the subjects to the twelve questions. Figure 11 shows the subjective rating in the

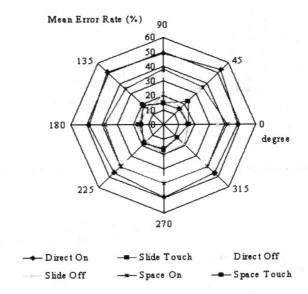

Figure 10: Mean error rate for each strategy according to direction.

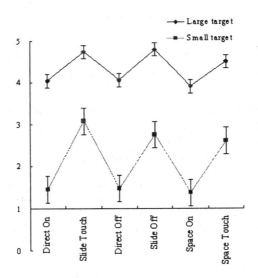

Figure 11: The results of the subjective evaluation for the six strategies according to target size (1 = lowest preference, 5 = highest preference).

experiment. The Slide Touch and Slide Off strategies were rated highly for both large targets and small targets. When selecting a small target, the Slide Touch strategy was the most preferred (mean = 3.08).

From the marks left in Figure 2 by all subjects, we determined that the smallest radius (39 pixels) and the medium radius (131 pixels) were the most popular pen-movement-distances. These radii were determined by a preliminary experiment. Though they were radii in which the movements of the hand were few, nevertheless significant differences in the six strategies were observed. There was also a significant difference between the six strategies at the maximum outside radius of 160 pixels. Furthermore, 135, 180 and 225 degrees of pen-movement-direction could be comfortably accommodated.

5 Discussion

5.1 The Best Strategy

Based on analyses of selection times, error rates and the subjective evaluations, the Slide Touch strategy was the best strategy of the six. This result is the same as the result obtained in another experimental study (Ren & Moriya, 1997a). We have verified again that the Slide Touch strategy is the most efficient of the six strategies for selecting a small target.

5.2 Target Size

Regarding target size, there were significant differences between the six strategies in terms of both selection time and error rate for target sizes of 3 pixels and 5 pixels. On the other hand, in the case of the target size of 9 pixels, no significant difference in error rate between the six strategies was observed. The significant differences between strategies were changed by changing the target size. In other words, the error rates were influenced by the selection strategies when the targets were small. As the amount of information displayed on the screen is increasing, users have to select smaller targets because the width and height of screens is limited. This tendency is especially obvious in portable pen-based systems, in particular, personal digital assistants (PDAs), personal information managers (PIMs), and other pocket-sized pen-based applications. Therefore, the experimental results are important factors in the design of strategies for selecting small targets in pen-based systems.

5.3 Pen-Movement-Distance and Pen-Movement-Direction

It was shown that there were significant differences between the six strategies in both selection time and error rate caused by each of the pen-movement-distances and each of the pen-movement-directions.

This means that there was a significant difference even when the distances and directions were changed, i.e. significant differences remained in all directions and all distances.

These results offer some hints for the design of selection strategies. The influence of pen-movement-distance and pen-movement-direction on both error rate and selection time should be considered in pen input strategy design.

Regarding pen-movement-directions, the vectors of 135, 180 and 225 degrees were preferred by most of the subjects. We assumed that the reason for this was that these vectors were on the left side of the initial position and they could be easily seen by these right-hand subjects.

6   General Consideration and Future Study

6.1   Usage of Selection Strategies

When the screen is a 2D surface, and where other targets exist near the target, the Direct On and Direct Off strategies can be used. For instance, the Direct Off strategy is the same as for the familiar mouse technique. Here the selection is made when the pen contacts the surface of the screen and, after visual confirmation, is moved into the target area. However, hand/eye coordination is essential when using the Direct On and Direct Off strategies. For the Direct Off strategy the pen must be inside the target (that is, 'catching' the target) when the pen is removed from the screen. In the Direct On strategy the pen approaches the screen and target area and it is in the target area only momentarily.

In situations where other targets do not exist near the target, and also in situations where other targets do not exist near one side of the target (e.g. the top), the Slide Touch and Slide Off strategies are useful. For instance, in the Slide Touch strategy, contact with the target may be affected after landing on the screen outside the target area. However, in the Slide Touch strategy, selection is affected on contact with the target area thus making visual confirmation essential since the first target contacted will be selected. In this situation the Slide Off strategy can be used because selection does not depend on the point of removal from the screen. Therefore the pen may, for example, pass through the target which will not be selected until the pen is removed from any point on the screen.

When using an electronic-tablet, a target on the screen can be designed as a 3D target. Thus the Space On and the Space Touch strategies may be used in the same situation. In the Space On and Space Touch strategies the pen can affect the target before it makes contact with the screen.

6.2   Additional Analyses Planned

The additional analyses below will be conducted:

Analyses of interactions between strategies and parameters: we plan to conduct comprehensive ANOVA tests for interactions between strategies and target size; strategies and target distance; and strategies and target direction.

Analyses of differences between pairs of strategies: in this paper, we have observed the effect of target size, distance and direction on the six strategies considered together. We plan to conduct an ANOVA test to look at whether there was a significant effect on the differences between each pair of strategies due to changes in target size, distance and direction.

Fitts' law issues: we plan to plot the selection time against the Index of Difficulty (ID) with different selection strategies.

These analyses will further define the specific effects of variations in parameters on each of the interactions observed.

6.3   Future Research Challenges

Target shapes: we used circular targets to keep the distance to the edge of a target constant in all directions. It has been reported elsewhere that differences in target shapes influence the selection time (Sheikh & Hoffmann, 1994). Thus, various target shapes could be used to compare selection strategies. It is also necessary to investigate the relationships between strategies and target shapes, and to find strategies which are suitable for specific shapes.

Isolated targets and dense targets: the effect of neighbouring targets was not considered in this experiment. Consideration must be given to small isolated targets and small targets in dense displays.

The Slide Touch strategy and other selection strategies: comparisons   between the Slide Touch strategy and other interaction selecting/pointing techniques proposed by other studies — for instance, (Kabbash & Buxton, 1995; Worden et al., 1997) — may be conducted to improve the performance of small target acquisition tasks.

Acknowledgements

The authors gratefully acknowledge the earlier contribution of Erei Miyajima and Masaya Hagihara to this work. We are grateful to Akira Igawa, Yasuharu Takenaka, and John Cahill for their helpful comments, and the members of the Moriya Lab at Tokyo Denki University for their warm support. We wish to thank the subjects for their participation and patience. We wish to thank the three anonymous referees of HCI'98 for their valuable comments on the draft paper. The helpful reviews have greatly improved the presentation of the paper.

We also wish to thank the Telecommunications Advancement Foundation (TAF) for supporting the first author to present this paper.

References

Buxton, W. (1990), A Three State Model of Graphical Input, *in* D. Diaper, D. Gilmore, G. Cockton & B. Shackel (eds.), *Proceedings of INTERACT'90 — Third IFIP Conference on Human–Computer Interaction*, Elsevier Science, pp.449–56.

Fitts, P. (1954), "The Information Capacity of the Human Motor System in Controlling Amplitude of Movement", *British Journal of Educational Psychology* **47**(6), 381–91.

Kabbash, P. & Buxton, W. (1995), The 'Prince' Technique: Fitts' Law and Selection using Area Cursors, *in* I. Katz, R. Mack, L. Marks, M. B. Rosson & J. Nielsen (eds.), *Proceedings of CHI'95: Human Factors in Computing Systems*, ACM Press, pp.273–9.

MacKenzie, I. S., Sellen, A. & Buxton, W. (1991), A Comparison of Input Devices in Elemental Pointing and Dragging Tasks, *in* S. P. Robertson, G. M. Olson & J. S. Olson (eds.), *Proceedings of CHI'91: Human Factors in Computing Systems (Reaching through Technology)*, ACM Press, pp.161–6.

McClintock, M. & Hoiem, D. (1993), Minimal Target Size in a Pen-based System, *in Abridged Proceedings of 5th International Conference on Human–Computer Interaction*, Elsevier Science, p.243.

Potter, R., Weldon, L. & Shneiderman, B. (1988), Improving the Accuracy of Touch Screens: An Experimental Evaluation of Three Strategies, *in* E. Soloway, D. Frye & S. B. Sheppard (eds.), *Proceedings of CHI'88: Human Factors in Computing Systems*, ACM Press, pp.27–32.

Ren, X. & Moriya, S. (1995), The Concept of Various Pointing Strategies on Pen-based Computers and their Experimental Evaluation, *in Proceedings of the Eleventh Symposium on Human Interface*, pp.565–74.

Ren, X. & Moriya, S. (1997a), The Best Among Six Strategies for Selecting a Minute Target and the Determination of the Minute Maximum Size of the Targets on a Pen-based Computer, *in* S. Howard, J. Hammond & G. K. Lindgaard (eds.), *Human–Computer Interaction — INTERACT'97: Proceedings of the Fifth IFIP Conference on Human–Computer Interaction*, Chapman & Hall, pp.85–92.

Ren, X. & Moriya, S. (1997b), The Strategy for Selecting a Minute Target and the Minute Maximum Value on a Pen-based Computer, *in* S. Pemberton (ed.), *Proceedings of CHI'97: Human Factors in Computing Systems*, ACM Press, pp.369–70.

Sears, A. & Shneiderman, B. (1991), "High Precision Touchscreens: Design Strategies and Comparisons with a Mouse", *International Journal of Man–Machine Studies* **34**(4), 593–613.

Sears, A., Plaisant, C. & Shneiderman, B. (1992), A New Era for High-precision Touchscreens, *in Advances in Human–Computer Interaction*, Vol. 3, Ablex, pp.1–33.

Sheikh, I. & Hoffmann, E. (1994), "Effect of Target Shape on Movement Time in a Fitts' Task", *Ergonomics* **37**(9), 1533–47.

Worden, A., Walker, N., Bharat, K. & Hudson, S. (1997), Making Computers Easier for Older Adults to Use: Area Cursors and Sticky Icons, *in* S. Pemberton (ed.), *Proceedings of CHI'97: Human Factors in Computing Systems*, ACM Press, pp.266–71.

Zhai, S., Buxton, W. & Milgram, P. (1994), The 'Silk Cursor': Investigating Transparency for 3D Target Acquisition, *in* B. Adelson, S. Dumais & J. Olson (eds.), *Proceedings of CHI'94: Human Factors in Computing Systems*, ACM Press, pp.459–64.

A Study of Two Keyboard Aids to Accessibility

Shari Trewin & Helen Pain

*Department of Artificial Intelligence, University of Edinburgh,
80 South Bridge, Edinburgh EH1 1HN, UK.*

Tel: *+44 131 650 2728*
Fax: *+44 131 650 6516*
EMail: *{shari, helen}@dai.ed.ac.uk*
URL: *http://www.dai.ed.ac.uk/daidb/people/staff/*

Sticky Keys **and** *Repeat Keys* **are two important keyboard configuration facilities intended to improve keyboard access for users with motor disabilities. While the value of such facilities has long been recognized, there has been very little empirical research examining their use.**

This paper reports on a study in which both facilities were found to be effective in eliminating certain input errors. While *Repeat Keys* **did not introduce any difficulties in the tasks studied, some important difficulties with** *Sticky Keys* **were observed. Suggestions for modifications to** *Sticky Keys* **which may reduce users' difficulties are made.**

Keywords: disability access, keyboard configuration, sticky keys, repeat keys, motor disabilities, empirical studies of users.

1 Introduction

Motor impairments cause some users to experience difficulty in the manipulation of keyboards and mice. Configuration facilities are software procedures which allow users to alter some aspect of the keyboard or mouse response in order to avoid such difficulties.

Many configuration facilities originated as system add-ons or replacement device drivers. They are now becoming integrated into mainstream operating systems. While the value of these facilities has long been recognized, very little empirical research has examined the benefits they can provide, and the trade-offs involved in using them. Data indicating potential savings in time or effort, reduction of errors, and ease of use of the facilities would be useful to developers of disability access software, operating system designers, potential users of these facilities, and to teachers, funding agencies, and professionals working with computers and people with motor disabilities.

This paper examines two of the best known and most useful keyboard configuration facilities: *Sticky Keys* and *Repeat Keys*. It presents a study of twenty keyboard users with motor disabilities, and ten keyboard users with no motor disability, and examines the effects of these facilities on input errors occurring and time spent correcting errors in a simple copy typing task. Difficulties encountered in using the facilities are also reported.

2 Repeat Keys

The ability to repeat a character by holding down a key is generally considered to be a useful feature of ordinary keyboards. For some people with motor disabilities, however, the short default time before a key starts to repeat can cause many unwanted errors. In this paper such errors are referred to as *long key press errors*. Brown (1992) observes that unwanted characters generated by key repeats can present a "serious obstacle" to accessibility. They are one of the major problems observed in formal and informal reports of keyboard usage by people with motor disabilities (Brown, 1992; Vanderheiden, 1992; Millar & Nisbet, 1993; Poulson et al., 1996; Trewin & Pain, in press).

For example, the following shows the characters generated in typing the word 'with', for someone whose key press length tends to produce two copies of each character. Individual keystrokes are separated by spaces:

> ww <delete><delete> ww <delete> ii <delete><delete> i tt hh
> <delete><delete> <delete><delete> t hh <delete><delete> hh
> <delete>

The word was eventually correctly typed, using sixteen keystrokes. Had this person opted to use a spelling checker instead of making manual corrections, the word presented to the checker would have been 'wwiitthh' The spelling checker for Microsoft Word 6 makes the suggestions 'wittier' and 'witty', given this input — production of the correct word would have required manual editing of these suggestions, reintroducing the original problem. A better solution is to eliminate such errors at source.

The *Repeat Keys* facility, available in some form in most modern operating systems, takes this approach. It allows a user some control over the delay before a key starts to repeat, and the rate at which repeat characters are generated. It is also possible to prevent keys from repeating altogether.

3 Sticky Keys

The second access facility considered in this paper is *Sticky Keys*, also available in most modern operating systems. *Sticky Keys* is designed to support people who type with one hand, or with a mouthstick, or anyone who finds it difficult to hold down one key while pressing another. When activated, this utility allows modifier keys to be pressed prior to the key to be modified, rather than simultaneously. It also allows locking of modifier keys.

Utilities performing the function of *Sticky Keys* were among the first keyboard configuration facilities to be developed. The 1-Finger program developed by the TRACE Centre in the early 1980's (Novak et al., 1991) is one example.

In the absence of a facility like *Sticky Keys*, some people who find simultaneous key presses difficult utilize the *Caps Lock* key where possible. Others try to avoid modified key presses altogether, or resort to awkward, uncomfortable movements. They may make dropping errors: releasing the modifier key before the key to be modified has been pressed down. Brown (1992) asserts that such difficulties can render a program "virtually inaccessible", while Millar & Nisbet (1993) describe *Sticky Keys* as a very basic access requirement. Vanderheiden (1992), Poulson et al. (1996) and Trewin & Pain (in press) report similar difficulties with the use of modifier keys.

On the Macintosh, *Sticky Keys* deactivates automatically when a modifier key is pressed simultaneously with a character. In Windows 95, this is the default behaviour, but the facility can be disabled.

Sticky Keys implementations usually include a locking mechanism, whereby a modifier key can be locked down, and all subsequent characters are modified. Locking is activated by pressing the modifier key twice, and deactivated by pressing a third time.

4   A Study of Users

The data described here were gathered as a side effect of a larger study.

4.1   Participants

Thirty unpaid volunteers took part in the study. Twenty had some disability affecting their typing (participants D1–D20), while ten had no relevant disability (participants N21–N30). There were seventeen men and thirteen women, aged between 19 and 73.

Disabilities affecting use of the keyboard included cerebral palsy, effects of stroke, spasms, nerve damage, incomplete tetraplegia, multiple sclerosis and arthritis. The effects of these disabilities on keyboard use included tremor and spasm in the hands and fingers, coordination difficulties, loss of dexterity, weakness and pain when pressing keys.

The keyboard experience of the participants ranged from none at all to 37 years of daily use. There was no significant difference between the disabled and non-disabled groups in terms of age ($t = -1.669$, $p = 0.106$) or experience level ($t = -0.162$, $p = 0.872$). Experience was measured as the number of years of daily computer use each participant had had, where daily was considered to be five days a week or more. For participants who used computers less frequently, a daily use figure equivalent to their actual use was calculated.

4.2   Materials

Four matched text passages were used. Each required 625 keystrokes, and included 21 capital letters and 9 punctuation marks requiring the use of the *Shift* key.

Macintosh 475 8/160 and Power Macintosh 6100/66 machines, and the SimpleText word processor were used. The key repeat delays provided by *Repeat Keys* on the Macintosh are 12/60, 16/60, 24/60 and 40/60 seconds. Alternatively, the key repeat facility can be deactivated. In the default keyboard configuration, the key repeat delay is 16/60 seconds, and *Sticky Keys* is inactive.

On the keyboards used in the experiment, the *Caps Lock* key could be used to generate capital letters, but not punctuation marks which normally required the use of *Shift*.

4.3   Procedure

Experimental sessions were limited to two hours, and extended only if the participant chose to continue. Participants were free to stop or rest at any time.

Participants were asked to copy one of the passages as accurately as possible using the default keyboard configuration. They were free to make corrections if they wished, or to ignore their errors. Negative transfer of learning effects are to be expected for participants used to a different configuration, and these effects in this and other typed passages will be identified and discussed at various points in this analysis.

Depending on the keyboard difficulties observed during this task, the participants were then asked to copy up to three further passages, each with a particular access facility enabled. Due to constraints imposed by the larger study, *Repeat Keys* was most often the first facility considered, and *Sticky Keys* was most often the last.

Participants were informed what changes were made each time. When *Sticky Keys* was activated, participants were told that they should generate capital letters by pressing and releasing *Shift* exactly once, and then pressing the desired character, or by using *Caps Lock* if preferred. They were not instructed on the more advanced features of *Sticky Keys*, such as the locking mechanism. Their attention was not drawn to the visual feedback *Sticky Keys* provides on the current status of *Shift*. They were not required to activate the utility themselves.

The intention here is to examine the use of the alternative mechanism for generating modified characters, provided by *Sticky Keys*, and to note any difficulties in the use of this mechanism. The usability of the utility as a whole requires further research.

Ideally, participants would also have been asked to copy a final passage with the default configuration, in order to allow proper measurement of practice/fatigue effects. In practice this was not feasible. Many participants did not complete three passages due to fatigue or time constraints. A further passage would have extended the experiment time beyond the acceptable limit for many of the participants.

All participants typed passages in a single session, with breaks between passages, with the exception of Participant D8, who typed two passages on two separate sessions, having become too tired to continue after the initial passage on the first session.

The order in which the text passages were presented was varied between participants, in order to counteract any passage-specific effects.

4.4 Data

For each participant, the following data were recorded:

- *An automatically generated log of input events*, including time stamped key down and key up events.

- *A video of the participant's hands typing* at the keyboard. This was used to help distinguish between difficulties in use of modifier keys, and errors due to other causes.

- *Observations made during the tasks.* For each participant, the same observer (the first author) recorded impressions of the difficulties experienced by the user, and noted examples of long key press errors, dropping errors, difficulties in using modifier keys, and other relevant events.

- *Background information about the participant.* This included details of their previous keyboard experience, and their previous awareness of *Sticky Keys* and *Repeat Keys*.

4.5 Analysis

The observations made and video evidence were used to manually annotate the recorded log files, indicating types of errors made and time spent correcting errors of each type. This process included differentiation between dropping errors, and cases where a participant who usually uses *Sticky Keys* deliberately released *Shift* before pressing down the key to be modified. Any difficulties in using the utilities were also annotated.

The annotated log files were then automatically filtered and the Systat statistical package (SYSTAT, 1992) used to perform the analyses. Non-parametric statistics were used, as the variables under examination do not, or cannot be assumed to, have normal distributions.

5 Results

5.1 Repeat Keys

Prior to the experiment, ten of the participants with motor disabilities and four with no disability were aware of *Repeat Keys*, or knew that the key repeat delay could be altered. Nine of those with a disability and one other had chosen to alter the key repeat delay on their usual machine. All had either increased the delay or disabled repeats altogether.

5.1.1 Long Key Press Errors

It is difficult to identify long key press errors with accuracy where they occur on the *Delete* key, or the arrow keys, where repeats may be used intentionally. As a result, where this paper presents error rates, these represent the percentage of key presses other than modifier keys, *Delete*, and the arrow keys which were long key press errors.

Participant	Error rate (%)	Time correcting (%)
D3, D4, D8, D17	14.0–74.4	21.4–44.8
D1, D2, D5	3.8–6.4	2.9–4.7
D6, D9, D11, D12, D14, D15	1.1–2.3	0.4–9.0
D10, D16, D20, N21, N22, N27	0.2–0.6	0.0–1.4

Table 1: Long key press errors observed.

In the first passage typed all participants used the default key repeat delay of 16/60 seconds. Sample sizes were in the range 568–761 keystrokes.

Table 1 shows the long key press error rates, and time spent correcting these errors, for the sixteen participants with non-zero error rates. Thirteen of the sixteen had a motor disability. The highest error rate observed was 74.4%. The highest for a participant with no motor disability was 0.3%. The four participants with the highest error rates ($> 10\%$) accounted for 81.7% of the long key press errors observed, and each spent over 20% of their time correcting these errors.

There was no significant correlation between experience and error rate in either the disabled or non-disabled group.

Some of the errors observed were due to negative transfer of learning effects, where participants were used to a longer key repeat delay. Comments from participants with high error rates included:

> "This is far more sensitive ... this is like working on a PC." (Participant D3)
> "This doesn't normally happen to me. Have you changed the settings?" (Participant D8)
> "I'm getting frustrated!" (Participant D17)

The very high error rates observed suggest that these participants were unable to adjust to the shorter delay.

5.1.2 Fatigue and Practice Effects

In this paper, increases in a user's key press length over time are referred to as *fatigue effects*, while decreases are *practice effects*.

Fatigue and practice effects were examined using the Mann–Whitney U test to check for significant ($p < 0.05$) increases in key press lengths between passages for each participant, using all the passages they typed. In order to eliminate potential interference with passages typed using *Sticky Keys*, modified keys were excluded, in addition to those keys mentioned previously. Some passages were typed using a facility which affected the keyboard's response to adjacent overlapping keystrokes. It has been assumed that the use of this facility has no effect on key press lengths.

Table 2 shows the number of participants with and without disabilities whose key press lengths significantly increased, did not change, or decreased during the session. Eight participants, all with a disability affecting their typing, showed a

Participant group	Increase (fatigue)	No significant difference	Decrease (practice)
Disabled	8	7	5
Non-disabled	0	7	3

Table 2: Changes in key press length over time.

significant increase in key press lengths over time. For seven of these participants, the observed change cannot be attributed to the use of *Repeat Keys*, since all either typed a further passage after having used an altered key repeat delay, or did not use an altered delay in any passage.

Of the thirty participants, eight exhibited a significant reduction in key press length over time. Two were novice keyboard users, three were occasional users, and three usually used a PC platform with a key repeat delay longer than 16/60 seconds. The two most extreme examples are Participant D4, whose error rate was 14.0% in the first passage typed, and 6.7% in the final passage typed, and Participant D11 whose error rates were 1.1% and 0.3% in the first and final passages typed. Practice effects, while reducing error rates, do not necessarily eliminate them.

5.1.3 Increasing the Key Repeat Delay

Ten people (nine with some motor disability) tried a delay longer than the default setting of 16/60 seconds. All had non-zero error rates in the initial passage. Participant D2 chose to disable key repeats altogether. For the remaining participants the delay used was determined by a computer model, described by Trewin & Pain (1997), which uses information about the key press lengths in the initial passage to choose an 'ideal' delay value. An ideal value is one which minimizes long key press errors while still allowing keys to repeat as quickly as possible. The actual delay imposed was the nearest available setting at or above the model's recommendation. Three participants used a delay of 40/60 seconds, and six used a delay of 24/60 seconds.

Table 3 shows, for each of these participants, the delay value they used, their initial error rate, and their error rate under the new delay. The final column of the table shows whether the participant's key press lengths were changing significantly over time, irrespective of use of *Repeat Keys*. Entries in brackets indicate that the participant typed only two passages. For these participants, changes over time could therefore be attributable to the use of *Repeat Keys*, or to practice or fatigue effects.

Error rates with the new delay ranged from 0% up to 0.6%, and the maximum time spent correcting errors was 2.2%. Only two of the ten participants showed a decrease in key press lengths over time, and so for the remainder the error reduction can be clearly attributed to the increased key repeat delay.

The four participants with error rates over 10% in the original passage, had error rates of up to 0.3% using the increased delays, and spent up to 0.2% of their time correcting these errors. Comments from these participants included:

Participant	Delay tried (1/60 sec)	% errors with default delay	% errors with new delay	Significant changes in key press length between passages
D2	off	4.7	0.0	no change
D17	40	74.4	0.3	(increasing)
D8	40	21.0	0.0	(no change)
D3	40	19.0	0.0	no change
D4	24	14.0	0.2	decreasing
D9	24	2.1	0.3	increasing
D12	24	1.4	0.6	increasing
D11	24	1.1	0.0	decreasing
D20	24	0.6	0.0	increasing
N22	24	0.2	0.0	no change

Table 3: Increasing the key repeat delay.

> "It's amazing the difference." (Participant D3)
> "This feels a lot better." (Participant D4)

For two participants, there appeared to be some effect of increasing the key repeat delay on key press lengths. When the repeat delay was increased, the Mann Whitney U test showed a significant ($p < 0.05$) increase in key press lengths for Participants D3 and D17. As mentioned previously, Participant D17 only copied two passages, so it is not known whether this effect was due to *Repeat Keys* or fatigue effects. However, Participant D3 typed three passages. There was no significant difference ($p = 0.569$, Mann–Whitney U test) between her key press lengths in the first and third passages. While using an increased key repeat delay, her key press lengths were significantly longer than those in the first and third passages ($p = 0.003$ and $p = 0.028$ respectively, Mann–Whitney U test).

5.2   Sticky Keys

Five of the thirty participants, all with a motor disability, typed with one hand only. A further seven, six with a motor disability, typed predominantly with one hand but could employ the other hand for modifier key presses. The remaining eighteen typed using both hands. Three of the two-handed typists, all with no disability, were novice touch typists.

Prior to the experiment, eleven of the participants with motor disabilities and one with no disability were aware of *Sticky Keys*. Six participants always or sometimes used *Sticky Keys*. All *Sticky Keys* users had a disability affecting their typing. Three typed with one hand only, one typed mainly with one hand, and two typed with both hands.

5.2.1   Use of Modifier Keys

The number of uses of *Shift* observed for each person varied between 11 and 38, the average being 28. For each participant, a dropping error rate was calculated as the

Participant group	Dropping errors	*Caps Lock* errors	Error rates > 10%	Time correcting
Disabled	45	3	5	39 seconds
Non-disabled	1	0	0	0 seconds

Table 4: Errors in the use of modifier keys.

average number of dropping errors observed per use of the *Shift* key. Table 4 shows the errors observed, and number of participants in the disabled and non-disabled groups with error rates greater than 10%.

All five one-handed typists (D1, D2, D4, D6, D12 and D16), and one inexperienced participant (D12) used *Caps Lock* for single capital letters. The use of *Caps Lock* to produce capital letters can introduce errors. As shown in Table 4, on three occasions a participant using this technique forgot to deactivate the lock, and a total of 16.3 seconds was spent correcting this error.

Almost all of the 46 dropping errors, and all 3 errors in the use of *Caps Lock*, occurred among the group with disabilities. Five participants had error rates of 10% or greater. Participant D6 made 31 dropping errors, giving an error rate of 100% — on average one error for every use of *Shift*. No other participant made more than three dropping errors.

In the majority of dropping errors observed, the key to be modified was not pressed, no input was generated, and therefore no error correction was required. Only one participant spent time (22.7 seconds) correcting dropping errors in which a character was generated.

There was no significant correlation between experience and dropping error rate among the participants. There was, however, a significant inverse correlation between dropping error rate and typing style (Spearman Rho = -0.488, n = 30, p < 0.01). For the purposes of this analysis, typing style was measured on an ordinal scale of four points corresponding to one-handed, mainly one-handed, two-handed and touch typing styles.

5.2.2 Fatigue and Practice Effects

When using modifier keys, fatigue and practice could affect both the dropping error rate and the participants' ease of use of modifier keys. While practice may reduce dropping errors, the lack of observed correlation between previous keyboard experience and dropping error rate suggests that practice cannot eliminate the problem. Conversely, if fatigue were to increase users' difficulty in using modifier keys, and increase dropping error rates, the need for an alternative mechanism such as *Sticky Keys* would increase. During experimentation it was observed that some users spent time (and effort) manoeuvring themselves into an appropriate position before making simultaneous key presses. These efforts are highly likely to induce fatigue, but such effects were not measured in this experiment.

Fatigue and practice could also affect the ease of use of *Sticky Keys*, and corresponding error rates. Because of the short period of time spent using *Sticky Keys*, these effects cannot be examined. As with *Repeat Keys*, fatigue and practice will act to degrade or improve performance. These effects are assumed to be present

Typing style	Faster with *Sticky Keys*	No significant difference	Slower with *Sticky Keys*
One-handed	0	5	0
Mainly one-handed	1	4	2
Two-handed	0	6	6

Table 5: Effect of *Sticky Keys* on time taken to produce modified characters.

in some, but not all participants. The results presented in the following section are intended to give an overview of the use of the utility by a range of different people, in a range of stages of fatigue or experience.

5.2.3   Using Sticky Keys

Sticky Keys offers an alternative mechanism for generating modified key presses, which is effective for all modifier keys, eliminates dropping errors, and does not require any movements other than single key presses.

This section examines the use of *Sticky Keys* by twenty-four of the thirty participants, including fifteen with some motor disability. Of the latter group, five typed with one hand only, six typed predominantly with one hand, but could use the other for modifier key presses, and four used both hands. Among the nine participants with no disability, one typed mainly with one hand while the remainder, three of whom were novice touch typists, used both hands.

Some participants previously unaware of the utility commented that they found it "much easier" than the original method for generating modified characters. One predominantly one-handed typist described it as "more fluid", since he didn't have to stop to place his thumb on the *Shift* key. Some thought it would be easy to learn to use it, while others felt they were too used to the original method.

It is feasible that the use of *Sticky Keys* allows modified characters to be generated more quickly for some users. The time taken to produce modified key presses was measured as the total time between completion of the previous key press, and initiation of the following key press. Significant ($p < 0.05$) differences when using *Sticky Keys*, as indicated by the Mann–Whitney U test, are shown in Table 5, where the participants are grouped according to their typing style (e.g. one- or two-handed).

For only one participant (D15) were modified characters generated significantly faster when using *Sticky Keys* ($p < 0.05$, Mann–Whitney U test). Furthermore, for eight participants, including two mainly one-handed typists, modified characters were generated significantly more slowly when using *Sticky Keys*. None of this group of eight were previously familiar with *Sticky Keys*. Two of them typed predominantly with one hand, the remaining six used both hands to type.

Dropping errors can no longer be generated when using *Sticky Keys*. In addition, none of the participants used the *Caps Lock* key to generate capital letters when *Sticky Keys* was activated, so no errors associated with this technique were observed. However, two new errors were introduced, and the error numbers observed are

Typing style	Deactivation of *Sticky Keys* (average)	Accidental locking (average)
One-handed	0.20	0.60
Mainly one-handed	1.29	0.43
Two-handed	2.47	0.08

Table 6: Errors introduced with *Sticky Keys*.

summarized in Table 6. The most frequent of these was unintentional deactivation of the facility by pressing a modifier key simultaneously with another key. When this happened, the experimenter reactivated *Sticky Keys* using the control panel. The second error occurred when participants pressed *Shift* more than once before pressing their chosen letter. Most often this occurred when a participant paused after having pressed *Shift*, forgot that they had already pressed it, and pressed it again. This activated the locking facility of *Sticky Keys*, causing future typing to be unexpectedly capitalized. When this occurred participants were given instruction on how to deactivate the lock.

Fourteen participants, including six with a motor disability, deactivated *Sticky Keys* accidentally a total of 34 times. On average, the two-handed typists made 2.47 accidental deactivations each, the predominantly one-handed typists 1.29, and the one-handed typists 0.20. Only once did a one-handed typist deactivate *Sticky Keys*.

There was no significant correlation between the participants' previous experience of *Sticky Keys*, measured on a four point ordinal scale: "never heard of it", "tried and rejected it", "sometimes use it" or "always use it" and the number of times they deactivated it accidentally (Spearman Rho = -0.282). The experiment did not measure the time that participants would have taken to discover that they had accidentally deactivated *Sticky Keys*, and to reactivate it.

Seven unintentional activations of the locking facility were observed while participants were using *Sticky Keys*. No participant reported noticing the visual feedback provided by *Sticky Keys*, which may have helped in avoiding errors of this kind. A total of 209.2 seconds was spent correcting errors of this type.

6   Discussion

6.1   Repeat Keys

Under the default key repeat delay, some participants with motor disabilities had very high long key press error rates. Participants without disabilities showed low error rates. For those participants with the highest error rates under the default delay, the use of an increased delay produced substantial savings in time and effort. No participant experienced difficulty in using the longer delay settings. Reductions in error rate were observed for all participants who tried an increased delay, overriding fatigue effects found in four of this group.

The fatigue and practice effects observed in sixteen of the thirty participants over a two hour typing period suggest that for many individuals, their ideal key repeat delay is not static. Furthermore, the lack of correlation between experience and error rates implies that the ideal repeat delay does not alter in a predictable way with experience. While users prone to long key press errors could control their error rates by setting the key repeat delay to the maximum they anticipate requiring, or by disabling repeats altogether, this slows or prevents the deliberate use of repeats, for example when using arrow keys for positioning. The effect of using long key repeat delays on word processing tasks has not been examined here. It has been assumed that the minimum delay which eliminates long key press errors is the optimal setting. The results presented here suggest that dynamic alteration of the key repeat delay is sometimes necessary, if an ideal setting is to be maintained.

The use of *Repeat Keys* itself can also affect key press lengths. Participant D3 made longer key presses when the delay was increased. This suggests that her natural, most comfortable key press length was often above the default, but that she could reduce her key press length to some extent to accommodate a shorter repeat delay when necessary. The participants' own comments suggest that the keyboard was much easier to use with a longer delay. *Repeat Keys*, therefore, can not only reduce errors but also make the keyboard more comfortable to use.

Even in this small sample, the full range of available increased repeat delay settings were used. Even with the maximum available delay of 40/60 second, one participant still showed long key press errors. This suggests that an increased range of settings, including settings greater than 40/60 second, would be beneficial for some users.

Half of the participants were previously aware of the utility, and one third had used it. It was primarily used by participants with disabilities, but one non-disabled user was also found. Of the 16 previously unaware of the facility, 12 had non-zero error rates, and may have benefited from using it.

These results are encouraging, indicating that in the absence of any difficulty in activating and setting *Repeat Keys*, the facility can make an effective contribution to keyboard accessibility for computer users with motor disabilities.

6.2   Sticky Keys

Sticky Keys was found to be effective in tackling dropping errors and eliminating the need for awkward simultaneous key presses. However, many users found errors occurring through the use of the utility itself. The time participants spent recovering from these errors was much greater than the time spent recovering from dropping errors and errors in the use of *Caps Lock*, despite assistance from the experimenter. While the incidence of such errors was lower among the one-handed or predominantly one-handed typists, this may have been partly because the majority of the one-handed typists were already familiar with the utility. Furthermore, two of the two-handed typists were *Sticky Keys* users, so difficulties experienced by this group are worthy of attention.

Sticky Keys did not, in general, appear to reduce the time taken to produce modified characters significantly, in fact an increase in time was more often observed. The timing information on which these results are based also included times taken to read the next word and check previous work, and these, together with fatigue and learning effects, may have swamped any effects due to *Sticky Keys*. It is probable that the major benefit of *Sticky Keys* is in reducing the effort required to produce modified characters, rather than the time taken to type them.

Participants all typed at least one passage using the default method for generating modified characters before trying *Sticky Keys*. This was a methodological limitation imposed by the larger study. The initial use of the default mechanism could have lead to transfer of learning effects, particularly for novice keyboard users, which may have influenced the number of accidental deactivations of *Sticky Keys* observed. However, this is actually a more general problem — the majority of novice keyboard users are likely to learn the default method first, and similar negative transfer effects would be expected when transferring to *Sticky Keys*. In this respect, then, the experimental methodology may have mirrored the real world experience of many users. The automatic deactivation of *Sticky Keys* when users revert to the default method is intended as a form of automatic configuration. However, these results suggest that it may well work against users who are new to *Sticky Keys*, as it is easy for them to deactivate the utility without realizing it, and may become confused when it suddenly fails to work. It would, perhaps, be an improvement if the utility was less easy to deactivate. One suggestion would be to allow automatic deactivation only after a long break in input. Alternatively, this aspect of *Sticky Keys* could be deactivated.

The participants in this study were given only minimal training in the use of the utility, and sometimes stumbled upon more advanced features — the locking mechanism in particular. This lead to confusion, and could potentially cause users to reject the utility, if no support was available. For some users it would be useful to be able to disable these advanced features. For others, training in the use of *Sticky Keys* may be helpful. Awareness of the utility was much higher among participants with disabilities, but there was one one-handed typist who was unaware of it. Unfortunately, the relevant Macintosh on-line documentation is difficult for a novice user to find. In Windows 95, only some of the functionality is described in the on-line help documentation. The user is left to infer the available functionality from the options in the control panel, which provides only incomplete information. For example, the user can choose that two presses on *Shift* will cause it to lock, but no explanation is given as to how to deactivate the lock! The options available to users of configuration facilities should be more explicitly described in on-line help systems.

These potential difficulties for novice users of *Sticky Keys* may partially explain why the rate of uptake among those aware of *Sticky Keys* is lower than that for *Repeat Keys*. Certainly, the interface of the utility as a whole requires further empirical examination.

7   Summary

We have described several aspects of the use of *Sticky Keys* and *Repeat Keys*, two of the best known and most popular keyboard configuration facilities intended to support keyboard users who have motor disabilities.

The use of *Repeat Keys* to increase key repeat delays reduced error rates from a maximum of 74.4% under the default delay, to a maximum of 0.6% under a delay suited to each participant. For four participants, this represents a potential time saving of over 20%. Participants had no difficulty in using an increased delay. It has been observed that the ideal delay for an individual may vary over time, and is not correlated with keyboard experience.

The use of *Sticky Keys* to produce modified characters eliminated dropping errors, and errors in the use of *Caps Lock*, and was reported to require less effort by some participants. However, significant savings in time were not shown. Furthermore, the use of *Sticky Keys* introduced two new error types, caused by advanced features of the facility itself. The minimal training given to these participants was not sufficient to allow them to recover quickly from such errors. Further investigation of the *Sticky Keys* interface and potential mechanisms for reducing these difficulties is required.

The facilities have been used by users with and without motor disabilities affecting their use of the keyboard. They have been found useful to participants who do not necessarily exhibit the difficulties these facilities were designed to overcome. This supports observations by previous researchers that facilities designed to improve disability access are often more generally useful (Vanderheiden et al., 1987; Glinert & York, 1992; Newell et al., 1995).

These two configuration facilities can potentially have a significant impact on keyboard accessibility for users with motor disabilities. In the case of *Sticky Keys*, however, the full potential of the mechanism is not currently realized.

Acknowledgements

The authors would like to thank the University of Edinburgh for funding this research; all the volunteer participants and those who helped in contacting participants, particularly Annalu Waller, the Herald and Post, and the Thistle Foundation; Lothian Regional Council and the Hands on Technology project for providing access to much of the equipment used; Simon Kelly and Mike Ramscar for their assistance and helpful feedback; and several anonymous reviewers of an earlier version of this paper for particularly thoughtful comments and suggestions.

References

Brown, C. (1992), "Assistive Technology Computers and People with Disabilities", *Communications of the ACM* **35**(5), 36–45.

Glinert, E. P. & York, B. W. (1992), "Computers and People With Disabilities", *Communications of the ACM* **35**(5), 32–5.

Millar, S. V. & Nisbet, P. D. (1993), *Accelerated Writing for People with Disabilities*, CALL Centre and Scottish Office Education Department, CALL Centre, University of Edinburgh. ISBN 1 898042 01 2.

Newell, A., Arnott, J., Cairns, A., Ricketts, I. & Gregor, P. (1995), Intelligent Systems for Speech and Language Impaired People: A Portfolio of Research, *in* A. D. N. Edwards (ed.), *Extra-Ordinary Human–Computer Interaction: Interfaces for Users with Disabilities*, Cambridge University Press, chapter 5, pp.83–101.

Novak, M., Schauer, J., Hinkens, J. & Vanderheiden, G. (1991), Providing Computer Access Features Under DOS, *in Resna'91: Proceedings of the 14th Annual Conference*, Resna Press, pp.163–5.

Poulson, D., Ashby, M. & Richardson, S. (1996), *Userfit: A Practical Handbook on User-centred Design for Assistive Technology*, European Commission, Brussels-Luxembourg. TIDE 1062 USER project.

SYSTAT (1992), *SYSTAT: Statistics, Version 5.2 Edition*.

Trewin, S. & Pain, H. (1997), Dynamic Modelling of Keyboard Skills: Supporting Users with Motor Disabilities, *in* A. Jameson, C. Paris & C. Tasso (eds.), *User Modeling: Proceedings of the Sixth International Conference*, Springer-Verlag, pp.135–46.

Trewin, S. & Pain, H. (in press), "Keyboard and Mouse Errors Due to Motor Disabilities", *International Journal of Man–Machine Studies* .

Vanderheiden, G. (1992), "Making Software More Accessible for People with Disabilities", University of Wisconsin-Madison. Release 1.2.

Vanderheiden, G., Lee, C. & Scadden, L. (1987), Features to Increase the Accessibility of Computers by Persons with Disabilities: Report from the Industry/Government Task Force, *in Resna'87: Proceedings of the 10th Annual Conference*, Resna Press, pp.750–2.

Design: Process, Task Analysis, Requirements and Specification

Combining Goals and Functional Requirements in a Scenario-based Design Process

Hermann Kaindl

Siemens AG Österreich, Geusaugasse 17, A–1030 Wien, Austria.

Tel: *+43 1 71600 288*

Fax: *+43 1 71600 323*

EMail: *hermann.kaindl@siemens.at*

While promising approaches to early system design using *scenarios* **have been proposed, no design process is available that guides scenario-based development. We present a model that combines scenarios both with functions and goals. Functions are required to make the desired behaviour of some scenario happen in order to achieve one or more goals. Using this model, we propose a systematic and concrete design process that is both model-driven and data-driven. Our design process supports the transition from the current to a new system and guides the design of a new system. In addition, this process makes it possible to detect redundancy and to improve both completeness and understandability of the resulting design. We have applied our approach in real-world projects, and our experience suggests the utility of this approach.**

Keywords: scenarios, design techniques.

1 Introduction

Early system design is widely believed to be well supported by the use of *scenarios* — see for example the collection (Carroll, 1995). Such interaction scenarios have been proposed (among others) for capturing and representing the interactions of potential users with a computer system that has yet to be built. When these usage descriptions are concrete, scenarios help to discuss use and to design use.

Unfortunately, such scenarios are mostly isolated. In particular, the goals of users to be achieved in the course of applying such a scenario are typically left implicit. Being aware of the goal(s) of some sequence of (inter)actions, however, facilitates their understanding. So, our approach makes the relation of scenarios to goals explicit.

While scenarios are very popular these days, their wide-spread use is more recent than the use of functional specifications. It may seem now that these are strictly opposing and even conflicting approaches to system design. However, it is already recognized that both approaches are needed and should complement each other (Mack, 1995). In order to address this issue, in our approach functions of the computer system are attached to scenarios. While in theory functional specifications should be formal in contrast to more or less informal scenario descriptions, in practice also functional requirements are mostly described in natural language. So, we do not discuss issues of formal vs. informal representations in this paper, but focus on these attachments from the perspective of integrating functional with behavioural representations.

Still, "functional specifications can become divorced from user's needs and requirements" (Mack, 1995). Therefore, we combine scenarios both with functions and with goals in this paper. In particular, we define a relation of functions of a computer system yet to be built to goals of its users. This relation shows how these functions will be used — in scenarios — to achieve these user goals.

We utilize this combined model for defining a systematic and concrete *design process* based on scenarios. It guides usage-centred design of a new interactive system. Since this process relates goals, scenarios and functions in both the new and the current system, the evolution of how people carry out a task can be tracked. In addition, the resulting design representation is more structured and complete as well as less redundant and better understandable than a representation that contains only scenarios.

This work was performed in the larger context of our approach named RETH (Requirements Engineering Through Hypertext). For an overview of this method and its supporting tool (including its architecture) as well as some real-world experience, the interested reader is referred to (Kaindl, 1996b; Kaindl, 1997).

Our approach has been applied in several real-world projects both outside and inside of our company. We selected one of the larger projects for summarizing our experience, in particular that of using the combined model and the design process as presented in this paper.

As a running example in this paper, however, we prefer to use the ATM (automated teller machine) domain, since we can assume familiarity with ATMs from their daily use. Unfortunately, for this reason it is difficult to imagine that we are working on a design of an ATM as though such machines did not exist yet. For the same reason, however, this example is useful for the purposes of this paper, since this familiarity helps us explain the notions and concepts discussed. Finally, this kind of example is ubiquitous in the literature, and so its use facilitates the comparison of our approach with previous work.

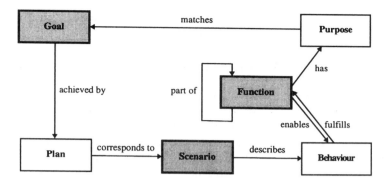

Figure 1: Some important notions and their relationships.

This paper is organized in the following manner. First we present our new combined model of functions, scenarios and goals. Then we show how this model can be used for a design process as well as for improving some design qualities. After this theoretical discussion, we summarize our experiences of applying our approach in a selected real-world project. Lastly, we relate our approach to existing work.

2 Our Combined Model

Figure 1 shows the key notions that we use for the explanation of our combined model. Lines between boxes representing notions indicate that there is a direct relation between these notions.

We discuss these relations shortly, and based on them we discuss the indirect relation between functions and goals that is important in our combined model. Typically, someone requires *functions* from some proposed computer system — functional requirements. Once available, these functions allow this computer system to act appropriately in interaction scenarios — they enable its external *behaviour*. These scenarios can be viewed as corresponding cooperative *plans*: the computer system and actors in its environment execute these plans together when interacting in these scenarios. These plans help to achieve *goals* (when executed without failure). So, functions of the proposed software/hardware system and goals of its users are related indirectly, essentially through some behaviour.

The effects achieved by the behaviour described in interaction scenarios can be represented by *functions* of the encompassing composite system[*]. That is, such behaviour fulfils a composite or aggregated function. The functions provided by the computer system are sub-functions — part of these functions — and so are the functions required from the other actors (Kaindl et al., 1998). The aggregated functions of the composite system have some *purposes*[†] for actors with goals — these

---

[*]The composite system is the set of objects that perform the user's task and include the proposed software/hardware system, the user and other objects needed to complete the task.

[†]The notions goal and purpose are often used synonymously. So, it may seem to be strange to make

purposes match (sub-)goals of the actors. An important point is that we must look at the respective system that fulfils a function: the computer system to be built or the encompassing composite system that contains it as well as actors with goals. In this paper, we focus on the functions of the proposed computer system that has yet to be built.

Now let us present the essential relations of our combined model. These are relations among functions, scenarios and goals, the key concepts shown in shaded boxes in Figure 1. In the ATM example, the function *Cash Provision* is required from the ATM (among others) in order to make the scenario *Get Cash from ATM* happen. Figure 2 illustrates this example through the link from Step 10 of the scenario *Get Cash from ATM* to the separate description of the function *Cash Provision*. We view functions attached to steps of the system to be built as functional requirements, since they make explicit what functionality is required from the system to be built in a scenario to enable it fulfilling its part in the required interactions. In addition, more information on a requirement is necessary in practice (Kaindl, 1997), and there is the possibility of integrating a formal Specification right here.

Since the relations are very important for understanding the design process based on them, we treat them also more formally here. The example above can be written more formally as *(Get Cash from ATM, Cash Provision)* ∈ *By-Function*. That is, this tuple is an element of the relation *By-Function* ⊆ *Scenario* × *Function* — see also (Kaindl, 1995; Kaindl, 1997).

The attachments in Figure 2 are of the form "By-Function *Function Name*". It is adapted from *functional representation* (Chandrasekaran et al., 1993). In this scenario description in natural language, it can be viewed as a kind of pseudocode.

Although this is the only such link illustrated explicitly in Figure 2, it actually shows attachments of functions to steps both of the user and the system to be built. While the attachment of a function to a step of the system to be built means a functional requirement, we also discuss attachments of functions to steps that are to be performed by the user. Functions attached to steps of the human user document what the user will have to contribute during successful execution of the specific sequence of interactions of this particular scenario. From the perspective of designing the user interface, they focus on what is to be supported through this user interface (to be built). It makes even more explicit the selection processes of user interface elements to given scenarios described in (Constantine, 1995; Johnson et al., 1995). Once the functions needed from the user are explicitly known and represented, defining *use contexts* and finally concrete user interface components becomes a more conscious process. Our experience with this approach suggests that it can help to provide better user interfaces and thus improve usability, but this issue is beyond the scope of this paper.

In general, each scenario may require several functions, and each function may be required in several scenarios. For instance, also the function *Cash Card Acceptance* is required from the ATM (among others) in order to make this scenario

---

a distinction here. Still, the *function* of some system or device appears to be more closely related to its *purpose* for a user than to the *goal* of that user which is matched by this purpose. For this reason we make this distinction here, but without any general claim about this distinction.

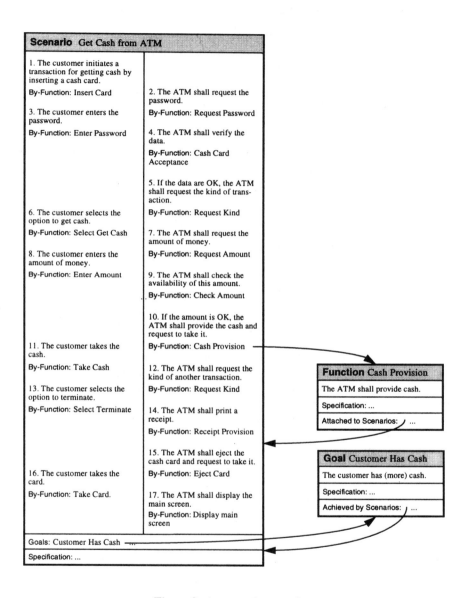

Figure 2: An example scenario.

happen, as well as another scenario for using the ATM to transfer money between accounts. Therefore, *By-Function* is in general a many-to-many relation.

Overall, we want to combine functions and goals via scenarios. So, we additionally need a relation between scenarios and their goals. In the ATM example, the goal *Customer Has Cash* is achieved by the scenario *Get Cash from ATM*. Figure 2 illustrates this example through the link from Goals of the scenario *Get Cash from ATM* to the goal *Customer Has Cash*.

More formally, this can be written as *(Customer Has Cash, Get Cash from ATM)* ∈ *By-Scenario*. That is, this tuple is an element of the relation *By-Scenario* ⊆ *Goal* × *Scenario*.

In general, each goal may be achieved by several scenarios, and each scenario may achieve several goals. In the ATM example, there may be variations in the way the amount is entered: typing it in completely or using a fast cash button[‡]. Another goal is that the customer has a receipt. Therefore, *By-Scenario* is in general a many-to-many relation.

An important reason why goals and scenarios should be explicitly related is that knowledge about the goals of the interactions described in a scenario helps us understand them. For example, when we watch someone approaching an ATM and inserting a cash card, we know the potential goal(s) of these actions. Otherwise, they would not make sense to us. This may seem obvious, because we know ATM machines so well from our daily use. Consider, however, what someone coming from Mars might think about such observations. So, in the process of design and requirements capture for a *new* and yet unknown system, such information is crucial for someone not involved in the scenario development to get an understanding.

In our combined model the indirect relation between goals and functions is important. It is simply the composition of the relations *By-Scenario* and *By-Function*. This relation shows how the functions of a system to be built will serve goals of its users. For instance, it shows that the function *Cash Card Acceptance* of an ATM is required for achieving the goal *Customer Has Cash*, through its use in the scenario *Get Cash from ATM*.

Conceptually, this combined model serves as *metamodel* in the sense that it models how the corresponding part of a design model should look like. This approach does not, however, determine the exact form of such a representation. Natural language descriptions are still commonplace in practice, but even these can be significantly improved using explicit references that represent these relations informally. We have proposed using hypertext with links that are known to the machine (Kaindl, 1996b), and object-oriented associations (Kaindl, 1996a). Another useful approach may be to directly represent these relations in a (relational) database system. The concrete representation is, however, not important in the context of this paper.

[‡]The example shown in Figure 2 abstracts from these details (Constantine, 1995), while it already involves a cash card as a concrete means of customer identification. So, scenario descriptions may actually vary within a spectrum from concrete to abstract. This issue is different, however, from determining the system boundary between the proposed computer system yet to be built and its environment.

3   A Design Process Based On Our Model

Based on this model that explicitly relates functions, scenarios and goals, we define a systematic and concrete design process in the sense of *how* to acquire design information. Conceptually, we follow the approach according to (Dardenne et al., 1993): *acquisition processes* are viewed as ways of traversing the metamodel graph to acquire instances of its various nodes and links. These instances make up the design model[§]. In this paper, we focus on a simple graph according to the relations *By-Function* and *By-Scenario* as defined above.

While we attempt to provide a prescription for the acquisition process that is easy to follow for a user of our approach, we do not find it useful to prescribe exactly one strict sequence of traversing the graph — e.g. it is not generally recommended to always start with acquiring and describing scenarios first. Therefore, we prescribe *partial* sequences only, that depend on the information already known at some point in time. Whenever through executing such a partial sequence other information becomes known, another one will be triggered, etc.

In effect, the resulting process is both model-driven and data-driven. Both the metamodel and what is already known determine the next step to be taken.

Below, we discuss three cases of what is already known at some point in time: goals, scenarios and functions. For each of these cases we define (conditional) sequences of steps to be performed when using our approach. Since the metamodel graph that we focus on here is very small, the resulting process might be considered trivial.

When information about an old (current) system is available in addition to information about the new system that contains the system to be built, the design process becomes more complicated. In fact, our design process addresses the important problem of how to utilize information about the old system for designing a new one, i.e. design evolution. Information available about the way how work is currently performed can usefully influence the design of the new system. Several steps below intend to make the best use of information about the old system in the course of designing the new system. If there is no information about an old system available, however, then the respective steps below can just be omitted.

3.1   Known Goals

We first discuss the case when information about one or more goals is available. It may have been acquired through interviews or one of the ideas discussed in (Antón, 1996). We only deal here with 'direct' goals of potential users of the system to be built (e.g. the goal that the customer has cash). That is, we neither cover the whole goal structure of the user (e.g. including goals that are to be achieved through having the cash like having some procured item) nor the goals of some institution that will provide the system to be built for the users (e.g. making profit through the bank fees related to the use of an ATM).

In case some goal is known, we propose the sequence of steps as given in Figure 3. The last of these steps is in general the most difficult one, since it requires some creativity for its execution. Since scenarios can be viewed as cooperative

---

[§] In an object-oriented view, these are instances of metaclasses, i.e. they can be classes on their own.

1. **If some goal is known from the old system, then figure out whether this is still a valid goal in the new system that will include the system to be built.**

   e.g. let us assume an old system that 'just' contains human cashiers. The goal of meeting a friendly person (hopefully, the human cashier was friendly) is not a valid goal in a new system that would contain ATMs only. The goal *Customer Has Cash*, however, is still a goal in the new system containing ATMs (in fact, this is the primary goal for users of an ATM).

2. **If some goal is known for the new system, then try to link it to one or more scenarios for the new system that are already known.**

   e.g. if the goal of having a receipt becomes known and the scenario *Get Cash from ATM* as illustrated in Figure 2 is already known, this new goal just needs to be linked to this scenario — of course, one needs to determine first whether this goal is indeed achieved by this scenario.

3. **If some goal that is known for the new system cannot be linked to any scenario for the new system, then develop one or more such scenarios and link them to the goal.**

   e.g. if the goal *Customer Has Cash* becomes known but no scenario for achieving it is yet known, a scenario like *Get Cash from ATM* is to be developed.

Figure 3: Sequence of steps for known goals.

plans, developing scenarios for achieving goals can be viewed as a plan construction process. This means that the interactions between human users and the computer system to be built are viewed as steps in a cooperative plan for achieving the goals. This view helps us and people applying our approach to focus the design of interactions towards explicit goals. If some scenario is known for the old system, the scenario for the new system may be developed using analogies (see Step 2 in Figure 4).

3.2   Known Scenarios

Now let us discuss the case when information about one or more scenarios is available. These may be scenarios for the old system as well as scenarios for the new system.

In case some scenario is known, we propose the sequence of steps as given in Figure 4. For executing Steps 1 & 4, the technique of *systematic question asking* — in particular the *why*-questions — helps to identify the goals of a given sequence of interactions (Carroll et al., 1994). Domain modelling can be viewed as narrative understanding. Much as understanding a narrative involves building an elaborate concept map of an event by observing a selected set of specific events, domain modelling using scenarios involves building an elaborate concept map of a problem domain. The knowledge of these goals helps people understand the sequence of interactions.

---

1. **If some scenario is known for the old system, then identify the goals that are achieved through it.**

   e.g. if the scenario of getting cash involving a human cashier is known from a system where ATMs are yet unavailable, the goal *Customer Has Cash* is to be identified from this scenario.

2. **If some scenario is known for the old system, then try to develop an analogous scenario for the new system.**

   e.g. if a scenario of getting cash involving a human cashier is known from a system where ATMs are yet unavailable, a scenario like *Get Cash from ATM* is to be developed by analogy.

3. **If some scenario is known for the new system, then try to link it to one or more goals and functions for the new system that are already known.**

   e.g. if the scenario *Get Cash from ATM* is known as well as the goal *Customer Has Cash* and the function *Cash Provision*, they are to be linked as shown in Figure 2.

4. **If some scenario that is known for the new system cannot be linked to any goal for the new system, then identify one or more goals and link them to the scenario.**

   e.g. if the scenario *Get Cash from ATM* is known but neither of the goals of having cash nor of having a receipt, one or the other or preferably both goals are to be inferred and to be linked to the scenario.

5. **If one or more actions of some scenario that is known for the new system cannot be linked to any function for the new system, then develop one or more such functions and link them to the scenario.**

   e.g. if steps do not yet have functions linked to them (like most of them in Figure 2) and when representations of such functions are not yet available, these are to be developed and to be linked to the respective steps of the scenario.

Figure 4: Sequence of steps for known scenarios.

This view of *understanding* is actually dualistic with *planning* (Schank & Abelson, 1977). Planning means here generating a plan for achieving some given goal, and a plan is mostly viewed as a sequence of actions. Plan understanding occurs in the dualistic situation: when some actions are observed, one tries to identify some related goal. The plan is understood when the right goals are known.

For executing Step 5, the technique of systematic question asking — in particular the *how*-questions — helps to elicit more detailed elaborations of a given sequence of interactions. These can be useful for developing the functions to be attached to the steps of the known scenario.

As prescribed in Step 2, we suggest trying to make use of a scenario for the old system by developing an analogous scenario for the new system. The analogy to an existing scenario makes it much easier to construct a new scenario. Extra care is required here, however, not to prevent innovations through this approach; e.g.

1. **If some function is known from the old system, then figure out whether this is still a valid function in the new system that will include the system to be built.**

   e.g. let us assume an old system that uses cash cards for the identification of customers like today's typical ATM. If in the new system customers shall be identified by their finger prints, the old function *Cash Card Acceptance* is not valid in this new system. The function *Cash Provision*, however, is still valid as a function of the new system to be built.

2. **2. If some function is known for the new system, then try to link it to one or more scenarios for the new system that are already known.**

   e.g. if some function Check Amount is known and the scenario *Get Cash from ATM*, it is to be linked to Step 9 of this scenario as given in Figure 2.

3. **3. If some function that is known for the new system cannot be linked to any scenario for the new system, then develop one or more such scenarios and link them to the function.**

   e.g. if some function for money transfer between accounts is known to be required for an ATM but no scenario that can be linked to it, a scenario for performing such money transfer is to be developed.

Figure 5: Sequence of steps for known functions.

---

when not even questioning the current way of customer identification through a cash card, the alternative of using finger prints instead may never be considered. So, for developing scenarios by analogy, their level of abstraction vs. concreteness may be relevant.

When the focus is 'just' to acquire the functional requirements of the system to be built, only the steps of this system are to be linked to descriptions of functions. For a better definition of the concrete user interface, however, also the functions to be performed by the user should be defined and attached.

3.3   Known Functions

Finally, we discuss the case when information about one or more functions is available. We focus here on functions required from the system to be built, since for these it is important to show that and how they can be used in at least one scenario to achieve at least one goal of the user. Known functions from the old system are to be checked whether they make still sense in the new system. In case some function is known, we propose the sequence of steps as given in Figure 5.

In practice, people often come up with functional requirements on the proposed computer system without saying anything about the way these functions will be used. In such a case, it may be difficult to understand these functions and in particular their intended use. There is even the danger that such a function does not really make sense for achieving a goal of the user. This danger also exists when such a function is said to be required just because this or a similar function is available in the old system.

Therefore, we propose to ask about potential uses in concrete envisioned situations. The answers result in (links to) scenarios that make clear why a certain function of the system to be built is required.

While the technique of systematic question asking starts with scenario descriptions, this shows that starting from functional descriptions is similarly useful. In this sense, we extend this technique here. Our extension helps to avoid that "functional specifications can become divorced from user's needs and requirements" (Mack, 1995).

4   Detecting Redundancy and Improving Completeness and Understandability

When this process of acquiring design information is followed thoroughly, some redundancy can be detected and some completeness and understandability of the resulting design is achieved:

1. *Each of the user's goals is linked to at least one scenario that can achieve it.* So, each known goal is considered in the design.

2. *Each scenario is linked to at least one goal.* In this way, the scenarios are shown to make sense, and they are better understood.

3. *Each action in each scenario is linked to some function.* So, no function is missing in the known scenarios.

4. *Each function is linked to at least one action in some scenario.* In this way, the functions are shown to make sense, and they are better understood.

While we found that these conditions reduce redundancy and improve on the completeness and understandability achieved without using our approach, they are of course no full guarantee. Conditions 1 and 3 are necessary conditions for completeness, but extra goals and functions may just be missing, and the set of scenarios is always potentially incomplete. Conditions 2 and 4 are necessary conditions for 'non-redundancy' in the design, but it can be redundant in many other ways. These latter conditions also improve the understandability, but there may be other ways for improving it. However, achieving these conditions is better than having lose ends and redundant functions or scenarios in the design representation.

5   Real-world Experience with Our Approach

Now let us present some real-world experience with this approach in a selected project. This application was performed in a logistics project called LLS that included several organizations in Austria and Germany. (LLS is a German acronym for "Logistik-Leitsystem", which denotes a proposed control system for logistics.) More precisely, we dealt with the user requirements on and the external design of the proposed computer system within the LLS. In the project it is called "DV-System LLS", and we call it in English here "LLS IT".

As usual in the course of designing such a system, several people participated in various roles:

> LLS IT shall be able to convert a message into the message format of the
> receiver of this message (like a clearing centre). These formats are based
> on existing standards such as, e.g. EDI and EDIFACT. The conversion
> must include both syntactic and semantic checks.

Figure 6: Textual description of the function *To convert message*.

- *user representative*: a representative of potential users of LLS, with a very good understanding of logistics, but without much knowledge on requirements engineering or human–computer interaction;

- *system designers*: specialists partly of logistics and partly of computer science, but also without deep knowledge on requirements engineering or human–computer interaction;

- *requirements engineer*: the developer of the overall method published, e.g. in (Kaindl, 1996b; Kaindl, 1997) and of the general design process defined above (this author); in this project the role of a requirements engineer was defined just to guide the concrete process happening and to look at the evolving design from this perspective, but not directly to define requirements or to make design decisions.

We focus in this case study on the use of our design process based on the combined model as presented in this paper. In order to illustrate the process and the model as well as their utility, we provide some few concrete examples of their use in this project.

When the requirements engineer became involved in this project, many functional requirements on the proposed computer system LLS IT were already acquired through a cooperation of the user representative and the system designers. Examples are functions of managing the storage of goods, of logistic information change management, and of 'open clearing'. The latter functions encompass the more obvious analysing and distributing of messages as well as, e.g. the less obvious function *To convert message* as shown in Figure 6[1].

However, usage scenarios and goals of using such a system have largely been left implicit. So, the part of our design process for known functions as prescribed in Figure 5 was triggered. In this project this meant that the requirements engineer asked the related questions in order to instantiate the general process under the given conditions. The first step was not applicable (dealing with functions known from the old system), as there was no old computer system like LLS IT yet. The second step was not successful (having no scenarios for the new system available to link the given function to). So, the third step (developing scenarios) was initiated.

In particular, the requirements engineer asked about envisaged interactions of users with LLS IT, where the previously elicited functions are indeed needed.

---

[1] The wording was generally rather elaborate and given in German. So, we do not directly include the original text here but paraphrased and slightly shortened text in English.

Triggered by this question for interactions, the user representative and the system designers discussed how they envisaged the concrete use of the proposed LLS IT system. At this point it became apparent that and how the user representative and some of the system designers made use of their well-founded knowledge of logistics. In particular, they used knowledge on how goods are shipped *without* having LLS IT available. That is, they made use of (yet implicit) *scenarios for the old system.*

So, scenarios were made explicit, which triggered the part of our design process for known scenarios as prescribed in Figure 4. According to its first step, the requirements engineer asked about goals to be achieved through these scenarios in the old system. Performing this step made explicit the primary goal of logistics in general: the safe and timely arrival of some goods from some dispatcher to some receiver. In addition, it revealed the goal of proper and timely information management related to transportation of goods, which is most often not achieved in today's practice. In fact, this was a major incentive for designing LLS and in particular LLS IT.

The second step of this part of our design process suggests to make direct use of a given scenario for the old system and to develop an analogous scenario for the new system. Implicitly, this was somehow done before by the user representative and the system designers, anyway. But according to the explicit suggestion from the requirements engineer, this analogical transfer became conscious. So, it was easier to focus on the new functionality to be provided by LLS IT, e.g. to serve as a central repository. In effect, the user representative and the system designers together developed several scenarios of how LLS IT should be used. These included scenarios for the distribution as well as for the procurement of goods, via some transport medium (or several transport media). A concrete example was a scenario developed for the procurement of collected goods via railway that envisaged the use of LLS IT. A fragment of this scenario called *Procuring collected goods via railway* is shown in Table 1.

According to the third step of the part of our design process as prescribed in Figure 4, these scenarios were linked with the already known functional requirements. The information about scenarios and functional requirements on LLS IT was fit together through attaching the functions to the scenarios according to the relation *By-Function.* For example, most of these scenarios included one or more actions of converting messages to various message formats used by certain receivers. Once the function *To convert message* as shown in Figure 6 was attached to these actions in the scenarios, it became clear how this function of LLS IT will be used (in the scenarios just developed, e.g. *Procuring collected goods via railway* as shown in Table 1). So, the potential risk was reduced that such a function is isolated from user's needs.

Strictly speaking, however, the goals of using LLS IT (according to the scenarios) were not yet explicit at this point in time. So, they could not yet be linked to the scenarios. According to the fourth step, such goals were to be identified. So, the requirements engineer asked (using *why*-questions) for the goals of users of LLS IT that should be achieved by these scenarios. Typical *goals* of various kinds of users revealed by the *why*-questions are the following:

Scenario *Procuring collected goods via railway*			
1. The **receiver** of goods transfers a procurement message to LSS IT.			
	2. **LLS IT** shall acknowledge the receipt of this message to the receiver and analyse it. Then LLS IT shall convert this procurement message and distribute it to the railway organization and to the dispatcher of the goods. LLS IT shall also store the message. *By-Function: To acknowledge receipt of message, ... To convert message , ...*		
		3. The **dispatcher** acknowledges the receipt of this message to LLS and transfers his freight data about the goods to be shipped to LLS IT.	
		...	
			9. The **railway organization** transfers a message to LLS IT that it got the goods for transportation.
	10. **LLS IT** shall acknowledge the receipt of this message to the railway organization and inform the dispatcher. In addition, LLS IT shall transfer the freight data in advance to the freight forwarder responsible for delivering the goods to their receiver. *By-Function: To acknowledge receipt of message, ... To convert message , ...*		
		...	
Goals: *Availability of information on goods to be shipped, ...*			

Table 1: A tabular representation of a specific LLS scenario.

> Freight forwarders want to have as much information as possible about goods to be shipped in advance. The availability of such information results, e.g. in improved planning and scheduling in order to minimize the mileage.

Figure 7: Textual description of the goal *Availability of information on goods to be shipped.*

- Dispatchers of goods (from the shipping industry) want to have information about whereabouts of the goods dispatched.

- Receivers (in the general public or in industry) want to have information about the date and time of delivery.

- Freight forwarders want to have information about goods to be shipped.

A description of the last of these goals can be found in Figure 7. These goals were linked to the scenarios according to the relation *By-Scenario.*

Note, that all of these goals are sub-goals of the larger goal of proper and timely information management related to transportation of goods as already revealed before (for the old system without LLS IT). These goals appear to have been mentioned since they relate to the envisaged improvements through building LLS IT. The primary goal of the safe and timely arrival of goods from some dispatcher to some receiver, however, was not given as a reply to the *why*-questions.

At this point in time, the requirements engineer found it useful to trigger the part of our design process for known goals as prescribed in Figure 3. Performing its first step confirmed, of course, that the original goal of the arrival of goods is still a valid goal in the new system. For those with in-depth knowledge about logistics, it was just too obvious to be mentioned again. Performing the second step just meant to install the links between this goal and the relevant scenarios according to the relation *By-Scenario.* Since all the known goals were linked in this way with at least one scenario for the new system including LLS IT, the third step was not applicable.

After that, the requirements engineer returned to the part of our design process for known scenarios as prescribed in Figure 4. Performing its fifth step revealed that some few actions in the scenarios could not be linked to any function. Most of these missing functions had been considered obvious before, but according to our systematic process they were finally made explicit. In this way, the representation was made more complete.

As a result of carefully applying our design process, all this information on functions, scenarios and goals was already represented and linked according to our combined model. In particular, the information about scenarios and functional requirements on LLS IT was fit together through attaching the functions to the scenarios according to the relation *By-Function* The scenarios were linked to the goals according to the relation *By-Scenario.*

In this way, the functions were linked via scenarios to the goals of the users. As a concrete example, the function *To convert message* was shown to be relevant for achieving, e.g. the goal of freight forwarders for *Availability of information on goods to be shipped.* This indirect relation is simply the composition of the relations of this function and this goal with, e.g. the scenario *Procuring collected goods via railway.*

Technically, all this design information and its links were represented in the form of hypertext in our tool RETH. Since RETH can export this representation (automatically) into a WWW (World-Wide Web) representation, the people involved were able to browse the design information using their favourite web browser, and even from distant places concurrently. In fact, such export was performed from time to time already for intermediate representations, which made intermediate stages of the design accessible in this way.

For the official delivery, still a 'linear' document was required. Since today such conventional documents are typically needed, our tool RETH supports their construction as described in (Kaindl, 1996b). In essence, RETH performs a depth-first traversal of the various structures of classes and subclasses (of scenarios, goals, etc.) as represented in hypertext nodes, and extracts the respective text chunks. The resulting document contains page references in place of hypertext links.

Of course, it is difficult to objectively compare the achievements in a real-world project like this one with those of other approaches. The only fair comparison possible here is with the other sub-projects. Our approach helped in this sub-project through guiding the development according to our design process based on the underlying combined model. Combining both functions with scenarios and scenarios with goals was necessary and useful to achieve this result. The application of our design process achieved a more structured representation of relevant information, and a more complete, less ambiguous and better understandable definition of the design of the interactions between the computer system to be built and its human users. In particular, the application of our design process helped to make clear how the functions of LLS IT will contribute to serve goals of the various users through scenarios. So, this sub-project resulted in a better requirements specification than the others.

The major lessons learned from this case study can be summarized as follows:

- Our design process is flexible enough to be carried out usefully in a real-world context. It derives this flexibility from being both model-driven and data-driven. Because of this flexibility, however, it is not yet clear whether and how this process can be carried out successfully when no requirements engineer is involved.

- In addition to guiding the design of a new system, our design process supports the transition from the current to the new system. By relating goals, scenarios and functions in both the current and the new system, the system evolution can be clearly tracked.

- Our combined model of goals, scenarios and functions serves well as a basis for our design process. The relations *By-Scenario* and *By-Function* among these concepts allow the navigation between them. From applying our process, instances of these concepts as well as links among them result, that represent a (partial) design of the interactions of potential users with a proposed computer system.

6 Related Work

It is infeasible here to give a comprehensive overview of all the work proposing uses of *scenarios*. A selection of important work related to human–computer interaction can be found in (Carroll, 1995). The focus in our paper is on those scenarios that support the generation of design ideas, which are called *envisioner* scenarios in (MacLean & McKerlie, 1995). Only recently scenarios were discussed in relation to goals (Carroll et al., 1994; Potts, 1995). While most of the previous work on scenarios leaves their goals implicit, our approach emphasizes explicit representation both of goals and of their relations to scenarios and functions.

Goals have previously been dealt with explicitly in many approaches to *task analysis* — for an overview see, for example (Preece et al., 1994, Chapter 20). A task can be viewed as a piece of work that a person or other agent has to perform (or wishes to). Concrete ways of performing tasks can be described in scenarios such as those in our approach. Similar constructs to scenarios have occasionally been called *methods* or *plans* in the context of task analysis. An example of an approach to task analysis known as TKS (Task Knowledge Structures) supports the process of identifying what people currently do in their work within a given domain. Its authors also dealt with scenarios, which in this context describe human activity (Johnson et al., 1995). Another role of scenarios in this approach is in depicting an account of a proposed course of action. Our approach explicitly relates scenarios to goals, and it contributes a detailed design process that also addresses the important problem of relating the current way of performing tasks to the design of a new system, i.e. the transition from old to new system.

According to our view of a scenario as a cooperative plan, developing a scenario can be viewed as a plan construction process, and this view helps us and people using our approach to focus the design of interactions towards goals. The problems with the plan execution approach of an expert help system for using a photocopier as analysed in (Suchman, 1986) are to be taken seriously. But they do not invalidate every planning approach and in particular not a planning *view* as taken in our approach. Our scenarios are still scenarios much like those described, e.g. in the collection (Carroll, 1995), and we do not even assume that any reasonable set of scenarios can be complete for a real-world problem. So, our view of scenarios as cooperative plans tries to make use of cognitive theories of planning and understanding like the one described in (Schank & Abelson, 1977) and it is useful for relating scenarios with goals, but it does not detract from the usefulness of the scenario approach.

Many approaches to requirements engineering have been proposed, and recent work on scenarios in the context of requirements engineering — see for example (Potts et al., 1994) — made useful contributions. The metamodel of (Dardenne et al., 1993) contains goals, and the meta-concept of a scenario is shortly mentioned. However, no direct connection to the goals is present in their metamodel, while our approach especially emphasizes the relationships between scenarios and goals and the use of goals for developing scenarios. Although our approach to the acquisition process follows their approach in the sense of traversing the metamodel graph, ours is more flexible in being both model-driven and data-driven. As described in (Dardenne et al., 1993), a 'strategy' in their approach may well start from goals, but once started it is model-driven only.

In the context of object-oriented analysis and design, *use cases* are the basis of at least one approach (Jacobson et al., 1992) and have been included in others. Use cases are mostly considered as classes of scenarios in the literature on object-oriented development, while there is also the view that "a use case is a type of scenario" (Mack, 1995). Anyway, use cases in these approaches have been neither related to goals nor attached with functional requirements. Some of the work already referred to above (Carroll et al., 1994) relates to object-oriented software development as well.

In summary, our combined model is unique in its approach to combining scenarios with both functions and goals. According to our best knowledge, our design process based on this model is the first systematic and concrete scenario-based design process. It encompasses the *systematic question asking* technique (Carroll et al., 1994), that it builds upon. While this technique only starts from scenarios, our process can additionally start from known functions or goals, and it is therefore also driven by what is currently known. In addition, our design process deals with design evolution from old to new system. Still, further improvements should be possible through integration of various scenario approaches such as shown in (Sutcliffe, 1995) and the use with other techniques such as design rationale to explore requirements.

7 Discussion

Finally, let us discuss some important issues related to our approach. As indicated above, it deals with goals that will be directly achieved by use of the proposed computer system, such as the goal that the customer has cash after using an ATM. In case that other possibly more strategic goals are known, the goal structure will first have to be elaborated in order to reveal the directly achievable goals. In fact, determining which goals are to be directly supported is another highly important aspect of designing a composite system.

Of course, we can never be sure that all the users' goals are known and specified for systems that have not yet been built. We argue for having at least one user representative involved like in the case study reported above, but still there is no guarantee that some goals may not yet be known or just stay hidden. The approach described in this paper strives for a certain completeness in itself in the sense that for each envisaged usage scenario at least one of the goals to be achieved through its execution is specified. Inferring goals from scenarios may reveal some that may otherwise be forgotten or unspecified. Our real-world experience suggests that this systematic approach improves the completeness also in regard to the specified goals.

Goals may also be in conflict, especially when different kinds of users are involved. We deal with conflicting goals in the same way as with conflicting requirements (which is sketched in (Kaindl, 1997)). Essentially, closely related information is grouped together through classification (performed by humans). This improves the chance that conflicting items — in this case conflicting goals — are discovered. In the tool representation, conflicting goals are linked by a special relation until this conflict is resolved.

An important issue in our approach and more generally in the design of interactive systems is deciding which functions are to be allocated to the computer system and which to the human users. In a recent report on a case study (Kaindl et al., 1998), we focused on functional decomposition using scenarios. Of course, the issue is not only how to decompose the overall functionality required for achieving goals, but also responsibility assignment in the sense of allocating sub-functions to the computer system and to the human users, respectively. In fact, this involves determining the system boundary between the proposed computer system yet to be built and its environment. Envisioning usage scenarios helps to discuss concrete and alternative function allocations and therefore supports design rationale for determining the system boundary.

While the scenario-based design process proposed in this paper is systematic and still flexible, its adoption in real-world practice requires a good understanding of the metamodel and of the overall approach. Since we cannot yet assume such an understanding when this new approach is applied for the first time, we currently insist on being involved in applications as facilitators, such as in the role of the requirements engineer in the case study presented above. In the course of the first application we assume that the people involved have gained the required understanding, so that our involvement will not be necessary in subsequent applications. In addition, we currently work on machine support for guiding the process.

During the application of our design process, the people involved systematically think about the given problem and the design of the composite system from different perspectives. The outcome of using this process is a specification that includes functional requirements on the proposed computer system as well as related scenarios and goals. Our real-world experience suggests that this specification may be better than others that are not created using our approach. Having a better specification of the composite system, there is a higher chance of building the right computer system. When errors at this stage can be avoided, this means high savings compared to having to re-design and re-implement after the deployment.

8 Conclusion

The essence of the approach proposed in this paper is that scenarios should be combined *both* with functions *and* goals. Our combined model helps to show how the functions of a system to be built will serve goals of its users through their use in scenarios. The concrete design process based on this model guides the system design.

Since our approach primarily strives for being useful in practice, it uses known ideas about dealing with scenarios from other approaches. However, this paper also introduces some new ideas, primarily the following:

- *a combined model of functions, scenarios and goals*: based on previous work that linked either functions with scenarios or scenarios with goals, our combined model explicitly relates functions with goals through scenarios; this relation shows how the functions of a computer system yet to be built will serve goals of its users;

- *a systematic and concrete design process based on this model*: our design process uses and extends the *systematic question asking* technique; it provides guidance for designing a new interactive system and relates the resulting design with information from the current system.

By relating goals, scenarios and functions in both the current and the new system, the evolution of how people carry out a task can be clearly tracked. In addition, we have shown how the thorough use of our combined model and of our design process based on this model achieves certain conditions for completeness, 'non-redundancy' and understandability of the resulting design. These theoretical considerations were confirmed by our experience in several real-world projects. Especially the combination of scenarios both with functions and goals was necessary and useful. Therefore, we confirm the utility of scenarios that was reported previously. In addition, we propose to use our approach that extends the previous use of scenarios in several ways.

In summary, we focused in this paper on a design process based on scenarios in human–computer interaction. For improving system design we have successfully combined scenarios both with functions and with goals.

Acknowledgement

The LLS project has been partially funded by the Austrian ITF (Investitions- und Technologiefonds). We thank our partners in this project for their great cooperation, in particular Johann Schuster. The discussions with Stefan Kramer and Mario Hailing on possibilities of machine support for novice users of our tool RETH supporting our approach to requirements engineering helped to make the process of acquiring information according to the combined model more concrete. Andrew Monk provided very useful comments to earlier drafts of this paper.

References

Antón, A. I. (1996), Goal-based Requirements Analysis, *in* C. Shekaran & J. Siddiqi (eds.), *Proceedings of the Second International Conference on Requirements Engineering (ICRE'96)*, IEEE Computer Society Press, pp.136–44.

Carroll, J. M. (ed.) (1995), *Scenario-Based Design: Envisioning Work and Technology in System Development*, John Wiley & Sons.

Carroll, J. M., Mack, R. L., Robertson, S. P. & Rosson, M. B. (1994), "Binding Objects to Scenarios of Use", *International Journal of Man–Machine Studies* 41(1/2), 243–76.

Chandrasekaran, B., Goel, A. K. & Iwasaki, Y. (1993), "Functional Representation as Design Rationale", *IEEE Computer* 26(1), 48–56.

Constantine, L. (1995), "Essential Modeling: Use Cases for User Interfaces", *ACM Interactions* II.2, 34–46.

Dardenne, A., van Lamsweerde, A. & Fickas, S. (1993), "Goal-directed Requirements Acquisition", *Science of Computer Programming* 20, 3–50.

Jacobson, I., Christerson, M., Jonsson, P. & Övergaard, G. (1992), *Object-Oriented Software Engineering: A Use Case Driven Approach*, Addison–Wesley.

Johnson, P., Johnson, H. & Wilson, S. (1995), Rapid Prototyping of User Interfaces Driven by Task Models, *in* Carroll (1995), pp.209–46.

Kaindl, H. (1995), An Integration of Scenarios with their Purposes in Task Modeling, *in* G. Olson & S. Schuon (eds.), *Proceedings of the Symposium on Designing Interactive Systems: Processes, Practices, Methods and Techniques (DIS'95)*, ACM Press, pp.227–35.

Kaindl, H. (1996a), How to Identify Binary Relations for Domain Models, *in* T. Maibaum & M. Zelkowitz (eds.), *Proceedings of the Eighteenth International Conference on Software Engineering (ICSE-18)*, IEEE Computer Society Press, pp.28–36.

Kaindl, H. (1996b), "Using Hypertext for Semiformal Representation in Requirements Engineering Practice", *The New Review of Hypermedia and Multimedia* 2, 149–73.

Kaindl, H. (1997), "A Practical Approach to Combining Requirements Definition and Object-oriented Analysis", *Annals of Software Engineering* 3, 319–43.

Kaindl, H., Kramer, S. & Kacsich, R. (1998), A Case Study of Decomposing Functional Requirements Using Scenarios, *in* D. Berry & B. Lawrence (eds.), *Proceedings of the Third International Conference on Requirements Engineering (ICRE'98)*, IEEE Computer Society Press, pp.156–63.

Mack, R. L. (1995), Discussion: Scenarios as Engines of Design, *in* Carroll (1995), pp.361–86.

MacLean, A. & McKerlie, D. (1995), Design Space Analysis and Use Representations, *in* Carroll (1995), pp.183–207.

Potts, C. (1995), Using Schematic Scenarios to Understand User Needs, *in* G. Olson & S. Schuon (eds.), *Proceedings of the Symposium on Designing Interactive Systems: Processes, Practices, Methods and Techniques (DIS'95)*, ACM Press, pp.247–56.

Potts, C., Takahashi, K. & Antón, A. I. (1994), "Inquiry-based Requirements Analysis", *IEEE Software* 11(2), 21–32.

Preece, J., Rogers, Y., Sharpe, H., Benyon, D., Holland, S. & Carey, T. (1994), *Human–Computer Interaction*, Addison–Wesley.

Schank, R. & Abelson, R. (1977), *Scripts, Plans, Goals and Understanding*, Lawrence Erlbaum Associates.

Suchman, L. A. (1986), *Plans and Situated Actions*, Cambridge University Press.

Sutcliffe, A. G. (1995), Requirements Rationales: Integrating Approaches to Requirements Analysis, *in* G. Olson & S. Schuon (eds.), *Proceedings of the Symposium on Designing Interactive Systems: Processes, Practices, Methods and Techniques (DIS'95)*, ACM Press, pp.33–42.

Understanding a Task Model: An Experiment

Nadine Ozkan, Cécile Paris & Sandrine Balbo

CSIRO/MIS, Locked Bag 17, North Ryde, NSW 1670, Australia.

Tel: *+61 2 9325 3100*

Fax: *+61 2 9325 3200*

EMail: *{Nadine.Ozkan, Cecile.Paris,*
Sandrine.Balbo} @cmis.csiro.au

URL: *http://www.cmis.csiro.au/*
{Nadine.Ozkan, Cecile.Paris, Sandrine.Balbo}/

The HCI community advocates task analysis as a useful technique for user requirements analysis and system design, and has shown that task models should be developed collaboratively with users. The question of the usability and readability of task models for end-users is therefore an important one. In addition, we were specifically interested in this question in the context of our current project, Isolde*. Isolde is an authoring tool for technical writers whose user interface relies heavily on a specific task notation, DIANE+. We undertook an empirical study aimed at testing the readability and usability of DIANE+. Two experimental tasks are performed by end-users with no previous exposure to task models. Results show that DIANE+ is largely readable but that its usability is somewhat more problematic. This can be attributed to the task description notation rather than to the concepts themselves.

Keywords: task analysis, task modelling, usability of task models, empirical study.

---

*An Integrated Software and On-Line Documentation Environment.

1 Introduction

The main reason for the adoption of task analysis in the HCI domain is the claim that task models are closer to the user's perspective than the traditional models used in software engineering (state diagrams, data models, etc.), which focus on internal system functioning. Task analysis and task modelling have been among the most successful contributions of the HCI community to systems engineering. Task modelling is used for user requirements analysis (Barthet, 1988; Scapin & Pierret-Golbreich, 1989), system design (Hartson & Hix, 1990; Lim & Long, 1994) and usability evaluation (Card et al., 1983). Recently, it has also been shown to be useful to produce end-user documentation — for example (Tarby, 1994; Paris et al., 1991; Paris & Vander Linden, 1996a; Balbo & Lindley, 1997). When task analysis is used for user requirements analysis or system design, and when task models are developed collaboratively with users, the question of their usability and readability for end-users is an important one. This paper addresses this question for a graphical task representation notation, DIANE+ (Barthet, 1988). (The question of the generality of these results to other types of notation is raised in the discussion section.) We present an empirical study of how DIANE+ is manipulated by users with no previous exposure to task models. This study was done in the context of the design of Isolde, an authoring tool for technical writers (Pemberton, 1996; Paris & Vander Linden, 1996b; Paris et al., in this volume). The first section describes the aims of the study in relation to the design of Isolde. The second section describes the DIANE+ task notation. The third section describes the methodology we employed for the study. Finally, we present the results in the fourth section, followed by a discussion, the conclusion and future work.

2 Context and Aims of the Study

This study was done in the context of the design of the Isolde authoring tool for technical writers. The aim of the Isolde tool is the automatic generation of portions of an application's on-line help. Building on Drafter (Paris et al., 1991; Paris & Vander Linden, 1996a), a previous project concerned with the automatic production of multi-lingual hard copy manuals, we are developing an interactive on-line help drafting tool to be integrated into both the technical writers' working environment and the software design process. On-line help and documentation typically refers to end-users' tasks, that is what the end-users are trying to do with the software system at use, and how they can achieve their goals with the system. To generate on-line help automatically then, we need to represent the software system's functionality in terms of these end-users' tasks. We have already shown in (Paris et al., 1991; Paris & Vander Linden, 1996a) that documentation could be generated from task models. In that work, we used a simple plan/goal representation as often employed in AI planning systems, e.g. (Sacerdoti, 1977). As this representation was limited, we wished in our current project, Isolde, to exploit representation models with greater expressiveness, such as the task notations developed in the HCI community. On-line help is generated automatically from the task model, and the draft is presented to the technical writers for corrections or approval. Writing on-line help using such a support tool, then, requires technical writers to create task models, as well as manipulate and understand them. In this context, the aim of the study presented in this paper was thus threefold:

- to test the usability and readability of task models for people outside the HCI community and not computer professionals;

- to reveal the strategies that would be used by technical writers to create task diagrams; and

- to guide the design of the Isolde user interface.

This paper addresses the first of these.

3   The Adopted Task Notation: DIANE+

A variety of task representation notations are available – for example, UAN (Hartson & Hix, 1990), MAD (Scapin & Pierret-Golbreich, 1989), DIANE+ (Barthet, 1988), GOMS (Card et al., 1983), Petri Nets (Palanque et al., 1993), TKS (Johnson, 1992). State charts (Harel, 1987) have also been used for the generation of documentation (Thimbleby & Addison, 1996). DIANE+ was chosen within Isolde for the following reasons:

- DIANE+ is a task modelling notation which is claimed by its authors to be user-centred as opposed to system-centred.

- The notation is suited to system design (as opposed to system evaluation), and is applicable for a variety of design tasks.

- DIANE+ was designed with the explicit aim of bridging the gap between the software engineering and the human factors community. In fact, current work is underway by the authors of DIANE+ to use it as the basis for the automatic generation of user interfaces (Tarby, 1994). The fact that DIANE+ is formal enough to enable code generation, while still providing a usage perspective on systems, is particularly well aligned with our goal in Isolde.

- There are several claims in the literature on DIANE+ about its high level of readability and usability (Barthet, 1988). Because of its graphical nature, the authors of DIANE+ claim that it is easier to understand than other language-based formalisms such as UAN (Hartson & Hix, 1990), or other more formal, albeit graphical, representations such as Petri Nets (Palanque et al., 1993). This study acts as an initial validation of the claims of readability and usability, although the comparison with other types of formalisms remains to be done.

- DIANE+ has been used as the basis for the automatic generation of contextual help (Tarby, 1994), which links in well with Isolde's objectives.

As for expressive power, like several other notations, DIANE+ expresses the following:

- user tasks (called manual tasks);

- system tasks (called automatic tasks);

- tasks requiring both user and system input (called interactive tasks);

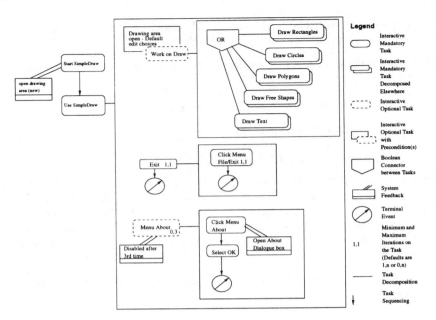

Figure 1: The high-level tasks of SimpleDraw in DIANE+.

- mandatory and optional tasks;

- task hierarchical decomposition in sub-tasks;

- system feedback to a user action;

- sequencing of tasks;

- parallelism of tasks;

- Boolean relationships between tasks; and

- the cardinality of a task, that is the maximum and minimum numbers of times a task can be executed.

Based on discussions with technical writers, on previous work (Paris & Vander Linden, 1996a) as well as on an analysis of on-line help and documentation — e.g. (Hartley & Paris, in preparation), this information is considered necessary and sufficient to provide end-user documentation. DIANE+ is thus suitable for our specific application. Figure 1 shows an example of part of the DIANE+ diagram for SimpleDraw, a simple 'toy' drawing application developed in-house for experimental purposes. In the DIANE+ notation, horizontal links denote task decomposition and vertical links denote task strict sequencing. (Figure 1 is fully described in the next section.)

4 Methodology

4.1 Choice of Method

We adopted an experimental method whereby we devised tasks to be performed by a group of technical writers and analysed their process and their output. Other types of methods are available, such as structured interviews, semi-structured interviews or observation of work practices. The choice of an experimental approach was motivated by the following factors:

- The user population does not normally use formal task models. We could therefore not resort to direct observation of current work practices.

- The study related in this paper was only part of the activities undertaken to design the Isolde interface. Other activities included semi-structured interviews and observations. This paper, however, is not focussed on the methodology for design but only on one of its activities, namely the assessment of the usability and readability of DIANE+.

4.2 Participants and Tasks

Five technical writers participated in the study. They are representative of future Isolde end-users. They specialize in writing end-user documentation for software systems. One is novice, with less than one year experience in technical writing. The others have at least 10 years experience. In Australia, technical writers are trained in communications and writing rather than in technical domains. None of the participants have computer science or HCI background, although two use flowchart diagrams in their work.

After an one-hour introduction to DIANE+ where its different concepts (listed in the previous section) and their graphical representation were presented, two successive tasks were given to the technical writers. The first involved the interpretation of a DIANE+ diagram. The second involved the creation of a DIANE+ diagram. The interpretation of a model being generally easier than the generation of a model, the interpretation task was given first.

For the interpretation task, the technical writers were presented with a DIANE+ model of the SimpleDraw application (see Figure 1 for part of that model[†]) and asked to produce the end-user documentation in one hour. They did not have access to the system itself, but only to its DIANE+ model.

As is shown in Figure 1, SimpleDraw allows the user to draw various types of shapes (square, circle, polygon, etc.) and to write text. SimpleDraw is a very straightforward application and did not require the use of the more difficult features of DIANE+ (such as the constraints on the minimum and maximum number of times a task can be executed). We therefore made its DIANE+ model somewhat more complex to make sure that all the DIANE+ features were actually present in the tested model.

Two difficulties were added to SimpleDraw. First, we introduced a restriction on the number of times the information on SimpleDraw (the 'About SimpleDraw'

[†]We built this model to match the functionality of SimpleDraw.

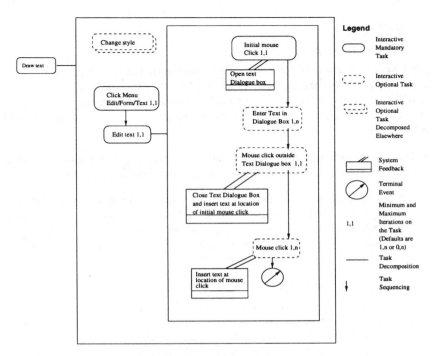

Figure 2: The partial DIANE+ model of SimpleDraw: The DrawText function.

text) could be invoked in one session (a maximum of three times). Secondly, we changed the functionality of the Draw Text function to make it awkward and counter-intuitive. This was to ensure that technical writers were actually reading the DIANE+ diagram and not going on reasonable assumptions of how SimpleDraw should work. The Draw Text function, as it is described in the model (Figure 2), is the following. After having chosen the Text option from the appropriate menu, the user must click in the work area where the text is to appear. SimpleDraw responds by opening a text dialogue box. The desired text must be typed in the dialogue box. A click outside the dialogue box indicates that editing is terminated. The text is then displayed at the location of the initial mouse click. The same text can be placed in other locations by clicking appropriate places in the work area.

For the generation task, the technical writers were presented with a running application, the Unix calendar manager, and had individual demonstrations of its functionalities. They were then asked to produce its DIANE+ representation. They were provided with the definition of DIANE+, two examples of DIANE+ diagrams (of other applications), and the running Calendar Manager application, all of which they could consult at will.

For the interpretation task, we only gathered the technical writers' final production (i.e. the documentation) for analysis. For the generation task, on the other hand, we asked the technical writers to 'think aloud' in order to obtain, in addition to the resulting diagram, the process which lead to it, with its intermediary steps and any comments. This information was used to help guide the Isolde user interface design.

We had to impose a time limit of one hour to the performance of each of the two experimental tasks. Of course, this limit is both artificial and arbitrary, but it was necessary: our participants are time-conscious professionals working under pressure in an industrial environment. We could have ran the experiments with people who don't have such time constraints (students for example) and this would have permitted the 'normal' completion of each task. However, in the trade-off between unconstrained time and representative users, we favoured the latter. Nevertheless, it may be noted that one hour was sufficient time to produce 'stable' instruction texts for the tasks for which interpretation was attempted. Similarly, for the generation task, 'stable' diagrams were produced within the hour allotted for the experiment. What we mean by a stable production is one which acts as a basis for further work, essentially addition or enhancement (i.e. very little or minor revision). For the generation task for example, we observed that diagrams produced in the first 15 to 30 minutes were subject to many fundamental changes. Once the participant 'understood' or 'got the hang' of DIANE+ modelling, the remaining time was spent on adding to the diagram, not revising what had already been produced. The time taken to obtain a 'stable' production was less for the interpretation task.

Of course, this artificial time limit is accounted for in the analysis: no measure of task completeness is taken into account when assessing performance.

5 Results

5.1 Interpretation Task

The results of the interpretation task are summarized in Table 1, and an example of the instructions produced is given in the Appendix. Eleven SimpleDraw modules were to be documented. We marked as *correct* documentation which described the same functionality as that expressed in the DIANE+ diagrams, and as *incorrect*, documentation which described functionality different from the DIANE+ documents. The great majority (88%) of the documentation that was attempted was correct.

All the documentation sets produced were, if not complete for lack of time, at least accurate for the 'standard' modules of SimpleDraw (that is, the modules whose functionality was not altered for the purposes of the experiment, as described in the previous section). The representations of sequencing, decomposition, parallelism, system feedback, optional and mandatory tasks were all accurately interpreted. As for the two difficulties which we introduced, the limit on the number of times the 'About' text could be looked at was picked up by all the technical writers, whereas the awkward behaviour of the 'Draw Text' function was described completely by only two of them. Two others described it incorrectly and the remaining technical writer did not attempt it due to confusion.

In addition, it is interesting to note that most technical writers (including the one who was confused by the 'Draw Text' function) made the written comment that they found the DIANE+ model easy to understand . This comment was offered spontaneously, as no instructions were given to this effect. It thus seems that the

SimpleDraw Modules to be described	P1	P2	P3	P4	P5
SimpleDraw Overview		I		C	C
Starting SimpleDraw			C	C	C
Draw rectangle	C	C	C	C	C
Draw circle		C	C		
Draw polygon					
Draw free shape		C			C
Draw text	I	I	C		C
Change colour	C	C			C
Change line thickness	C	C			C
Exit	C		C	C	
Get info about	I			C	

	P1	P2	P3	P4	P5	Average
Out of 11 descriptions of modules						
Proportion of correct descriptions	36%	45%	45%	45%	64%	47%
Proportion of faulty descriptions	18%	18%	0%	0%	0%	7%
Proportion of descriptions left blank	45%	36%	55%	55%	36%	45%
Out of the attempted descriptions						
Proportion of correct descriptions	67%	71%	100%	100%	100%	88%
Proportion of incorrect descriptions	33%	29%	0%	0%	0%	12%

P1, ..., P5: Participant1, ..., Participant 5
C: Attempted and correct except for cardinality
I: Attempted and incorrect
blank cell: not attempted

Table 1: Results of the interpretation task.

---

results of the experiment confirm the technical writers' positive overall impression of DIANE+ readability.

These results show that straightforward features are interpreted without difficulty, while more intricate features can pose problems for interpretation. Nonetheless, the overall performance on the interpretation was very good.

5.2 Generation Task

As expected, performance on the generation task was somewhat lower than on the interpretation task. For each of the possible Calendar Manager functions, we checked that the various features of DIANE+ were used correctly (that is, they were used when they were necessary, and left out when they were not) and that they accurately represented the functionality of the Calendar Manager. We must note, in analysing the resulting diagrams, that the same functionality may be expressed in several ways using DIANE+ so that several different DIANE+ diagrams may, in fact, be correct. As is shown in Table 2, of the attempted models, 65% were correct. (A sample of the models produced is given in the Appendix.)

Calendar Manager Functions	P1	P2	P3	P4	P5
Enter New Appointment					
precondition	C	C	C	C	C
sequencing	C	C	C	C	C
boolean connector	C	C	C	C	C
decomposition	I	C	C	C	C
end state	I	I	I	C	I
cardinality	I	I	I	I	I
system feedback	C	C	C	C	C
task attributes					
Set Time (Start, End)					
precondition	C	C		C	C
sequencing	C	C		C	I
boolean connector	C	C		C	I
decomposition	I	C		C	I
end state	C	C		C	I
cardinality	I	I		I	I
system feedback	C	I		C	C
task attributes					
Write a Message					
precondition	C		C		
sequencing	I		C		
boolean connector	C		C		
decomposition	I		C		
end state	C		I		
cardinality	I		I		
system feedback	C		C		
task attributes					
Set Alarm Options					
precondition	C		C		C
sequencing	I		I		I
boolean connector	C		C		I
decomposition	I		I		I
end state	C		I		I
cardinality	I		I		I
system feedback	C		C		I
task attributes					
Accept Input	C	C	C	C	C

Of the attempted descriptions	P1	P2	P3	P4	P5	Averages
Proportion of correct ones	62%	73%	64%	87%	41%	65%
Proportion of incorrect ones	38%	27%	36%	13%	59%	35%

P1, ..., P5: Participant1, ..., Participant 5
C: Attempted and correct except for cardinality
I: Attempted and incorrect
blank cell: not attempted

Table 2: Results of the Generation task.

For this task, only one technical writer (P4) produced an accurate diagram (excluding task cardinality, which is discussed below). For the others, the types of errors produced in the DIANE+ diagrams can be grouped in the following categories:

1. Ignored task attributes. Task cardinality as well as other task attributes such as optional or mandatory, manual or automatic were largely ignored.

2. Sequencing versus decomposition. Three models showed confusion between these two types of relationships between tasks. For example, a downward arrow was used to indicate either of those relationships, making them indistinguishable. However, this confusion was not systematic throughout each model. For example, a valuable observation was that the portions of the model which were created by looking at other examples of DIANE+ models did not show this confusion.

3. Influence of other system representation schemes. For example, one technical writer uses flow charts extensively in his work practice. His diagram clearly did not take advantage of a task perspective but resembled more a flow chart expressed using DIANE+.

6   Analysis and Discussion

The results of the interpretation task indicate that DIANE+ is indeed largely readable. Difficulties are observed regarding complex tasks, but, based on this experiment, it seems likely that these difficulties will disappear as the technical writers acquire expertise with task models.

The results of the generation task are revealing of the usability aspects of DIANE+. A major difficulty here seems to lie with the confusion between relationships of decomposition and of sequencing between two tasks (as those two relationships are fundamental in building task models). The usability of DIANE+ seems therefore to be deficient.

We believe that the source of this confusion lies with the DIANE+ representation and potentially with the new conceptual task (constructing a model of the software's functionality instead of documenting it) rather than with the concepts themselves (e.g. decomposition, sequencing, etc.). This is supported by several observations. Firstly, the confusion did not occur systematically in any one model: the same model could exhibit both correct and incorrect representations of task decomposition. (It is interesting to note that, often, the correct portions were generated based on an example of a correct DIANE+ model.) In addition, task decomposition is a notion which is well mastered by technical writers who write on-line, task-oriented documentation, in the style promoted in (Carroll, 1990). In fact, one of the technical writers who used sequences to indicate decomposition also found means to distinguish the two types of links graphically. (This is illustrated in the samples given in the Appendix.) This made his DIANE+ diagram very unorthodox, but had the merit of showing us that the concepts were distinct for him. Lastly, the fact that the concepts are clear and that the confusion lies with their DIANE+ representation is also supported by the absence of this type of confusion in the interpretation task.

The same conclusion can be derived regarding another feature of DIANE+ which generated poor performance, namely task cardinality (the minimum and maximum number of times a task can be executed). Task cardinality was interpreted correctly by only one of the technical writers and not attempted by most of them. As for generation, task cardinality was left out of all the DIANE+ models except one. However, the concept of repeating a series of tasks for a fixed number of times is again one which is routinely used by technical writers.

In summary, our study indicates that:

1. The DIANE+ notation is largely readable by users outside the HCI community.

2. Its usability is more problematic: Our study shows that some features of DIANE+ induces problems regarding task attributes, task cardinality as well as a confusion between sequencing and decomposition.

3. However, the concepts of task analysis (task decomposition, task sequencing, task parallelism, etc.) are clear for technical writers.

In conclusion, these experiments seem to show the influence of representation on the manipulation of concepts which are, by themselves, well understood. Further work would be required to confirm this influence as opposed to the effects of difficulties in performing a new task.

Nevertheless, and despite the limitations in the DIANE+ representation which were uncovered, the experiments support one of the hypothesis of the Isolde project, namely that task models are appropriate representations for technical writers. Isolde's user interface will need to address the shortcomings of DIANE+.

We now turn to examining the generality of the results we have presented in this paper: in what measure can they be applicable to other end-users and to other task notations? We believe that the results should hold for classes of users with similar characteristics as technical writers, namely people:

- with no technical training;

- with great familiarity with computers as users; and

- with some exposure to modelling techniques.

As to other types of task notations, again we hypothesize that the results should hold for graphical notations — such as MAD (Scapin & Pierret-Golbreich, 1989), which are similar to DIANE+, but not necessarily for other 'families' of notations, such as statecharts (Harel, 1987), Petri nets (Palanque et al., 1993) or language based ones, e.g. UAN (Hartson & Hix, 1990). This is corroborated by previous experience (Balbo & Lindley, 1997), where we observed, albeit not in a systematic fashion, that the MAD graphical task notation was found to be largely readable and served as a communication tool among software engineers, HCI specialists and technical writers.

7   Current and Future Work

We are currently working collaboratively with the technical writers on the design of Isolde's user interface. The design must palliate to the difficulties with DIANE+ found in our experiment, and in particular to the confusion between task decomposition and sequencing. Two rounds of paper prototyping and validation took place before settling on an interface design. We now have a first working prototype ready for evaluation. We expect a few more rounds of prototype validation before its design is finalized.

   We are also planning to provide Isolde users with some initial specification of the tasks to be documented. As Isolde is to be used in conjunction with a CASE (Computer Aided Software Engineering) system, we are currently attempting to obtain as much information as possible from the specifications of the software system as embodied in the CASE tool, and to import these into Isolde (Lu et al., 1998). This means that the technical writers will be provided with an initial model of the task, which they will then need to augment or modify. The results reported in this paper indicate that this should help them create task models, given the observation that the number of errors in the generation task was significantly lower when technical writers based their model on an example.

Acknowledgements

We thank the team of technical writers from IBM Global Services and especially Pamela Manning and Flor Bonifacio, as well as Necola Hoare for their enthusiastic participation to our study. We also thank the other members of the Isolde team, Shijian Lu and Keith Vander Linden, and Anthony Hartley for his useful comments on drafts of this paper. This work is supported in part by the Office of Naval Research (ONR), by the Grant N00014-96-1-0465 in the Programme for User Centered Direct Interaction Systems.

Appendix: Sample Data from the Experiments

1. Sample Production for the interpretation task
(Note that comments in *italics* are addressed to the Isolde team members)

Starting Simple Draw

- Double-click on SD icon *presumed method*
  SD displays the main drawing area

Exiting Simple Draw

- Click on File in the menu bar, then choose Exit

Drawing rectangles

- Make sure you have selected the colour and thickness you wish to use for the rectangle
  Refer to Changing line colour *link*
       Changing line thickness *link*

- Click on Edit in the menu var, then choose Form, then Rectangle
  SD displays *??*

- Position the cursor where you wish the upper left-hand corner of the rectangle to appear

- Click the mouse button, hold it down and drag the mouse until the rectangle is the desired size, then release the mouse button

2. Sample Productions For the generation task

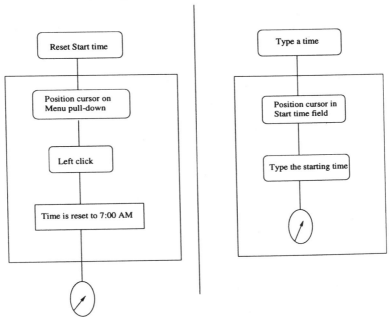

Note: Decomposition and sequencing relationships are both denoted by a vertical line segment. However, subtasks are enclosed within a box.

References

Balbo, S. & Lindley, C. (1997), Adaptation of a Task Analysis Methodology to the Design of a Decision Support System, *in* S. Howard, J. Hammond & G. K. Lindgaard (eds.), *Human–Computer Interaction — INTERACT'97: Proceedings of the Fifth IFIP Conference on Human–Computer Interaction*, Chapman & Hall, pp.355–61.

Barthet, M.-F. (1988), *Logiciels interactifs et ergonomie, modèles et méthodes de conception*, Dunod Informatique Ed., Paris.

Card, S. K., Moran, T. P. & Newell, A. (1983), *The Psychology of Human–Computer Interaction*, Lawrence Erlbaum Associates.

Carroll, J. M. (1990), *The Nurnberg Funnel: Designing Minimalist Instruction for Practical Computer Skill*, MIT Press.

Harel, D. (1987), "Statecharts: A Visual Formalism for Complex Systems", *Science of Computer Programming* **8**(3), 231–74.

Hartley, A. F. & Paris, C. L. (in preparation), Towards an Empirical Characterization of the Discourse of Software Instructions, Technical Report, ITRI, University of Brighton. See also Hartley, A.F. & Paris, C.L. (1995) Drafter: French Corpus Analysis and Grammatical Description, WP14/WP15 Deliverable, Drafter Project IED4/1/5827, EPSRC grant number J19221.

Hartson, H. R. & Hix, D. (1990), "The UAN: A User-Oriented Representation for Direct Manipulation Interface Designs", *International Journal of Man–Machine Studies* **8**(3), 181–203.

Johnson, P. (1992), *Human–Computer Interaction: Psychology, Task Analysis and Software Engineering*, McGraw-Hill.

Lim, K. & Long, J. (1994), *The MUSE Method for Usability Engineering*, Cambridge University Press.

Lu, S., Paris, C. & Vander Linden, K. (1998), Towards Automatic Construction of Task Models from Object-Oriented Diagrams, *in* S. Chatty & P. Dewan (eds.), *Proceedings of the IFIP Working Conference on Engineering for Human-Computer Interaction 1998*, Kluwer.

Palanque, P. A., Bastide, R., Dourte, L. & Sibertin-Blanc, C. (1993), Design of User-driven Interfaces Using Petri Nets and Objects, *in* C. Rolland, F. Bodart & C. Cauvet (eds.), *Proceedings of CAISE'93 (Conference on Advance Information System Engineering)*, Vol. 685 of *Lecture Notes in Computer Science*, Springer-Verlag, pp.569–85.

Paris, C. & Vander Linden, K. (1996a), "DRAFTER: An Interactive Support Tool for Writing Multilingual Instructions", *IEEE Computer* **29**(7), 49–56. Special Issue on Interactive Natural Language Processing.

Paris, C. & Vander Linden, K. (1996b), An Overview of On-Line Documentation and CASE Tools, Technical Report ITRI-95-16, ITRI.

Paris, C., Vander Linden, K., Fischer, M., Hartley, A., Pemberton, L., Power, R. & Scott, D. (1991), A Support Tool for Writing Multilingual Instructions, *in Proceedings of the Fourteenth International Joint Conference on Artificial Intelligence (IJCAI'95)*, Morgan Kaufmann, pp.1398–404. Also available as ITRI report ITRI-95-11.

Pemberton, L. (1996), Requirements from Technical Writing, Technical Report, ITRI.

Sacerdoti, E. D. (1977), *A Structure for Plans and Behaviour*, Elsevier Science.

Scapin, D. & Pierret-Golbreich, C. (1989), Toward a Method for Task Description: MAD, *in Proceedings of Work with Display Units '89*, Elsevier Science, pp.371–80.

Tarby, J.-C. (1994), The Automatic Management of Human–Computer Dialogue and Contextual Help, *in* B. Blumenthal, J. Jornostaev & C. Unger (eds.), *Proceedings of EWHCI'94: The East–West International Conference on Human–Computer Interaction*, Springer-Verlag.

Thimbleby, H. & Addison, M. (1996), "Intelligent Adaptive Assistance and Its Automatic Generation", *Interacting with Computers* **8**(1), 51–68.

Analysing Requirements to Inform Design

Michele Ryan & Alistair Sutcliffe

Centre for HCI Design, School of Informatics, City University, Northampton Square, London EC1V 0HB, UK.

Tel: *+44 171 477 8993*

Fax: *+44 171 477 8859*

EMail: *M.Ryan@city.ac.uk*

Publications, guidelines and methodologies have proliferated on usability engineering in the HCI literature while an extensive literature exists on methods in requirements engineering. Requirements analysis and usability are inextricably linked yet few methods exist to integrate the two approaches. In this paper we propose a framework for analysing requirements of systems and user interfaces, and report its use in requirements capture. Inadequacies resulting from the application of the framework are described leading to development of a method for requirements elaboration. Use of the method is illustrated by applying it retrospectively to the requirements capture exercise.

Keywords: reuse, usability, evaluation, frameworks, methods, requirements gathering.

1 Introduction

Software engineering process models such as the Spiral Model (Boehm, 1988) recommend that several iterations of requirements gathering, design and implementation are necessary. The Star Model (Hix & Hartson, 1993) proposes cycles of prototyping and evaluation which have become the norm for a user centred approach and recognize the iterative nature of design and evaluation (Bevan, 1996). However, the design process is complex and poorly understood. Requirements analysis concerns itself with questions of what is required; what users need to know and so on (Sutcliffe, 1996), whereas, design is concerned with how these things can be achieved (Preece et al., 1994). However, exposure to design solutions is frequently a necessary part of clarifying requirements. In HCI, requirements capture either occurs through task analysis or is an ad hoc phase of system development. Process guidance is limited to recommendations for various techniques that may be applied, e.g. interviews, card sorts, protocols, etc. (Johnson, 1992; Preece et al., 1994). There are also checklists, design rules and guidelines which focus on operational usability (Ravden & Johnson, 1989; Shneiderman, 1992; Nielsen, 1993; Bevan, 1996) to assist the designer at various stages.

In spite of these methods and techniques many systems don't work, are unusable or fail e.g. London Ambulance Service system, Camelot and ASSIST (Collins, 1997). In a retrospective analysis of a healthcare information system we found that usability was a major cause of poor system quality; however, many usability errors were functional in nature (Sutcliffe et al., in press). In our previous work, we have developed a method of scenario-based requirements analysis (SCRAM (SCenario-based Requirement Analysis Method) — (Sutcliffe, 1995)) but this work did not specifically address the integration of usability and functionality during requirements analysis. The purpose of this paper is to propose a requirements analysis method from a HCI perspective. We show how the application of the method contributes to the design process and solution.

Following this introduction, Section 2 describes a requirements analysis framework. To put the work in context, Section 3 provides an overview of the case study project and early requirements and evaluation activities. Section 4 reports on later requirements gathering activities. In Section 5 we describe a preliminary method for analysing requirements using the proposed framework (in Section 1). The final section summarizes the lessons learned and contains a brief conclusion.

2 Analytical Framework of Requirements

Requirements gathering is the process of finding out what a client or customer wants from a software system and is therefore one of the key factors which influence design. Requirements are frequently categorized into three types: functional requirements, which specify what the system must do; data requirements, which specify the information that must be available for processing; and usability requirements, which specify the acceptable level of user performance and satisfaction with the system (Preece et al., 1994). More extensive taxonomies are reported in the Requirements Engineering literature (Robertson, 1997). The framework we propose in Figure 1, takes a HCI perspective and therefore expands on the definition of usability requirements and includes requirements that profile the user population.

3 Multimedia Broker Early Requirements and Evaluation

In this section we describe how requirements were gathered on the Multimedia Broker project. Multimedia Broker is a web based application for searching, retrieving and publishing information from multiple, multimedia databases on the World Wide Web. The role of the Broker is to assist users find relevant information and to help the publishers design, configure and maintain on-line services and products. There are three user partners on the project who provide domain expertise in the fields of transport and planning, publishing educational material and books.

Functional requirements — *which specify the things that the system must do, that is, the tasks it must perform.*

   1. Perform application tasks (non user specific tasks)

   2. Manage data — process data in some way

   3. Failure recovery

User functional requirements — *which concern the tasks specified by the users which they want to perform using the system, and their associated requirements such as task support and feedback.*

   4. Task support

   5. Provide feedback

Usability requirements — *which specify the acceptable level of performance and user satisfaction.*

   6. Efficiency — must be efficient to use

   7. Memorability — must be easy to remember

   8. Learnability — must be easy to learn and understand

   9. Errors — must have a low error rate

  10. Satisfaction — must be satisfying to use

  11. Ease of use — must be easy to use

  12. Comprehension — must make sense and be easy to understand

User Interface Requirements — *which concern the operation of the user interface.*

  13. Information presentation — concerns what information is presented and how.

  14. Dialogue and behaviour — (e.g. whether to use a scroll bar).

User Requirements — *which are concerned with requirements relating to user needs, experience, knowledge and expectations (e.g. Different user levels must be supported).*

  15. Needs (e.g. for training, different user levels)

  16. Experience (e.g. previous experience)

  17. Expectations

Data Requirements — *which specify the application structure and the data that must be available.*

  18. Input — the type of data entering the system

  19. Output — the type of data output by the system

Non-functional Requirements — *which concern non task related characteristics of the system (e.g. Speed is very important).*

20. Security	25. Cost	29. Environment (e.g. Legal)
21. Speed	26. Timescales	
22. Robustness	27. Software	30. Political
23. Accuracy		
24. Maintainability	28. Sales	31. Client

Figure 1: Framework of requirement types.

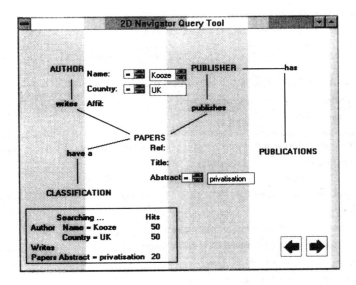

Figure 2: 2D Map Navigator. Shows Entities and Relations in a query by pointing user interface.

3.1 Early Concept Demonstrator

A feasibility study carried out in advance of the project identified a number of functions which should be included in the system. There were four main categories: information retrieval, brokering, payment and administration, and pre-press authoring. The feasibility study guided the design of the early concept demonstrator which illustrated different user interface designs.

In supporting information retrieval the concept demonstrator offered different ways of browsing and navigating the information space. The options include 3D and 2D graphical interfaces, world maps, and text-based interfaces. Interactive screens for constructing and modifying queries were displayed which involved picking items from categories or using constrained natural language. Figure 2 shows an interactive top-down 2D Entity Relation Map Navigator, while Figure 3 shows constructing a query using a natural language template.

Human brokers refine their knowledge of user, requirements and constraints by asking a structured sequence of questions. The system provided fill-in templates or invoked a mini knowledge-based system to support negotiation with the user. We wanted to find out what sort of support tools users wanted (e.g. did they want help to clarify their needs, did they want to be advised on possible courses of action and choices, did they want the system to match their requirements to suitable media resources?). In Authoring Support we wanted to find out what sorts of tools authors needed (e.g. Would a report writing tool that enabled users to create their own multimedia documents be useful?). The screen in Figure 4 illustrates such a tool for creating multimedia documents.

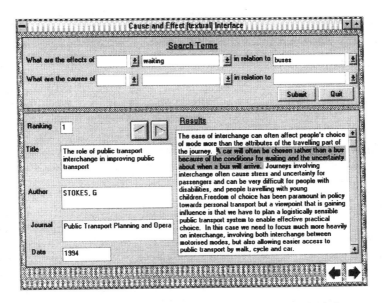

Figure 3: Constrained NL interface which searches causal relations.

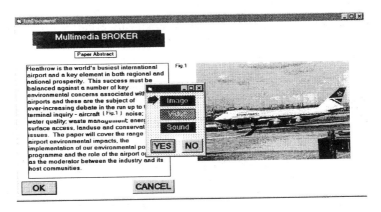

Figure 4: Tool for creating multimedia documents.

The demonstrator was used to elicit users' views and obtain feedback on functional and non-functional requirements. Trade-offs between options were discussed to elicit reasons for users' preferences, for example, a 3D interface may look visually pleasing but it might be difficult and time consuming to use.

3.2   Evaluation

Two evaluation sessions on the concept demonstrator were carried out in August and November 1996. Five users from PTRC, a publisher in the transport and planning industry participated. They were information professionals who were computer literate and experienced in the domain.

We used SCRAM (Sutcliffe, 1995; 1997) a scenario requirements analysis method that involves presenting the concept demonstrator which is illustrated in a scripted sequence and linked to scenarios (sequence of realistic tasks). Possible functionality and interface designs are explained to the users. Each feature of the concept demonstrator is described by a facilitator who asks a small group of users probing questions about their requirements. Design options are explained in terms of their trade-offs. The users are encouraged to clarify any points they found ambiguous and elaborate any further requirements. The final stage of the method involves a brainstorming session between the users and the facilitator where key facts are summarized into a requirements map. Users also complete a pre-session questionnaire about their computer use experience, and a post-session questionnaire providing feedback.

3.3   Results

We report detailed results for two sessions carried out with PTRC's users on the 19th August 1996, and the 27th November 1996, see Tables 1 & 2. Requirements and associated comments verbalized by users are summarized and analysed according to the framework presented in Figure 1.

The requirement types were not always mutually exclusive, for example, one might consider the requirement, "You shouldn't impose a geographical view right at the start", to be a user interface information requirement, but it might also be a usability requirement, concerned with the user's interaction with the application. In analysing the requirements according to the framework we have allocated a single type to each requirement statement.

The next section in this paper reports a follow up study using a later concept demonstrator.

4   Further Requirements Using Scenarios and Focus Groups

The initial set of requirements were high-level so the next step was to build on these by eliciting requirements for specific domains and user groups. Our first task was to specify a set of typical user tasks (scenarios) for users from the transport domain. The next step was to develop more detailed scenarios of use with the our three user partners and develop further concept demonstrators supporting the functionality of the scenarios. We describe the scenarios and concept demonstrator developed for PTRC who specialize in publishing material in the transport industry.

Interface screen	Summary of requirements and associated comments verbalized	Requirement type
Navigation 3D Browser	Today people expect to see a good presentation.	User — expectations
	Speed is very important.	Non functional — speed
	Today people want a 3D interface.	User — expectations
	It must be technically correct (i.e. terminology must be correct and precise) but it must also be interesting.	Non functional — accuracy/ Usability — satisfaction
Services	The different ways of accessing the data are useful.	User functional — task support
	The system must allow the user to input their own terms, pulling an item off a list is not enough.	User functional — task support
	Mapping users terms to system terminology is necessary.	Functional — perform application tasks
Querying	Users want to be able to narrow (shrink) results.	User functional — task support
2D Map showing entities/ relations	Users want to be able to use key phrases (such as 'stated preferences') as well as key words.	User functional — task support
	Will the system be indexed in such a way so as to cope with both key words and key phrases?	Functional — manage data
2D Topic map	Users want the full range of Boolean operators.	User functional — task support
Natural language interface	People are always interested in the consequences of certain actions, particularly before and after events, such as before and after effects of a roundabout improvement.	User functional — task support
	There is a place for this NL representation but an example is needed.	Usability — ease of use
	There are many different levels of users that need to be catered for.	User — needs
	Initially the screens must be simple so that users are not scared off, also they need hand holding with examples.	Usability — ease of use
	The textual NL screen was considered easier to use and more logical than the graphical one.	Usability — ease of use
SQL	Very few of PTRC's users will be able to use SQL.	User — experience
Form Fill	PTRC's users will be used to using Form Fill interfaces.	User — experience
	If English is used to express ANDs and ORs it has to be precise.	Usability — comprehension
Query Library	A query library is useful for saving and re-using queries.	User functional — task support
Query by example	Approximate match on a chunk of text (or a number of keywords) is useful.	User functional — task support
Thesaurus/ Spell-checker	Both are useful tools for users.	User functional — task support

Table 1: Session 1 (19.08.96) — PTRC's analysed requirements from comments recorded on video.

Screen Category	Summary of requirements and associated comments verbalized	Requirement type
Intro Screen	The categories must be readable.	Usability — ease of use
Navigation	It is important to have different strategic views (of the data).	User interface — info presentation
World map	You shouldn't impose a geographical view right at the start.	User interface — info presentation
2D map showing entities/ relations	I think it's hard when you go to a library and you've got all these separate headings. You don't know if yours is classified as a journal, paper, proceedings or whatever. You want the computer to hide that, to sort it all out.	Usability — ease of use $\longrightarrow$ functional
2D Topic Map	It is quite important to make this level of abstraction of the data itself be flexible, and not to hard code it.	Non functional — software
	There are different levels of user. They will want the capacity themselves to adjust the way in which they view the data.	User — needs/ User functional — task support
List of Tables	I just want to know a system and be familiar with it, it depends on how often I was using it. I don't think I'd care about whether it was graphical or form filling.	Usability — ease of use
	Ideally one would like to have both (graphical and form filling) styles of interface.	User interface — dialogue and behaviour
3D Interface	(U1) If the visualization actually adds functionality and enables you to do something then that's fine, otherwise in itself it's not useful.	Usability — efficiency
	(U2) Not necessarily. Screen savers are irritating but sell!	Non functional — sales
Services	Defining the categories is the most intellectualizing aspect of it all, it is absolutely crucial to get it right.	Non functional — client
	How would you restrict people so that they didn't retrieve information without paying for it?	Non functional — security
Querying 2D Map showing entities/ relations.	It is very useful to have the number of hits being displayed as you incrementally construct the query.	User functional — task support

4.1   Scenario 1

The user is a transport consultant seeking to obtain information on Traffic calming. She constructs a query using keywords, submits it to the database and is presented with a set of results. The results set is quite long so the system helps the user to narrow the query by offering context sensitive narrowing advice. This is presented in a series of steps, the user is free to skip steps and can complete the process anytime by selecting the Finish button. There are seven steps in total. In Step 1, the user is asked to specify which domain she is interested in. Using the user's search terms the system looks up meta data information for details of possible domains. In Step 2, the system asks the user to specify the geographical area she might be interested in, see Figure 5.

Screen Category	Summary of requirements and associated comments verbalized	Requirement type
Intelligent Advice Help to reformulate query.	This sort of advice would be good, very useful. Particularly if you had been down lots of paths.	User functional — task support
Finding similar to a retrieved item.	Extracting terms from the retrieved item and submitting back as part of the query would be useful.	User functional — task support
Presentation Planning	(U2) It's really nice to see each bit of the results.	User interface — info presentation
Bar chart of results by query component.	(U1) You don't need a bar chart to represent this information. Better as a list.	Usability — ease of use
Horizontal/ Vertical Spatial linking.	Very useful. But you don't need both horizontal and vertical linking. Just one way.	User interface — info presentation
Search within results.	Useful to be able to search in different ways, by location, by price, etc.	User functional — task support
Brokering/ Negotiation	Don't want the system to take decisions on my behalf unless I know how/why it is taking these decisions.	User functional — task support

Table 2: Session 2 (27.11.96) PTRC's analysed comments recorded on video.

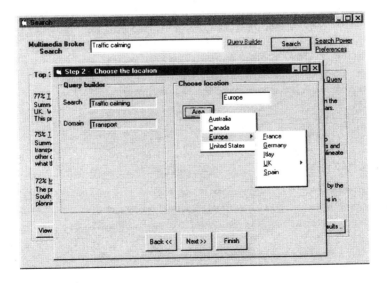

Figure 5: Step 2 — Narrowing by area.

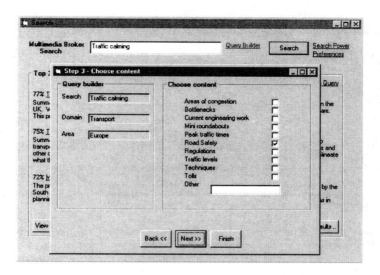

Figure 6: Step 3 — Content narrowing advice.

In Step 3 the system uses the initial results set to create a list of relevant key words which the user can add to the query for specialization. Using specific dictionaries, keywords and phrases are picked from the results set and offered as content specifiers (see Figure 6). In the fourth step the system prompts the user to choose from key words or phrases which are stored by the system from previous queries. In the fifth step the system allows the user to restrict the search to a particular author, range of dates or media type. The results will contain papers which are closest to the user's specification ranked by relevance.

When reviewing papers for purchase the user is given free abstract information. If she decides to buy a paper she is prompted with information on the content of any graphics files, see Figure 7.

When ordering the Broker completes the details of the user's name and address from her login record. The user can encrypt the order for maximum security. At this point the user enters her credit card number and then submits the order, which is acknowledged by the system.

4.2   Scenario 2

The user is an author who has written a paper for the Traffic Management and Road Safety stream which has been accepted for the annual conference. She now must upload the abstract, the paper and the graphics. On the left-hand-side of the uploading files screen (see Figure 8) is a window displaying the contents of the selected ETF directory on her C: drive. She selects the source files she wants to upload, then the stream, then clicks the Upload button. The selected files are copied to the stream as shown in the bottom-right window. The user is notified that the transfer is successful.

Another scenario for registration by email was also developed but is not illustrated.

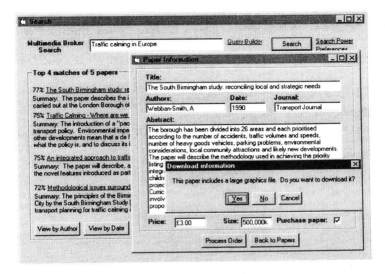

Figure 7: Paper abstract information.

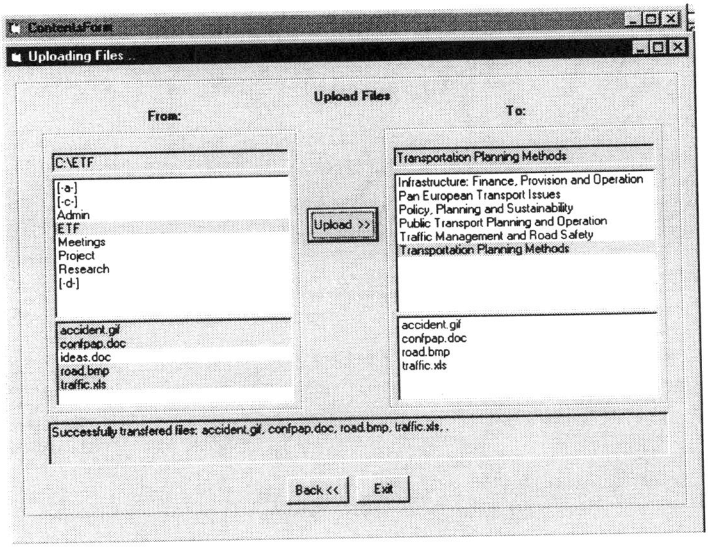

Figure 8: Uploading documents.

Scenario A

- Consultants who have portables don't use search engines because they are too difficult to use and produce too many irrelevant results. Consultants want to retrieve bits of relevant information and they want a very fast and efficient way of doing this.

- Consultants don't do general searches but specific ones. A key Broker aim should be to reduce redundancy.

- A typical consultant, living out of a suitcase, would not want a complex web search engine which would produce masses of documents. The search process needs to be targeted to the particular user.

- Typing in keywords/phrases. The system must be able to accept American spelling as well as English.

- Context sensitive support for key word/phrases searches is needed. The user should be able to type in part of a key word or phrase and the system should respond by providing a list available terms.

Figure 9: Requirements feedback from focus group session.

4.3   Evaluation

A focus group evaluation session was carried out using the concept demonstrator. A focus group is an informal assembly of users to elicit perceptions, feelings, attitudes and ideas of participants about a selected topic (Nielsen, 1993). The first ten minutes of the session involved giving the audience an overview of the Multimedia Broker project, and providing suggestions as to how the Broker might help them be more efficient and productive in their work. This was followed by an interactive discussion with users around a number slides of the interface designs for the three scenarios. Approximately six users attended the session and most considered themselves to be potential end-users of the system.

4.4   Results

Due to space constraints only an extract of the users' feedback is shown in Figure 9. For more detail see Table 3 in the next section where their requirements are analysed in detail.

The requirements were categorized with the framework to investigate the distribution of the users' concerns, see Table 4.

In Session 1 the users were most concerned with functionality and user needs, experience and expectations. In the second session users were more concerned with non-functional requirements (software, sales, client and security) than those in the first session. They were, in common with the first group, concerned with usability. They also raised a number of user interface design issues. Users' priority in the third session were data and functional requirements. Even though the volume of requirements was similar in the three sessions their distribution was different.

In analysing the requirements according to the framework we identified the 'gaps', that is, categories of requirements which were not captured, for example, for non functional requirements: cost, legal, political or time scale requirements were not considered. For usability, users were primarily concerned with ease of use. Memory

Focus group requirements	Requirement	Follow up questions	Reusable generic requirements
Consultants want to retrieve bits of relevant information ...	User functional — task support	What information is required? How should the information be presented to the user? What are the links between items and how should these be represented?	Domain specific Information Retrieval (IR); preformed queries, hypertext structures, starfield displays.
... and they want a very fast and efficient way of doing this.	Usability — efficiency	What are the alternative ways of performing the task and their relative advantages? What task support is needed?	Fast path, low response time. macros, defaults, economic user interface dialogue.
A key Broker aim should be to reduce redundancy.	Functional — manage data	What techniques can be used to reduce redundancy? How can duplicates be identified?	Text matching algorithms, stemming and truncation, synonym tables.
The search process needs to be targeted to the particular user.	User — needs	Who are the users and what are their characteristics? How should the user interface be customized? How can users be monitored? What UI properties should be changed?	Adaptability/ configurability methods, user stereotypes, preference files, set UI levels, customization facilities.
The system must be able to accept American spelling as well as English.	Data — input	What range of input is required? How should it be checked and interpreted?	Language default. User customized dictionaries.
The user should be able to type in part of a key word or phrase and ...	Data — input	What range of input is required? How should it be checked and interpreted?	Keyword/ phrase spotting, stop lists, simple parsers, classifiers.
... the system should respond by providing a list available terms.	Data — input + User functional — provide feedback	What range of input is required? How should it be checked and interpreted? What task support should be provided and how intelligent should the system be?	Stemming truncation techniques, predict words from frequency distribution, domain specific lexicons.
If the system goes down while an order is in process, how would the user know? The system must give appropriate feedback.	Functional failure recovery + User functional — provide feedback	How does the system monitor failures, how does it log transactions, how are recovery processes organized? How and when should the user be notified?	Transaction logs, recovery and roll back processes, providing user feedback, transaction status.

Focus group requirements	Requirement	Follow up questions	Reusable generic requirements
A method for obtaining payment by subscription was required so that users would not have to pay by credit card.	User functional — task support	What task support do users need? What procedure is needed for order processing? What payment scheme is used? Are credit terms, discounts offered?	Order transaction processes, progress tracking, discount calculations. Payment processing techniques.
How would the Broker stop other people from using their logins and ordering goods on their account?	Non functional — security + Functional — perform application tasks	What monitoring processes could be set up to detect threats? What assets are threatened? How can they be defended? What is the origin of threats?	Barrier security, passwords, bio-identification techniques, access logs, audits.
It is important that the Broker system provides plenty of feedback and confirmation so as to inspire trust and confidence in it's users.	User functional — provide feedback	How and when should the user be notified? What issues concern users? How can their fears be dealt with?	Status displays, consistent user interface.
A comments space is required, for example, to request accommodation for couples.	Data — input	What range of input is required? How should it be checked and interpreted?	Special requests by users.
Feedback that registration has actually taken place is required.	User functional — provide feedback	How and when should the user be notified? What should the feedback message contain?	Feedback displays — salience and location, status indicators.
Could mathematical symbols be lost or corrupted? The Broker should be able to read the various types of files to ensure that this would not happen.	Data — input	What types of files might be imported? What file formats should be supported? Are communication protocols necessary? Will the data format need transforming?	Data transformation facilities, file formatters, standards.
A CD ROM of the ETF proceedings would be a good idea.	Data — output	What information should be output, on what medium? How and when should output be produce? Who and where is its destination?	Matching output to media, ranking, sorting and formatting procedures.
It was suggested that a guided tutorial and on-line task based support should be provided.	User functional — task support	What subject matter needs to be learned? Will learning needs change, be varied?	Guided tours, wizards, tutorial examples, helps systems.

Table 3: Summary of analysed requirements.

Requirement category	Session 1 19.08.96	Session 2 27.11.96	Session 3 focus group 02.09.97	Total
Functionality	2	1	3	6
User functional	9	3	7	19
Usability	5	8	1	14
User interface	–	5	–	5
User	5	1	1	7
Data	–	–	6	6
Non functional	2	4	1	7
Total	23	22	19	64

Table 4: Number of requirements and type for Session 1, 2 & 3.

load and numbers of errors were not explicitly considered. Furthermore when the requirements gathering dialogues were inspected several opportunities were missed when requirements should have been elaborated with further questions.

Threads in the formation of requirements were traced where one requirement triggered a number of sub requirements. For example, "I think it's hard when you go to a library and you've got all these separate headings. You don't know if yours is classified as a journal, paper, proceedings or whatever" (see Table 2), concerns usability and then triggered the functional requirement: "You want the computer to hide that, to sort it all out". In many cases requirements were elicited but not followed up or elaborated later in the session.

The framework enabled the designer to relate the requirements to different aspects of the design — functionality, user interface, usability — but it does not really help the designer develop a solution from the requirements stated. For example, we know from Table 1 that, 'users want to be able to narrow (shrink) results', but we don't know how they want to do this and what task support would be useful. In addition the framework does not give procedural guidance for questioning in requirements sessions and omissions could have been discovered by follow-up questions. More guidance is needed, in the form of a checklist or follow up questions to aid the designer in developing a software solution.

In the next section we propose a preliminary method for analysing requirements to inform design. We apply the proposed method to the requirements elicited in the third session.

5   Analysis Method

Initial requirements are captured and analysed according the framework presented in Figure 1. Follow up questions elaborating the requirements help the designer to understand the stated requirements in more detail and to identify dependencies. Following user centred design lifecycles an early prototype of the system is developed. Iterative evaluation of a functional prototype leads to the final design, see Figure 10.

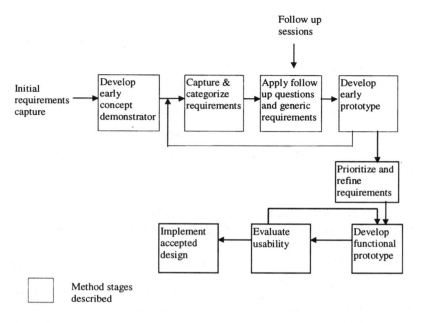

Figure 10: Requirements capture process showing major activities.

Many requirements will affect different aspects of the design. For example, a user functional requirement will have implications for the user interface. In order to bring requirements together into an effective solution it is essential to look at each requirement in turn and consider how it will affect the design.

We extended the framework presented in Figure 1 to provide generic requirements linked to follow up questions directed to requirements of a particular type. For user functional requirements, the following issues should be considered:

- How can the system support the user's task?

- What are the dependencies on achieving that support?

- How intelligent should the system be in user support?

- What collaboration is necessary between the system and the user?

For information requirements the questions direct attention to the information required to support the user's task, and how it should be presented to users. Data requirements for input are linked to questions about validation requirements, while system output of data has follow up questions on the medium, timing and destination of output. User interface requirements are linked to questions that follow the spirit of cognitive walkthroughs (Wharton et al., 1994), i.e. predictability of actions and adequacy of feedback. The follow up questions were developed from the perspective of our experience, although they are intended to be general in scope. Table 3 shows the requirements table which contains the requirements type in Column 2, linked to follow up questions and reusable requirements that point to potential design solutions in Column 4. The table has been applied to the requirements captured during the focus group session reported in Section 4.

The follow-up questions and generic requirements suggest several design options which could be discussed with users, thereby leading to new requirements. In the Multimedia Broker project we have proceeded from the requirements listed in Tables 1 & 2 to prototype development. Further evaluation will discover how many requirements were omitted or incorrect in the current design that the method may have captured.

6 Conclusion

Our main contribution in this paper is a framework for classifying requirements, including usability issues, with a preliminary method for cross referring these to follow up questions and re-usable generic requirements.

We presented a framework for analysing requirements and illustrated its use. The framework enabled the designers to relate requirements to different aspects of the design — functionality, user interface, usability — but didn't really help the designer develop an effective design solution from the requirements stated. One problem is the interdependencies between requirements e.g. functional requirements can have implications for usability. Another is that only high level requirements may be captured leaving the designer to resolve the detail. While detailed requirements may be resolved by prototyping and evaluation cycles, we argue this can be inefficient as many designs have to be discarded. If designers could get prototypes nearly 'right first time' development productivity should increase. The method we propose attempts to address this problem with follow up questions as hints for the designers, and generic requirements expose the user to the space of possible design solutions.

We reported generic follow up questions and reusable requirements linked to the taxonomy. We have also developed more a specific set tailored to information retrieval and brokering. Clearly there is a trade off between the generality of the questions and reusable requirements and their power in any one domain. We expect that whereas follow-up questions may prove useful across domains, reusable requirements may be more targeted. We are researching this approach by creating models of generic models of application classes which embed reusable requirements as one approach to this problem (Sutcliffe & Maiden, 1998). Another approach is to translate reusable requirements and questions into claims (Carroll & Rosson, 1992) that can be applied to domains of interest and potentially reusable artefacts. Claims, however, are specific to a task-artefact context, so we are investigating how they can be transformed for more general application (Sutcliffe & Carroll, in this volume).

In our future work we plan to develop the questions and reusable requirements tables to handle a range of domains. This paper has made a modest start in this direction by describing a framework and a process whereby requirements analysis and usability engineering may converge and reusable requirements for both can enhance productivity.

Acknowledgements

The authors would like to thank partners on the Multimedia Broker project (SISU, PTRC, LIBER, Coopers & Lybrand, Brameur, and IMT) for their cooperation and help in this study. The Multimedia Broker project (No. IE2093) is funded by the European Union's Information Engineering Multimedia Telematics Applications Program. Many thanks also to Simon Attfield for designing the natural language interface screen (Figure 3), and to Tim Miller for developing the concept demonstrator of the tool for creating multimedia documents (Figure 4).

References

Bevan, N. (1996), INUSE European Usability Support Centres. Telematics Applications Project IE 2016. Information Engineering Usability Support Centres, Technical Report, National Physical Laboratory. Kirakowski, J. (ed), Human Factors Research Group, University College, Cork.

Boehm, B. (1988), "The Spiral Model of Software Development and Enhancement", *IEEE Computer* **21**(5), 61–72.

Carroll, J. M. & Rosson, M. B. (1992), "Getting Around the Task–Artefact Framework: How to Make Claims and Design by Scenario", *ACM Transactions on Office Information Systems* **10**(2), 181–212.

Collins, T. (1997), *Crash*, Charles Scribners and Son.

Hix, D. & Hartson, H. R. (1993), *Developing User Interfaces: Ensuring Usability through Product and Process*, John Wiley & Sons.

Johnson, P. (1992), *Human–Computer Interaction: Psychology, Task Analysis and Software Engineering*, McGraw-Hill.

Nielsen, J. (1993), *Usability Engineering*, Academic Press.

Preece, J., Rogers, Y., Sharpe, H., Benyon, D., Holland, S. & Carey, T. (1994), *Human–Computer Interaction*, Addison–Wesley.

Ravden, S. & Johnson, G. (1989), *Evaluating Usability of Human–Computer Interfaces: A Practical Method*, Ellis Horwood.

Robertson, S. (1997), "Requirements Made to Measure", Presentation at City University.

Shneiderman, B. (1992), *Designing the User Interface: Strategies for Effective Human–Computer Interaction*, second edition, Addison–Wesley.

Sutcliffe, A. G. (1995), Requirements Rationales: Integrating Approaches to Requirements Analysis, *in* G. Olson & S. Schuon (eds.), *Proceedings of the Symposium on Designing Interactive Systems: Processes, Practices, Methods and Techniques (DIS'95)*, ACM Press, pp.33–42.

Sutcliffe, A. G. (1996), "A Conceptual Framework for Requirements Engineering", *Requirements Engineering Journal* 1, 170–189.

Sutcliffe, A. G. (1997), A Technique Combination Approach to Requirements Engineering, *in* J. Mylopoulos (ed.), *Proceedings of 3rd International Symposium on Requirements Engineering RE'97*, IEEE Computer Society Press, pp.65–74.

Sutcliffe, A. G. & Maiden, N. A. M. (1998), "The Domain Theory for Requirements Engineering", *IEEE Transactions on Software Engineering* 24(3), 174–196.

Sutcliffe, A. G., Economou, A. & Markis, P. (in press), "Tracing Requirements Errors to Problems in the Requirements Engineering Process", *Requirements Engineering Journal* Centre for HCI Design Report HCID/97/24.

Wharton, C., Reiman, J., Lewis, C. & Polson, P. (1994), The Cognitive Walkthrough Method: A Practitioner's Guide, *in* J. Nielsen & R. L. Mack (eds.), *Usability Inspection Methods*, John Wiley & Sons, pp.105–140.

Generalizing Claims and Reuse of HCI Knowledge

Alistair Sutcliffe[†] & John Carroll[‡]

[†] *Centre for HCI Design, School of Informatics, City University, Northampton Square, London EC1V 0HB, UK.*

Tel: *+44 171 477 8411*
Fax: *+44 171 477 8859*
EMail: *a.g.sutcliffe@city.ac.uk*
URL: *http://www.soi.city.ac.uk/research/hcid/index.html*

[‡] *Department of Computer Science, 660 McBryde Hall, Virginia Tech (VPI&SU), Blacksburg, VA 24061–0106, USA.*

Tel: *+1 540 231 6931*
Fax: *+1 540 231 6075*
EMail: *carroll@cs.vt.edu*

A framework for classifying claims and indexing them for reuse with generic models is proposed. Claims are classified by a schema that includes design issues, dependencies, usability effects, with links to scenarios and the artefact associated with the claim. Generic models describe classes of application and tasks. Claims are associated with appropriate model components. Models which match a new application are retrieved from a library by using keyword searches or browsing the model hierarchy. Claims are reused on applications sharing the same generic application. Artefacts associated with claims may also be reused although user interfaces need customizing because of domain specific features. Claims evolution and reuse are illustrated with an information retrieval case study.

Keywords: knowledge reuse, task-artefact cycle, domain models, claims, design process.

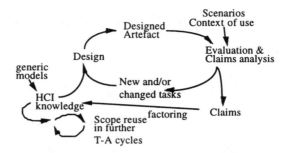

Figure 1: Task-artefact cycle, evolved from Carroll & Rosson (1991), showing the derivation of claims and factoring for reuse in related task-artefact contexts.

---

1   Introduction

A core problem in human–computer interaction is expressing relevant knowledge (models and theories, specific research results, lessons from experience) in forms that are accessible to designers and are applicable in design. In a series of papers, Carroll & Rosson (1991; 1992) have elaborated the *task–artefact cycle* in which new designs evolve as responses to requirements for supporting human activities, and usability evaluation of the support provided by artefacts. Their approach to managing this co-evolution of tasks and artefacts is to enumerate defining scenarios of use, and to explicitly detail the causal relations implicit in those scenarios, describing the problems and affordances encountered by users. A simple example of a claim within a scenario context is the assertion that "animated demonstrations encourage learning by exploration in a scenario where an experienced programmer is wondering what sort of project to work on first in a new programming environment".

While scenarios can provide relevant and vivid context for identifying and interpreting claims, the specificity of scenarios militates against generalization of a claim's applicability beyond the context in which it was derived. This is an obstacle to reuse of claims as HCI knowledge. This paper proposes an ontology by which claims can be indexed in a library of generic, reusable domain models in order to increase their potential reuse. We first present an ontology of claims and the domain models. We then present a brief case study illustrating the reuse of claims in an Internet-based information retrieval system.

2   An Ontology for Claims Knowledge

Figure 1 illustrates the elaborated task-artefact cycle we propose. In the centre of the figure, task scenarios that have been empirically evaluated and/or subjected to claims analysis provide requirements for the design of new artefacts. The elaborations which concern this paper are categorizing claims identified in particular design and use contexts for storage in a repository of HCI knowledge, enabling retrieval and reuse in subsequent and different design contexts.

The major knowledge-related components are claims, scenarios and models of generic application classes that provide the reuse context for a claim. Claims assert trade-offs (upsides and downsides) that pertain to design features. Scenarios set claims in a specific context of use while generic models scope the applicability of claims in terms of application classes to which a claim may apply.

The claim description schema has a number of slots which are filled by narrative information such as the claim's author, and by a set of terms following the practice of controlled vocabularies in faceted classification. The claims format from previous publications, i.e. a claim description followed by one or more upsides (benefits) and one or more downsides (disadvantages or potential problems) was expanded as follows:

1	Claim ID	unique identifier for the claim
2	Title	name given by claim author
3	Author	researcher(s) who developed the original claim
4	Artefact	brief description of the product/application in which the claim originated
5	Description	text explanation of the claim
6	Upside	positive effect of using claim on a system goal or usability
7	Downside	negative effect of using claim on a system goal or usability
8	Scenario	scenario in which the claim was derived or is currently used
9	Effect	desired and measurable system goal/usability effect that the implemented claim should achieve
10	Dependencies	other design problems that have to be solved to achieve the claim's effect
11	Issues	design issues influenced by the claim
12	Scope	generic models of application classes or tasks to which the claim applies

Slots 6 and 7 are typically iterated, as two or three upsides and downsides to alert the designer to trade-offs, while scenarios in Slot 8 are specialized into two sub-classes according to whether the claim is based on observation of a problem with an artefact or a redesign to address the problem:

- Usage scenarios: these scenarios describe a usability problem encountered by a user and are based on empirical evidence.

- Projected usage scenarios: describe interaction as it should occur with the redesigned artefact. These scenarios may be based on the designer's expectations or may be grounded in actual observation of user interaction.

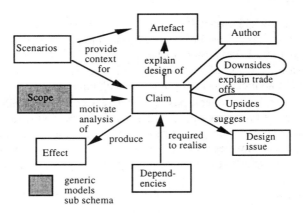

Figure 2: Claims description schema components with relationships to show how different arguments can contribute to the classification.

Links to multimedia (e.g. screen dumps, video of the artefact being used) or the product itself are provided for Slots 4 and 8. The classification schema for each claim is extended by hypertext links to relevant design documents, artefacts as well as to related claims. Slot 9 describes the desired, and measurable, usability effect, while Slot 10, dependencies describes design problems that must be solved to enable satisfactory implementation of the claim. The issues in Slot 11 records design issues that are not directly addressed by the claim but are inherent in the artefact. Slot 12 is filled by generalizing the claim's original task/artefact context using a set of generic models to scope a set of future reuse contexts. The claims schema components and relationships are illustrated in Figure 2.

To broaden a claim's scope, the attributes of the claim, the usage scenario, and its associated artefact are compared with a set of general models of applications and tasks to establish which problem types the claim may address. Claims are attached to one or more generic models, so designers can browse a library for models that match their current design problem and then follow links in a hypertext database back to appropriate claims for explanations of usability trade-offs, design advice and a potentially reusable artefact. Having outlined the claims classification framework, we now describe the generic models in more depth.

3   Generalizing Claims

The approach taken is to establish whether a claim may be applicable to a general set of artefacts that share the same underlying abstract problem. If claims could be associated with analogous problems then a wider range of reuse may be possible. To solve this problem we associate claims with generic domain models. The properties of claims and their associate tasks and artefacts are matched to properties of generic models that describe classes of applications. Claims are linked to generic models or components thereof. The models and their associated claims may be retrieved

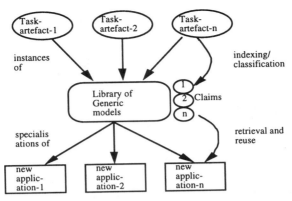

Figure 3: Framework for classifying and reusing claims via generic models of the domain theory.

---

from the library by keyword searching on their properties or by browsing the class hierarchy of models. This enables users to select claims that are applicable to their current problem by searching a library of generic models that describe application classes and tasks. In addition to keyword searching, a more sophisticated matching tool is provided that retrieves appropriate generic models from a minimal set of facts describing the new application. This tool has been described in detail by Sutcliffe & Maiden (1998). Space precludes a complete description of the domain classification schema and library of generic models (see Sutcliffe & Maiden (1994), in press for more detail), but in summary three types are proposed; grounded domains, meta-domains, and generic tasks. Claims are linked to grounded domains if they concern problems of transaction processing and real world interaction; for instance, many human factors problems concerned with monitoring user interfaces belong to the grounded domain class for Object Sensing models. Other examples are claims for task support functionality in hiring/loans, sales order processing, and logistics/distribution application classes. The domain theory classes are introduced in the following section. Claims derived in training and decision support applications are associated with meta-domains, for instance claims linked to design support and tutorial systems. If claims pertain to a particular task then they are indexed to generic tasks that match to their original context; for instance, claims based on a medical expert system for diagnosis or television fault diagnosis would be indexed as supporting the diagnostic generic task. As more applications are analysed claims are recruited to the library. The process of claims classification and reuse is illustrated in Figure 3.

4 Grounded Domains

Grounded domains can be located in the real world in that the work task takes place at some location. Grounded domains are characterized by a physical existence and observable objects and actions, the tasks they contain, and how users interact with a system to achieve a common objective.

Level-2 class Spatial Object sensing

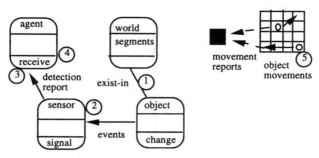

Figure 4: Object Sensing Model illustrated as an informal diagram and in Object oriented analysis notation. Claims are attached to either the whole model (as in Figure 5) or specific components depending on their intended usability effect on the associated artefact.

Grounded domains are abstract models of problems rooted in a real world context which can be mapped to specific applications that share a common purpose, structure and behaviour. This approach is anchored in models of analogical reasoning (Gentner, 1983) and categorical memory (Rosch, 1983). An example of a grounded domain, illustrated in Figure 4, describes sensing the behaviour or movement of objects or agents in a physical space. This domain model maps to specific monitoring applications in air traffic control, road traffic monitoring, ship-borne radar systems, etc. Ten families of grounded domains describe systems of cooperating objects that cover applications that span hiring/loans, inventory-stock control, accounting, booking-allocation, logistics, manufacture and assembly, monitoring and sensing, command and control, simulations and games. Each model family contains specializations of the generic model, specified as a set of cooperating objects in modelling language composed of attributes, actions, agents, objects, container structures, tasks, events and states. The domain models represent the requirements or essential model (McMenamin & Palmer, 1984) for an application class, i.e. a set of cooperating objects and activities that achieve a system goal. Each family has a set of generic properties that describe the design issues and dependencies necessary for implementing computer systems to satisfy the requirements. Claims are mapped to generic model via a combination of the properties and goals, agents, etc. that constitute the model components.

To illustrate the process, claims derived from our previous research into safety critical user interface design (Sutcliffe, 1996) are associated with object sensing generic models. The claims originated in an instrument monitoring application and describe how displays may be designed to improve the reliability of human monitoring and interpreting events. For instance, Claim 1 in Figure 4 relates to trade-offs in displaying a model of the monitored world, whereas Claim 2 describes trade-offs in filtering detected events, while Claim 3, automatically highlighting rare events has the upside of making events more noticeable but the downside of decreasing user awareness by detecting too many false alarms. Claims are linked to

the components in the model that provides the closest match to their properties.
The factored description for this claim is:

> *Claim ID*: SF3.
> *Title*: Rare event monitor.
> *Author*: A. G. Sutcliffe.
> *Artefact*: User interface for a chemical analysis instrument control system
> *Description*: infrequent, dangerous events are detected by the system and a warning is issued to the user, in this case operational failures in a laser gas chromatograph.
> *Upside*: automatic detection of dangerous events relieves the user of constant monitoring; automatic detection and warning gives the user time to analyse the problem.
> *Downside*: issuing too many warnings may lead the user to ignore critical events; automated monitoring may lead to user overconfidence in the automated system and decrease their situation awareness.
> *Scenario*: when an abnormal event is detected by the laser emission, power supply or sample container sensors, the system gives an audio warning to the user and visually signals the location of the problem on a diagram of the instrument.
> *Effect*: the user is aware of the dangerous event and its location, error monitoring is more dependable.
> *Dependencies*: reliable detection of dangerous events — multiple evidence, filtering false warnings, detecting locus of events.
> *Issues*: warning message and feedback given to the user Scope Object sensing, Agent control models.

The above claim shared properties of <detecting events, issuing warnings and providing feedback> with the generic model, in addition the claim and its originating artefact both have agents <power supply, etc. sensors> for detecting and reporting events <voltage and emission fluctuations> to users <laboratory technicians>. The claim and model are matched by inquiring which class the specific agents, objects and tasks belong to and investigating the matching between specific design issues and generic design properties.

5 Meta-domains

Meta-domains are used to describe the agents, major objects and cognitive tasks that transform or plan action within grounded domains. The definition of meta-domain emphasizes human activity in problem solving, analysis and creative design which achieves a purpose.

Currently there are six families of meta-domains which are training/instruction, research, management, authoring and design. Meta-domains, in contrast to grounded domains, are not concerned with transactions; instead they constitute human activity that is applied to the grounded domains. For instance, one can teach people how to

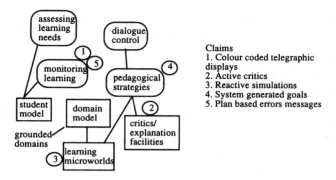

Figure 5: Learning/tutorial meta-domain showing major system components and associated claims.

operate a stock control system, or design a new one. Since meta-domains support complex human activity, they are modelled as conceptual architectures composed of functions and models based on analysis of previous systems belonging to that class. Figure 5 illustrates an architecture model for the training meta-domain and its associated claims. Some of these claims have been reported in our previous research on tutorial support environments (Singley & Carroll, 1996); for instance, system generated goals describes trade-offs in providing the learner with an explicit representation of learning goals, while plan based error messages and colour coded telegraphic displays are related to design of feedback to help users monitor their own learning. Other claims are extracted from the other authors' research, in this case trade-offs between active and passive critiquing styles which allow learners to make mistakes and offer suggested corrections vs. critics which try to prevent learners making the mistake in the first place or trade-offs between constructive simulations which you have to construct yourself instead of ready built simulations (Fischer et al., 1993). As with grounded domains, meta-domains are indexed with a set of properties that describe the design issues and dependencies that need to be addressed for implementation of the conceptual architecture. Matching claims to meta-domain models uses these properties as well as investigating the fit between user-agents and their tasks.

To illustrate one claim in more detail, the colour-coded telegraphic display (Singley & Carroll, 1996), applies to artefacts that provide feedback on the student's progress in learning systems.

> *Claim ID*: Colour-coded Telegraphic Display.
> *Author*: Singley, M. K.; Carroll, J. M.
> *Artefact*: MoleHill tutor — Goalposter tool.
> *Description*: A colour-coded telegraphic display of goals.
> *Upside*: provides persistent feedback on the correctness of actions as well as access to further information.
> *Downside*: learners must learn the display's feature-language and

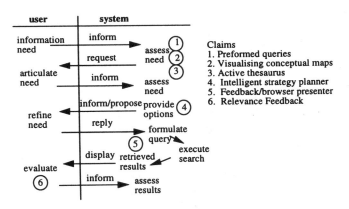

Figure 6: Interaction pattern for the information searching generic task. Claims are attached to either the whole task or specific components depending on the original task/artefact context.

controls.

Scenario: the presentation of individual goals in the window is telegraphic, several words at most. However, the learner can expand any of the telegraphic goals (through a menu selection) to display a fuller explanation of why the goal is worthwhile pursuing or not. Thus the system provides both shorthand feedback on correctness and access to further help.

Effect: improved learning by provision of appropriate feedback.

Dependencies: tracking user's progress in learning task, known goal structure.

Issues: feedback display, colour-coding, user initiative.

Scope: feedback for learning assessment and progress tracking in tutorial systems.

The desired effect of the design is to improve learning by provision of appropriate feedback, although this depends on tracking user's progress in learning tasks with a known goal structure. Matching between the claim and model components was driven by the issues of providing feedback in the learning process and encouraging active learning by problem solving. As the issues in meta-domains are complex a glossary is used to facilitate the mapping.

6   Generic Tasks

Generic tasks are carried out by agents to achieve a goal and may form components of either grounded or meta-domains. Generic tasks cause state changes to objects or agents in grounded or meta-domains; for instance, a diagnostic task changes the state of a malfunctioning object (e.g. human patient) from having an unknown cause to being understood (symptom diagnosed). Generic tasks are organized in a class hierarchy and are specialized into specific tasks. Currently seven families of generic tasks have been described; diagnosis, information searching, reservation, matching-allocation, scheduling, planning, analysis and modelling. Two examples of generic tasks are diagnosis: determining the cause of some malfunction in a system, locating its cause and proposing remedial treatment that maps to medical diagnosis of electrical equipment fault finding, and information searching: articulating a need, formulating queries, evaluating results, revising queries as necessary. Tasks are described as interaction diagrams depicting event flows between agents (including automated systems), following use case notations. The advantage of this is twofold. First it enables claims to be reused more easily within object oriented development methods, and secondly, specification as use case scripts facilitates mapping to scenarios. Scenarios in original claims are instances of interaction that can be generalized to use cases. A generic model of information searching is illustrated in Figure 6 with associated claims based on research into information seeking behaviour (Sutcliffe & Ennis, in press) and information visualization (Sutcliffe & Patel, 1996).

The first three claims describe trade-offs for design features which help query formulation by either providing libraries of preformed query libraries, conceptual maps of the database or an active thesaurus with suggests alternative query terms. The second claim, conceptual maps was derived from research on information display artefacts (Sutcliffe & Patel, 1996) and is described in more detail as follows:

Claim ID: IR-VIS2.
Title: Visual conceptual maps.
Author: U. Patel, A. G. Sutcliffe.
Artefact: Camerawise information display system.
Description: A graphical map displays a model of the database contents so the user can query by pointing to concept-keywords on the map.
Upside: visualizing the database helps the user browse and explore the available information; query by pointing to categories is simple.
Downside: finding specific items in large maps is difficult; maps can become cluttered as databases scale up so wayfinding becomes difficult; expressing complex queries by pointing is not possible.
Scenario: The user wishes to find information on camera aperture settings. They scan the map to find the category camera settings and follow links to apertures. The user double clicks on this category node to retrieve information from the database.
Effect: The user can scan the map display to locate required information quickly.
Dependencies: well structured information space which can be modelled.
Issues: design of map layouts and information categories that match the users' conceptual model, event interpreter for query by pointing.
Scope: information seeking tasks, sub class browsing.

A glossary of design issues and synonym tables aid identification of generic tasks when classifying claims; for instance, functional requirements of an artefact expressed as searching, seeking, retrieval, information access or browsing all point to the information searching generic task.

7 Reusing Claims

In the section we demonstrate the reuse and evolution of claims. The claims library is applied to research prototypes developed in the INTUITIVE project (Sutcliffe et al., 1995) and MultimediaBroker projects (Sutcliffe & Ryan, 1998).

The INTUITIVE system consisted of a set of reusable information retrieval services that could be embedded in a variety of applications. Two demonstrator applications were developed. The first version was a decision support system for shipboard emergency management, and the second was a training system for shipboard emergency management. The first step is to establish the generic domain and tasks that are generalizations of applications. Then claims are linked to the appropriate generic domain/task model that matched to their originating, domain-specific context. The mappings between a specific application and the generic models can be established in several ways. Heuristics can be used to decide which abstraction is appropriate (Sutcliffe, 1997), or keyword searches can be performed on the scenario narratives that accompany the original claim and descriptive texts associated with each generic model; however, this requires a lexicon that maps concrete terms to their corresponding abstraction, (e.g. resource holder <supplier, inventory manager>). Alternatively, the domain model library may be browsed using explanation tools to help establish mappings (Sutcliffe & Maiden, 1998). There are only a small number of meta domains which are easily identified from their descriptions- in this case tutoring. Generic tasks are discovered by examining task specifications for similarities with the generic models and by investigating the dependencies and issues clauses. The application tasks were diagnosing the problem that caused the emergency; planning the response to deal with the emergency; searching for information on the hazards, dangerous cargo and emergency procedures; and planning training sessions.

Once the mappings have been discovered the claim's locus of application has to be decided. Here the schema helps. The issues and dependencies clauses indicate design components in the generic models to which the claims should be attached. Claims are generalized by adding new scenarios that expresses usage with the generic models and by removing domain specific references in the upsides/downsides. References to specifics in the originating domain should be replaced by more general assertions. The extent of the generalization is left to the developer's judgement.

Taking one grounded domain as an example, the rare event monitor claim is relevant to the object sensing part of the application. The sensing system user interface functions and scenario of use match with the rare event monitor claim. The new artefact will be designed by reuse of the claim and its originating artefact. This claim highlights design trade-offs for automatic detection of hazardous events that may be transferable from the gas laser, gas chromatograph control system to a fire detection artefact in INTUITIVE. Both artefacts have in common the functionally of rare event detection and signalling the locus of the event on a diagram, although the originating artefact detected several events of different types. The downside draws

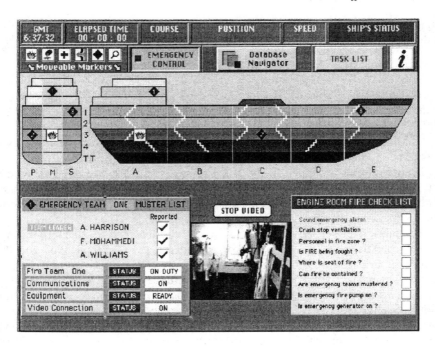

Figure 7: INTUITIVE shipboard emergency decision support system, showing the checkbox artefact (bottom right) and preformed queries as diamond icons leading two the answer box (bottom left).

attention to problems of reliability of detection and the danger of false warnings. Detection reliability could be dealt by tuning the sensor to prevent false alarms and using different sources of evidence, for instance, using heat and smoke sensors to detect fire. The new artefact gives the warning by a fire icon symbol displayed on the diagram of the ship (see Figure 7) so the feedback is presented with context information to mitigate the claim downside of lack of situation awareness. Other suggestions were detecting different event types such as types of fires and other shipboard hazards such as chemical spillage (prompted by the artefact), using multiple sources of evidence to improve event detection reliability, e.g. using smoke and heat to detect fires (prompted by the dependencies). However, the claim/artefact combination has user interface features which are not easily transferred. For instance the original display used a diagram of the gas chromatography to locate the fault. Clearly, this domain specific information is inappropriate for fire location on ships. In spite of this clash the HCI knowledge contained in the issues and dependencies clause can be reused (detecting locus of events, giving contextual feedback to the user). In the new design, the locus of the event is depicted by a fire icon on the ship diagram, but this will require usability testing to validate the claim's effect in the new design. This illustrates one of the problems of reusing claims. Whereas the HCI knowledge embodied in the claim may transfer across domains, this is less certain for claim–artefact combinations because the artefact user interface frequently contains domain specific details. However with configurable user interfaces this downside may be mitigated.

For the training version of the application, claims indexed on the instruction/training meta-domain were matched as before using design issues, agents and their tasks. We illustrate this with the colour coded telegraphic display (Singley & Carroll, 1996). The desired effect of the design is to improve learning by provision of summary, but expandable, feedback; although this depends on tracking user's progress in learning task and a known goal structure. The learning task in this case is the fire fighting procedure and the artefact consisted of a monitoring process that tracked the users' completion of an operation and signalled progress in a simple checkbox display (see Figure 7).

The Goalposter tool and its companion claim could be reused to improve the checklist display; however, the dependencies point out that detecting updates in the task may be a problem. If updates can be easily recorded the display will give improved feedback for the captain, but the downside is that the captain will have to learn the cryptic labels and display colour-coding needs to be considered. This might not be appropriate for the decision support task of emergency control; however it could be suitable for the tutorial system. Notice that the original claim was motivated by support for learning. The check box display in the training system was also used in the decision support version. Evaluation of the artefact demonstrated that the progress tracking checklist was a useful aid memoir for ship's captains during training and ordinary task operation.

The claims reuse library is being applied in the Multimedia Broker project which is developing a set of services to help multimedia title authors find and acquire resources over the World Wide Web. The system functionality consists of information searching, browsing, negotiation support, resource matching, and purchasing control. The Broker system maps to the grounded domains of object inventory, sales transaction, and object allocation for resource matching services with a generic task of information searching. Claims indexed on the generic information seeking task are reused; for instance, the conceptual maps claim, is reused to show the space of available resources in two views, conceptual categories and geographical location of suppliers. Development of two views was prompted by the claim's issue clause that draws attention to the importance of basing map designs on the user's conceptual model. Once again the user interface design has to be re-interpreted in the new domain context, so in this case one model described the media resources and the other the resource suppliers. Another reused claim which originated from information retrieval research, and was also applied in INTUITIVE, is the preformed query claim:

> *Claim ID*: Preformed query claim.
> *Author*: Sutcliffe A. G.
> *Artefact*: Preformed query library (Intuitive class) and UI menu selector.
> *Description*: A preformed query is attached to an icon or placed in a menu.

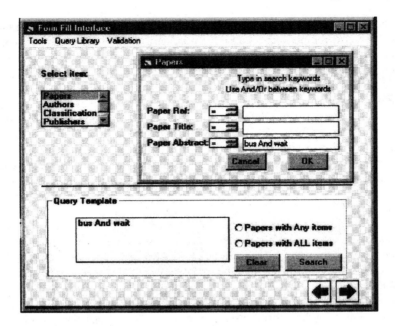

Figure 8: Multimedia broker prototype, showing the preformed queries interface.

Upside: provides rapid access to information; saves users effort in articulating queries.

Downside: finding queries in a large library can be difficult; queries inflexible, can not be adapted.

Problem scenario: the user needs to retrieve information for a known need.

Usage scenario: the user interface presents a menu of queries which can be reused. The user selects a query that matches their need by selecting an icon or a menu option, and the system retrieves the information for presentation.

Effect: The user can retrieve information by reusing familiar queries.

Dependencies: Information needs and queries must be known, future information needs must be predictable.

Issues: Query format, customizability of values and constraint clauses, addressing queries to different databases.

Scope: information seeking tasks with predictable needs.

The Multimedia Broker prototype embodying this claim is illustrated in Figure 8. In this case not only the claim but also its associated software artefact could be reused by customizing the Intuitive class. The basic functionality of the reusable query class and its components, i.e. a library of queries, a selection mechanism for the user and a means of submitting the query to a database could be transferred to the Broker; however, the new requirements also specified tailorable queries. In INTUITIVE the user interface manifestation (see Figure 7) of preformed queries were icons that enabled hypertext-like query by pointing. The user interface manifestation of the preformed query is different in the Broker system as the query buttons have been redesigned as mini-menus allowing limited customization of the preformed query. In addition the user can enter a limited set of keywords to customize the query. This mitigates one of the claim's downsides (inflexible queries) but the claim now appears in a different user interface context and has new functionality in the keyword additions. This indicates a new child claim may have to be developed from the preformed query parent. When to evolve new claims is a matter of judgement about how the original claim and artefact fits the new application requirements. If reuse initiates functional redesign it will require usability evaluation of the new task-artefact combination and this will initiate a new task artefact cycle. The usability payoff of the original claim may be compromized by changes in the user interface; however, the continuity of the artefact design for a the same task context gives reasonable confidence, if not a guarantee, that reuse in Multimedia Broker will pay off.

8 Discussion

This paper has contributed a method for generalizing claims to increase the reusability of HCI knowledge. It has done so by synthesizing claims evolution from the task artefact cycle with the domain theory (Sutcliffe & Maiden, 1998), to provide a means for indexing claims with a generic model that describes their scope of potential application. In addition we have reported a schema for describing claims knowledge and an outline of the process of generalizing claims themselves, although this work is reported more extensively in a forthcoming paper (Sutcliffe & Carroll, 1997). As a consequence claims may be understood in two contexts. First in the usage scenario of the original artefact and secondly in a relationship to a generic model describing a wider scope of application. This provides a conceptual framework for more systematically capturing and applying HCI knowledge in the context of design, with the conceptual elements of a causal theory of artefacts in use.

The claims framework of reusable psychological design rationale offers an open ended mechanism by which many authors can contribute to a common library of HCI knowledge. The domain theory library of generic application models provides a common means for indexing and retrieving claims. It could be argued that reuse could be delivered by indexing claims with a faceted classification, as practised in software component libraries (Prieto-Diaz, 1991); however, we believe the added value of generic models is providing a design and usage context of interpreting the generality of claims. Although the library is as yet modest, it demonstrates an approach which we believe will scale up. The domain theory models have been empirically validated (Maiden et al., 1995) and the library has remained stable over a number of years (Sutcliffe & Maiden, 1994; 1998). Reusing claims has posed several problems. One highlights the relationship between the claim and the artefacts functionality and user interface. User interface design may transfer at the high level but domain specific detail means that many aspects of presentation, and possibly dialogue design will not. This leads us to speculate another dimension of claims and artefacts exists that map to generic user interface components rather than whole systems or tools. Some examples are design of window managers, undo facilities and visual maps which are reported in this paper. In related work we are developing an approach to evolving claims at different levels of abstraction (Sutcliffe & Carroll, 1997). We do not envisage claims superseding other approaches e.g. theoretically grounded modelling. On the contrary, claims provide a conduit for wider utilization and dissemination of such knowledge. Take the label following effect reported by (Kitajima & Polson, 1997). This can be recapitulated as a claim that 'command and object labels should be visible and relevant to the user's task'. This claim is strongly grounded in the LICAI predictive theory that can explain upsides and downsides of the claim, such as users are strongly cued by labels for task actions that they expect to do; but they might find locating labels more difficult when many similar labels are present. This research poses further questions about the granularity of claims, scenarios that represent behaviour instances, and generic models that describe abstractions of design problems. The proposed ontology and process of reusing claims knowledge elaborates the task artefact cycle to enable a wider scope of knowledge and artefact reuse, but it does so at a cost of weakening the context within which the original claim was validated. Evaluation of evolving claims is thus vital for maintaining the integrity of a claims/artefact reuse library. Evaluation studies are continuing on the Multimedia broker project so we can validate the effectiveness of claims reuse, and gain further insights into the transferability of HCI knowledge and associated interactive artefacts. Understanding the relationship between HCI knowledge expressed in a claim and its accompanying artefacts, as well as how well generic models proscribe the applicability claims remains for our future research agenda. We will develop the claims library as well as refining the generic domain models that define the reuse scope. The claims library and extent of reuse so far is modest; nevertheless, we have demonstrated a mechanism for generalizing claims for reuse that offers a systematic and open ended framework for the development and application of HCI knowledge. To the extent that reuse becomes a more dominant paradigm for software development, and inter alia, user interfaces, we believe such a framework will become essential.

Acknowledgements

This work was partially supported by EU telematics project IE 2093 Multimedia Broker and a sabbatical for Alistair Sutcliffe at Virginia Tech.

References

Carroll, J. & Rosson, M. (1991), "Deliberated evolution: Stalking the View Matcher in Design Space", *Human–Computer Interaction* **6**(3-4), 281–318.

Carroll, J. M. & Rosson, M. B. (1992), "Getting Around the Task–Artefact Framework: How to Make Claims and Design by Scenario", *ACM Transactions on Office Information Systems* **10**(2), 181–212.

Fischer, G., Nakakoji, K., Otswald, J., Stahl, G. & T., S. (1993), Embedding Computer-based Critics in the Contexts of Design, *in* S. Ashlund, K. Mullet, A. Henderson, E. Hollnagel & T. White (eds.), *Proceedings of INTERCHI'93*, ACM Press, pp.157–63.

Gentner, D. (1983), "Structure-mapping: A Theoretical Framework for Analogy", *Cognitive Science* **7**, 155–70.

Kitajima, M. & Polson, P. (1997), "A Comprehension-based Model of Exploration", *Human–Computer Interaction* **12**(4), 345–89.

Maiden, N., Mistry, P. & Sutcliffe, A. (1995), How People Categorize Requirements for Reuse: A Natural Approach, *in* P. Zave & M. D. Harrison (eds.), *Proceedings of 2nd International Symposium on Requirements Engineering RE'95*, IEEE Computer Society Press, pp.148–57.

McMenamin, S. & Palmer, J. (1984), *Essential Systems Analysis*, Yourdon Press (Prentice–Hall).

Prieto-Diaz, R. (1991), "Implementing Faceted Classification for Software Reuse", *Communications of the ACM* **34**(5), 88–97.

Rosch, E. (1983), Prototype Classification and Logical Classification: The Two Systems, *in* E. K. Scholnick (ed.), *New Trends in Conceptual Representation: Challenges to Piaget's Theory?*, Lawrence Erlbaum Associates, pp.76–83.

Singley, M. & Carroll, J. (1996), Synthesis by Analysis: Five Modes of Reasoning that Guide Design, *in* T. P. Moran & J. M. Carroll (eds.), *Design Rationale: Concepts, Techniques and Use*, Lawrence Erlbaum Associates, pp.241–65.

Sutcliffe, A. (1996), User-centred Safety Critical Design, *in* J. Dobson (ed.), *Proceedings of CSR Conference: Human Factors in Safety Critical Systems*, Centre for Software Reliability, University of Newcastle and City University.

Sutcliffe, A. (1997), Using Domain Knowledge in Interactive System Design, Technical Report 97/12, Centre for HCI Design, School of Informatics, City University, London, UK.

Sutcliffe, A. & Carroll, J. (1997), Designing Claims for Reuse in Interactive Systems Design, Technical Report 97/17, Centre for HCI Design, school of Informatics, City University, London, UK.

Sutcliffe, A. & Ennis, M. (in press), "Towards a Cognitive Theory of Information Retrieval", *Interacting with Computers* . To appear in *Interacting with Computers*, special issue on Information Retrieval.

Sutcliffe, A. & Maiden, N. (1994), Domain Modelling for Reuse, *in* W. Frakes (ed.), *Proceedings of 3rd International Conference on Software Reusability*, IEEE Computer Society Press, pp.169–73.

Sutcliffe, A. & Ryan, M. (1998), Experience with SCRAM: A SCenario Requirements Analysis Method, *in* J. Mylopoulos (ed.), *Proceedings of 3rd International Symposium on Requirements Engineering RE'98*, IEEE Computer Society Press, pp.164–72.

Sutcliffe, A., Bennett, I., Doubleday, A. & Ryan, M. (1995), Designing Query Support for Multiple Databases, *in* K. Nordby, P. H. Helmersen, D. J. Gilmore & S. A. Arnessen (eds.), *Human–Computer Interaction — INTERACT'95: Proceedings of the Fifth IFIP Conference on Human–Computer Interaction*, Chapman & Hall, pp.207–12.

Sutcliffe, A. G. & Maiden, N. A. M. (1998), "The Domain Theory for Requirements Engineering", *IEEE Transactions on Software Engineering* **24**(3), 174–196.

Sutcliffe, A. G. & Patel, U. (1996), 3D or not 3D: Is it Nobler in the Mind?, *in* A. Sasse, R. J. Cunningham & R. Winder (eds.), *People and Computers XI (Proceedings of HCI'96)*, Springer-Verlag, pp.79–94.

Detecting and Resolving Temporal Ambiguities in User Interface Specifications

Paul Chesson, Lorraine Johnston & Philip Dart

Department of Computer Science, The University of Melbourne, Parkville, Victoria 3052, Australia.

EMail: *{chesson, ljj, philip}@cs.mu.oz.au*

Temporal ambiguities occur in user interface specifications when the application of multiple requirements can be interpreted in more than one way depending on when their conditions are evaluated. This paper discusses the resolution of temporal ambiguities using two approaches. The first approach involves the writer clarifying the intention of statements in an informal natural language specification. The second approach involves the use of a principle of *ordered events* to guide the writing and rewriting of the specification to avoid the ambiguity. A method for automatically detecting such ambiguities is presented, using an abstract specification model based on the language FLUID.

Keywords: user interface, dialogue specification, requirements.

1 Introduction

User interface dialogue specification is concerned with describing the structure of dialogue between an interactive system and its users. The process and result of formally specifying a user interface is aimed at facilitating the understanding and communication of the design between the participants in software development. Specifications can also enable developers to analyse features related to the usability of an interface.

An informal specification can be produced using a set of statements or rules (henceforth referred to as requirements) which describe the behaviour of an interface under various conditions. While understanding a single requirement by itself is usually straight forward, difficulties can arise when a reader tries to interpret the combined behaviour of multiple requirements. In some cases, the conditions dealt with in a requirement may be changed as a result of other requirements, and the result may differ according to the order in which requirements are applied. This is referred to as a *temporal ambiguity*.

The expression of temporal relationships at the syntactic and task levels in user interface specification languages has been approached in a number of ways. Temporal Logic can be used to express system behaviour in terms of temporal constraints (Johnson, 1990), while LOTOS and CSP can express temporal relationships by modelling a system in terms of processes which are able to synchronize with one other — for example, (Alexander, 1990) and (Paterno' et al., 1997). User Action Notation (UAN) has an explicit set of operators which are able to directly capture ideas such as interleavability, interruptions, and order independence (Hartson & Gray, 1992).

Languages may also use more implicit representations to address common temporal relationships in graphical user interfaces. Jacob's specification language for direct-manipulation interfaces (Jacob, 1986) allows interleaving by the suspension and resumption of coroutines, each responsible for describing the syntax of a screen object. TADEUS Dialogue Graphs (Elwert & Schlungbaum, 1995) allows the modelling of high level dialogue views (windows) which may be viewed and manipulated sequentially, concurrently, and in a modal fashion.

Section 2 of this paper explores the problem of temporal ambiguities and their causes. Section 3 presents two approaches for avoiding or remedying a specification containing a temporal ambiguity. Finally, Section 4 outlines a method for automatically detecting temporal ambiguities by the use of an abstract specification model based on the language FLUID.

2   An Introduction to Temporal Ambiguities

This section will present two examples of temporal ambiguities which can arise from user interface requirements. These requirements will be expressed using natural language for ease of understanding. It should be noted that the occurrence of temporal ambiguities is not limited to informal specifications. Although formal specification languages have well defined semantics, a system defined in such a language may have unintended behaviour resulting from the interaction of requirements. For example, an interface may be specified incorrectly because some scenarios were overlooked. This problem is compounded when the set of requirements for the user interface are being continually updated. Analysis of a formal specification like the one presented here, is required in order to detect potential defects such as ambiguity, as well as incompleteness and inconsistency.

The examples presented in this paper will consist of small sets of individual requirements from a larger specification. These requirements, though related, may not necessarily be grouped together in the specification document in the same manner as shown here. Instead, they may be placed in different parts of the document in order to emphasize other equally important relationships between requirements. This means that ambiguities may be more difficult to notice than they appear here, and reorganizing requirements may not be possible without de-emphasizing other relationships.

A number of rule-based languages will be discussed to illustrate how such languages can be used to distinguish between ambiguous interpretations. However, the approaches employed by these languages have limitations which will be discussion in Section 3.1.

Consider the following requirements for an interactive visualization system:

Example 1

   a. If the scale of the image is changed, then the viewing window is redrawn.
   b. If the viewing window is redrawn while the scale of the image is large enough to display a granularity scale, then the granularity scale is drawn in the viewing window.

The second requirement may be applied in isolation (for example, when the user explicitly requests that the entire screen be redrawn) or in the context of the first requirement (for example, when the user zooms in on the image and the viewing window needs to be redrawn to display the image at its new scale). However, in the context of the first requirement, it is not explicit whether the condition that "the scale of the image is large enough to display a granularity scale" is evaluated before or after the scale of the image is changed.

The intended interpretation of the requirements in the case of Example 1 is that the size of the image scale is checked after the scale of the image is changed. This follows the interpretation that the condition of a rule must be evaluated after all other rules which may affect that condition, have been applied. Such a property is useful in that requirements behave in a transitive manner (i.e. if *a* causes *b* and *b* causes *c*, then *a* causes *c*). ERL (Event Response Language) (Hill, 1986) supports this property to a limited extent by allowing a set of high priority rules (called ε-rules) to be fired, causing a change in state, before a set of regular rules is applied.

However, in other cases, it may be desirable to use the state of the user interface only at a particular instant in time to evaluate conditions. Typically, this instant is when an external event is received by the interface. Example 2 shows one such case where pressing a pause button causes an animation to toggle between the paused and playing states. In this case, the intention is that the state of the animation is evaluated at the instant before the pause button is pressed, otherwise if the pause button is pressed while the animation is playing, then the second requirement may undo the effect of the first requirement.

Example 2

   a. If the pause button is pressed while an animation is playing, then the animation is paused.
   b. If the pause button is pressed while an animation is paused, then the animation is played.

As illustrated, this form of interpretation is useful in cases where selection between a number of alternative behaviours is required. ERL also supports such interpretations by applying all ε-rules simultaneously, according to the current state of the interface (indicated by a set of flags). The same procedure is repeated for the set of normal rules.

3   Resolving Temporal Ambiguities

3.1   Objectives and Approaches

An important property which we believe should be supported in specifying user interfaces is that individual requirements be treated as independently from each other as possible. The motivation for this is to minimize the amount of complexity caused by the coupling of requirements during the development, communication, comprehension, and maintenance of a specification.

The order in which multiple rules may be applied is a similar issue to the problem of conflicting rules in rule-based formalisms. Proposition Production System (PPS) (Olsen, 1990) uses an ordered set of rules to specify a system. The ordering is needed to determine the outcome when multiple rules are fired which contradict one another. The same idea could be used to determine the order in which the effects of multiple rules are applied.

While supporting the goal of independent requirements, such mechanisms can be avoided by enabling requirements to be interpreted without direct reference to the rest of the specification. Although such approaches deal more directly with the problem than most non-rule-based approaches, a preferable goal is to have requirements which could be interpreted unambiguously without reference to the rest of the specification. For example, Dialogue Specification Notation (DSN) (Curry & Monk, 1995) disallows multiple rules from being fired simultaneously. While this idea has merits in its own context, if it is used to remove transitive effects like those in Example 1, the end result may require the contents of rules to be duplicated.

We have defined two methods for approaching the goal of resolving temporal ambiguities. The first method involves being more explicit in stating the temporal relationships between events and conditions. This is accomplished by altering the natural language description of the ambiguous requirements after they have been identified. The second method involves writing the specification according to a specific principle which can be used to interpret ambiguous sets of requirements. The principle we have used is to apply events in the same order as they are produced. This is called the *principle of ordered events* and is also supported in ERL through the use of event queues.

It should be noted that many subtle interpretations can be reached from requirements written in natural language, and although rewriting the specification may improve its clarity, it cannot guarantee that only one interpretation remains.

3.2   Using Natural Language

In the two examples presented in Section 2, rules are expressed in terms of an event occurring under a particular condition (requirement 1a occurs under all conditions). The event defines the exact moment at which the rule is applied, and as such is the critical point in time referred to in the requirement. Each condition may be fulfilled in one or more of the following ways:

1. It may be true at the instant of the event;

2. it may become true as a result of the event itself; or

3. it may have been true until the event itself.

Case (1) is the simplest, and occurs when the condition does not change during the application of the requirement. In such a case, temporal ambiguity does not exist. The verbs *is* (singular) and *are* (plural) are used in the phrase to describe such conditions. These verbs were used in the original requirements, and should be used by default until it is established that a temporal ambiguity exists.

In Case (2), words such as *will be* are used in the condition phrase to indicate that the condition be evaluated *after* any possible changes in the state of that condition. In Requirement 1b, the intention is that the scale of the image is checked after any possible changes, so the disambiguated specification of the two requirements reads:

Example 1′

  a. If the scale of the image is changed, then the viewing window is redrawn.

  b. If the viewing window is redrawn **and** the scale of the image **will be** large enough to display a granularity scale, then the granularity scale is drawn in the viewing window.

In Case (3), verbs such as *was* and *were* are used in the condition phrase to indicate that the condition be evaluated *before* any possible changes in the state of that condition. This is used in Example 2 where the state of the animation needs to be referred to, before it is changed.

Example 2′

  a. If the pause button is pressed while an animation **was** playing, then the animation is paused.

  b. If the pause button is pressed while an animation **was** paused, then the animation is played.

In addition to the state of a boolean condition, temporal ambiguities may occur in relation to the state of a data value. Consider the following requirements for a visualization system which allows the user to select between two types of scales (metric and imperial):

Example 3

  a. If a scale selection button (metric or imperial) is pressed, then the selected scale type is changed to the corresponding selection.

  b. If a scale selection button is pressed while the visibility of the scale is off, then the visibility of the scale is turned on.

  c. If the visibility of the scale is turned on, then scales of the currently selected type are drawn.

If one of the scale selection buttons is pressed while the visibility of the scales is off, then the selected scale type is changed and the visibility of the scales is turned on. However, the order in which these events occur is not known, so it is not clear if the scales are drawn according to the scale type just selected, or the previous selection.

Similarly to boolean conditions, it needs to be indicated whether any data value being referred to should be evaluated before or after any possible changes. Notice here that the data value is referred to in the consequent of the requirement instead of the condition. Data values may also be referred to in the condition phrase in the same manner. In fact, a more explicit representation of the requirement would refer to the value in the condition and bind the result to the output. For example, we could rewrite Requirement 3c as, "If the visibility of the scale is turned on, and the selected scale type is x, then scales of type x are drawn." This representation is useful because it explicitly shows that the currently selected scale type is an 'input' to the rule. This is important when requirements are formally modelled, as shown in Section 4.1.

To adjust the wording of requirements containing ambiguous data values, the requirements are written in their explicit form which supports the use of words such as "will be" and "was" to be used. Requirement 3c can be rewritten as, "If the visibility of the scale is turned on, and the selected scale type *will be* x, then scales of type x are drawn."

3.3   Using the Principle of Ordered Events

If care is taken to write a specification which follows the principle that events may only be applied to requirements in the same order in which they are produced, then in many cases requirements are able to be correctly interpreted. To illustrate how this works, consider Example 1 again. If the scale of the image is changed, resulting in the viewing window being redrawn, then the redrawing of the window will occur after the scale has been changed. With this assumption, the condition in requirement 1b will be evaluated using the new scale of image (as was the intention). In Example 2, if the pause button is pressed, resulting in the animation being paused, then the pausing of the animation will occur after the button is pressed. With this assumption, the condition in Requirement 2b is evaluated using the original state of the animation (as was the intention).

Although following this principle of ordered events can prove useful in the writing of a specification and the subsequent resolution of temporal ambiguities, it does not always have the desired effect. Consider the following user interface requirements for the control panel of a machine whose speed setting may only be altered when the machine is not operating:

Example 4

   a. If a speed selection button (0, 1, 2, or 3) is pressed while the machine is not operating, then the selected speed of the machine is changed.
   b. If the 'speed 0' selection button is pressed while the machine is operating, then the machine stops operating.
   c. If the start button is pressed while the machine is not operating and the selected speed of the machine is 1, 2, or 3, then the machine starts operating at the currently selected speed.

In this case, if the 'speed 0' selection button is pressed when the machine is operating, then the machine will stop operating, but the selected speed will not be changed since the event of stopping the operation of the machine occurred after the button was pressed. If this was not the intended behaviour, then the specification will need to be rewritten. In this case, the writer needs to be more explicit about the behaviour of the 'speed 0' selection button, instead of trying to generalize it:

Example 4′

 a. If a speed selection button (**1, 2, or 3**) is pressed while the machine is not operating, then the selected speed of the machine is changed.
 b. If the 'speed 0' selection button is pressed while the machine is operating, then the machine stops operating **and the selected speed of the machine is changed to 0**.
 c. If the start button is pressed while the machine is not operating and the selected speed of the machine is 1, 2, or 3, then the machine starts operating at the currently selected speed.

Such a rewrite of the requirements can often prompt the designer to reevaluate the way the interface is intended to be understood by the user. In this case, a cue is given that the 'speed 0' button may be better served as a 'stop' button to distinguish it from the other speed selection buttons. Alternatively, consideration could be given to splitting the dual functionality of the button into two separate buttons.

The principle of ordered events does not guarantee that an ambiguous specification will be resolved. In Example 3, the order in which the selected scale type is changed and the visibility of the scale is turned on is not known. Once again, the requirements need to be rewritten to clarify the intention:

Example 3′

 a. If a scale selection button (metric or imperial) is pressed, then the selected scale type is changed to the corresponding selection.
 b. If **a property of the scale is changed (e.g. type)** while the visibility of the scale is off, then the visibility of the scale is turned on.
 c. If the visibility of the scale is turned on, then scales of the currently selected type are drawn.

In this case, Requirement b is refined to show that the real reason why the scale is made visible is because one of its properties has changed. This in turn clarifies the intention that the selected scale type should be updated before the scale is redrawn. To reinforce this intention, natural language is used in the ambiguous requirement c in the same manner outlined in the Section 3.2.

3.4   Summary

The principle of ordered events provides a useful heuristic for testing the clarity of the relationship between requirements. If the principle does not support the intentions, then the requirements involved in temporal ambiguities should be checked to ensure that the generalizations and causal relationships are expressed in a logical and easily understandable manner. Requirements expressed in natural language (or even formally represented requirements which are supplemented with natural language) can also help clarify the intention at the level of single requirements.

4 Automated Detection of Temporal Ambiguities

It is non-trivial to discover the existence and source of temporal ambiguities in a set of requirements, but this can be aided by analysis on a formal representation of the requirements. An abstract representation of requirements can be constructed based on the language FLUID (Chesson & Johnston, 1996). FLUID was developed to support the philosophies of user interface specification outlined in Section 3.1, and follows the principle of ordered events. Although the abstraction reduces a FLUID specification to a simple non-deterministic set of rules, the complete specification from which it is derived has a well defined meaning and is typically more expressive than the rule-based languages which have been cited here.

This section describes the abstract representation of requirements and the process by which they can be analysed to detect temporal ambiguities. The model used to represent requirements was specifically developed for the specification of user interfaces, and although it may be used for non-interactive systems where event-based modelling is appropriate, no claim is made regarding its suitability. Issues relating to the presentation of the analysis results are discussed, and an example is given within the context of a supporting tool. Note that each temporal ambiguity typically involves just a small number of requirements, and the example only lists one such set of requirements which would be found in a larger specification by such a tool.

4.1 The Black-box FLUID Specification Model

Individual requirements in FLUID are represented by *sub-dialogues* which are described using two tables and a coloured Petri net. Sub-dialogues are related to each other using a *constraint hierarchy* which describes the constraints between requirements. It is a directed, acyclic graph consisting of a sub-dialogue at each node. Events are propagated from the top of the hierarchy and are processed by each sub-dialogue which is reached. As a result of processing, a sub-dialogue may block an event from being passed on to sub-dialogues beneath it. This enables constraints to be placed on the access to application or interface functionality which is invoked from the sub-dialogues at the lower levels.

Analysis will be performed on an abstract representation of FLUID sub-dialogues called *black-box*. The black-box representation only states the events and actions referred to in each sub-dialogue, without including details of how they are used. Each sub-dialogue is may react to an event from a given set of inputs, and potentially produce one or more events or actions from a given set of outputs. The set of input events are partitioned into two subsets: *trigger* events, and *conditional* events. Trigger events may produce output events or actions as a direct result of processing. Conditional events are events which do not directly produce output events or actions, but may affect the state of the sub-dialogue, thereby affecting the processing of future trigger events received by the sub-dialogue. Any events which affect the state of the condition by their definition, must be included in the set of conditional events. In addition, any events which affect the data values referred to in the output events or actions, must also be included.

As a consequence of the black-box representation, no assumptions can be made regarding the relationship between the events which are received by the sub-dialogue and the resulting events which are generated. All possible behaviours of the black-box sub-dialogues (a superset of all behaviours which may occur in practice) will need to be analysed. As a result, temporal ambiguities may be detected during analysis which cannot occur in practice, but all temporal ambiguities which do exist will be found. The extraneous ambiguities detected may be dismissed if sufficient justification can be provided.

4.2   Detecting Ambiguous Sub-dialogues

In order to analyse temporal behaviour of a black-box FLUID specification, the precise sequence of steps in the processing of each event needs to be described. This sequence of steps is called a *trace*. However, the processing of events in FLUID is non-deterministic. Therefore, more than one trace may exist for the processing of a given event.

The flow of control in a black-box FLUID specification is the propagation of events between sub-dialogues in the constraint hierarchy. This means that a trace can be characterized by recording specific occurrences of an event being received by a sub-dialogue. Each such occurrence is represented by a *trace-node* in the trace, and a trace is represented by an ordered sequence of nodes. Additionally, the idea of a *sub-trace* will be introduced. A sub-trace is a trace which only includes the nodes for a specific event propagating through the constraint hierarchy.

The overall strategy which will be used to generate the set of traces produced by the processing of a user or application event (henceforth referred to as a *raw* event) can be informally described as follows:

1. Construct a set of sub-traces for the raw event.

2. Examine each trace-node from each of these sub-traces in turn, and if that node represents an event which may generate output events from a sub-dialogue, then:

    (a) Determine all possible sequences of events which may be produced from the sub-dialogue. Note that it is possible that no events may be produced.

    (b) For each event in a sequence of generated events:

        i. Construct a set of sub-traces for the generated event.

        ii. Merge each sub-trace with the trace it was generated from to form a new set of traces. The traces produced by merging must be valid within the semantics of FLUID.

        iii. Repeat for each sub-trace for the generated event.

    (c) Repeat for each event in each sequence of generated events, by merging their sub-traces into the new traces.

3. Repeat for each trace-node in each of the new traces.

In summary, a set of sub-traces is computed for the raw event, and each trace-node in the sub-trace is checked for new events. If new events are able to be generated, their sub-traces are added. This process is recursive, producing a growing number of more detailed traces as new permutations are considered. A specification must guarantee that any event does not directly or indirectly generate an event of the same type. This ensures that the process will terminate. Assessing the need for recursion and reducing this need, are currently under investigation.

In order to detect possible temporal ambiguities in a black-box FLUID specification, sub-dialogues need to be found which can receive both trigger and conditional events in either order, when processing a particular raw event. This is done by searching for traces which demonstrate that both orderings are possible.

A formal specification of the computation of traces and the subsequent detection of temporal ambiguities, is presented in (Chesson et al., 1997).

4.3   *Presentation of Results*

Once an ambiguity is detected for a particular sub-dialogue and raw event, it can be presented to the writer of the specification using two traces: one which demonstrates how a trigger event can be received by the sub-dialogue before it receives a conditional event, and one which demonstrates how a conditional event can be received by the sub-dialogue before it receives a trigger event. In order to present the traces in a useful manner, a number of steps can be employed.

When a sub-dialogue can receive trigger and conditional events in a particular order, it can typically be demonstrated in more than one trace. However, the differences between these traces are a result of combinations of event processing, which lead to the same effect, and extraneous events which are generated but have no bearing on the actual ambiguity. It is desirable to present the parts of the trace which can demonstrate the ordering of events as concisely as possible. To do this, only the section of a trace up to the point where the ambiguous ordering is demonstrated is considered. Secondly, trace nodes which represent conditional events being received by sub-dialogues not relevant to the ambiguity are removed, as these events are unnecessary for presentation purposes. This leaves traces with nodes representing events being received by the sub-dialogue where the ambiguity exists, and nodes representing the generation of new events. From this set of candidates, the shortest trace is chosen, thereby eliminating traces which deal with extraneous details.

A final consideration for presenting the traces is to be able to show which events are generated and when (recall that trace nodes representing the generation of events only record the trigger event and sub-dialogue). This additional information can be recorded for each trace during its construction, but is not needed during analysis.

A tool has been implemented to demonstrate the detection of temporal ambiguities using the method presented in this section. Figure 1 shows a file representing a black-box FLUID specification for Example 3. Figure 2 shows the corresponding output from the tool.

5   Conclusion

Temporal ambiguities occur in user interface specifications when the application of multiple requirements can be interpreted in more than one way according to when

```
// Requirement A
// If a scale selection button (metric or imperial) is pressed, then the
// selected scale type is changed to the corresponding selection.

SelectScale                          // sub-dialogue name
  press_scale_select                 // trigger event
                                     // no conditional events
  change_scale_type                  // output event

// Requirement B
// If the scale selection button is pressed while the visibility of the
// scale is off, then the visibility of the scale is turned on.

ShowScale                            // sub-dialogue name
  press_scale_select                 // trigger event
  change_scale_visibility            // conditional event
  change_scale_visibility            // output event

// Requirement C
// If the visibility of the scale is turned on, then scales of the
// currently selected type are drawn.

DrawScale                            // sub-dialogue name
  change_scale_visibility            // trigger event
  change_scale_type                  // conditional event
  DrawScales                         // action
```

Figure 1: Black-box FLUID specification of Example 3.

```
Temporal ambiguity in "DrawScale" from event "press_scale_select".
  Trace where conditional event is received before trigger event:
    "press_scale_select" received by "SelectScale".
    "change_scale_type" generated.
    "change_scale_type" received by "DrawScale" (conditional).
    "press_scale_select" received by "ShowScale".
    "change_scale_visibility" generated.
    "change_scale_visibility" received by "DrawScale" (trigger).
  Trace where trigger event is received before conditional event:
    "press_scale_select" received by "ShowScale".
    "change_scale_visibility" generated.
    "change_scale_visibility" received by "DrawScale" (trigger).
    "press_scale_select" received by "SelectScale".
    "change_scale_type" generated.
    "change_scale_type" received by "DrawScale" (conditional).
```

Figure 2: Output of temporal ambiguity detection tool for Example 3.

---

their conditions are evaluated. FLUID offers a foundation for addressing this problem by providing a formal abstraction which is able to model individual requirements. The automatic procedure outlined here for analysing a specification can determine the conditions under which temporal ambiguities can occur, as well as the requirements which caused them. Resolving these ambiguities by applying the principle of order events may reveal unclear design rationale. In addition, modifying the corresponding informal statements in the specification can clarify the correct intention to the reader.

References

Alexander, H. (1990), Structuring Dialogues using CSP, *in* M. D. Harrison & H. W. Thimbleby (eds.), *Formal Methods in Human–Computer Interaction*, Cambridge Series on Human–Computer Interaction, Cambridge University Press, chapter 9, pp.273–95.

Chesson, P. & Johnston, L. (1996), FLUID: Specifying Data Flow and Control for User Interfaces, *in* L. Yong, L. Herman, Y. Leung & J. Moyes (eds.), *Proceedings of the First Asia-Pacific Conference on Computer–Human Interaction*, Information Technology Institute, pp.171–80.

Chesson, P., Johnston, L. & Dart, P. (1997), Detecting and Resolving Temporal Ambiguities in User Interface Specifications, Technical Report 97/29, Department of Computer Science, The University of Melbourne.

Curry, M. & Monk, A. (1995), "Dialogue Modelling of Graphical User Interfaces with a Production System", *Behaviour & Information Technology* **14**(1), 41–55.

Elwert, T. & Schlungbaum, E. (1995), Modelling and Generation of Graphical User Interfaces in the TADEUS Approach, *in* P. Palanque & R. Bastide (eds.), *Design, Specification and Verification of Interactive Systems*, Springer-Verlag, pp.193–208.

Hartson, H. & Gray, P. (1992), "Temporal Aspects of Tasks in the User Action Notation", *Human–Computer Interaction* **7**, 1–45.

Hill, R. (1986), "Supporting Concurrency, Communication, and Synchronization in Human–Computer Interaction — The Sassafras UIMS", *ACM Transactions on Graphics* **5**(3), 179–210.

Jacob, R. (1986), "A Specification Language for Direct-manipulation User Interfaces", *ACM Transactions on Graphics* **5**(4), 283–317.

Johnson, C. (1990), Using Temporal Logic to Prototype Interactive Systems, *in* D. Diaper, D. Gilmore, G. Cockton & B. Shackel (eds.), *Proceedings of INTERACT'90 — Third IFIP Conference on Human–Computer Interaction*, Elsevier Science, pp.1019–20.

Olsen, D. (1990), Propositional Production Systems for Dialog Description., *in* J. C. Chew & J. Whiteside (eds.), *Proceedings of CHI'90: Human Factors in Computing Systems*, ACM Press, pp.57–63.

Paterno', F., Mancini, C. & Meniconi, S. (1997), ConcurTaskTrees: A Diagrammatic Notation for Specifying Task Models, *in* S. Howard, J. Hammond & G. K. Lindgaard (eds.), *Human–Computer Interaction — INTERACT'97: Proceedings of the Fifth IFIP Conference on Human–Computer Interaction*, Chapman & Hall, pp.362–9.

The Design of New Technology for Writing On-line Help

Cécile Paris, Nadine Ozkan & Flor Bonifacio[†]

CSIRO/MIS, Locked Bag 17, North Ryde, NSW 1670, Australia.

Tel: *+61 2 9325 3100*

Fax: *+61 2 9325 3200*

EMail: *{Cecile.Paris, Nadine.Ozkan}@cmis.csiro.au*

URL: *http://www.cmis.csiro.au/{Cecile.Paris, Nadine.Ozkan}/*

[†] *IBM Global Services Australia, 55 Coonara Avenue, West Pennant Hills, NSW 2125, Australia.*

Tel: *+61 2 9354 4860*

Fax: *+61 2 9354 7766*

EMail: *florb@au1.ibm.com*

This paper presents an instance of the design of new technology in the domain of technical writing. We are proposing a novel tool for technical writers called Isolde*. Isolde has the potential to change substantially the technical writing process as well as the place of technical writers in a software development team. Consequently, Isolde has been designed through the collaboration of end-users and human computer interaction specialists. This paper shows how its design has evolved from technical and user related considerations, ensuring that Isolde is both feasible and desirable. The paper also discusses the use and place of this new technology in the technical writers' work environment.

Keywords: participatory design, technical writing, task modelling, emerging technology, requirements analysis, work practices.

---

*An Integrated Software and On-Line Documentation Environment.

1   Introduction

The role of technical writers is currently changing, as is highlighted by the Trends Report of STC International (Sayers, 1996), which specifies that new models for the process of technical writing need to emerge. Furthermore, as the invited speech of the 1996 STC conference pointed out (Parkinson, 1996), there is a pressing need for technical writers to seize opportunities presented by new technology. In this spirit, researchers in software engineering, human computer interaction (HCI) and language technology from CSIRO, the Australian national research institute, and the Information Design and Development group of IBM Global Services Australia have established a close relationship. We had already collaborated on the design of a major software system using state-of-the-art techniques in HCI (Balbo & Lindley, 1997), and we concluded that collaboration was useful and led to a quality product.

The two groups are currently collaborating on the design of the user interface of a novel tool for technical writers called Isolde. The aim of this paper is to describe how the design of Isolde has been shaped from a convergence of two types of considerations:

- technical considerations related to the current state of technology; and

- user-driven considerations related to the cognitive and collaborative processes of technical writing.

The next section, Section 2, examines the current trends in the tools available for technical writers. Section 3 describes Isolde and discusses its fit within these trends. Section 4 describes our design methodology for Isolde's interface. We then discuss two major features of Isolde and show how each is motivated by both technical and end-user considerations. Section 5 focuses on the type of help generated by Isolde, and Section 6 on the user input to Isolde (task models). The paper then goes on to explore the consequences of introducing a tool such as Isolde in the technical writers' work environment.

2   Trends in Tools for Technical Writing

In writing documentation, technical writers typically use a number of electronic tools or ancillary aids. They can be classified according to the type of task they can perform (Hartley & Paris, 1996):

Project Management Tools: These tools help *manage work flow processes* — e.g. Lotus Notes, and QMX.

Document management tools: These tools do not help with the document writing process itself but with *managing the documents*.

Word and Text processing tools: These help with the writing process, but affect only the *mechanical part* of that process, not its output, i.e. the document.

Tools to enforce consistency in the vocabulary, grammar and style employed in a document: Such tools affect the document produced, but mostly at the levels of *syntax* and *graphology*. These tools are employed both to avoid errors and to ensure consistency of style throughout the documentation. They include grammar checkers, style checkers, and tools based on controlled language. These tools may be user-definable (in that the technical writers have control over them), or set by a company to conform to a specific style (and the technical writers cannot customize them). They may be interactive. Tools in these categories need not be computational; they could, instead, be in the form of style guides and style sheets that writers must follow.

Tools to structure the documents: especially for on-line help: these tools also help with the mechanical part of the writing process, but with a view of helping with the *organization* (or *structure*) of the text, especially if hypertext-based documentation is to be produced. These tools also may be computational (e.g. HDK), or templates that the writers must follow to present the information. These templates may help with both the structure of the text to be written (e.g. the order in which to present the information) and its information content (i.e. what information to present).

While potentially complex in terms of their software implementation, these tools are still fairly simple conceptually, in terms of the support they offer technical writers. Yet, we already see three shifts over time in this support:

- from supporting the mechanics of document production and management to supporting the writing proper;

- from helping with the syntactic level of the text to helping with the structure and content of the text; and

- towards the design, development and deployment of tools to be employed earlier in the documentation writing process.

At the convergence of the first two shifts are tools which help with the more abstract linguistic levels of the text, i.e. structure and, to some extent, information content.

3   Description of the Isolde Prototype System

Today, advances in software engineering, language technology and HCI allow us to envisage furthering the shifts discussed in the previous section with more sophisticated tools to support the technical writing process. Drawing on these disciplines, the CSIRO team is currently developing Isolde, a research prototype for an authoring tool for technical writers. Isolde takes as input a high-level description of the functionality of the software to be documented (such as a task model, as defined in HCI — see Figures 4 & 8) and automatically generates hypertext for a subset of its on-line documentation. Hence Isolde envisages that instead of producing text directly, technical writers proceed in two stages. First they produce a description of the system functionalities (in DIANE+, a task modelling notation). Second, once the text is generated automatically, they revise and correct it as appropriate. Isolde thus supports the authoring process at yet an earlier stage, that of defining the knowledge that is to be contained in a text, and provides help at all linguistic levels of the text, by generating the text automatically.

3.1   Isolde's Architecture

The Isolde design is based on previous work in natural language generation (Paris et al., 1991; Paris & Vander Linden, 1996a), and on the collaboration between CSIRO and technical writers. Figure 1 shows the current architecture for the Isolde system. Isolde contains three main modules:

1. **An interface to the technical writers:** It is through this interface that the technical writers control the authoring tool. The interface design was based on an analysis of the technical writers' work and an assessment of how they would work with task models (Ozkan et al., in this volume). At this point, the interface allows technical writers to import, create and manipulate task models in the DIANE+ notation. When the task model is created, it can be exported to the hypertext generator for the on-line help to be generated. Once fully implemented, the interface will also enable technical writers to edit the text after it has been generated.

2. **A transformer module:** This module derives a draft task model from the output of a Computer Aided Software Engineering (CASE) tool when available (Lu et al., 1998). The technical writer can then revise and augment this draft model.

3. **A hypertext generator:** This module is responsible for producing the on-line help for the selected task (Paris et al., in press). It takes as input the task model as defined by technical writers and produces its corresponding documentation. This module is based on extensive work in natural language generation. It exploits a number of resources:

   - A library of concepts both about the domain of the software and the software interface (such as interface objects). This is linked to the task model and to the lexicon to provide the conceptual knowledge and its linguistic realization necessary to form appropriate text.
   - A set of linguistic resources that includes:
     - discourse plans, or information about what constitutes a how-to text and how to organize the information;
     - one (or several) grammar(s) — several if multi-linguality is required; and
     - one (or several) lexicon(s) — i.e. the vocabulary to be employed.

     Style guides could be used to control the linguistic resources and thus ensure that only the specified vocabulary, grammar and style are employed. Similarly, rules concerning formatting can be included.

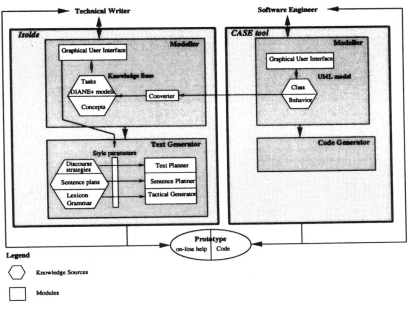

Figure 1: The Isolde architecture.

3.2 Usage of Isolde

Technical writers can use Isolde in two modes:

1. **In a stand-alone mode**. In this mode, technical writers can use Isolde to formally specify the functionality of the software, i.e. to create task models, manipulate them and generate on-line help from them. This mode is used when no usable models of the software functionalities exist already.

2. **Coupled to a Computer Aided Software Engineering (CASE) tool**. In this mode, Isolde can bootstrap the process of constructing a task model by constructing automatically a draft model from the information contained in the CASE tool.

The latter mode is the more complex case and is described in this paragraph. To produce on-line documentation with Isolde, technical writers first import information from a CASE tool. This enables Isolde to build an initial task model, filtering out information related to programming details as opposed to the end-user's task (Lu et al., 1998). The result of this step is a draft of the task model representing the functionality of the software to be documented. This task model is checked and revised by technical writers, using the task model editor contained in the interface. At any point, technical writers can ask Isolde to produce the on-line documentation for the task model or some part of it. Once the documentation is produced, writers can go back to the task model to correct or refine it. The text is re-generated, reflecting

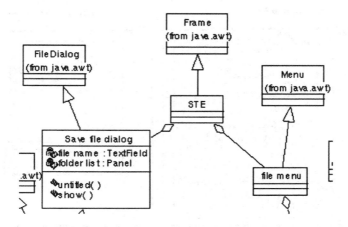

Figure 2: A portion of the UML class structure for STE.

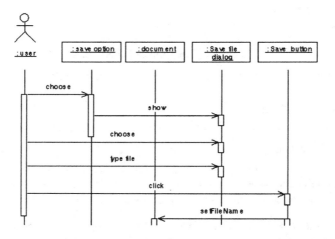

Figure 3: A portion of the UML scenarios for STE.

the changes. When the on-line help text is judged appropriate, it can be integrated with the prototype that resulted from working with the CASE tool.

This mode of producing on-line help with Isolde is illustrated with Figure 2, 3, 4 & 5. In Figures 2 & 3, we see portions of the models that would be specified in a CASE tool, written in the Unified Modelling Language (UML) (Rational Software Corporation, 1997). This example uses Rational Rose, and the models are for STE, a Simple Text Editor written in Java that we have used for prototyping. Figure 4 shows a portion of the DIANE+ task model that would be derived from these models. Finally, Figure 5 shows the text that Isolde would generate for the modelled tasks.

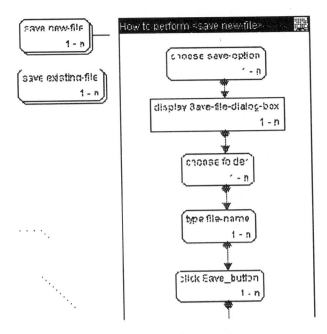

Figure 4: The task model in DIANE+ for the Save function.

From the designer's perspective, Isolde's functionality is the product of collaborative design. The design method is described in Section 4. From the technical writers' perspective, the main features of Isolde are the following:

- the type of documentation Isolde can produce;

- the type of input Isolde requires (task models in the DIANE+ notation); and

- the quality of the generated text.

These features are likely to be determining factors in the usability of Isolde itself and to have an impact on both the cognitive process of technical writing and the interaction of this process with other processes in software development. Sections 5 & 6 examine the features above and show how they address both technical and user-driven considerations.

4 The Design Methodology

Isolde was designed in three phases, which are described in this section. The purpose of the first phase was to gain an understanding of the technical writing process and of the formalisms, if any, used by technical writers. This was done through a series of observations and structured interviews. Two rounds were performed with six technical writers in individual sessions.

To use STE.
What would you like to do?

- Create a file.
  How?

- Save a file.
  How?

- Open a file.
  How?

- Print a file.
  How?

- Close a file.
  How?

To save a file.
What would you like to do?

- Save a new file.
  How?

- Save an existing file.
  How?

To save a new file.

1. Choose the save option from the file menu.
   The system will display the save file dialogue box.

2. Choose the folder.

3. Type the file name.

4. Click the save button.
   The system will save the document.

Note If you would like to create a new folder in which to save your document, you can click on the **New Folder** button on the top of the dialogue box.

Figure 5: The generated hypertext.

During the interviews, four types of questions were asked: (1) general questions on the nature of the process of technical writing, (2) questions regarding the models used by technical writers, (3) questions regarding their work setting and (4) prospective questions on the use of new tools. They are detailed below:

1. General questions:

   - What are the major steps you go through when you get involved in a project to write on-line documentation?

   - Can you tell me about a typical project or about the last project in which you were involved? Let's go step by step with that project.

   - What do you do in your actual own documenting activity (as opposed to when you're interacting with the team): Steps, tools, etc.

- What different types of projects are there? What makes the difference between projects (time frame, project size, when you get involved, etc.).

2. Models:

   - Do you document what you do — either for yourself or to share with others, and if yes, how?
   - What is the main purpose of these documents for you?
   - If you use specific notations, can you show me an example for a recent project?
   - If several notations are used, what are the differences between them (representational power, appropriateness, etc.)?

3. Work setting:

   - Where do you work (always the same room or does it vary with projects)?
   - Where physically is the software design team in relation to you?
   - How do you communicate with the software design team? (e.g. meetings, e-mail, paper memos, informal discussions, electronic project room, etc.)?
   - What is the content of those meetings (e.g. discuss help content or structure, exchange models, exchange impressions, formal reporting)?
   - Is your involvement in a project punctual or are you present during the whole development phase?

4. Prospective questions:

   - How would you feel about a tool such as Isolde — would it be easy for you to work in this way, would it facilitate your task, would it integrate smoothly with your current work practices, etc.?
   - How would you feel about an electronic tool which would allow you to communicate with the designers and give them feedback on the design?

As for the observations, they were of two types:

- observations of what is physically done during the documentation activity: meetings, manipulation of models, exploring a prototype, etc.; and

- observations of the cognitive aspect of the task, using the think aloud protocol.

The second phase was a verification of the usability of DIANE+, the task notation which was selected by the design team as a potential notation for Isolde's user interface. The usability and readability of DIANE+ for technical writers was tested experimentally and proved to be adequate. A full description of the experimental methodology can be found in (Ozkan et al., in this volume). The results of the testing are briefly described in Section 6.3.

Open a document on your hard disk or a network

1. Click **Open**.

2. In the **Look in** box, click the drive, folder, or Internet location that contains the document.

3. In the folder list, double-click folders until you open the folder that contains the document you want.
   If you can't find the document in the folder list, you can search for it
   How?

4. Double-click the document you want to open

Figure 6: Example of procedural help from MS Word97. Part of the screen for "How to open a file from the hard disk".

The third and last phase was prototyping. Drawing on the knowledge acquired from the first two phases, a first prototype of Isolde's user interface was designed. It was tested using a 'white board' prototype: both the static and the dynamic aspects of the user interface were tested, with the system functionality being simulated by a design team member. Six technical writers were given several tasks to perform with the prototype. Each session was video recorded and the technical writers' difficulties and misunderstandings were recorded and analysed. The results were fed into the next round of design. The prototype underwent two iterations of prototyping before the final system specifications were issued. The user interface of the current Isolde system still remains to be evaluated in terms of usability.

5 Help Generated by Isolde: Technical and End-user Motivations

5.1 Types of On-Line Help

In order to scope the type of help that could be addressed in Isolde and to understand its place in the process of writing on-line help, our group of technical writers and computer scientists have collaboratively developed a model of this process. This model is expressed in DIANE+ (Tarby & Barthet, 1995), our chosen task modelling notation (briefly described in Section 6.2). The high-level tasks which constitute the process of writing on-line help are presented in Figure 8[†]. For the purposes of this paper, let it suffice to say that writing documentation involves writing three types of help:

- **Procedural help** basically enumerates the series of steps required to perform a user goal, as well as other relevant goals that can be achieved from a given state. Procedural help can be seen as an answer to the question "How to?". Figure 6 shows an example of procedural help from MS Word97.

- **Conceptual help** defines the concepts used in an application. Conceptual help can be seen as an answer to the question "What?". Figure 7 shows an example, the concept of a readability score from MS Word97.

[†]For a complete presentation of the model, refer to (Paris et al., 1997).

Readability scores

When Word finishes checking spelling and grammar, it can display information about the reading level of the document, including the following readability scores. Each readability score bases its rating on the average number of syllables per word and words per sentence.

Flesch Reading Ease score

Rates text on a 100-point scale; the higher the score, the easier it is to understand the document. For most standard documents, aim for a score of approximately 60 to 70.

Flesch–Kincaid Grade Level score

Rates text on a US grade-school level. For example, a score of 8.0 means that an eighth grader can understand the document. For most standard documents, aim for a score of approximately 7.0 to 8.0.

Figure 7: Example of conceptual help from MS Word97. "What is a readability score?"

- **Business** help relates to how the software application is embedded in its context of use. Business help can be seen as answering questions beyond the direct scope of the software. An example is information about the business rules which govern the use of the application.

5.2   The Focus of Isolde: Procedural Help

Isolde addresses procedural help. The reasons for this choice are described below. The first of these is technical, the others are user-driven:

- **Feasible automation**: Because procedural help describes system functions in terms of user actions on the user interface, it is highly structured and heavily based on the programmed behaviour of the system. It thus seems realistic to automate its production. This is supported by other work, such as (Paris et al., 1991; Paris & Vander Linden, 1996a; Thimbleby & Addison, 1996).

- **Significance within the help system**: The significance of procedural type of help is supported by the current trend towards 'minimalist instructions' (Carroll, 1990). The philosophy of minimalist instructions is based on the argument that learning software is more effective if software documentation is short, simple and directed towards real work activities. In the light of this philosophy, procedural help, which is task-oriented and therefore focussed on the user's activities, is a central type of help.

- **Routine and time-consuming task**: From the technical writers' perspective, writing procedural help is the easiest and the most routine part of the technical writing process: it requires that the technical writers explore the possible commands for performing a task and document them. This is done in a systematic fashion and does not require much personal input or creativity. By contrast, the other types of help (business and conceptual) call upon a good, global understanding of the software application and of its place in its context of use. Writing these two types of help allows technical writers to exploit more fully their knowledge, judgement and experience. However, the writing of procedural help can often be the most time-consuming activity of the technical writing process.

In summary, as well as being technically feasible, the automatic production of procedural help addressed by Isolde is important and relevant. Its manual production is both time-consuming and relatively uninteresting. Isolde offers the opportunity for technical writers to spend more time on the equally important and more mentally challenging aspects of document production, namely the conceptual and business types of help information.

6   Task Models as Input to Isolde: Technical and End-user Motivations

6.1   Why a Task Modelling Notation?

In order to produce help texts, Isolde's text generator requires as input some description of the functionalities of a system. It is this description which will be input by the technical writers using Isolde. As indicated previously, the notation selected for this description is a task modelling notation called DIANE+ (Barthet, 1988; Tarby & Barthet, 1995). The reasons motivating the choice of a task modelling notation are both technical and user-driven:

- Task models come from the HCI community and are designed to reflect the user's perspective on a system. Since on-line help is also based on this perspective, they are very appropriate for our purpose.

- Our own work in other projects has shown that task models can be used to guide technical writers with the design of on-line help (Balbo & Lindley, 1997).

- The HCI community advocates the use of task models at the beginning of the software development life cycle, for the analysis of user requirements. The use of task models by technical writers would promote their early involvement in the software life cycle, as well as facilitate their communication with the members of the software development team. This is in line with the trends in technical writing (see Section 2).

Given that we wanted to use a task modelling notation, we had to ensure that the one which we chose could meet both technical requirements and user-driven ones. On the one hand, it had to allow the representation of all the information contained in on-line help; On the other hand, it had to be easily manipulated by technical writers. Sections 6.2 & 6.3 respectively examine those two sets of requirements and how they are met by DIANE+.

6.2   The Expressiveness of DIANE+

Tasks in DIANE+ are represented graphically and decomposed hierarchically. Figure 8 is a high-level description of the technical writing process and is used here to illustrate the DIANE+ notation. The features of DIANE+ appearing in this figure are the following[‡]:

- Tasks requiring both user and system input (called interactive tasks). Interactive tasks are represented by a rounded box.

- Mandatory and optional tasks. Mandatory tasks are represented by boxes with solid lines and optional tasks are represented by boxes with dashed lines.

- Task decomposition into sub-tasks. Task decomposition is represented as an horizontal link between a mother task and its subtasks, which are enclosed in a box. Then a task is decomposable but its decomposition is not shown in a diagram, a double line indicates that the decomposition is given elsewhere.

- Sequencing of tasks. Task sequences are expressed using downwards arrows between tasks.

- Parallelism of tasks. Tasks with no link between them are parallel tasks.

DIANE+ can also represent system tasks (called automatic tasks), boolean relationships between tasks, and the task cardinality, that is the minimum and the maximum number of times the task can be executed.

We believe that this information is necessary and sufficient to provide end-user procedural help. This is supported by previous work (Paris et al., 1991; Paris & Vander Linden, 1996a; Pemberton, 1996; Paris & Vander Linden, 1996b; Pemberton et al., 1996) as well as our own corpus analysis of on-line help and documentation (Hartley & Paris, in preparation). Lastly, another reason for using DIANE+ is its current use in other work to generate automatically a subset of on-line help (Tarby, 1994).

6.3 The Readability and Usability of DIANE+

From the users' perspective, DIANE+ is prominent in Isolde's user interface. In order to ensure that it could be easily manipulated by technical writers, we tested its readability and usability with a group of six technical writers. The readability of DIANE+ was tested by presenting this group with a DIANE+ diagram and asking them to generate the corresponding set of instructions. The usability of DIANE+ was tested by presenting this group with a running software application and asking them to produce the corresponding DIANE+ diagram. These experiments are described in detail in (Ozkan et al., in this volume). The results indicate that DIANE+ is certainly readable (an average of 88% of the tasks which were represented were successfully interpreted) and largely usable (an average of 65% of the tasks which the writers tried to represent was successfully modelled using DIANE+). It is thus realistic to think that technical writers could work with task models given appropriate training.

[‡]Features not illustrated in Figure 8 are omitted. The reader is referred to (Barthet, 1988; Tarby & Barthet, 1995) for a full description of the notation.

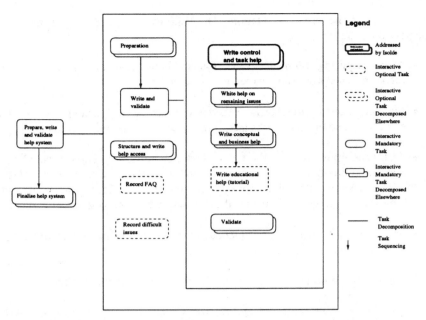

Figure 8: The high-level tasks in the process of writing on-line help, using the DIANE+ notation.

Among the results of these experiments[§], we wish to relate here two important observations, which have had an important impact on the design of Isolde's functionality. Results showed that:

- it is easier to understand DIANE+ diagrams than to generate them; and

- it is easier to generate DIANE+ diagrams from examples than from scratch.

These two observations thus confirm the desirability of coupling Isolde to a CASE tool to provide the technical writers with an initial task model of the system to be documented, rather than requiring them to produce the task model from scratch.

7   The Scope of Use for Isolde

As explained previously, Isolde provides support in specifying the content of a document, that is, it provides support early in the process of documentation writing. It also provides support at several levels: at the selection of the appropriate pieces of information to include in a specific text, and at the levels of text organization, wording and formatting. Although Isolde is potentially a powerful tool for producing documentation, it does require the creation or modification of a task model, which may be a difficult and time-consuming activity, and it may require post-editing of the

---

[§]An analysis of those features of DIANE+ which pose problems was undertaken in order to address them in Isolde's user interface. However, this is not the focus of this paper.

generated text. It is therefore important to understand its scope of use and limitations. We outline here the conditions under which such a tool could be useful:

- Software projects in which a user requirements analysis is done at the onset of the project: in these cases, task models would already be available (at least partially), thus reducing the burden on the technical writers.

- Software projects developed through the use of CASE tools and for which the software designers defined a series of scenarios: this would allow Isolde to automatically obtain some partial representation of the task models, once again reducing the burden on the technical writers.

- General purpose software rather than software aimed for a specific context. As Isolde does not address business help, its use for software which relies heavily on specific business practices is limited.

- Software projects in which previously defined task models can be re-used extensively. This may be either within the software development life cycle (i.e. from one prototype to another, or from one release version to the next), or outside it (i.e. different applications share some tasks, as in an integrated environment). A task model can be re-used when it does not change drastically but instead is partially modified (some elements are revised) or expanded. Under these conditions, having a formal model of the task is useful both to represent the updates formally and also to produce the updated documentation in a consistent manner.

- Companies requiring documentation written according to a set of strict style guidelines that can be embodied in rules. In such cases, using a tool like Isolde would strictly enforce the rules and the consistency of the documentation.

- Software projects for which the specification of the system's functionality is comprehensive enough to produce automatically a major part of the procedural help.

- Software projects which need a range of documentation material, all containing similar information but presented differently.

- Software projects for which the documentation needs to be presented both in hardcopy and soft copy.

- Software projects requiring the documentation be appropriate for a wide range of users, or using different styles, if these styles can be embodied in rules.

- Software projects requiring documentation in several languages.

Finally, it is also important to recognize that the impact of Isolde will also depend on its linguistic resources and the quality of the text produced, as this will impact on the amount of post-editing required.

8 Discussion

There are a number of other implications of using an authoring tool like Isolde. Firstly, although our experiments show that technical writers are able both to understand and to manipulate task models, they will require some training before they can become proficient at it. Given that writers already learn to use computational tools and, in some cases, to read diagrams such as flow-charts, we believe this training would not be a major issue.

Secondly, this authoring tool would be one more tool to be used by technical writers. It would thus be important to ensure that it is well integrated with the other tools, providing writers with a whole documentation environment (Hartley & Paris, 1996). While we are not yet addressing this issue, it has been the objective of two European research projects (DOCSTEP, 1995; INDOCREN, 1995).

Thirdly, the use of a tool like Isolde, whose core information is a task model, might engender better communication among all members of a software development team, i.e. software analysts and programmers, HCI specialists and technical writers, as it would provide them with a common representation and language. This hypothesis has in fact been shown valid in an earlier project, in which one of the uses of task models was to serve as a communication tool among members of the team (Balbo & Lindley, 1997). In addition, the presentation of an explicit task model or its construction could help the technical writers with their understanding of the system to be documented.

Finally, and most importantly perhaps, with an authoring tool like Isolde, documentation becomes more integrated into the software development life cycle, as it is coupled with software development tools. With Isolde, writing the procedural documentation involves the development and use of task models. As a result, technical writers can be involved at an early stage in the software development life cycle and contribute to the design of the application. Indeed, as end-users' advocates, they could provide crucial feedback to the software development team to develop a better product. Their role then would be a more central one. In this scenario, the production of a software product and its documentation would be a team effort in information design, involving for example the functions of an analyst, a programmer, an HCI specialist, a technical writer and a graphic artist. This 'new' role for the technical writer and this novel approach of writing documentation are in fact in alignment with the new trends in the work place as well as advances in technology (Hartley & Paris, 1996).

In conclusion, the Trend Report Committee of STC International (Parkinson, 1996) pointed out the need for new models for the process of technical writing, ones in which there is much more information re-use, where the models are streamlined and value is added by technical writers. All these are supported by an authoring tool like Isolde: information re-use is a key point; the process is streamlined by integrating the documentation writing process into the software development life cycle and moving it to an earlier phase in that cycle; technical writers can provide crucial input into the software design. The report also points out the skills required of technical writers in the future. These include:

- analytical skills for task analysis, needs assessment and audience analysis; and

- information architecture skills.

These would cover the skills required to use a tool like Isolde. While Isolde is a research project, and as such, is still prospective and experimental, this may be an exciting technological development. It is our intention to study the real impact of a tool like Isolde in terms of the re-organization of the work flow, the re-distribution of roles in an integrated, multidisciplinary software design environment and its effect on cognitive workload.

Acknowledgements

This work is being supported by a grant to CSIRO from the Office of Naval Research (ONR), in the Programme for User Centered Direct Interaction Systems Grant N00014096-1-0465. We gratefully acknowledge the participation of all members of the Isolde team: Sandrine Balbo, Shijian Lu, Keith Vander Linden, Valery Anciaux, Christophe Plier, and Necola Hoare. We are also thankful for the support of Pamela Manning at IBM Global Services Australia and the members of the Information Design and Development Group: Jane Childs, Colin Dawson and Carolyn Knight. Finally, we thank Anthony Hartley, for the fruitful discussions about the changing role of technical communicators and the new trends in the work place as well as for his comments on earlier drafts this paper, and the anonymous reviewers for their comments on the submitted draft.

References

Balbo, S. & Lindley, C. (1997), Adaptation of a Task Analysis Methodology to the Design of a Decision Support System, *in* S. Howard, J. Hammond & G. K. Lindgaard (eds.), *Human–Computer Interaction — INTERACT'97: Proceedings of the Fifth IFIP Conference on Human–Computer Interaction*, Chapman & Hall, pp.355–61.

Barthet, M.-F. (1988), *Logiciels interactifs et ergonomie, modèles et méthodes de conception*, Dunod Informatique Ed., Paris.

Carroll, J. M. (1990), *The Nurnberg Funnel: Designing Minimalist Instruction for Practical Computer Skill*, MIT Press.

DOCSTEP (1995), "DOCSTEP: Product Documentation Creation and Management using STEP", MLAP-94 Project 63557; Project Summary published in the Project Fact Sheet Directory, Second Language Engineering Convention, London, November 1995.

Hartley, A. F. & Paris, C. L. (1996), Automatic Text Generation for Software Development and Use, *in* H. Somers (ed.), *Terminology, LSP and Translation: Studies in language engineering in honour of Juan C. Sager*, John Benjamins., Amsterdam/Philadelphia, pp.221–42.

Hartley, A. F. & Paris, C. L. (in preparation), Towards an Empirical Characterization of the Discourse of Software Instructions, Technical Report, ITRI, University of Brighton. See also Hartley, A.F. & Paris, C.L. (1995) Drafter: French Corpus Analysis and Grammatical Description, WP14/WP15 Deliverable, Drafter Project IED4/1/5827, EPSRC grant number J19221.

INDOCREN (1995), "INDOCREN: Intelligent Document Creation Environment", MLAP-94 Project 63033; Project Summary published in the Project Fact Sheet Directory, Second Language Engineering Convention, London, November 1995.

Lu, S., Paris, C. & Vander Linden, K. (1998), Towards Automatic Construction of Task Models from Object-Oriented Diagrams, *in* S. Chatty & P. Dewan (eds.), *Proceedings of the IFIP Working Conference on Engineering for Human-Computer Interaction 1998*, Kluwer.

Paris, C. & Vander Linden, K. (1996a), "DRAFTER: An Interactive Support Tool for Writing Multilingual Instructions", *IEEE Computer* **29**(7), 49–56. Special Issue on Interactive Natural Language Processing.

Paris, C. & Vander Linden, K. (1996b), An Overview of On-Line Documentation and CASE Tools, Technical Report ITRI-95-16, ITRI.

Paris, C., Ozkan, N. & Balbo, S. (1997), "Novel Uses of Task Models: Two Case Studies", NATO/ONR Workshop on Cognitive Task Analysis, Washington DC, November.

Paris, C., Vander Linden, K. & Lu, S. (in press), A Practical Approach to the Generation of On-line Help, *in Proceedings of Natural Language Processing and Industrial Applications*.

Paris, C., Vander Linden, K., Fischer, M., Hartley, A., Pemberton, L., Power, R. & Scott, D. (1991), A Support Tool for Writing Multilingual Instructions, *in Proceedings of the Fourteenth International Joint Conference on Artificial Intelligence (IJCAI'95)*, Morgan Kaufmann, pp.1398–404. Also available as ITRI report ITRI-95-11.

Parkinson, A. (1996), "Highlights — 43rd STC Annual Conference", url:http://stc.org/region7/cwc/www/coastlines/conference.html.

Pemberton, L. (1996), Requirements from Technical Writing, Technical Report, ITRI.

Pemberton, L., Gorman, L., Hartley, A. & Power, R. (1996), Computer Support for Producing Software Documentation: Some Possible Futures, *in* M. Sharples & T. van der Geest (eds.), *The New Writing Environment: Writers at Work in a World of Technology*, Springer-Verlag, pp.59–72. Also available as the ITRI Technical Report number ITRI-94-10.

Rational Software Corporation (1997), *Unified Modelling Language, Notation Guide, v.1.0.*

Sayers, K. (1996), "A Look at Trends of the Profession", url: http://stc.org/region7/cwc/www/coastlines/trends.html.

Tarby, J.-C. (1994), The Automatic Management of Human–Computer Dialogue and Contextual Help, *in* B. Blumenthal, J. Jornostaev & C. Unger (eds.), *Proceedings of EWHCI'94: The East–West International Conference on Human–Computer Interaction*, Springer-Verlag.

Tarby, J.-c. & Barthet, M.-F. (1995), The DIANE+ Method, *in* J. Vanderdonckt (ed.), *Proceedings of the 2nd International Workshop on Computer-Aided Design of User Interfaces*, Presses Universtaires de Namur, pp.95–119.

Thimbleby, H. & Addison, M. (1996), "Intelligent Adaptive Assistance and Its Automatic Generation", *Interacting with Computers* **8**(1), 51–68.

Visual Interfaces

Representation Matters: The Effect of 3D Objects and a Spatial Metaphor in a Graphical User Interface

Wendy Ark, D Christopher Dryer, Ted Selker & Shumin Zhai

IBM Almaden Research Center, 650 Harry Road, San Jose, CA 95120, USA.

Tel: *+1 408 927 1912*

EMail: *{wsark, dryer, selker, zhai}@almaden.ibm.com*

As computer graphical user interfaces (GUIs) are loaded with increasingly greater numbers of objects, researchers in HCI are forced to look for the next step in constructing user interface. In this paper, we examine the effects of employing more 'natural' representations in GUIs. In particular, we experimentally assess the impact of object form (2D iconic vs. 3D realistic) and layout (regular vs. ecological) have on target acquisition time. Results indicate that both form and layout significantly affect performance; subjects located targets more quickly when using interfaces with 3D objects and ecological layouts than they do with 2D objects and regular layouts. An interface with an ecological layout, realistic objects, or both may be an improvement over traditional interfaces.

Keywords: 3D interface, graphical interface, spatial metaphor, icon, ecological layout, regular layout.

1 Introduction

What is the next step in the evolution of the graphical user interface? One possible step is the move from predominantly iconographic, 2D representations to more realistic, 3D representations. The implicit assumption underlying the increasingly popular attempts to develop compelling 3D environments is that users will find it natural and intuitive to navigate virtual spaces (Reeves & Nass, 1996).

The specific advantages, however, of realistic 3D GUIs are unclear. Moreover, it is also unclear which attributes about a realistic 3D GUI would make it more useful. Note that we do not use the term 3D in the sense of a virtual reality display, but we are talking about a normal, everyday desktop computer screen. Clearly, a 3D GUI should not merely be the traditional GUI enhanced with the depth dimension. In the natural 3D world, there are many different factors that 'codify' objects. Many of these factors are visually salient attributes that have us to recall objects. If we transfer these factors onto the interface, the interface is more likely to involve a non-regular placement, differing external shapes, enhanced colour, landmarks, connectivity, and potential semantic associations than is a 2D GUI. In general, 3D GUIs may provide more dimensions to distinguish and identify objects. The more redundant dimensions available to the user, the greater the chance of the user being able to choose an attribute to which to relate. As a result, users might find and recall the objects more quickly in such a 3D GUI than in a 2D GUI. In this study, we examine whether and which factors of a 3D GUI affect how quickly users can acquire target objects in a laboratory experiment.

2   Theoretical Background

2.1   *Placement*

There is an large amount of research stating the importance of location having a direct effect on the recall of information. Mandler et al. (1977) and Hasher & Zacks (1979) indicated that people automatically encode spatial information. When recalling where a file is located, people want to expend the least amount of cognitive efforts as possible so they can focus on the tasks they want to accomplish once they retrieve the file. If forming spatial associations is a pre-attentive process, designers should use this to their advantage when creating interfaces.

Kaptelinin (1993) showed that experienced users do not need to read menu item names while working with the system. As novices, they primarily rely on the names of the menu items to accomplish simple tasks. After the learning period is over, the location of the item names seems to be encoded and the selection actions start to become automatic. Moyes (1995) and Kaptelinin (1993) both agree that users focus on local attributes initially (e.g. icon form) but over time switch to identifying attributes which are global, or require the user to consider the interface as a whole (e.g. the icon's relative position among all other icons on the screen).

Hess et al. (1984) also noticed the effect spatial placement has on recalling information. In their study, they showed that spatial separation of items on a screen aids memory for a task requiring that the items being monitored be available separately in memory.

Individual object locations are not the only concern in this study. More importantly, this experiment will focus on the effects of object layout, or how individual objects are placed in relation to each other. In particular, we are interested in the effect an office-like metaphor will have on user performance. Ecology, the study of the habits of living organisms and their interactions with their environment, can be applied to the office metaphor. Ecological considerations are important as people draw important cues from their immediate environment and develop knowledge of the space over time and through the experience of interacting with it. Benyon & Höök (1997) refer to many various types of spatial metaphors for which designers use to represent vast amounts of information.

van der Veer (1989) suggests that adequate metaphors can facilitate the learning process. In turn, the learning process facilitates automatic actions and; hence, the cognitive load has been reduced. The idea of organizing information by spatial metaphors have been advocated by many (Bolt, 1978; Cole, 1982; Malone, 1983). Although such an idea seems to be in agreement with the general theories, such as method of loci, some laboratory studies have not supported spatial interface advantage. In particular, Jones & Dumais (1986) had subjects read news articles and file them based on a certain condition (name only, location only, name and location, or name and location separate). The subjects were then given a passage from one of the ten articles (per condition) and were given three guesses as to where they had previously filed it. The performance of the subjects led to the conclusion that the location only condition did not have any significant advantage over the name only condition. The results also indicated that in the location and name combined condition, the article was more easily found. These results demonstrate that more semantic information provided for the objects (name plus location) will aid in the retrieval process. It is important to recognize that there are two cognitive processes involved in this study: the recognition task and the recall task. Jones & Dumais take measurements from both of these tasks which requires the subjects to not only recall the spatial location of where the article has been filed, but also from which article the passage was contained. However, in this experiment, we focus only on the recall task.

Objects in an ecological layout not only have their individual locations, but also form connectivities that make physical sense. For example, in the office metaphor, a monitor is on the desk and the hardware is attached to the monitor and the keyboard and the mouse are attached to the hardware. We propose these connections will facilitate target acquisition.

2.2 External Shapes

Another characteristic of realistic objects is the differing external shapes. The 2D iconic representation has a 'framing' effect. The rectangular box surrounding each of the icons gives them a uniformity which does not help to differentiate the icons. Having different shapes is a desirable quality when a distinguishable feature is needed quickly.

2.3 Colour

Colour is another important feature of a realistic object. There is a large amount of research about when colour is helpful and when it is distracting and which colours are better to use than others. A particularly interesting review of comparing the usefulness of colour against various achromatic codes (size, shape, etc.) gave evidence that a colour-coded target was more accurately identified than the codes monochrome, size, shape, and brightness (Christ, 1975). However, if colour is not the target, then colour becomes a shortcoming and a distraction on the screen.

2.4   Landmarks

Landmarks are inherent in any situation. The difficulty in developing a good test to study landmarks is the fact that landmarks are a personal discrepancy. We expect that unchanging features on a GUI such as a table or a bookshelf in the form of what can be called visual landmarks will improve a person's memory for where things are located. Groupings of any kind, be they caused by a rim or window around objects or by spatial separation could be considered landmarks and might improve performance.

Landmarks may serve as external memory aids and we know that external aids to memory are often employed when other, intervening, cognitive events might interfere with the processes of learning and recall, when accuracy is at a premium, and when memory load is to be minimized to facilitate the allocation of attention to other activities. It seems that, in general, individuals prefer to use external aids to memory rather than rely upon their own internal memory. This suggests that the effort occasioned by the use of external memory props is less demanding than the cognitive effort required to encode and retrieve information from internal memory sources (Findlay et al., 1988). However, Jones & Dumais (1986) did not find any significant data relating to landmarks.

2.5   Semantics

Rothkopf et al. (1982) improved upon the claims of Mandler et al. (1977) and Hasher & Zacks (1979) by stating that location provides especially privileged cues and that not all content-correlated background stimuli are equipotent cues in associative learning. Lansdale et al. (1987) also stresses the important factor in the utility of a cue enricher which seems to be the ability of the subject to form a meaningful association with the relevant document. The more semantic information provided related to the object, the more cues a person has from which to extract a useful meaning. In 1996, Lansdale et al. (1996) discovered that even though there were many differences between cues subjects used when describing characteristics of an object they recently saw, they were consistent with cues which they had previously used.

3   Method

To examine the relative contributions of different factors distinguishing two styles of interfaces (3D, ecological and realistic vs. 2D, regular and iconic), we operationalized two independent factors. The first, 'layout', varies from regular object placement with no landmarks and no connectivity ('regular') to non-regular placement with landmarks and connectivity ('ecological'). The second, 'object representation', varied from similar shape, simple colour, and shallow potential semantic associations ('2D iconic') to different shapes, complex colour, and rich potential semantic associations ('3D realistic').

In order to test the hypotheses described above, the interfaces developed were the best representations for a traditional 2D iconic interface and a new 3D realistic interface. The interfaces were based on the interfaces used in a pilot study (Selker et al., 1997).

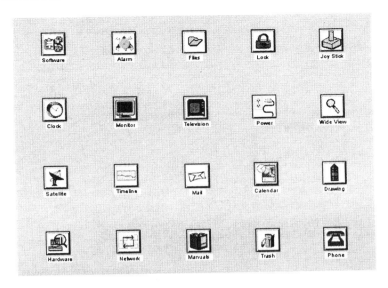

Figure 1: 2D regular.

3.1 Design

There were many issues which had to be taken into account when designing the interfaces used in the experiments. We attempted to make each of the two styles of interface resemble the most typical features of their own class. The 2D iconic representations were in 8-bit colour and were surrounded by identical rectangular boxes.

The regular layout consisted of rows and columns typical to a user interface. The ecological layout portrayed an office metaphor in which the computer monitor and hard drive were located in the centre of a desk with a bookshelf on the desk to the left of the computer. The ecological layout contained the 3D interface attributes previously described. The desk and the bookshelf served as visual landmarks while the computer monitor had connectivity with the hard drive which were also connected to the keyboard.

In order to account for the size discrepancies between the 2D and the 3D icons and also the difference in the placement of the icons, Fitts' (1954) law was used to calculate a regression slope to normalize our results.

The four experimental conditions were: 2D with regular placement (Figure 1), 2D with spatial placement (Figure 2), 3D with regular placement (Figure 3) and 3D with spatial placement (Figure 4).

The test was written in Macromedia's Lingo and displayed using Director on an IBM desktop computer with a standard mouse.

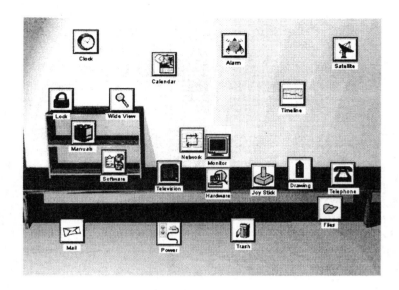

Figure 2: 2D ecological.

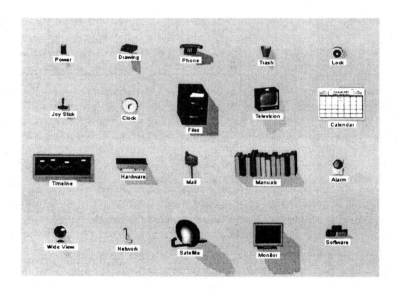

Figure 3: 3D regular.

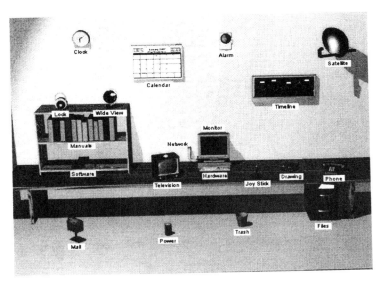

Figure 4: 3D ecological.

3.2 Subjects

Twelve subjects were used. Nine were male and three were female. All used computers on a daily basis.

3.3 Procedure

The experiment used a balanced, within subjects design. The subjects were asked to find an object as quickly as they could and then select the object by using the mouse to click on the object or the object's label. The subjects were assigned by a Latin square equally into one of four groups where each group consisted of a different order of the four conditions.

There were ten objects to locate per condition and three trials within each condition with the sequences varying per trial. The subject repeated the same test on a separate day (within a twelve to thirty-six hour time period).

The test consisted of an instruction screen which was followed by the name of an object to find. When the subject was ready, they were asked to click on a 'GO' button so as to position the cursor in the centre of the screen. Once the subject clicked on the object or its label, the test continued to the next object. The refreshed scene forces the subject to get reoriented to the interface and does not give way to any advantages for neighbouring objects. Errors were recorded along with the time it took to find each object.

Also, after the second day of the test, the subjects were given pictures of the four conditions and were asked to rate the pictures on a scale of 1 to 5 (1 easy; 5 hard) based on how hard it was to find the object they were looking for in each condition.

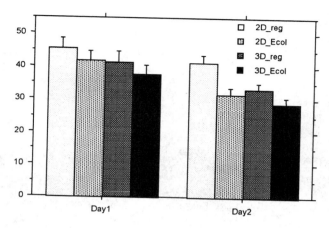

Figure 5: Mean completion time (seconds) with standard error bars.

4 Results

We were interested in whether object representation (2D iconic or 3D realistic) and layout (regular or ecological) would impact the time it takes users to search for and click on objects. To start, we examined whether other differences among the four conditions might impact our participants' performance. In particular, the distance to a target (amplitude) and the size of a target (width) can determine the time it takes to acquire a target, as described by the well-studied Fitts' Law. A transformation of this ratio (amplitude/width), called Fitts' index of difficulty, has been shown to be linearly related to target acquisition time.

To rule out the possibility that any differences in performance between experimental conditions were due to differences in Fitts' index of difficulty, we examined the mean of the indices across the ten targets for the four conditions. These means were 1.68, 1.62, 1.69, and 1.63 for the 2D Regular, 2D Ecological, 3D Regular, and 3D Ecological respectively. A descriptive analysis provides a measure of the comparability of the groups. A 2 (2D vs. 3D) by 2 (regular vs. ecological) analysis of variance on the indices revealed no significant main effects or interactions. The statistic for the explained variance is $F(3,36) = 0.040$, p non-significant. These analyses suggest that the four conditions are not meaningfully different in their average Fitts' indices of difficulty.

We also examined the variance of the ten targets across the four conditions. The standard deviations were .41, .54, .78, .48 for the 2D Regular, 2D Ecological, 3D Regular, and 3D Ecological, respectively. A test of heteroscedasticity revealed no significant differences in the distribution of indices across conditions; Levene statistic $(3,36) = 1.91$, p non-significant. This analysis suggests that the four conditions also share similar variance in the Fitts' indices of difficulty.

To examine the impact of object representation and layout of subject performance, we looked at the mean completion times over the three trials and

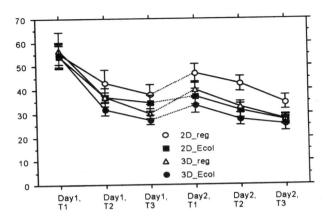

Figure 6: Learning and retention over separate days (completion time in seconds).

---

two days by each of the four conditions. These results are illustrated below in Figure 5.

We analysed these data with a 2 (object representation) × 2 (layout) × 2 (day) × 3 (trial) repeated measures analysis of variance with the order of the experimental conditions as a four level between subjects factor. The Fitts' indices of difficulty were added as a covariate to control for any possible variance accounted for by target size and distance.

This analysis revealed a main effects for object representation and layout; for object representation $F(1,8) = 41.02$, $p < 0.001$, and for layout $F(1,8) = 45.60$, $p < 0.001$. Subjects found objects more quickly when they had 3D realistic representation than they did when they had 2D iconic representations. Similarly, subjects found objects more quickly when the objects had an ecological layout than they did when they had a regular layout. The interaction between object representation and layout was not significant; these factors aided performance independently. Subjects performed best when objects had a 3D realistic representation in an ecological layout and worst when objects had a 2D iconic representation in a regular layout.

Other effects were also significant in this analysis. The main effect for trial was significant; $F(2,16) = 234.96$, $p < 0.001$. Subjects tended to perform better on latter trials than they did on earlier trials. The main effect for day was also significant; $F(1,8) = 11.99$, $p < 0.01$. Subjects tended to perform better on the second day than they did on the first. The interaction between day and trial was significant as well; $F(2,16) = 58.69$, $p < 0.001$. In general, the effect of trial was greater on the first day than it was on the second day. The day factor also interacted significantly with the layout factor; $F(1,8) = 18.94$, $p < 0.01$. Generally speaking, the day factor had a bigger impact for the ecological layout conditions than it did for the regular layout conditions (Figure 6).

Finally, the interaction among order, trial, object representation, and layout was significant; $F(6,16) = 9.05$, $p < 0.001$. We can offer no meaningful interpretation of this result. All other main effects and interactions, including the effect of the covariate, were not significant.

5 Discussion

The results indicate a user will search for and acquire objects more quickly if they are presented with a 3D ecological, realistic interface rather than a 2D regular, iconic interface. Specifically, an ecological layout (as opposed to a regular layout) and a 3D realistic representation of objects positively affected experimental task performance.

Interestingly, the effects of ecological layout and 3D realistic representation are additive. That is, the subjects' performance was better when either the ecological layout or the 3D realistic representation was present, and they performed best when both were present. Moreover, the interaction between these factors was not significant; their contributions to the interface are independent.

These results have important implications for interface design. For tasks which require identifying and learning the place of objects, 3D realistic interfaces along with ecological layouts will provide increased performance time. Interface designers can draw upon either factor. In applications where a regular layout is necessary, 3D realistic objects may still be useful. In applications where 2D icons are necessary, an ecological layout could still improve the usability of the interface. In other words, these results suggest that an interface need not be completely 3D to be an improvement over the traditional 2D iconic interface.

We would like to explore the other issues in the 2D vs. 3D comparison. We hope independently investigating shape, colour, landmarks and connectivity will provide insights into factors that can support the 3D realistic ecological representation as a favoured desktop interface.

Acknowledgements

We thank Ian May for his help in designing the initial interfaces.

References

Benyon, D. & Höök, K. (1997), Navigation in Information Spaces: Supporting the Individual, *in* S. Howard, J. Hammond & G. K. Lindgaard (eds.), *Human–Computer Interaction — INTERACT'97: Proceedings of the Fifth IFIP Conference on Human–Computer Interaction*, Chapman & Hall, pp.39–45.

Bolt, R. (1978), Spatial Data Management System, Final Technical Report, US Defense Advanced Research Projects Agency.

Christ, R. (1975), "Review and Analysis of Color Coding Research for Visual Displays", *Human Factors* **17**(6), 542–570.

Cole, I. (1982), Human Aspects of Office Filing: Implications for the Electronic Office, *in Proceedings of the Human Factors Society — 26th Annual Meeting*, Human Factors and Ergonomics Society, pp.59–63.

Findlay, J., Davies, S., Kentridge, R., Lambert, A. & Kelly, J. (1988), Optimum Display Arrangements for Presenting Visual Reminders, *in* D. M. Jones & R. Winder (eds.), *People and Computers IV (Proceedings of HCI'88)*, Cambridge University Press, pp.453–64.

Fitts, P. (1954), "The Information Capacity of the Human Motor System in Controlling Amplitude of Movement", *British Journal of Educational Psychology* **47**(6), 381–91.

Hasher, L. & Zacks, R. (1979), "Automatic and Effortful Processes in Memory", *Journal of Experimental Psychology: General* **108**, 356–88.

Hess, S., Detweiler, M. & Ellis, R. (1984), The Effects of Display Layout on Monitoring and Updating System States, *in Proceedings of the Human Factors and Ergonomics Society 38th Annual Meeting*, pp.1336–40.

Jones, W. & Dumais, S. (1986), "The Spatial Metaphor for User Interfaces: Experimental Tests of Reference by Location versus Name", *ACM Transactions on Office Information Systems* **4**(1), 42–63.

Kaptelinin, V. (1993), Item Recognition in Menu Selection: The Effect of Practice, *in* S. Ashlund, K. Mullet, A. Henderson, E. Hollnagel & T. White (eds.), *Proceedings of INTERCHI'93*, ACM Press, pp.183–84.

Lansdale, M., Scrivener, S. & Woodcock, A. (1996), "Developing Practice with Theory in HCI: Applying Models of Spatial Cognition for the Design of Pictorial Databases", *International Journal of Human–Computer Studies* **44**, 777–99.

Lansdale, M., Simpson, M. & Stroud, T. (1987), Comparing Words and Icons as Cue Enrichers in an Information Retrieval Task, *in* H.-J. Bullinger & B. Shackel (eds.), *Proceedings of INTERACT'87 — Second IFIP Conference on Human–Computer Interaction*, Elsevier Science, pp.911–6.

Malone, T. (1983), "How Do People Organize Their Desks? Implications for the Design of Office Information Systems", *ACM Transactions on Office Information Systems* **1**(1), 99–112.

Mandler, J., Seegmiller, D. & Day, J. (1977), "On the Coding of Spatial Information", *Memory and Cognition* **5**, 10–6.

Moyes, J. (1995), Putting Icons in Context: The Influence of Contextual Information on the Usability of Icons, PhD thesis, University of Glasgow.

Reeves, B. & Nass, C. (1996), *The Media Equation*, Cambridge University Press.

Rothkopf, E., Fisher, D. & Billington, M. (1982), "Effects on Spatial Context During Acquisition on the Recall of Attrivutive Information", *Journal of Experimental Psychology: Learning, Memory, and Cognition* **8**(2), 126–38.

Selker, T., May, I. & Zhai, S. (1997), "Representation Matters: Spatial Interface can Facilitate Target Acquisition", Presentation at the 6th International World Wide Web Conference.

van der Veer, G. (1989), "Individual Differences and the User Interface", *Ergonomics* **32**(11), 1431–49.

The Effect of Layout on Dispatch Planning and Decision Making

William B L Wong, David O'Hare[†] & Philip J Sallis

Department of Information Science, University of Otago, Dunedin, New Zealand.

EMail: *william.wong@stonebow.otago.ac.nz,*
PSallis@commerce.otago.ac.nz

[†] *Department of Psychology, University of Otago, Dunedin, New Zealand.*

EMail: *OHare@psy.otago.ac.nz*

This paper reports on an experiment conducted to determine whether the manner in which information is portrayed affects ambulance planning and dispatch decision making performance. Based the outcomes of a series of cognitive task analysis, deficiencies in an actual ambulance status display used for dispatch management was identified. The display was then re-designed by applying cognitive engineering principles to achieve task-to-display compatibility. The new display was then evaluated and it was found to improve dispatch decision making performance by 40%.

Keywords: display design, proximity-compatibility principle, mental model, ambulance dispatch management.

1 Introduction

This study investigates the hypothesis that the manner in which information is presented will affect human performance, and that this effect will be noticed particularly in more demanding dynamic decision making tasks. If information is portrayed in a manner that supports or conforms with the way the information is used in the decision making processes, one can expect the human decision maker to be more efficient at recognizing and integrating the necessary information cues to make a situation assessment. This is the approach taken by a significant body of research in developing display designs for the control of physical systems like chemical processing, and electricity generation (Bennett & Flach, 1992; Vicente & Rasmussen, 1992; Rasmussen et al., 1994; Wickens & Carswell, 1995; Woods, 1995). Such systems may be referred to as causal systems, i.e. the outcomes of changes in system states are predictable based on laws of nature. Whereas human activity systems like command and control and emergency dispatch management are intentional systems, i.e. the outcome of changes to the system are influenced by human intention, and are not predictable by laws of nature (Rasmussen, 1986). This research examines principles of display design in the context of intentional systems, and in particular ambulance dispatch management, an area of importance particularly following the deaths of patients who died waiting for ambulances in the UK (Page et al., 1993; Benyon-Davies, 1995) and in Australia (Evans, 1995; Yaman, 1995).

Appropriately sizing up the situation is a vital step in the naturalistic decision making process. With an appropriate assessment of the situation, the decision maker can devise, revise and adapt courses of action to suit the situation (Klein, 1989; Klein, 1990). The question is therefore, how do we portray the required information so that the display characteristics match the decision task characteristics of an emergency ambulance dispatcher? To address that question, it is necessary to understand:

1. The nature of such dynamic decision making environments.

2. The decision making process of the people operating in these environments.

3. The demands that such an environment places on the people who operate in these environments.

A cognitive task analysis (CTA) technique called the Critical Decision Method, or CDM (Klein et al., 1989; Klein et al., 1997) was used to identify the goals and decision strategies dispatchers in the Southern Regional Communications Centre of the New Zealand St John's Ambulance Service in Dunedin (Wong et al., 1997). The results of these studies have been reported elsewhere (Wong et al., 1995; Wong et al., 1996b).

These decision strategies and goal states, together with cognitive engineering principles like the Proximity-Compatibility Principle (Wickens, 1992; Wickens & Carswell, 1995) formed the basis on which a new ambulance dispatch screen was designed to co-locate information used in comparison-type decisions. The new design was intended to make the manner in which the information is portrayed more compatible with the manner in which the dispatcher assessed information cues during planning.

An experiment was then conducted to determine if the new screen improved human decision making performance in resource planning. 37 participants were allocated to two groups, one with the *old* screen and one with the *new* screen, in a randomized block design. There were three blocks of trials and each block comprised four trials. Each trial represented one of four levels of dispatch difficulty. The results indicate that the cognitively re-engineered layout improved user performance by 40%

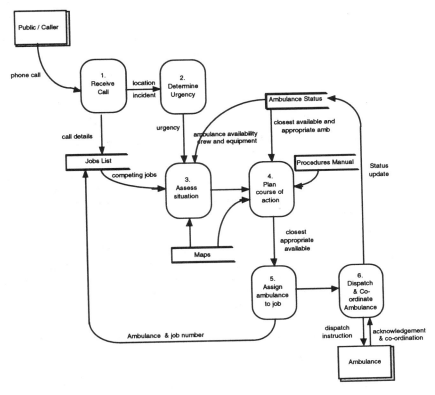

Figure 1: Task model of ambulance dispatch management.

in the more difficult conditions. This paper describes how the screen was re-designed, the procedures and outcomes of this experiment.

2   The Screen Re-design Process

This section describes the process through which the new screen was re-engineered. A task model, a data model, the goal states and decision strategies were first identified through the CTA. Deficiencies in the old screen were then identified by evaluating it against the understanding of how dispatch decisions are made. The screen was then re-designed using cognitive engineering principles.

2.1   Task Model of the Dispatch Management Process

Data flow diagrams (Gane & Sarson, 1979) were used to document the processes as a task model as shown in Figure 1. Data flow diagrams have been found to be useful representations for task models (Sutcliffe, 1997). The task comprises six processes which are described next.

2.1.1   Process 1 and 2: Receive Call and Determine Urgency

In the Dunedin-based Southern Regional Communications Centre (RCC), calls for help are received by a dispatch-trained ambulance officer. She records the call on the computer and interacts with the caller to determine the nature and the location of the incident. The dispatcher then assesses the urgency by considering the number of people injured, and the type of injuries sustained.

2.1.2   Process 3 and 4: Assess Situation and Plan Course of Action

The next step assesses the situation in terms of the current and immediate future jobs, compare the demands in the locality of the incident, and then identify the closest available resources to the incident. A plan of action is then developed. In simple cases, the plan can simply mean assigning an available ambulance to an incident in its immediate locality. Serious incidents take more time to plan and place greater cognitive demands on the operator. For instance, the dispatcher needs to see the 'bigger picture' in order to bring in ambulances to the area while not depleting neighbouring areas of ambulances, a process known as 'balancing the region'. In major disasters, dispatchers will also refer to a set of major incident standard operating procedures that specify agencies and officials to contact, the number of ambulances to dispatch, and the setting up of on-scene command posts and triage facilities. These procedures are usually kept beside the dispatcher's console and are largely textual supported with flowcharts. Another document that is often referred to is a topological and road map of the area to verify the location.

2.1.3   Process 5: Assign Ambulance to Job

Once the plan has been finalized, usually within a minute or two of receipt of the call, the dispatcher then assigns the ambulances to the job. This step involves indicating on the computer which ambulance has been tasked with the job. This act also automatically pages the ambulances. Finally, the assigned ambulance crews are contacted via radio or land lines and are given further instructions. The entire process takes no more than three minutes.

2.1.4   Process 6: Dispatch and Coordinate Ambulance

Following the dispatch of the ambulance, the dispatchers are often in close radio communications with the ambulance as it travels to the incident. Information like the time an ambulance has arrived on scene, and when it is available, is standard communication between the ambulance and the dispatcher. Other coordinating information include clarifying the location of the incident, updates on traffic conditions, or coordination with rescue helicopters. The task is completed when the dispatched ambulance has transported the casualty to the hospital or that the ambulance is back on station.

2.2   Data Model

Using data modelling techniques (Finkelstein, 1989), an entity-relationship model was derived from the original dispatch management screen (Figure 2). The data model was used to ensure that the re-designed screen contained the same data when testing whether layout had an impact on performance. ERMIA, Entity-Relationship Modelling for Information Artefacts (Green, 1991), a more involved modelling

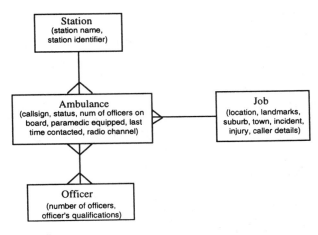

Figure 2: Entity-relationship diagram of dispatch management screen.

technique that accounted for display variations, was not considered necessary to ensure data consistency between different screen designs.

2.3   Goal States

The task analysis also investigated how individual dispatchers made dispatch decisions, what information cues were attended to, and what the purposes and rationales were for the decisions (Wong et al., 1996b).   The goal states are summarized below:

1. Notification of emergencies.

2. Maintain situation awareness.

3. Planning resource to task compatibility.

4. Speedy response to emergency calls.

5. Maintain history of developments for legal purposes.

2.4   Deficiencies in Old Interface Design

The ambulances in the Otago area are stationed in the towns indicated on the map of the Southern Region. The Southland (lower) half of the Southern Region was not included in the study. Together the Otago and Southland regions cover a total land area of about 54,000 square kilometres (Wong, 1997).

The original ambulance dispatch screen shows the ambulances and their availability status grouped by stations (Figure 3). The display is laid out in three columns. The name and unique identification number of an ambulance station is in light blue capitals against a blue band. The rows following each band are the ambulances deployed at that station. Each ambulance is represented by a callsign field, a status field, a radio channel field, a time last contacted field, and a job assigned

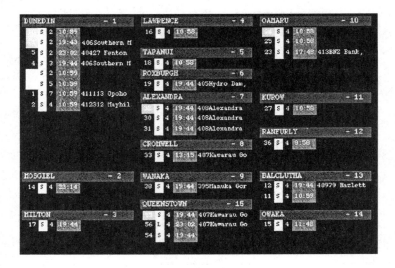

Figure 3: Screen shot of the original dispatch management screen.

field. The callsign field has been colour-coded to convey additional information like the equipment carried, the number of ambulance officers on board, and whether at least one of the crew is a paramedic.

The Dunedin station is presented on the top left, or in the western half, of the display although Dunedin is geographically in the east of the region. This is probably because it is the main station and it has the highest level of ambulance activity in the Region, following presentation guidelines that suggest placing more frequently used information at the place where English-speaking users would 'naturally' start reading. The Mosgiel and Milton stations are similarly displaced, though not for the same reason. It appears more because they are closely situated to Dunedin. Some of the remaining ambulance stations, e.g. Balclutha and Owaka, are mapped to their spatial locations in the region, while others, Kurow and Ranfurly, are not. While the Dunedin and Oamaru stations are geographically situated next to each other (Oamaru is the next closest station north of Dunedin), the display portrays the two stations as oriented east to west with the Lawrence station in between.

This represents an incompatibility between the information that is displayed and what is actually on the ground, and will lead to two difficulties:

1. It will be more effortful to learn the layout and spatial relationships between stations as demonstrated by the above cognitive task analysis comment.

2. That without a clear mental model of the spatial relationships between the stations, it is more effortful to make allocations between neighbouring stations, an identified decision strategy in dispatch management.

This observation is supported by a comment from a dispatcher during the study:

"The greatest difficult for me initially was where the hell are these [stations]. Where was Alexandra? There didn't seem to *be any logical sequence* ... they weren't alphabetically ordered, they were to a certain extent geographically ordered, and I couldn't understand, I couldn't find [the stations] initially." (Interview #7, line 576–9)

It is proposed that correction of these inconsistencies will lead to better performance.   The next section describes how cognitive engineering principles of design were applied to do this.

2.5   *Rationale for Re-design*

Having identified deficiencies in the old presentation, this section discusses the design rationale for the re-engineered presentation. The following two principles were used in the re-design of the screen:

1. the Proximity–Compatibility Principle; and

2. the Externalization Principle.

The Proximity–Compatibility Principle, or PCP, states that "... to the extent that information sources must be integrated, there will be benefit to presenting those dimensions in an integrated format" (Wickens & Carswell, 1995). Thus, if the information required by a task needs to be mentally integrated or combined (task proximity), then the information should be displayed in a physically integrated or combined manner as well (display proximity). This is the notion of display compatibility.   The PCP provides guidance on how information from different sources should be organized and placed on a display (Wickens & Carswell, 1995) so that its form is compatible with the level of integration in the task that the display is intended to support (Wickens et al., 1985).

The PCP also provides a basis for assessing task proximity.   Integration tasks require mental combination of information from different sources in order to successfully perform the task. Acts of mental combination of information sources include information condensation, computational and Boolean integration.   In dispatch tasks, information from different sources like neighbouring stations, jobs lists, location of incident, are compared simultaneously through Boolean operations to determine the appropriate ambulance to dispatch.   Such tasks are said to be of medium/high task proximity.

Displays can be designed to support such high proximity tasks by physically integrating or displaying close together different information sources that are used together. Such displays are said to possess high display proximity. Display proximity may be attained by controlling the display variables of spatial proximity, i.e. closeness between indicators; connections between or enclosures around indicators; source similarity, e.g. same colour, or orientation; code homogeneity, e.g. all quantitative information is displayed in analogue using the same display property; and object integration, where the arrangement of information sources so that they appears part of a single object. (Wickens, 1993; Wickens & Carswell, 1995). Although these guidelines are intended for designing object displays (Bennett et al., 1993; Wickens

& Carswell, 1995), the guidelines of spatial proximity, connections, source similarity, code homogeneity, are just as useful in guiding conventional display design.

While all the necessary data is available in the old screen, comparing the status of ambulances between neighbouring stations is effortful. If an incident occurs between neighbouring Dunedin and Oamaru, the dispatch must refer to extreme ends of the display to read the necessary information. This does not facilitate the comparison of status. The PCP suggests that better design is needed to bring information that is used together closer together on the display.

The literature has suggested that if the display representation is consistent with our mental model of a system, we can expect improvements in user performance when interacting with such a system (Staggers, 1993). Mental models are dynamic mental representations of the world that enables people to generate descriptions and explanations about systems and to make predictions about future events (Johnson-Laird, 1989; Preece et al., 1994). Mental models may be:

1. structural models that describe how a system works by defining the components and the relationship between those components; or

2. functional models that describe how to use a system by providing a task-action mapping between what is to be achieved and the functionality provided by the model.

Rasmussen & Vicente (1989) explains that the improvements can be achieved by externalizing or making perceptible, the user's mental model of the process being controlled so that abstract properties or relationships of the process is represented explicitly — the Externalization Principle. Thus, if a dispatcher has an understanding of the dispatch management system, one aspect of that understanding would be a structural model of the system. In designing the new screen, the user's structural model of the physical disposition of the stations was externalized. The procedure prescribed in (Carroll et al., 1988) was then used to translate the mental model into a design by identifying the task and goals that the display must support, and then designing the appearance.

2.5.1   The Task and Goals

In the earlier CTA, it was identified that when incidents occurred between two stations, the dispatchers decided on the ambulances to send by comparing the availability of the ambulances in these neighbouring stations. In terms of the PCP, the old display did not exhibit a display compatibility supportive of this medium/high proximity task.

2.5.2   The Appearance

To re-engineer the dispatch management screen, the locations of the stations were studied and four axes were identified to represent the relationship between the stations (Figure 4). The red axis represents the coastal stations, the yellow axis links the region's northern stations, the green axis links the western stations, and the blue axis forms a crescent linking the stations in the central part of the region.

The stations were re-aligned on the displays according to the identified axes (Figure 5). The visual cues of the colour-coded axes provide near-automatic perceptual processing of the relationship between stations (Wickens & Carswell,

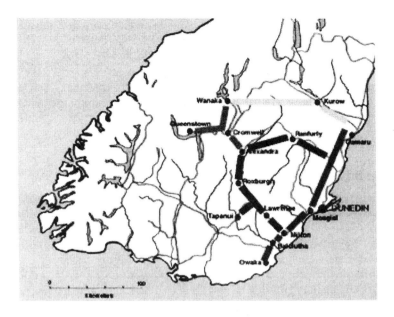

Figure 4: Externalizing the mental model: Map of area with axes.

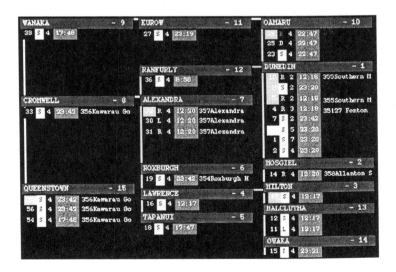

Figure 5: Re-engineered ambulance status screen with axes drawn in.

1995). There is no guessing or inferring to determine which station is related to which other stations. The dispatcher does not need to maintain in his working memory the stations that are closest to the incident in assessing the nearest available ambulance to send. The relationships have been made perceptible, and the information is directly compatible with the integration task she must perform.

The resulting screen satisfied the need to facilitate comparisons when identifying the nearest available ambulance, and for mapping the geographical disposition of the ambulance stations with their abstraction on the display. By using the same E-R model we ensured that there was no difference in the data contained within the new screen and the old screen. The only difference is the layout.

3   The Experiment

37 students participated in the experiment as part of class requirements for a course in Human Factors in Information Systems. The experiment was conducted in a mixed 2×4 factorial design, comparing two screen designs against four levels of task difficulty. There were three trials for each level of difficulty, giving a total of 12 trials. The trials were administered randomly. Participants were asked to respond to a simulated emergency call they would receive through a pop-up window on the system, by keying in the job details into the system, and then assigning an ambulance to the job.

All participants were novices to dispatch management. Novices were chosen over professional dispatchers in order to reduce the confounding effect experts (who were familiar with the old display) might have on the comparison between old and new designs.

3.1   *Displays and Apparatus*

Two test systems were built in SuperCard (Allegiant Technologies Inc., 1996). The 'Old' system was designed with the original screen layout of the ambulance status display, and the 'New' system was the re-designed layout with identical functionality. The system tracked the times all events occurred.

3.2   *Task*

Each task was designed to represent one of four levels of dispatch difficulty:

Category 1 'Simple Problem'(least difficult): The incident occurs within a town where the ambulance is stationed. No other ambulances are available. There is no choice in such problems.

Category 2 'Simple Trade-off Problem': The incident originates from within a station's area of responsibility. There is more than one ambulance available in that town. Some trade-off is required.

Category 3 'Boundary Problem': Such incidents occur mid-way between two stations. Either station could supply the ambulance.

Category 4 'Balancing Problem' (most difficult): A major incident usually requires dispatching ambulances from several stations to the scene. This depletes the

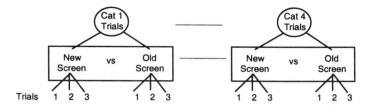

Figure 6: Approach to data analysis.

ambulance coverage of the immediate areas. Reinforcements are brought in from neighbouring stations and as a result 'gaps' in coverage occur, requiring dispatcher to bring in additional ambulances from stations further afield to 'balance' the ambulance coverage.

3.3 Procedure

Each group of participants was first briefed on the dispatch management process. Participants using the new screen were told how the stations mapped across from the geography to the display representation. Participants were shown how the four coloured axes related the stations to one another and how this mapping was used in the new screen. Although participants using the old screen were also told where the stations were on the map and on the screen, no explanation of the four coloured axes was given to them since there was no mapping in the old screen. Participants were subsequently asked to list or sketch where the stations are in relation to one another. Finally, the participants were briefed on how to assign ambulances. Following the briefing, participants were given a 10-minute practice run of four incidents. They were then administered the actual test scenarios.

3.4 Results

The data from the trials were extracted from the data collection module of the test systems, and then analysed in SPSS, a statistical analysis software package. This section reports on the outcome of that analysis.

3.4.1 Differences in Response Performance between Old and New

A separate MANOVA (multivariate analysis of variance) procedure (Hair et al., 1987; Tabachnick & Fidell, 1996) was performed on each of the four categories of task difficulty. The design of the analysis is illustrated in Figure 6.

Tabachnick & Fidell (1996, p.375) explains that while:

> "... ANOVA tests whether mean differences among groups on a single dependent variable are likely to have occurred by chance ... MANOVA tests whether the mean differences among groups on a combination of dependent variables are likely to have occurred by chance."

The procedure was performed to determine if the combination of mean differences in time to dispatch the ambulances from the set of trials between users of

Task Category	Wilks F statistic	F critical	d.f.	Significance
Category 1 Simple Problem	0.55753	2.92	3, 33	There is no difference.
Category 2 Simple Trade-Off	0.85051	2.96	3, 27	There is no difference.
Category 3 Boundary Problem	13.39780	2.92	3, 33	There appears to be a difference.
Category 4 Balancing Problem	15.34894	2.92	3, 33	There appears to be a difference.

Table 1: Summary of MANOVA results Old Screen vs. New Screen ($p = 0.05$).

Task Category	Old Response Time (seconds)	New Response Time (seconds)	Old – New (seconds)	Improved by:
Category 1	8.14	8.79	-0.65	-8%
Category 2	16.13	12.65	3.48	22%
Category 3	16.73	10.01	6.72	40%
Category 4	15.84	9.40	6.44	41%

Table 2: Mean response times Old Screen vs. New Screen.

the old screen and users of the new screen could have arisen by chance. A summary of the four MANOVA tests are presented in Table 1.

The results indicate that the observed mean differences in time to dispatch ambulances between participants using the new screen and old screen did not occur by chance. Participants using the 'New' screen were faster at dispatching ambulances than participants using the 'Old' screen only in the more difficult tasks (Category 3 and 4 levels of difficulty).

3.4.2   Size of the Improvement in Performance

We next determined how large the difference was in performance between the Old screen and New screen (Table 2). The mean performance difference increases as the task becomes more difficult. In Category 1 tasks (least difficult), the Old screen performed better than the New screen by about 0.65 seconds. The improvement of the New screen design ranged from an average of 3.5 seconds for Category 2 tasks to 6.7 seconds and 6.4 seconds respectively for the more difficult Category 3 and Category 4 tasks. This is a 40% improvement in the New screen users' performance under both more difficult task conditions.

3.4.3   Errors in Dispatch

The number of errors made in dispatching ambulances was also measured. An error was any response that violated the nearest available rule for ambulance dispatch. Overall, participants using the 'Old' screen made more errors for the number of ambulances they had dispatched, resulting in an error rate of 7.8% compared with a 5.1% error rate for participants using the 'New' screen (Table 3).

Category	Old Err	Total	%	New Err	Total	%
Category 1	5	44	11.4%	5	46	10.9%
Category 2	7	53	13.2%	1	44	2.3%
Category 3	6	80	7.5%	7	102	6.9%
Category 4	3	110	2.7%	6	178	3.4%
Total	21	287	7.3%	19	370	5.1%

Table 3: Number of Errors in 'Old' and 'New'.

	'Old' Screen	'New' Screen
Spatial sketch	78%	88%
Accuracy (places correct)	56%	76%

Table 4: Number of spatially oriented and correctly labelled model representations.

3.4.4 Mental Models of Disposition of Ambulance Stations

Before starting the trials, each participant was asked to sketch or write down how they thought the ambulance stations related to one another. These sketches were later examined for accuracy and representation, i.e. whether the stations were correctly named, and whether it was a spatial map type of representation or a text/table based representation. These illustrations suggest how participants stored the structural model of the ambulance dispatch system in their memories (Table 4).

The results shows that despite the lack of the explanation about the coloured axes in the old screen group, both groups tended to perceive a spatial metaphor as their representation of the structural model of the relationship between ambulance stations. However, only half of the Old screen group (56%) were able to correctly name the ambulance stations, compared with three quarters (76%) of the New screen group who were able to correctly name the stations.

4 Discussion

The results raises some questions which are addressed next.

Why were the improvements observed only under the more difficult conditions?

The results indicates that the manner in which information is portrayed does affect human performance, and this is particularly noticeable when the human is operating under more demanding conditions, like the more difficult Category 3 and 4 tasks. Under routine or simple task conditions, the results showed little difference in performance. (The 0.65 second decrease in performance in the Category 1 task is very small and will be interpreted as no difference.) Under these circumstances, the participant only has to deal with one ambulance and no choices are necessary. However, under the more difficult task conditions, the participant has to consider information about several stations (different information sources), juggling the comparative availabilities in working memory while evaluating which ambulances are the nearest available (integration and Boolean operations). She also has to consider the effect on coverage of deploying a particular ambulance to a job (planning). All these cognitive activities take up limited working memory and attentional resources, and hence performance can be expected to degrade if these resources are heavily taxed. Similarly, performance can be expected to improve if the demands of the task is off-loaded from these resources to the more efficient perceptual resources (Wickens, 1992; Wickens, 1993). The re-designed display performs this task of sharing the load, leading to the improvements we observed in the Category 3 and 4 task conditions.

Can the performance improvement be due to improvements in visual search performance?

Designing to optimize visual search is about designing a display that would enhance the speed with which a human user can locate a target piece of information. Tullis had developed a model to predict visual search performance and a set of design guidelines for laying out a display to take advantage of human perceptual capabilities, thereby optimizing visual search performance (Tullis, 1990). These guidelines inform on size of groups, the number of groups, separation between groups, layout complexity, and global and local display density. One shortcoming of that work is that the semantics of the information is not considered in the model. As long as the information, even a series of 'XXX' is organized according to the guidelines, the model will predict that visual search performance will improve. If the improvement was due to improved visual search, then dispatch performance should have improved across all conditions and not just in the more difficult cases. Therefore we cannot infer that the performance improvement is due to improvements to visual search performance.

How did knowing about the task and goals through the CTA help improve performance?

The cognitive task analysis (CTA) determined that complex dispatch decisions require comparisons between neighbouring stations to identify the nearest appropriate and available ambulances. Although the more proficient dispatchers tended to refer to their mental situation picture of where each ambulance is and is doing, most usually referred to the display and visually compared the availability of ambulances between stations, assessing which ambulances were the nearest. While all the necessary information for the decision is available, such a comparison is not explicitly supported by the way the information in the 'Old' screen is laid out, as explained earlier. The CTA helped by providing the understanding of the decision goals, and how the decisions were made. This lead to the insights that guided the development of the information co-location design of the new dispatch screen which explicitly facilitated the visual comparison strategy.

Why did participants using the 'Old' screen commit more errors?

The higher number of dispatch errors made by participants working with the 'Old' display can be attributed to their lack of knowledge of the region as demonstrated by the lower accuracy score on their mental model assessment. Many simply did not know where a station was in relation to their mental model, and hence which station was closest to an incident. The mis-match between the expectations of where to look for an ambulance station generated by their mental model, and what was actually presented on the display could have also lead to confusion as to which station was actually closer. Furthermore, the 'Old' design lacked a clear basis for the arrangement, leading to further confusion.

What process goals did the 'New' display support?

Several goals were identified in the CTAs. These include maintaining situation awareness; planning and in particular identifying available resources and matching them to incidents, minimizing disruption to on-going activities, planning ahead and filling in gaps; notification of emergencies; ensuring a speedy response; and keeping track of events. The design objective of the 'New' screen was primarily to support planning and resource deployment type of decisions. To complete a dispatch task, the operator had to be able to quickly identify the nearest available resource, often comparing ambulance availabilities between neighbouring stations, and be able to appreciate the consequences of that assignment in terms of gaps in coverage. The results suggest that the new screen design had been successful in supporting these decision tasks.

So, what do the results tell us?

The results indicate that by combining an understanding of the task and goals which we derived through a cognitive task analysis, with cognitive engineering principles of design, displays can be engineered so that they improve decision making performance in complex environments. Guidance from the cognitive engineering principles help ensure that the design of the displayed information is compatible with the nature of the task. This is known as display compatibility. The mental model defines the structure of the information required for the decision task, while knowledge of how the decisions are made guides the manner by which the information should be organized and portrayed.

5   Conclusion

Building on the understanding and insight we gained from an earlier CTA about how the decisions in complex and dynamic environment of ambulance dispatch are made, we evaluated an existing display design and re-engineered it based on cognitive engineering principles. The 'New' screen was then subject to an experiment and it was observed that the use of cognitive engineering design principles in designing interfaces could significantly improve performance in ambulance planning and dispatch decision making. This paper concludes with the following lessons learnt:

1. The manner in which information is laid out on a display is important to human decision making performance. Screens should be designed to facilitate information extraction and not merely make the required data available on the display. There should be compatibility between display and the task.

2. Cognitive engineering design principles can and should be applied to user interface design.

3. Cognitive task analysis is extremely useful in gaining the necessary understanding and subsequent insight with which to design display compatible interfaces.

4. While some have attempted it (Wong et al., 1996a), there is still no formal method to translate the understanding and insights gained from the CTA into screen designs.

The study started out to determine if layout could influence planning and dispatch decision making performance. While further work is being planned to verify this, the outcome of this study suggests that layout does affect decision making performance.

References

Allegiant Technologies Inc. (1996), *SuperCard version 3*.

Bennett, K. B. & Flach, J. M. (1992), "Graphical Displays: Implication for Divided Attention, Focused Attention and Problem Solving", *Human Factors* **34**(5), 513–33.

Bennett, K. B., Toms, M. L. & Woods, D. D. (1993), "Emergent Features and Graphical Elements: Designing More Effective Configural Displays", *Human Factors* **35**(1), 71–97.

Benyon-Davies, P. (1995), "Information Systems 'Failure': The Case of the London Ambulance Service's Computer Aided Despatch Project", *European Journal of Information Systems* **4**(3), 171–84.

Carroll, J. M., Mack, R. L. & Kellog, W. A. (1988), Interface Metaphors and User Interface Design, *in* M. Helander (ed.), *Handbook of Human–Computer Interaction*, North-Holland, pp.67–86.

Evans, M. (1995), "Inside Melbourne's Emergency Response CAD System", *GIS User: The Australian Geographic Information Systems Applications Journal* **14**, 28–30.

Finkelstein, C. (1989), *An Introduction to Information Engineering: From Strategic Planning to Information Systems*, Addison–Wesley.

Gane, C. & Sarson, T. (1979), *Structured Systems Analysis: Tools and Techniques*, second edition, Prentice–Hall.

Green, T. R. G. (1991), Describing Information Artifacts with Cognitive Dimensions and Structure Maps, *in* D. Diaper & N. Hammond (eds.), *People and Computers VI: Usability Now! (Proceedings of HCI'91)*, Cambridge University Press, pp.297–316.

Hair, Jr., J., Anderson, R. & Tatham, R. (1987), *Multivariate Data Analysis*, MacMillan.

Johnson-Laird, P. N. (1989), Mental Models, *in* M. Posner (ed.), *Foundations of Cognitive Science*, Lawrence Erlbaum Associates, pp.469–99.

Klein, G. A. (1989), Recognition-Primed Decisions, *in* W. Rouse (ed.), *Advances in Man–Machine Systems Research*, JAI Press, pp.47–92.

Klein, G. A. (1990), Recognitional Decision Making: Information Requirements, *in* A. P. Sage (ed.), *Concise Encyclopedia of Information Processing in Systems and Organizations*, Pergamon Press, pp.414–8.

Klein, G. A., Calderwood, R. & Macgregor, D. (1989), "Critical Decision Method for Eliciting Knowledge", *IEEE Transactions in Systems, Man and Cybernetics* **19**(3), 462–72.

Klein, G., Kaempf, G., Wolf, S., Thordsen, M. & Miller, T. (1997), "Applying Decision Requirements to User-centered Design", *International Journal of Human–Computer Interaction* **46**(1), 1–15.

Page, D., Williams, P. & Boyd, D. (1993), *Report of the Inquiry into the London Ambulance Service*, South West Thames Regional Health Authority.

Preece, J., Rogers, Y., Sharpe, H., Benyon, D., Holland, S. & Carey, T. (1994), *Human–Computer Interaction*, Addison–Wesley.

Rasmussen, J. (1986), *Information Processing and Human–Machine Interaction: An Approach to Cognitive Engineering*, North-Holland.

Rasmussen, J. & Vicente, K. (1989), "Coping with Human Errors through System Design: Implications for Ecological Interface Design", *International Journal of Man–Machine Studies* **31**(5), 517–34.

Rasmussen, J., Pejtersen, A. M. & Goodstein, L. P. (1994), *Cognitive Systems Engineering*, John Wiley & Sons.

Staggers, N. (1993), "Mental Models: Concepts for Human–Computer Interaction Research", *International Journal of Man–Machine Studies* **38**(4), 587–605.

Sutcliffe, A. (1997), "Task-related Information Analysis", *International Journal of Human–Computer Studies* **47**(2), 223–57.

Tabachnick, B. G. & Fidell, L. S. (1996), *Using Multivariate Statistics*, third edition, Harper Collins.

Tullis, T. S. (1990), The Formatting of Alphanumeric Displays: A Review and Analysis, *in* M. Venturino (ed.), *Selected Readings in Human Factors*, The Human Factor Society, pp.371–96.

Vicente, K. J. & Rasmussen, J. (1992), "Ecological Interface Design: Theoretical Foundations", *IEEE Transactions in Systems, Man and Cybernetics* **22**(4), 589–605.

Wickens, C. D. (1992), *Engineering Psychology and Human Performance*, Harper Collins.

Wickens, C. D. (1993), "Cognitive Factors in Display Design", *Journal of the Washington Academy of Sciences* **83**(4), 179–201.

Wickens, C. D. & Carswell, C. M. (1995), "The Proximity Compatibility Principle: Its Psychological Foundation and Relevance to Display Design", *Human Factors* **37**(3), 473–9.

Wickens, C., Kramer, A., Barnett, B., Carswell, M., Fracker, L., Goettl, B. & Harwood, K. (1985), Display/Cognitive Interface: The Effect of Information Integration Requirements on Display Formatting for C3 Displays, Technical Report EPL-85-3/AFHRL-RADC-85-1, Engineering-Psychology Research Laboratory, Aviation Research Laboratory, University of Illinois at Urbana-Champaign, Champaign, IL, USA.

Wong, W. B. L. (1997), Profiles of Selected Ambulance Dispatch Centres in New Zealand, Australia, and Singapore, Technical Report 97-2, Department of Information Science, University of Otago, Dunedin, New Zealand.

Wong, W. B. L., O'Hare, D. & Sallis, P. J. (1996a), Experimental Transformation of a Cognitive Schema into a Display Structure, *in* K. Lim, L. Herman, Y. Leung & J. Moyes (eds.), *Proceedings of the First Asia Pacific Conference on Computer–Human Interaction APCHI'96, Human Factors of IT: Enhancing Productivity and Quality of Life*, Information Technology Institute, pp.455–68.

Wong, W. B. L., O'Hare, D. & Sallis, P. J. (1996b), A Goal-oriented Approach for Designing Decision Support Displays in Dynamic Environments, *in* J. Grundy & M. Apperley (eds.), *Proceedings of OzCHI'96 The Sixth Australian Conference on Computer–Human Interaction*, IEEE Computer Society Press, pp.78–85.

Wong, W. B. L., Sallis, P. J. & O'Hare, D. (1995), Information Portrayal for Decision Support in Dynamic Intentional Process Environments, *in* H. Hasan & C. Nicastri (eds.), *HCI: A Light into the Future — Proceedings of OzCHI'95*, Ergonomics Society of Australia (Downer, ACT), pp.43–8.

Wong, W. B. L., Sallis, P. J. & O'Hare, D. (1997), Eliciting Information Portrayal Requirements: Experiences with the Critical Decision Method, *in* H. Thimbleby, B. O'Conaill & P. Thomas (eds.), *People and Computers XII (Proceedings of HCI'97)*, Springer-Verlag, pp.397–415.

Woods, D. D. (1995), Toward a Theoretical Base for Representation Design in the Computer Medium: Ecological Perception and Aiding Human Cognition, *in* J. Flach, P. Hancock, J. Caird & K. Vicente (eds.), *Global Perspectives on the Ecology of Human–Machine Systems*, Vol. 1, Lawrence Erlbaum Associates, pp.157–88.

Yaman, E. (1995), "Woman's Death Prompts Ambulance Service Changes", *The Australian* p.4. 14th June 1995.

Distortion-oriented Workspace Awareness in DOME

Philip Weir & Andy Cockburn

Department of Computer Science, University of Canterbury, Christchurch, New Zealand.

Tel: *+64 3 364 2987 x7768*
Fax: *+64 3 364 2569*
EMail: *weirp@acm.org, andy@cosc.canterbury.ac.nz*
URL: *http://www.cosc.canterbury.ac.nz/~andy/*

Distortion-oriented visualization techniques such as magnification-lenses, zooming functions and fish-eye views are useful in a wide range of single-user computing systems. They assist visualization of large information spaces by easing the transition between high-levels of detail in a local area of interest and the global context of the information space.

In real-time groupware environments, distortion-oriented visualizations offer additional benefits. By providing one distorted region for each user of a groupware workspace, users can maintain an awareness of the location and activities of their colleagues while simultaneously having a focused area of detail for their own work.

We describe the design and evaluation of DOME, a fully-functional distortion-oriented multi-user editor. Unexpected usability problems and potential solutions are discussed.

Keywords: groupware, collaborative workspace awareness, distortion-oriented visualization.

1 Introduction

One of the major problems confronting groupware designers is how to provide collaborative awareness between simultaneous users of a groupware information space. The simplest solution is to enforce strict-WYSIWIS (what you see is what I see) on the displays of all users. Strict-WYSIWIS has beneficial properties: it is relatively easy to implement and it is conceptually easy to use in that all users have precisely the same view. Unfortunately, it is a highly constraining style of collaboration in which the users are forced to work as a tightly coupled unit. This constraint fails to allow natural and dynamic styles of collaboration in which colleagues fluidly move between periods of close collaboration and periods of more autonomous work.

Experiments with relaxing the strict-WYSIWIS paradigm in order to increase the extent of user support have resulted in difficulties with users and designers misunderstanding the implications of the relaxations (Stefik et al., 1987). These difficulties, which manifest themselves in collaboration breakdowns such as mistaken deictic reference*, are largely due to the reduced mutual *workspace awareness* of colleagues' location and activities.

The problem, then, is to simultaneously provide users with a representation of their local area of work while simultaneously providing the 'right amount' of awareness of colleagues' location and activities. Current approaches to facilitating workspace awareness in synchronous groupware environments focus on 'awareness widgets' such as radar views (Gutwin et al., 1996) which provide renderings of the entire workspace within a miniature overview window; each user's location of activity is superimposed on the overview. The problems with miniaturization techniques are that they have limited scalability (a miniature rendering of an extremely large data-space will yield too little detail to be useful) and they provide a static level of detail, consequently limiting each user's ability to customize their awareness of colleagues.

In this paper we propose that distortion-oriented visualization techniques are a natural candidate for providing collaborative workspace awareness. In single-user systems distortion-oriented visualizations such as magnification-lenses, zooming functions and fish-eye views ease the transition between high-levels of detail in a local area of interest and the global context of the information space. In groupware environments they can be used to provide tailorable levels of awareness of co-workers while maintaining a focus on the local region of personal work. Our previous work (Greenberg et al., 1996a; Greenberg et al., 1996b; Greenberg et al., 1996c) has demonstrated several styles of distortion-oriented workspace awareness using point systems, but it has fallen short of evaluation. In this paper we describe a fully functional and robust distortion-oriented multi-user editor called DOME, and we discuss the results of its evaluation.

Section 2 describes DOME and its workspace awareness capabilities. Section 3 details the evaluation of DOME, and Section 4 discusses the findings of the evaluation and identifies directions for further work. Related work is reviewed in Section 5, and Section 6 concludes the paper.

---

*Deictic reference is a combination of reference by gesture and verbal reference such as 'this one' (Stefik et al., 1987).

2 DOME: A Distortion-Oriented Multi-user Editor

We built DOME to experiment with the effectiveness of distortion-oriented techniques for supporting workspace awareness in synchronous groupware environments. We strongly believe that in order to test the effectiveness of distortion-oriented workspace awareness it is necessary to provide a full-functionality and robust environment that offers a polished and professional interface. Point systems with minimalist interfaces such as those constructed as part of our earlier research (see Section 1) are inadequate for realistic usability evaluation[†].

DOME's main window is shown in Figure 1. As a single-user system it is a functionally rich text-editing environment that supports extensive facilities for annotation (described in Section 5) as well as the normal text-editing facilities such as undo, cut, copy and paste. LATEX documents and Tcl/Tk programs are automatically parsed and their structure can be displayed in a graphical tree that allows shortcuts to portions of the document or program.

In the sections below we describe several of DOME's groupware support facilities: the workspace awareness provided by its fisheye views, its support for tightly coupled collaboration, and its support for loose collaboration through shared and private annotations.

2.1 Fisheye Views for Tailorable Workspace Awareness

Fisheye views were first proposed by Furnas (1986) to provide a 'focus plus context' view of information spaces. Visualizations of the data-space are distorted according to the users 'degree of interest' in regions of the information space. Related work on the fisheye view concept is discussed in Section 5.

In DOME each user has a fisheye view on their own region of work. Text within the fisheye is magnified or demagnified according to the configuration of their lens. Each user also has one fisheye view for each of the simultaneous users of the system. The design intention is that each user can control the amount of screen real-estate dedicated to their own area of interest, while simultaneously maintaining a tailorable level of awareness on the location and activities of their colleagues.

Each tailorable fisheye lens controls the degree and range of magnification. The degree of magnification or demagnification (the size of the text font) at any point within a lens is dependent upon the vertical distance that the text lies from the centre of a fisheye lens. The centre of each lens follows the location of the user's insertion cursor while typing. Users can also move their lens independently of the insertion cursor in the same way that most word processors allow users to scroll to other regions in the document without disrupting the location of the insertion point. Figure 2 provides an extreme example of the stepped magnification provided by one of DOME's lenses: the three central lines are very large and bold; there are two outer levels of magnification, each of 4 lines and each with slightly lower levels of magnification. It is important to note that each user's customization of their lenses (both their own lens, and their lenses onto their colleagues' workspaces) does not affect the other users' displays.

[†]This paper was written using DOME and the LATEX text formatting and typesetting system.

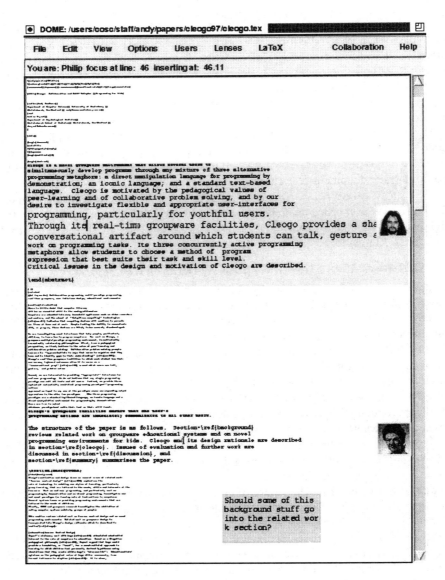

Figure 1: DOME's main window.

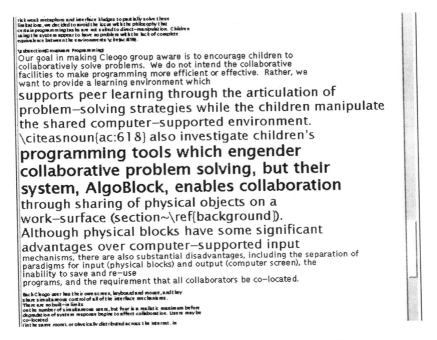

Figure 2: An extreme example of a lens's stepped magnification.

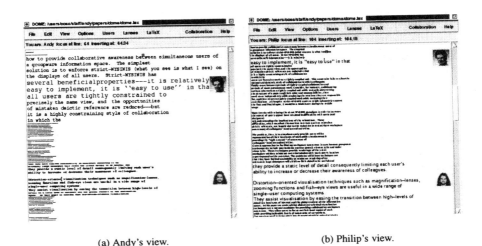

(a) Andy's view.

(b) Philip's view.

Figure 3: Two simultaneous views of the workspace.

Figure 4: Initiating tightly coupled collaboration in the 'Users' window.

Figures 3(a) & 3(b) show two users' simultaneous views of the document workspace using DOME. In the left-hand figure, Andy has configured his lenses so that he has a large legible region for his own text-area; his view onto Philip's work area is configured to provide a roughly paragraph-size legible viewport; and he has configured the background text to a sufficiently small size to give an extensive overall view of the document. In the right-hand figure, Philip has simultaneously configured his lens to provide a small region for his local text area, just one line for his view on Andy's work, and a just-legible font for the background text.

User configurable colours are used as an additional cue to the text region contained within each fisheye lens. Colours are used consistently across all users displays — if, for example, purple is used to denote Mary's region on one person's display, then Mary's region is purple on all displays. Consistent colour coding is intended to reduce the opportunity for mistaken deictic reference in expressions such as "the red bit of text at the top".

2.2 *Tailoring Levels of Awareness*

One of the major design intentions with DOME is to ease each user's transition between varying levels of awareness of colleagues.

There are several ways to configure awareness of specific users, but the most common way is through the 'users' window (Figure 4). This window shows an image of each user, the colour of their text region and their awareness level. There is also a menu under each user's image which allows the fisheye onto that user's region of activity to be set to one of six discrete awareness levels (from 'None' to 'Very High'). The precise configuration of the lens under each level can be tailored using 'lens handles' which allow the user to change a variety of lens properties, including the number of stepped magnification levels it provides, the range (number of lines) within each level, and the amount of magnification within each level. The default awareness level for new arrivals into a shared editing session can be tailored.

The discrete awareness levels allow users to rapidly move between, for instance, high levels of awareness for tightly coupled collaborative activity and low levels of awareness (or none) for more independent work.

The awareness features in DOME are highly configurable. Some of the configuration options are primarily intended to support our evaluation of different mechanisms for awareness, but others are intended to support user preferences, such as whether to display each user's image at their focal point.

2.3 Tightly Coupled Interaction

During tightly coupled collaborative work, 'awareness' of a colleague's activities may be insufficient. At such times users may need to revert to a strict-WYSIWIS mode of working in which all movements, actions and gestures are communicated between the users.

DOME provides four facilities to assist tightly coupled work. First, using the menu shown in Figure 4, a user can 'Goto' the location of any other user, causing their window to immediately display the location of their colleague. Second, a user may choose to 'Follow' another user, which slaves the user's screen location to that of the 'followed' user. Third, DOME provides 'semantic telepointers' (Greenberg et al., 1996d) which communicate to other users the region of text that a user points at with their mouse. The semantic telepointers assure that if one user points at a particular word, then his or her telepointer on the other users' displays will also point at that word. This is a significant improvement on geometry-based telepointers which simply point to the same window coordinates without accounting for differing window sizes, variations in word-wrap and non-aligned scroll locations. Finally, when a user selects a region of text, the selection is communicated to all other users by shading the text region.

2.4 Annotation

The workspace awareness facilities described above are primarily intended to support the users' dynamic awareness of the location and activities of colleagues who are concurrently working within the workspace. Issues of temporal awareness — the awareness of what information has changed in the workspace — are also important.

DOME provides powerful annotation facilities which can be used for a variety of purposes including temporal awareness of document modifications and meta-comments about the underlying text. Annotations in DOME are based on a 'sticky-note' metaphor that closely maps to common paper-based editing practices. DOME's annotations provide extensions beyond the real-world metaphor to assist a variety of collaborative and personal editing strategies.

Annotations are created as either 'private' or 'shared'. Shared annotations are simultaneously editable by all users. Private annotations are shown only on the creator's window, but they can be shared between sub-groups of users (or all users) by sending them to others (see Figure 5).

Annotations can either be associated with a specific piece of text ('pinned to the text') or they can be unpinned and 'float' above the text with a constant geometry in the window regardless of the scrolled location. Pinned annotations are useful for comments about specific pieces of text (for instance, changes that have been made or should be made), and unpinned annotations are useful as general communication portholes between users.

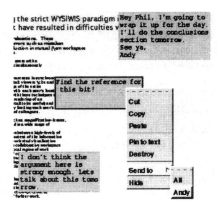

Figure 5: Three annotations: sending a private annotation to another user.

3 Evaluation

A primary design intention with DOME was to create a thoroughly polished editing environment that could be used to evaluate distortion-oriented workspace awareness. We strongly felt that the rudimentary interfaces of the demonstration systems used in our prior work (see Section 1) would obscure any evaluation.

The fourteen subjects in the evaluation were all postgraduate Computer Science students and Computer Science academics, and were randomly assigned to pairs. All subjects were familiar with the concepts of groupware systems, but none had previous experience with DOME. Each pair participated in a single one-hour video-taped session. During the evaluations the users were seated alongside one-another, approximately one and a half metres apart. We selected the side-by-side setting to illuminate failings in the workspace awareness: if users frequently looked at their partner's screen, it would indicate a failing in the awareness features.

In each session approximately twenty five minutes was spent introducing DOME's features and familiarizing the subjects with the distortion-oriented views. Although this is a relatively long time to dedicate to familiarization, we felt it was worthwhile to ensure that users were settled to the concept of the fisheye view prior to engaging in the evaluation tasks. Fifteen minutes were then spent on each of two tasks, and five minutes were allocated to a post task interview.

The first task involved re-ordering a jumbled structured document. It was introduced to the users as follows:

> A production of "The Tragedy of Macbeth" by William Shakespeare is due to be performed tonight. The problem is that the script was emailed to the production company in parts, and assembled automatically by an email reassembler. The software malfunctioned and assembled the messages based on the order in which they arrived, rather than the sequence in which they were sent.

Your task is to work together with your partner to reassemble the text so the play can go on. The file `macbeth.tex` contains the jumbled text.

In the second task the subjects were given a template document and were asked to complete the sections, and in particular to summarize these sections in a table at the end of the template. The task was introduced as follows:

Your second task is to fill-in the details of a document on the fourth year Computer Science papers offered in our department. The structure of the paper is provided in the file `course.tex`. Be sure to complete the summary table at the end of the document.

The two tasks were selected to generate differing requirements for workspace awareness. The first task was intended to require frequent transitions between collaborative work and independent work as the users moved from negotiating which scene to collect next (which we presumed would be a collaborative activity) to retrieving and repositioning the text (which we presumed would be an independent activity). The second task was selected to generate a need for workspace awareness in more tightly coupled collaborative activity. Although some of the sections in the template could be completed independently, we believed it would be necessary to collaborate in order to produce the summary table.

3.1 Observations

Overall the subjects' reactions to the distortion-oriented workspace awareness features were negative. The subjects reported, and we observed, some substantial limitations of the fisheye mechanisms which will have to be amended before subsequent evaluation. These difficulties are reported in the following sections.

Not all of our observations were negative, and there were many interesting and promising uses of the awareness features. During the second task, in which the subjects were writing about courses and lecturers, we noted several occurrences of subjects laughing. When asked, the subjects reported that they had seen what their partner had written about a particular course or lecturer. Although the information communicated through the awareness facilities was frivolous (in this case), it demonstrates that the subjects were aware of each others actions. Several of the pairs also made successful use of the shared annotations for mediating collaborative activity, such as keeping track of assigned tasks.

3.1.1 'Jumping' Text caused by Fish-eyes

The biggest problem, reported by all of the subjects, was caused by the small amount of unwanted text-motion that occurs when the fisheye lenses are moved. This problem arises as a result of two types of user action.

First, when a user moves their own insertion point their fisheye view moves to the new location. The text around the new location is immediately magnified according to the current configuration of their lens. This causes a small offset (both horizontal and vertical) between the coordinate clicked and the resultant location of the I-beam insertion point. The magnitudes of the horizontal and vertical offsets, which are formally expressed in Equations 1 & 2, show that the offsets are caused by

simultaneously develop programs through any mixture
of three alternative programming metaphors: a direct
manipulation language for programming by
demonstration; an iconic language; and a standard
text-based language. Cleogo is motivated by the
pedagogical values of peer-learning and of
collaborative problem solving, and by our
desire to investigate flexible and appropriate

manipulation language for programming by
demonstration; an iconic language; and a standard
text-based language. Cleogo is motivated by the
pedagogical values of peer-learning and of
collaborative problem solving, and by our
desire to investigate flexible and appropriate
user-interfaces for programming, particularly for
youthful users. Through its real-time groupware

(a) Text before clicking.   (b) Text after clicking.

Figure 6: Unwanted text motion when repositioning the insertion point. The I-beam is displaced from the clicked coordinate.

$$\delta_x = \sum_{c=0}^{clickChar} w_R(c) - w_I(c) \tag{1}$$

where:

- δ_x is the horizontal offset between the clicked location and the resultant location of the I-beam.

- c takes the value of each character from the start of the line to the clicked character.

- $w_R(x)$ gives the width of character x at the resultant (magnified) font-size. Note that this value is the same for all characters in fixed-width fonts.

- $w_I(x)$ gives the width of character x at the initial (background) font-size.

$$\delta_y = \pm \left((h(1) - h(b)) * \frac{lines(1)}{2} + \sum_{l=2}^{numLevels} (h(l) - h(b)) * lines(l) \right) \tag{2}$$

where:

- δ_y is the vertical offset between the clicked location and the resultant location of the I-beam. δ_y is negative (the I-beam appears below the clicked location) when the user clicks a text location above the current location of the fisheye. It is positive when the user clicks below the fisheye.

- $h(x)$ gives the font-height at magnification level x.

- b is the background magnification level.

- l takes one value for each of the stepped lens levels of magnification, from the 2nd stepped level to the outer-most level. Level 1 is the lenses centre of magnification.

- $lines(x)$ gives the number of lines contained within lens magnification level x.

Equations 1 & 2: The horizontal and vertical offsets between the clicked location and the resultant location of the I-beam.

the difference between the text sizes before and after repositioning the lens. Figure 6 demonstrates the problem: the cross hair in the left figure shows the location about to be clicked; the cross-hair in the right figure shows the unchanged location of the click; and the I-beam in the right-hand figure shows the resultant location of the insertion point. Consequently, having clicked at a particular point in the text, the user must search for the resultant (close-by) location of the I-beam. Users reported that although this was initially disturbing, they quickly became used to this small motion.

The second cause of text-motion was more disturbing for the users because it arose from the actions of their partners' and was therefore seen as 'unpredictable'. Whenever a colleague moved from a location above a user to a location below the user (or from below to above) their action would cause a small vertical offset in the user's view. This offset is due to the relocation of the colleague's lens. The effect is most noticeable when awareness of colleagues is set at high levels, and when the background text size is small. Equation 2 concisely describes the cause and magnitude of the effect. Methods of reducing this problem are discussed in Section 4.

3.1.2 Location versus Semantic Distortion

We observed several occurrences of subjects becoming disoriented in the document, typified by accompanying comments such as: "Now, where's the sub-section gone?" The problem was explicitly identified by one pair but, according to our observations, affected several pairs. It was caused by the absence of semantically oriented distortion in the fisheye lens.

DOME's fisheye lenses magnify text purely according to the vertical distance that the text lies from the centre of the lens. The distortion functions do not account for the semantic importance of the underlying textual units. Furnas used the term 'a priori importance' to capture this notion of semantic importance within information spaces (Furnas, 1986). In written articles there is a high level of a priori importance associated with the structural tags of the document such as section headings, titles, captions and so on. Users who are familiar with WYSIWIS word processors will expect to see these document elements displayed in a format that is similar to their final rendering — normally large and emboldened text.

In our observations, there were clear periods of conflict between the text that the subjects' expected to see magnified and the text that was magnified. The problem was particularly pronounced when the subjects had selected extremely small background text-sizes, and when section or subsection headings rolled out of the magnified region of the lens.

4 Discussion and Further Work

We are not overly discouraged by the results of our evaluation. We believe that the worst problem encountered by the subjects (the unwanted vertical text motion caused by the actions of partners) can be significantly reduced or eliminated by ensuring that the vertical location of the insertion point remains constant whenever lenses move. Small amendments to the vertical scroll location can be used to correct the δ_y offset (see Equation 2). Retaining the horizontal location of the insertion point is more problematical. One approach to correcting the δ_x offset would be to use horizontal scrolling. This is unlikely to be acceptable, however, because part of the text line would have to be scrolled out of the viewable area. Wide margins at low levels of magnification could overcome the need for scrolling, but they would be extremely wasteful of screen real-estate. Other potential solutions would be to dynamically modify the line-wrap of the text, but this is also unlikely to be popular because of the amount of dynamic text-modification that would be necessary.

We will not correct horizontal displacement (δ_x offsets) in the next version of DOME. In our study, it was the vertical offsets caused by other users that most severely disrupted interaction. Subsequent evaluations will determine whether fixing the vertical offsets is sufficient for user acceptance.

The 'location versus semantic content' problem can be viewed as an issue of insufficient functionality in the current version of the system. DOME already has the ability to parse and amend the semantic units within LaTeX documents and Tcl/Tk programs, and consequently it should not be difficult to add magnification functions based on a priori importance: for instance, ensuring that section or procedure headings are always displayed larger than the surrounding text.

Having made these modifications to the system we will re-initiate evaluation in a similar style to that described in Section 3. Provided that the modifications result in a system that is acceptable to the users, we will undertake a longitudinal evaluation study to investigate how the awareness features are used by collaborators who are thoroughly familiar with the system.

5 Related Work

Research on distortion-oriented visualizations and on fisheye views stems from Furnas's (1986) seminal work which describes a mechanism for representing the user's "neighbourhood in great detail, yet only major landmarks further away". A recent review of distortion-oriented presentation techniques can be found in Leung & Apperley (1994). The work reported here is concerned with a new application area for distortion-oriented techniques: the provision of workspace awareness.

In one of the earliest papers on the importance of mutual awareness in synchronous groupware environments Stefik et al. (1987) reported on a variety of WYSIWIS mechanisms for providing focused interfaces for collaboration. The substantial usability problems of their Colab meeting environment were later reported in Tatar et al. (1991). The problems arose from users misunderstanding exactly what each other could see on their screens, and from mistaken deictic references.

Within editing environments Dourish & Bellotti (1992) note the dual requirements of "understanding the activities of others" while maintaining a "context for your own activity". Towards this end, Gutwin et al. (1996) explored the development and usability of widgets specifically designed to provide an awareness of other users in the workspace. These widgets include 'shared telepointers' which show the precise location of each user within the workspace and 'gestalt-viewers' which provide a miniature overview of the entire workspace.

Our previous work (Greenberg et al., 1996a; Greenberg et al., 1996b; Greenberg et al., 1996c) demonstrated a variety of distortion-oriented mechanisms for workspace awareness in text-based and graphical workspaces. The systems described in these works were purely intended to demonstrate the types of awareness that distortion-oriented mechanisms could provide, and they were inadequate for evaluation.

May & Barnard (1995) provide an interesting analysis of problems associated with "presentationally complex interfaces". Their work, which derives interface design guidance from an Interacting Cognitive Subsystems analysis of cinematography, would have predicted the problems that DOME users encountered with text movement.

6   Conclusions

Distortion-oriented visualization techniques appear to have the potential to satisfy collaborators' needs for workspace awareness in real-time groupware environments. They allow users to focus on their local area of work while simultaneously offering a viewport onto the work of colleagues. By tailoring the distortion provided by the visualization scheme, users can tailor their level of awareness of colleagues. The tailoring capability promises to bridge the gap between differing styles of collaborative work: from largely independent asynchronous collaboration, through semi-synchronous 'awareness', to tightly coupled and fully synchronous WYSIWIS collaboration.

Our distortion-oriented multi-user editor, DOME, has been designed and constructed to provide a fully-functional environment for experimenting with and evaluating distortion-oriented workspace awareness. The first evaluation of DOME, reported in this paper, illuminated several substantial usability problems with our implementation of awareness capabilities through 'fisheye' distortion. Although these problems overwhelmed the evaluation results, we are encouraged by evidence of successful uses of the awareness features. Our further work will ease the usability problems and continue evaluation.

Acknowledgements and Availability

DOME is written in Tcl/Tk (Ousterhout, 1993) and GroupKit (Roseman & Greenberg, 1996). Its starting point was a fisheye text viewer developed by Saul Greenberg while on sabbatical at the University of Canterbury. DOME has been tested on Sun Sparc stations and on PCs running the Linux operating system. It is available on request from the second author.

References

Dourish, P. & Bellotti, V. (1992), Awareness and Coordination in Shared Workspaces, *in* J. Turner & R. Kraut (eds.), *Proceedings of CSCW'92: Conference on Computer Supported Cooperative Work*, ACM Press, pp.107–14.

Furnas, G. W. (1986), Generalized Fisheye Views, *in* M. Mantei & P. Orbeton (eds.), *Proceedings of CHI'86: Human Factors in Computing Systems*, ACM Press, pp.16–23.

Greenberg, S., Gutwin, C. & Cockburn, A. (1996a), "Applying Distortion-oriented Displays to Groupware", Video Programme of the ACM Conference on Computer Supported Cooperative Work.

Greenberg, S., Gutwin, C. & Cockburn, A. (1996b), Awareness Through Fisheye Views in Relaxed-WYSIWIS Groupware, in *Proceedings of 1996 Graphics Interface Conference.*, Morgan-Kaufmann, pp.28–38.

Greenberg, S., Gutwin, C. & Cockburn, A. (1996c), Using Distortion-oriented Displays to Support Workspace Awareness, in A. Sasse, R. J. Cunningham & R. Winder (eds.), *People and Computers XI (Proceedings of HCI'96)*, Springer-Verlag, pp.299–314.

Greenberg, S., Gutwin, C. & Roseman, M. (1996d), Semantic Telepointers for Groupware, in J. Grundy & M. Apperley (eds.), *Proceedings of OzCHI'96 The Sixth Australian Conference on Computer–Human Interaction*, IEEE Computer Society Press, pp.54–61.

Gutwin, C., Roseman, M. & Greenberg, S. (1996), A Usability Study of Awareness Widgets in a Shared Workspace Groupware System, in M. S. Ackerman (ed.), *Proceedings of CSCW'96: Conference on Computer Supported Cooperative Work*, ACM Press, pp.258–67.

Leung, Y. K. & Apperley, M. (1994), "A Review and Taxonomy of Distortion-Oriented Presentation Techniques", *ACM Transactions on Computer–Human Interaction* **1**(2), 126–60.

May, J. & Barnard, P. (1995), Cinematography and Interface Design, in K. Nordby, P. H. Helmersen, D. J. Gilmore & S. A. Arnessen (eds.), *Human–Computer Interaction — INTERACT'95: Proceedings of the Fifth IFIP Conference on Human–Computer Interaction*, Chapman & Hall, pp.26–31.

Ousterhout, J. K. (1993), *An Introduction to Tcl and Tk*, Addison–Wesley.

Roseman, M. & Greenberg, S. (1996), "Building Real Time Groupware with GroupKit, A Groupware Toolkit", *ACM Transactions on Computer–Human Interaction* **3**(1), 66–106.

Stefik, M., Bobrow, D. G., Foster, G., Lanning, S. & Tatar, D. (1987), "WYSIWIS Revised: Early Experiences with Multiuser Interfaces", *ACM Transactions on Office Information Systems* **5**(2), 147–67.

Tatar, D. G., Foster, G. & Bobrow, D. G. (1991), "Design for Conversation: Lessons from Cognoter", *International Journal of Man–Machine Studies* **34**(2), 185–209.

Innovative User Interfaces: Multimedia and Multi-modal User Interfaces, Wearable Computers and Virtual Reality

Towards Principles for the Design and Evaluation of Multimedia Systems

Peter Johnson & Fabio Nemetz

Department of Computer Science, Queen Mary and Westfield College, University of London, Mile End Road, London E1 4NS, UK.

Tel: *+44 171 975 5224*

Fax: *+44 181 980 6533*

EMail: *{pete, fabio}@dcs.qmw.ac.uk*

URL: *http://www.dcs.qmw.ac.uk/*

The rapid growth of multimedia technology has made it possible to deliver high quality audio, graphics, video and animation to the user. However, this growth in technology has not been met by a growth in design knowledge. While it is possible to have multimedia it is not at all obvious that we know how to design high-quality multimedia systems that are fully usable to the degree we should expect. To improve the situation much work is under way to develop guidelines, style guides and principles for multimedia design. This paper illustrates the problem facing designers (and users) of multimedia systems by examining some of the design mistakes that have been made in one public information system (as an example of one class of multimedia systems). We then consider what design features any such principles should address.

Keywords: multimedia system design, evaluation of multimedia systems, principles for multimedia design.

1 Introduction

Multimedia technology can considerably increase the options open to the user-interface designer (Alty, 1997). However, the lack of detailed design knowledge and widely available design experience make multimedia user-interface design and evaluation ill-defined and unprincipled activities.

Although many view multimedia just as the use of more than one medium to present information to users (Nielsen, 1995), multimedia is much more than this. In our research, we adopt a wider definition, encompassing both input and output media and focusing on human–computer interaction rather than on the technological aspects. In this way, we consider interactions with animations, gesture recognition, speech input, speech synthesis, haptic input and output and virtual reality as examples or special cases of multimedia. As Marmolin (1991) states:

> "A user centred definition would characterize multimedia systems as systems enabling the usage of multiple sensory modalities and multiple channels of the same or different modality (for example both ears, both hands, etc.), and as systems enabling one user to perform several tasks at the same time. That is, multimedia is viewed as a multi-sensory, multichannel, multitasking and multi-user approach to system design. In addition multimedia systems put the user in control, i.e. could be described as a user centred approach".

Traditional approaches to design for usability from HCI do not yet directly deal with the unique characteristics of multimedia systems: "while general usability criteria such as learnability, flexibility and robustness apply equally to single media and multimedia systems, they have little to say regarding the specific benefits and drawbacks of concurrent media input and output" (Bearne et al., 1994).

The use of multiple media, when well exploited by designers, potentially makes multimedia interfaces more exciting, more natural, more enjoyable and pleasant to use than traditional mainly text-based interfaces (Petersen, 1996). This occurs because multimedia provides us with richer forms of representing information in human–computer interactions. However, it does not necessarily follow that merely by increasing the richness of the media we will increase the utility and usability of information and computer systems. While in some cases the addition of more media will allow us to express concepts and information more fully, with greater clarity, and with greater accuracy than before, in other cases it will introduce ambiguity, confusion and contradiction.

Our research aims to define a set of principles to address the complexities of multimedia design and evaluation, in order to make multimedia systems useful and usable, rather than 'gimmicky' and ephemeral. The background theory involves research in cognitive psychology and media communication. Some issues that are under investigation by various researchers (Barnard & May (1994), Bearne et al. (1994), Williams (1996), Faraday & Sutcliffe (1996), Alty (1997), and many others) include:

- The effect of media on human cognition.

- Criteria for selection and combination of different media.

- How to identify and incorporate multimedia needs in usability requirements.

- How to design interactions involving multimedia.

- How to evaluate the effects of media in terms of utility and usability.

The principles that will emerge from our research are expected to support designers in making decisions about the various media so as to maximize the effectiveness and efficiency of the user-computer interactions. This will enable designers to build more usable multimedia systems, and help move HCI towards a stronger theoretical basis and more principled discipline of design.

In the next section, we present examples of the problem with multimedia systems. In section three, a set of multimedia features are presented which need to be considered in the development of multimedia design principles. Then, we discuss the basic steps involved in the continuation of this research. Finally, some conclusions about principles and features of multimedia design are drawn.

2   Is There a Problem with Multimedia Design?

It is all very well for us to argue that we need principles and the like to support the design of multimedia systems, but if it is the case that designers of such systems are getting it right without any such principles then we should not be over concerned. We have carried out an analysis of several classes of multimedia systems and from this we have arrived at the conclusion that there is indeed a problem. The classes of multimedia systems we have considered are not exhaustive but represent different types. We have considered applications on the world-wide web that provide information and guidance in a domain. Examples of these are guides such as tourist guides and the home page for the BCS HCI conference itself. This class of information is designed to let the user find particular information and to 'browse' through the information that is there. One example of a relatively good design we have come across of a web-based tourist guide is the Scotguide (http://www.scotourist.org.uk/contents.htm). First we consider this example.

This guide is a realistic and highly interesting public information system that is widely used. It is not chosen as being a really bad example of an information system or as one that has made outrageous use of multimedia. However, when we looked closely at the design of this system we quickly found some interesting features that exemplify the lack of design principles that seems to surround the use of multimedia. The system in question makes use of text, diagrams, maps, photographs, animation and hypermedia. In Figures 1, 2, 3 & 4, we show four examples taken from this system. These examples are a good reflection of the whole system, and the problems, which we illustrate here, are found throughout the particular design.

In Figure 1 we have shown part of the contents page to the guide. The page is well laid out and is very well designed in terms of the readability of the text and the structure of the information on it. However, the first point to make is the use that is made of animation on this page. It is not possible for us to show this in the figure but we will attempt to describe it. There are two uses of animation on this page. First, the compass in the top-left hand corner of the figure has a lid on it that opens and closes independent of the user doing anything. Second, the star-like compass points alongside the text rotate all by themselves without the user doing anything to them.

Figure 1: Scotourist contents.

Neither of these uses of animation have any function in the user interface other than perhaps to make the design more attractive. However, they have a detrimental effect on aspects of the system's usability. The compass has text written around the edges of it (this text is as follows: at the north point — 'the guide', at the east point — 'website plan', at the south point — 'magazine' and to the west point — 'winter escapes'). Each of these pieces of text at the four compass points is in fact a hypertext link to other pages of information. This was not apparent to us until by chance we moved the mouse pointer over the compass and one of us (not the one using the mouse) noticed a change in the text at the bottom of the Netscape browser. Later we noticed that the cursor had also changed. Just as we had discovered that these compass points were indeed links, the lid of the compass closed shut for only a few moments but enough to make it impossible to read the text and aim the mouse on to a link of interest (in fact we later discovered that you can still select the link even when the lid is closed and you cannot see the text links or the compass points at all). The problem here is that the animated opening and closing of the lid attracts your attention to the compass but then interferes with your ability first to perceive that the text at the four points of the compass are indeed links and, worse still, makes it difficult to select, read and aim at the links with the mouse cursor when (if) you do realize they are links and want to select one of them.

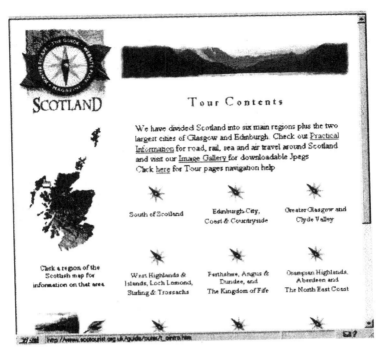

Figure 2: Scotourist tour contents.

This particular use of animation in multimedia seems to us to break a number of desirable features of design. First, it does not make a *significant contribution* to the quality or ease with which you can interact with the system nor does it convey any useful information. Second, it actually prevents the user from *exploring the system* because it obscures, through the animation itself, some of the navigable links of the system.

The second use of animation is on the smaller star-like compass points that are alongside the text in Figure 1. These are one of the first things that the user notices on the page. They all rotate at the same time and when you view the full page with all its rotating star-like compass points on it, they become very distracting and interfere with your reading and searching of the text. The star-like compass points themselves are selectable buttons that have the same function as the underlined text links in the adjoining text in Figure 1. This *redundancy* is a good thing as it increases the users' chances of finding or noticing something. However, the animation of these compass points and the opening and closing of the lid of the larger compass have a distracting and interfering effect upon the users' ability to read and select items of interest from the text. Again, the animation here does not make a significant contribution to the interaction with or interpretation of the information. Instead it *interferes with and distracts the user's attention.*

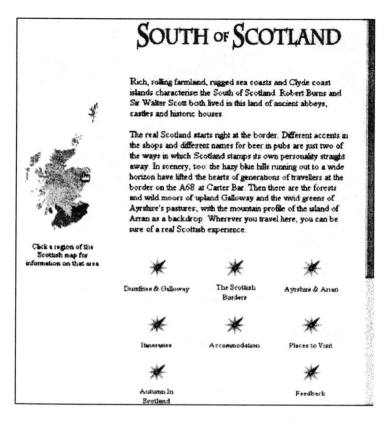

Figure 3: Scotourist guide — South of Scotland.

Also on this page we would like to draw attention to the map of Scotland that is just below the compass. On this page (Figure 1) the map itself is not interactive. On other pages (Figures 2, 3 & 4) it is. To tell the user this map is now interactive the designers insert text under the map (Figure 2) telling the user to "click on a region of the Scottish map for information on that area". This is fine on the pages where the text appears (as it does on all pages where the map is interactive). However, on the contents page the map looks as if it should be interactive and users do still try to select from it even though the text is not there (and even when they have seen the text previously on other pages).

The map presents further problems when it is interactive. In Figure 2 it can be seen that the map has regional boundaries on it and these represent different sectors of Scotland that you can gain information about. Good use is made here of *redundancy* and multiple routes for *exploration* of the information as further information about these regional areas can be reached from either the map or the rotating compass points (yes they are here again — nine of them this time spinning merrily away). There

Figure 4: Scotourist guide — Perth.

are nine selectable compass points, eight of these correspond to regions of Scotland and the ninth is labelled 'practical information'. A close look at the map gives the impression that there are five regions on the map divided by the boundary lines — where are the other three regions? Well, the Outer Islands constitute a sixth region, and Edinburgh is the seventh and Glasgow the eighth. You cannot identify where the three sectors of the Outer Islands, Edinburgh or Glasgow are and you do not know what the names of the five identifiable sectors are from the map unless you know Scotland. Even then you would have to read the text of the rotating compass points and work out where each of the sectors are on the map. There is clearly a problem with *consistency* across the two representations and with the *quality of the information representation* of the map itself.

When you select a region from the map you do not get any feedback from the map telling you which region you have selected. When that region is displayed, the map is redrawn with the other regions (the ones not selected) drawn in a lighter shade and with the regional boundary lines hidden (see Figure 3). The text below the map tells the user to click on a region of the map (as before) to select a new region but now the regional boundary lines that were there before have disappeared. Worse still, the user cannot make the selection from the hosts of rotating compasses to get to another region because these now relate to features and information about the selected region. At this point the user has to guess where the regions were on the map to select another region with no help at all from the interface. These design problems can be described as failing to maintain a consistent use of redundancy and not consistently allowing multiple routes of exploration.

One further problem is shown in Figure 4. Here the user has selected the 'places to visit' page on one of the regions (Perthshire, Angus & Dundee and the Kingdom of Fife). The user is presented with an attractive display including descriptive text and photographic images. The pictures provide a *high quality information representation* and a seemingly *natural* use of this medium. The text contains highlighted places that you can go to for further information about these particular places and alongside and below the selectable places are photographic images (good use of redundancy). The only problem is that the images are not of the places that you can select even though you might think they were. The upper image is of Blair Castle (a non-selectable place mentioned in the text) and Pitlochry (another non-selectable place mentioned in the text). Even worse still, Pitlochry is mentioned in the text before Blair Castle but the pictures are ordered so that Blair Castle is before Pitlochry. Consequently, we have further design problems caused by inconsistencies between the links and the pictures and in the relationship of the pictures to the text content. This lack of *referential alignment* causes confusion and ambiguity.

To summarize, our brief analysis of this rich and interesting information system has highlighted a number of points at which the system could be improved. We have attempted to stand back from the detail of the particular design problem and characterize these at a more general level of design problem such that we might identify from this analysis some more generally applicable design features. These design features noted are:

- Naturalness of the medium.

- Consistent use of media.

- Referential alignment.

- Redundancy.

- Significant contribution of the media.

- Exploration and navigation.

- Quality of information representation.

The two features of *consistent use of media* and *referential alignment* are themselves closely related and can be considered as sub-problems within the *allocation of media*.

From this brief analysis of a public information system it is clear that there is a need for design principles that can guide designers away from making such mistakes. We would like to stress the fact that this is one of the best public information systems we have found on the world wide web in terms of its information and coverage and yet it clearly has multimedia design problems that detract from the usability of the system. We also hope we have managed to show you something of what a beautiful place Scotland is.

We could go through more examples like this in different areas and uses of multimedia but in the context of this paper we now move on to consider each of the above features from which a set of principles might be usefully developed.

3   From Features Towards Multimedia Design Principles

In this section, each of the features above is considered in a more general context. Each feature is explained and considered together with some further questions it raises. A main source is Alty (1993), who has developed design guidelines for the use of multimedia in process control interfaces. Based on this work and our analysis of design problems we have generalized the features so that they can be used for multimedia in general. We have also augmented the expressiveness of the features, so that they can be further developed to guide design. The ultimate goal is to develop a small set of principles that can be used to aid and guide designers in their reasoning about multimedia systems.

The term *principle* is used in different ways in the literature. Shneiderman (1997) differentiates three kinds of guidance for designers: *high-level theories and models*, which offer a framework or language to discuss issues that are application independent, *middle-level principles*, which are useful in creating and comparing design alternatives, and *specific and practical guidelines*, which provide reminders of rules uncovered by designers. For instance, one of his middle-level principles is "Use the Eight Golden Rules of Interface Design" which includes eight design recommendations (e.g. enable frequent users to use shortcuts). This agrees with his statement that "the separation between basic principles and more informal guidelines is not a sharp line". Yet (Preece et al., 1994) consider principles as a special case of guidelines. For them, there are two kinds of guidelines: *high level guiding principles* and *low level detailed rules*. They consider principles as guidelines that offer high level advice that can be applied widely (e.g. know the user population). On the other hand, *principles* and *rules* are considered to be synonyms by Baecker et al. (1995): "collections of statements that advise the designer on how to proceed (e.g. know the user)", while guidelines are defined as "collections of tests that can be applied to an interface to determine if it is satisfactory (e.g. provide an average response time of less than one second)".

We take a principle to be some established fact that has a theoretical and empirical basis for its acceptance, that can be applied to a prescribed problem area in a well-defined manner and for which there is some indication of what the result of following the principle (or not) will be. At this stage in our research we identified a number of areas where we believe there is scope for developing a more principled understanding of interacting with multimedia and what features a set of principles for multimedia design must address. These features are developed further below.

3.1   Naturalness

Multimedia systems try to take advantage of human senses to facilitate human–computer interaction, and human–human, computer mediated communication. Considering that we live in a world of multimedia events (Rudnicky, 1992), "many people believe that multimedia communication is natural and corresponds more closely with how the brain has developed" (Alty, 1997), and, therefore, "multimedia exercises the whole mind" (Marmolin, 1991). In this viewpoint, the human brain is seen as having evolved in a multi-sensory environment, where simultaneous input on different channels was essential for survival. Thus, "the processing of the human brain has been fine-tuned to allow simultaneous sampling and comparison between different channels" (Alty, 1997). Multimedia systems have the potential to make appropriate and efficient use of human perceptual and cognitive capabilities by making our interaction with computers more natural.

A related feature to naturalness is *realness* or the degree of correspondence between the representation and the real thing. Naturalness and realness are similar but not the same. Naturalness is concerned with the mapping between the stimuli and the senses taking recognition of the fact that people normally gain information from the world from multiple senses (e.g. hearing an explosion would cause people to look for a cloud of smoke or flames). On the other hand, realness is concerned with how close the representation of the explosion corresponds to an actual explosion.

Two consequences for systems that possess these features appear to be that they show properties of *believability* (the closer they are to the real thing, the more believable they appear to be) and *fidelity* (the degree of detail).

To fully understand and exploit the naturalness feature, a better understanding of how our senses are affected by each medium and by their combination is needed. Moreover, we need to consider when and to what degree we need to attain particular levels of naturalness and realness in order to support appropriate levels of believability and fidelity. A flight simulator might require high degrees of naturalness and realness in order to effectively train the pilot. The system must be believably like the real thing and be of high fidelity to allow the appropriate levels of flying skills to be developed in the pilot. Similarly, in image guided neurosurgery the surgeon must have high degrees of naturalness and realness in the brain images that are guiding her as she removes a brain tumour. The fidelity and believability of the images are of extreme importance to the success of the operation.

3.2   Media Allocation

How, and on what basis, is a particular medium selected for the presentation of a particular piece of information? Each medium has both constraining and enabling features (Arens et al., 1993) and affords different interactions, offers different communicative intentions and has its own rules and conventions.

But is it enough to have a knowledge of each medium in order to make an adequate selection? Some argue that it also depends on the user's knowledge and experience of a domain and task: if the domain and task are new to the user, a concrete representation seems to be best; if the user has a lot of experience in the domain and task, then a more abstract form may be adequate — adapted from Marmolin (1991).

Alty (1993) adds that the usefulness of different media in presentation situations is closely related to the complexity of the idea being conveyed. He also states that the capabilities of the perceiver play an important role in the media allocation problem.

There is an important difference between 'abstract' and 'concrete' concepts. Abstract and complex concepts are more easily and completely represented by words than by pictures. In contrast, more concrete concepts, if represented by pictures and sounds, can improve the speed of understanding and comprehension over that of text representation. Moreover, the choice of medium also has to consider what information is intended to be conveyed and what is the intended effect of the information.

It is not easy to define a complete set of criteria to solve the media allocation problem. One aspect that should be investigated in detail is the relation between media and tasks. In other words, the main problem is to determine which media best transmit the information needed by the users to carry out their tasks.

Summarizing, it seems that multiple factors play a role in the media allocation decision (Arens et al., 1993):

- Characteristics of the media.

- Characteristics of the information.

- Goals and characteristics of the user.

- Goals of the producer.

Based on these factors, it is necessary to determine the enabling and constraining features of each medium, given the goals and characteristics of the user, the intended effect of the information and the characteristics of the information itself. Then, it will be possible to determine the media to be used.

In a training guide for would-be surfers there are several possible ways to show the manoeuvres employed to catch and ride a wave into the shore. In books, pictures or, more commonly, abstract sketches are used. In a multimedia system, real-time video and slow motion video, with annotated text and audio explanations would be used to show the movements of the surfer relative to the oncoming wave, the timing and positioning of the board, the timing and movements as the wave is caught, and then, as the surfer moves from a lying-down to a standing position. Of course, ideally, one would want to use a realistic simulator to enable the user to actually practice the various body movements in differing simulated sea and wave conditions. The instruction guide could match the media to the nature of the information, the goals and skills of the users and purpose of training.

3.3 Redundancy

Often considered useful in complex and cognitively laden tasks, redundancy is considered a significant phenomenon in multimedia systems (Vetere, 1997). It is well known that using both visual and audio channels simultaneously to explain a complex diagram is better than using only one channel; it is also true that people use the redundancy offered by multiple channels to improve their understanding of situations (Alty, 1991). Redundancy is a special case of overlap between channels

(Basil, 1994) and it occurs when information in one channel repeats or complements what is said in another channel.

In multimedia systems, redundancy is achieved through the integration and synchronization of different media. It can produce 'real-world' like conditions, and reduce the overload on working memory (e.g. video and audio, animated graphics and text overlay or sound commentary). Comprehension is directly affected by redundancy, since more of the information provided is understood. For instance, if there is confusion and misunderstanding as a result of misperception of information in one medium, then this can be supplemented by providing the same material in another medium, at the same time (or proximal close in time and space). It is through redundancy that we are able to overcome the ambiguity that otherwise could arise in deixis involving pointing and speaking and often eye and head movement, such as in the classic 'put that there' phenomenon, in which multiple forms of media are used to overcome the ambiguity of the referents 'that' and 'there'.

Understanding how effectively to use redundancy, is still a challenge for multimedia systems designers. If combined in a congruent (harmonic, synchronized) way, redundant different media are far more effective than using single media (Hoogeveen, 1997). However if combined in a non-congruent way, they are less effective (in this case, disruption, ambiguity and confusion occurs). Vetere (1997) states that presently there is insufficient knowledge to help designers manipulate these redundancies to improve interactions.

Even though redundancy plays a major role in multimedia systems, little is known about how to take full advantage of it. No methodology or criteria for how to apply redundancy in multimedia systems have been developed so far, let alone a theory of redundancy and its effects on usability.

For example, in neurosurgery the surgeon relies upon the redundancy of the many brain images, presented in different media, and located at different positions around the operating theatre as well as on the actual view of the brain through the microscope to keep her aware at all times of the location and intended path of the operation in the brain and to keep her aware of the adjacent parts, to the injured or diseased brain section, that must be avoided at all costs.

3.4   Significant Contribution of the Media

One of the main strengths of multimedia systems is the opportunity for providing richer forms of interaction and information access through the combination of multiple media. To be successful in improving the quality of the interaction and the efficiency of information access, different media must be combined and co-ordinated, otherwise there is a risk of increased complexity and interference to the user from high cognitive and perceptual-motor loadings caused by interaction and information overload (Alty, 1991). Just adding a new medium will not guarantee an improvement in the users ability to recognize and understand how to interact with a given system or the meaning of a particular piece of information. Adding extra media can cause the user to not even notice a relevant piece of information due to attentional overload or distraction by another, less relevant piece of information presented in a perceptually dominant medium (Bearne et al., 1994). Hence, additional media should be used only if they make a significant and relevant contribution in the transmission of a message. Otherwise, they can distract and interfere in many ways with the users' ability to perform their tasks.

It is important to observe that this kind of problem also occurs in everyday general communications. Our understanding of multimedia can greatly benefit from theories of communication. Grice's theory of implicature (Levinson, 1983), for instance, is concerned with the efficient and effective use of language in conversation. One of its maxims, the *maxim of quantity*, is related to the fact that, when making a contribution to a conversation, this contribution must carry all and only the necessary information, not more and not less than what is required. Another maxim, the *maxim of relevance*, states that one should make the contributions relevant.

Examples found in the Scottish Tourist guide described earlier clearly introduce animation for no useful reason. It serves to distract the user's attention away from the relevant pieces of information as it is perceptually domineering in the display. Animation could have been usefully used in other ways such as to demonstrate the routes to some of the destinations or to attract the user's attention to relevant parts of the information as in an explanatory guide.

3.5 Exploration

One of the main advantages of multimedia systems seems to be the increased level of interactivity* they provide. This is partly due to the use of our senses in a fuller and more orchestrated manner, and also because of a greater flexibility and freedom to explore the information. Ideally, neither the author nor the designer should force how the information should be viewed or processed; the user should be in control, exploring the interface and choosing the best media for the task.

Carroll (1990) has provided a good account of why exploration is a desirable property of a system and its interface. Exploration allows the user to discover for themselves, the workings, content and functional use of a system. Multimedia can be used to facilitate greater exploration in all these areas, but the media have to be designed to support exploration. The ability to support the user in exploration itself has to be designed; it does not just happen.

A high level of interactivity improves sensory stimulation, and thus facilitates human information processing (Hoogeveen, 1997). Alty (1993) adds that, for hidden goals (or goals not well understood), it is better to allow users to exploit the interface and choose the best media for the task. Bearne et al. (1994) suggest, in their usability guidelines for multimedia systems, that users must be given control over the appearance and the disappearance of each piece of information. The feeling of engagement produced by freedom of exploration is an important issue to take into consideration when designing a multimedia system.

One possible explanation for this phenomenon is that we are used to exploring our environment in an active way. Quoting Gibson (1966; 1979) as cited by Hoogeveen (1997), "we do not hear, we listen; we do not see, we look around". In other words, we actively search for information. That searching is guided by our cognitive understanding of the domain and by our knowledge of how to search. It is

---

*Level of interactivity, in this context, is the degree to which a computer system is responsive to the user's (explorative) behaviour (Hoogeveen, 1997)

also guided by the environment in which we are searching. In the case of multimedia systems, the system is the environment and the designer can provide the support and guidance for searching and exploring. The system must 'invite' the user to explore it, enable them to make guesses of what things might do and what they might find, provide feedback to each action taken in the process of exploration, and provide an easy way to reverse or undo any action taken, thus providing a safe and inviting environment for exploration. In the Scottish tourist guide, the exploration aspects of the system could have been improved by allowing the user to easily return from a given location and maintaining consistency in the navigation and interactions available. For example, once having used the 'map' to find information about one region, that same map could not subsequently be used to return from that location or to go to another location.

3.6   Quality of Information Representation

It has been argued (Hoogeveen, 1997) that the quality of the representation of multimedia information (e.g. graphic representation/photographic representation) can affect the way people interact with multimedia systems. Each medium has its own rules and conventions and will make its own special demands and requirements upon technology to enable that medium to be used optimally. Although literacy is required in every medium, most computer designers are not well skilled in film or video presentation languages (Alty, 1991). People are used to high-quality productions (such as in films, video or television) and could expect to see something of the same standard in a computer display.

Many current multimedia systems have lower quality audio and video presentation capabilities than a user might find on their TV or hi-fi unit. For many applications the quality of the audio and video is extremely important. However, the acceptable level of quality will vary according to the information being presented, the purpose to which it is to be put and the costs and benefits of providing it at a given level of quality. For example, the quality of audio signal received over a mobile phone is often poor and at times very poor. However, for the purposes of holding a conversation, and given the current costs of producing increased audio quality in mobile phones, it is often acceptable. If though, you were trying to listen (or worse still join in with) a musical quartet over a mobile phone then the audio quality would be inadequate for these purposes. Similarly, in using images, we do not always need high resolution, colour images that update in real-time. However, a neurosurgeon engaged in image-guided surgery would need far higher quality images of the brain than might be required of images of a face in a normal video-conferencing situation (unless of course the video conference was between a patient and a dermatologist trying to assess if the patient's facial blemish is cause for concern or not).

4   Next Steps, Small and Large

The features presented in this paper were developed from an extensive literature survey and reflect some of the main aspects of multimedia systems. There are of course attempts to develop standards for multimedia design (e.g. Draft Standard for Multimedia User Interface Design ISO/CD 14915-1). This ISO standard includes a number of general principles, namely; suitability for the task, controllability, self-descriptiveness, conformity with user expectations, error tolerance, suitability for individualization and suitability for learning. It also identifies some specific multimedia design principles, such as suitability for the communication goal, suitability for perception and understanding, suitability for exploration and suitability for engagement. These principles are not out of line with our design features, which we feel ought to be addressed by a set of multimedia design principles. At present the Draft ISO standard is not what we would call principles, but we note that they are still in draft form and it is encouraging that our research and theirs are converging on a common set of features that will result in a set of multimedia design principles. At the present stage, our design features represent a tentative formulation in need of further investigation. In this section, we present our plan for advancing the research.

First we need to refine these features into a set of principles, so that they can be expressed in a more complete and systematic manner, including examples, appropriate theoretical and empirical evidence, and predictions about their effects on usability.

The next step is to assess and refine the principles on different classes of multimedia systems, domains and tasks. In doing this, we will assess their:

1. *predictiveness and reliability* — through experimental testing; and

2. *applicability and usability* — through use in design context.

In this way we will be assessing if they apply to multimedia design problems, if they can predict usability issues and be applied to those issues, and if the principles themselves are usable by designers and evaluators to develop and assess the usability of systems using multimedia.

In the end, we should be able to propose evaluation and design methods or techniques that are principle-based. A method of evaluation would include appropriate criteria, forms of data, forms of analysis and techniques of interpretation to produce redesign recommendations. In the even longer term in order to support design creation, environments might be developed, which would include exemplars, guidelines and constraints derived from the principles.

5   Discussion and Conclusion

In this paper, we have showed that we need principles to support the design and evaluation of multimedia systems. Some examples from a system design were described that illustrate there is indeed a design problem. Then we proposed a tentative set of six features that were elaborated with evidences from the literature. The features are:

1. Naturalness.

2. Media allocation.

3. Redundancy.

4. Significant contribution of the media.

5. Exploration.

6. Quality of information representation.

This is an on-going research topic for us. In order to achieve our goals, these features need to be further refined, tested and used in real-world situations before they can emerge as principles for multimedia design.

Multimedia is a typical technological achievement that lacks an appropriate HCI theory basis to enable systematic reasoning about the utility and usability of particular multimedia design options.   Without an underlying conceptual development in our understanding of the HCI of multimedia, even using the most advanced technology in design, it will not be possible to improve current designs. Relying upon assumptions, beliefs and intuitions alone will not be enough to bring about a widespread improvement in the quality and usability of multimedia systems.

Our research aims to develop basic principles for the design and evaluation of multimedia systems. We believe that these principles will provide a consistent basis for user-interface designers to make better decisions and, hence, to build more usable and useful multimedia systems.

Acknowledgements

Peter Johnson's research is supported by EPSRC grant numbers: GR/K19211, GR/K79796 and GR/K79154. Fabio Nemetz is funded by CAPES/Brazil.
    Figures 1 to 4 are copyright of the Scottish Tourist Board.

References

Alty, J. L. (1991), Multimedia — What is It and How do We Exploit It?, *in* D. Diaper & N. Hammond (eds.), *People and Computers VI: Usability Now! (Proceedings of HCI'91)*, Cambridge University Press, pp.31–44.

Alty, J. L. (1993), Multimedia: We Have the Technology but Do We Have the Methodology ?, *in* H. Maurer (ed.), *Proceedings of Euromedia'93*, AACE, pp.3–10.

Alty, J. L. (1997), Multimedia, *in* A. B. Tucker (ed.), *The Computer Science and Engineering Handbook*, CRC Press, pp.1551–70.

Arens, Y., Hovy, E. & Vossers, M. (1993), On The Knowledge Underlying Multimedia Presentations, *in* M. T. Maybury (ed.), *Intelligent Multimedia Interfaces*, MIT Press, pp.280–306.

Baecker, R. M., Grudin, J., Buxton, W. & Greenberg, S. (1995), *Human–Computer Interaction: Toward the year 2000*, Morgan-Kaufmann.

Barnard, P. & May, J. (1994), Interactions with Advanced Graphical Interfaces and the Deployment of Latent Human Knowledge, *in* F. Paterno' (ed.), *Proceedings of the Eurographics Workshop on the Design, Specification and Verification of Interactive Systems*, Springer-Verlag, pp.15–48.

Basil, M. D. (1994), "Multiple Resource Theory I: Application to Television Viewing", *Communication Research* **21**(2), 177–207.

Bearne, M., Jones, S. & Sapsford-Francis, J. (1994), Towards Usability Guidelines for Multimedia Systems, *in Proceedings of Multimedia'94*, ACM Press, pp.105–110.

Carroll, J. M. (1990), *The Nurnberg Funnel: Designing Minimalist Instruction for Practical Computer Skill*, MIT Press.

Faraday, P. & Sutcliffe, A. (1996), An Empirical Study of Attending and Comprehending Multimedia Presentations, *in Proceedings of Multimedia'96*, ACM Press, pp.265–75.

Gibson, J. (1966), *The Senses Considered as Perceptual Systems*, Houghton-Mifflin.

Gibson, J. (1979), *The Ecological Approach to Visual Perception*, Houghton-Mifflin.

Hoogeveen, M. (1997), "Towards a Theory of the Effectiveness of Multimedia Systems", *International Journal of Human–Computer Interaction* **9**(2), 151–68.

Levinson, S. C. (1983), *Pragmatics*, Cambridge University Press.

Marmolin, H. (1991), Multimedia from the Perspectives of Psychology, *in* L. Kjelldahl (ed.), *Proceedings of the Eurographics Workshop on Multimedia*, Springer-Verlag, pp.39–52.

Nielsen, J. (1995), *Multimedia and Hypertext — The Internet and Beyond*, Academic Press.

Petersen, M. G. (1996), Evaluating Usability of Multimedia Interfaces, Master's thesis, Department of Computer Science, Queen Mary and Westfield College.

Preece, J., Rogers, Y., Sharpe, H., Benyon, D., Holland, S. & Carey, T. (1994), *Human–Computer Interaction*, Addison–Wesley.

Rudnicky, A. I. (1992), Introduction to Part II, *in* M. Blattner & R. M. Dannenberg (eds.), *Multimedia Interface Design*, ACM Press, pp.147–82.

Shneiderman, B. (1997), *Designing the User Interface: Strategies for Effective Human–Computer Interaction*, third edition, Addison–Wesley.

Vetere, F. (1997), Redundancy in Multimedia Systems, *in* S. Howard, J. Hammond & G. K. Lindgaard (eds.), *Human–Computer Interaction — INTERACT'97: Proceedings of the Fifth IFIP Conference on Human–Computer Interaction*, Chapman & Hall, pp.205–11.

Williams, D. (1996), Multimedia, Mental Models and Complex Tasks, *in* G. van der Veer & B. Nardi (eds.), *Proceedings of CHI'96: Human Factors in Computing Systems*, ACM Press, pp.65–6.

How Can Multimedia Designers Utilize Timbre?

Dimitrios I Rigas[†] & James L Alty[‡]

[†] *School of Computing and Mathematics, University of Huddersfield, Huddersfield HD1 3DH, UK.*

Tel: *+44 1484 472758*
Fax: *+44 1484 421106*
EMail: *D.Rigas@hud.ac.uk*

[‡] *LUTCHI Research Centre, Department of Computer Studies, Loughborough University, Leicestershire LE11 3TU, UK.*

Tel: *+44 1509 222649*
Fax: *+44 1509 211586*
EMail: *J.L.Alty@lboro.ac.uk*

When musical sound is required during development of auditory or multimedia interfaces, designers often need to utilize different musical voices or timbre (usually produced via a multiple timbre synthesizer or a sound card) in order to communicate information. Currently, there is a limited set of guidelines assisting multimedia designers to select appropriate timbre. This paper reports a set of recall and recognition experiments on timbres produced by a multiple timbre synthesizer. Results indicate that a number of instruments were successfully recalled and recognized. A set of empirically derived guidelines are suggested to assist multimedia designers in selecting timbre.

Keywords: user interfaces, multimedia, auditory, music, timbre, instruments.

1 Introduction

An important research question for a multimedia designer who wishes to use musical stimuli in an interface is how to choose appropriate musical voices or instruments. Using a number of musical instruments is obviously advantageous for communication purposes, but what capabilities does the average listener have? Can one distinguish a bassoon from a piano or a French horn from an organ? It is likely that complex problem domains will require the designer to use distinct timbres (different musical instruments). This is because the use of different musical instruments provides an excellent way of differentiating musical messages used in communicating different types of information in interfaces. For most HCI applications using music as an output mode, it is likely that more than one instrument will be required.

2 Relevant Work

Hearing characteristics include pitch, loudness and timbre. Pitch is the frequency of the sound. Low frequencies produce a low pitch and high frequencies produce a high pitch. Loudness is proportional to the amplitude of the sound. Timbre denotes the special set of characteristics associated with the sound of a particular instrument. For example, different instruments produce different timbres.

Experiments with trained musicians who were asked to rate the similarity of musical sounds produced by different musical instruments Grey (1982) showed that there were three families (with sub-families) in terms of instruments' similarity. Families identified with some of their sub-families include:

1. Family one. E-flat clarinet, soprano saxophone, bass clarinet, and English horn.

2. Family two. Oboe and mute trombone.

3. Family three. Bassoon, French horn, cello, trumpet, and flute.

Continuous music either on its own or with visual support has been utilized in algorithmic animation (Brown & Hershberger, 1992; Alty, 1995). It has also been reported that music may assist in program debugging (Vickers & Alty, 1996). Other forms of musical sound include earcons. Earcons are short musical structures following specific construction rules and guidelines (Blattner et al., 1989; Brewster et al., 1995a) and have been shown to successfully provide navigational cues in interfacing menu hierarchies (Brewster et al., 1996). Sound can also assist in interfaces for people with special needs such as the visually impaired (Edwards, 1987; Edwards, 1995; Rigas, 1996; Rigas & Alty, 1997). A set of guidelines for the use of timbre in earcons comes from Brewster (1994). The relevant guidelines for timbre which were revised in Brewster et al. (1995b), are:

- Use musical instruments.

- Multiple harmonics are suggested to avoid masking.

- Avoid similar instruments (e.g. violin1, violin2, violin3).

He remarks that:

"...instruments that sound different in real life may not when played on a synthesizer, so care should be taken when choosing timbres. Using multiple timbres per earcon may confer advantages when using compound earcons. Using the same timbres for similar things and different timbres for other things helps with differentiation of sounds when playing in parallel." (Brewster et al., 1995b)

3 Experiments with Timbre

First, some obvious considerations need to be addressed. There is a fundamental difference between memory recall and recognition. This paper refers to the process of memory recall *as the ability of subjects to draw from their memory the name of the instrument being heard in the absence of any memory aid in choosing the name.* The process of recognition, in contrast, refers to *subjects' ability to recognize names of musical instruments being heard from a set of names which are provided to them.*

Recall of instruments' names will be based on listeners' experience. For people who have not pursued a musical education, who only possess an average musical knowledge, the recall of a musical instrument will depend on two issues. The first is whether the sound of the instrument has been stored in an appropriate labelled location in their memory from previous experience, and the second is whether a successful comparison between the instrument heard and a previously stored 'sound' of the instrument can occur (Roederer, 1994). There are three possibilities which can happen when a person with an average musical knowledge hears an instrument. These are:

1. The sound of the instrument is well known to the listener, and the comparison is successful. The listener recalls the name of the instrument (i.e. with no aid to memory apart from the sound of the instrument itself).

2. The sound of the instrument is vaguely known to the listener, thus the comparison is not completely successful. The listener recalls a number of different names for the instrument heard.

3. The sound of the instrument is not known to the listener, thus comparison is not successful. The listener fails to recall the name of the instrument heard.

In using musical instruments to communicate information in an interface, one certainly needs to be able to say to users "<instrument A> will communicate one type of information, <instrument B> will communicate another type of information", and so on. However, there is a question as to how many instruments can be involved. Are listeners going to identify the instruments heard by name and, thus, being able to follow the musical messages? Are there any musical instruments which non musically educated listeners can identify by name when heard? If so, which are those musical voices that multimedia interface designers could use? In order to at least partially investigate these questions, the following experimental approach was taken:

Musical Instrument	% of confidence	Musical Instrument	% of confidence
Guitar	96	Xylophone	30
Piano	94	Trombone	30
Timpani	83	Pan Pipes	27
Violin	82	Tuba	20
Saxophone	76	Oboe	17
Flute	55	Piccolo	16
Harp	53	French Horn	13
Trumpet	42	Bassoon	10
Castanets	40	Celesta	3
Cello	37	Contrabass	3
Harmonica	37	Harpsichord	2
Organ	35	Mandolin	1
Clarinet	34	English Horn	1

Table 1: The results of the instrument survey in percentages.

1. An initial survey in which 100 people were requested to specify which instruments they thought they could recognize if heard.

2. A recall experiment in which 16 subjects were tested with 23 instruments. Subjects were offered no training in order to investigate the success rate of people recalling from their memory the names of the instruments being heard.

3. A recognition experiment in which 16 subjects were tested with 7 instruments. Subjects were not trained but they were provided with a list of the names of the seven instruments. They had to choose the instrument being presented.

4. Another recall experiment in which 10 subjects were tested with 10 instruments. Subjects were aided by an instruments' dictionary (i.e. names of instruments using synthesized speech and their sounds). The experiment aimed to identify any listeners' improvements in recalling the names of the instruments after a short training (i.e. presentation of the instruments' dictionary).

The subjects who participated in the recognition and recall experiments were not musicians. Their musical ability was examined via a musical questionnaire (Rigas, 1996).

3.1   Survey

A survey was first made with 100 people who were requested to list the musical instruments they thought they could be able to confidently recognize by name if they were heard. Participants selected the instruments from a provided list. The results of this survey are shown in Table 1. The table lists the percentages of people who were confident that they could recognize certain instruments.

Stimuli \ Recalled as	PIANO	PICOLO	HARP	ENGL. HORN	GUITAR	ORGAN	FR. HORN	CELESTA	CLARINET	SAXOPHONE	CELLO	TROMBONE	DRUMS	VIOLIN	HARMONICA	TUBA	CONTRA BASS	TRUMPET	XYLOPHONE	PAN PIPES	FLUTE	OBOE	BASSOON
PIANO	8		1		2	2		2								1							
PICOLO	2					9													2		1		
HARP	2		10		1												1						
ENGL. HORN					1						1			4	2						3	2	
GUITAR	6	1		2	2						1					1							
ORGAN				1		14					1												
FR. HORN		2	1	1	1		2		1		1					1		2					1
CELESTA	1		3		1						1					1			8				
CLARINET									8							1		1			3	1	
SAXOPHONE			1			1					1	2		4								1	
CELLO						1		1			4					1			1	1	1	1	
TROMBONE						2			2		1	1				2	3						
DRUMS													15										
VIOLIN											2	2		4								2	
HARMONICA							1		2	1				5	1						1	1	1
TUBA			1				1	1							1						1	1	1
CONTRA BASS											1			3	1	2	1					1	1
TRUMPET						2			1								4	2					1
XYLOPHONE																			16				
PAN PIPES		1														1				8	5	1	
FLUTE		8						1													3		
OBOE			1			1			3		1			5	1						1		
BASSOON			1				1	1			1				1			2				5	1

Figure 1: Results of the recall experiment with instruments. Numbers in boxes show the frequency of recalls (n = 16).

These results are no more than an indication of what people believe that they will recognize. Although, it cannot be argued that people will definitely recognize these instruments, it is likely that the ones at the top of the list will be the most popular and widely heard ones. People were not tested with the musical stimuli of each instrument and, thus, some experimentation to explore this topic further was required.

3.2 Recall Experiment

Will listeners have the same recall success when the instruments are actually heard? To investigate this, a recall experiment was performed in which 16 subjects were asked to recall from their experience, the names of 23 instruments presented to them. A short tune (eight notes) was played using the normal range of each instrument. Subjects were given 20 seconds to consider their answer and to note it on their answering sheet. The Roland MT32 multiple timbre synthesizer was used driven from the Sound Blaster Card and MIDI (Musical Instrument Digital Interface).

Families	Piano	Organ	Wind	Woodwind	Drums	Strings
Piano	65	4	2	0	0	3
Organ	1	15	3	4	0	5
Wind	8	4	18	11	0	11
Woodwind	4	15	5	58	0	13
Drums	0	0	0	0	15	0
Strings	2	2	5	8	0	14

Table 2: The results of the experiment organized in families. The numbers show the frequency of recalls. For example, when instruments from the piano family were played, 65 recalls were names of instruments from the piano family, four recalls were names of instruments from the organ family, two recalls were names of instruments from the wind family, three recalls were names of instruments from the strings family, and there were no recalls from the woodwind and drums families.

Results are shown in Figure 1. It can be seen that the successful recall rates were not uniform, and certainly not as good as subjects had predicted in the survey — see Section 3.1. For example — see Figure 1, when piano was heard, eight out of sixteen people recalled it successfully as a piano, one person recalled it as a harp, two people recalled it as a guitar, two people recalled it as an organ, two people recalled it as a celesta, and one person recalled it as a tuba.

Some instruments were almost uniquely recalled, for example *xylophone*, *drums* (timpani was used) and *organ*. Others had reasonably good recognition rates (up to 50%). Note that there are major differences between what subjects thought they could recognize — see Table 1 — and what they actually recognized. If we redraw Figure 1, grouping instruments together into their recognized families we get Table 2. The families used in table Table 2 were:

Piano:	piano, harp, guitar, celesta, and xylophone.
Organ:	organ and harmonica.
Wind:	trumpet, French horn, tuba, trombone, and saxophone.
Woodwind:	clarinet, English horn, pan pipes, piccolo, oboe, bassoon, and flute.
Strings:	violin, cello, and bass.
Drums:	drums.

We can expand the results of Figure 1 in terms of the above families. This is shown in Figure 2. One can see that recall by family is very successful. In other words, confusion usually occurs within a musical family than across families. The χ^2 values* of the experimental results organized in families (see Table 2) suggest that subjects did not recall the names of the instruments randomly.

These results (which basically follow music orchestration rules), indicate that multimedia interface designers should choose instruments from different families to

---

*χ^2 values are 271.65 for piano, 31.6 for organ, 22.71 for wind, 144.96 for woodwind, 75 for drums, df = 5, critical value 20.52 at 0.001.

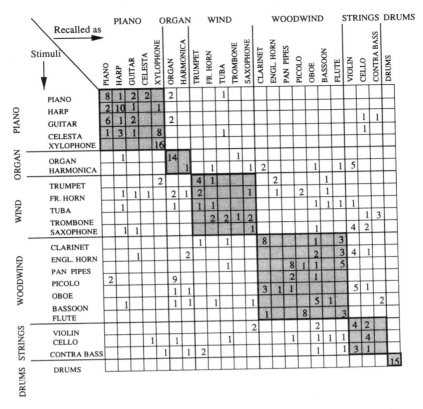

Figure 2: Results of the recall experiment with instruments grouped in families *piano, organ, wind, woodwind, strings* and *drums*. Numbers in boxes show the frequency of recalls.

avoid confusion. *Piano, organ, xylophone* and *drums* seem to be particularly well distinguished.

3.3 Recognition Experiment

In the recognition experiment, 16 subjects[†] were tested with 7 instruments. Subjects were presented with a short tune from each instrument and they had to recognize the name of the instrument from a list of names. The instruments presented were piano, guitar, drums (timpani was used), violin, saxophone, flute and harp.

As it can be seen in Figure 3, successful recognition rates were 81.2% for piano, 87.5% for guitar, 100% for drums, 87.5% for violin, 93.7% for saxophone, 87.5% for flute, and 31.2% for harp. These results demonstrate that recognition from a small set of possibilities (and not recall) has higher success rates.

The instruments chosen were one from each class, as specified above, but two were from the piano class chosen to explore the family interference issue. These were

---

[†]The same subjects who participated in the experiment discussed in Section 3.2.

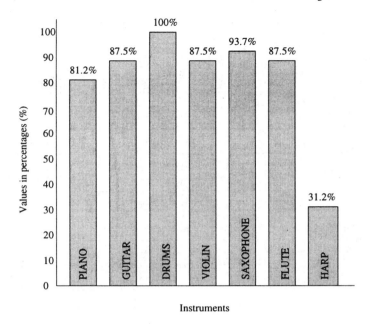

Figure 3: The results of the recognition experiment.

piano and harp which, as it can be seen in Figure 3, confused the subjects[‡]. The poor performance of the harp might be due to interference within the same family. However, it may also be due to poor synthesizer quality. Synthesizer quality may contribute significantly in the recognition of an instrument. To investigate the effect of synthesizer quality, another experiment was performed.

3.4   Recall Experiment Using a 'Musical Dictionary'

In this experiment 10 subjects[§] in were presented with a dictionary of instruments. The dictionary had entries for 10 instruments of the following form:

This is <the name of instrument> (a short tune played).

The dictionary was presented five times as described above. On completion of the dictionary presentation, subjects had to write the name of the instrument for every succeeding tune heard. The musical voices tested were piccolo, flute, pan pipes, clarinet, tuba, harmonica, trumpet, cello, celesta, and violin.

Some of the instruments had been selected because of their similarity, and some because of their distinctness, in order to examine the capability of participants in making successful comparisons and recalls after a short conditioning process (i.e.

[‡]χ^2 values are 6.25 for piano, 9 for guitar, 16 for drums, 9 for violin, 12.25 for saxophone, 9 for flute, and 2.25 for harp. These values (apart from harp) exceed the critical value of 5.41 at 0.02, df = 1.

[§]These subjects were not the same with the ones who participated in the experiments discussed in Sections 3.2 & 3.3.

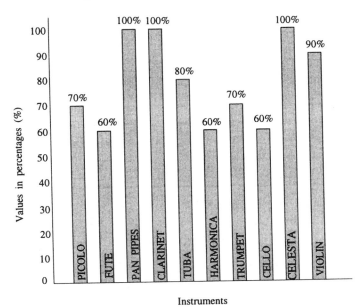

Figure 4: A graphical presentation showing successful recall rates of subjects (in percentages) of the recall experiment using the instruments' dictionary.

training). The results of this experiment are shown in Figure 4. The percentages of successful recalls were 70% for piccolo, 60% for flute, 100% for pan pipes, 100% for clarinet, 80% for tuba, 60% for harmonica, 70% for trumpet, 60% for cello, 100% for celesta, and 90% for violin. Flute, cello, and harmonica are not significant results[1]. The rest of the instruments are significant[||]. This experiment also suggests that trained people are more likely to recall some instruments than others (χ^2 value is 16.9, n = 10, critical value 14.68 at 0.1). One can see that some instruments which were poorly recalled in previous experiments — see Sections 3.2 & 3.3, were recognized reasonably in this experiment.

3.5 Discussion and Guidelines

Some multimedia interface designs may only require a single musical instrument to be used. The guideline for the selection of a single instrument is simple. First, one needs to identify the range of notes required in terms of pitch and octaves. Secondly, an instrument should be selected from the ones which provide the required pitch range. If one is not absolutely certain of the range then a musical instrument with a wide range of octaves should be chosen (e.g. piano, harp or organ).

[1] χ^2 values are 0.4 for flute, cello and harmonica (critical value of 1.64 at 0.20).
[||] χ^2 values are 1.6 for piccolo, 10 for pan pipes, 10 for clarinet, 3.6 for tuba, 1.6 for trumpet, 10 for celesta, and 6.4 for violin (critical value of 1.64 at 0.20).

However, it is more likely that two instruments will be used sequentially rather than a single instrument for most HCI applications. In using two musical instruments, one must ensure that the following conditions are satisfied:

1. The user must be in a position to identify the separate musical timbres and be able to recognize at least one by name.

2. The musical instruments should sound sufficiently convincing for a musically untrained ear. A good multi-timbre synthesizer must be used, and even then some voices are much better than others.

3. Instruments should be derived from different musical families.

The first condition ensures that the user can distinguish the two instruments and, also, can recognize one by name. The reason that it is a mandatory requirement for the user to recognize at least one is because this will allow them to follow the other instrument as well even if it cannot be recognized by name. The second condition ensures that the instruments are complementary in terms of voice quality, do not sound similar, or mask each other. Sound distortion or a poor synthesizer may make a piano sound like a harp! The third condition suggests the use of instruments from different families as our experimentation has suggested. These findings support existing guidelines for usage of timbre (Brewster et al., 1995b) — see also Section 2. Our experiments suggest that one instrument from each of the following families is likely to be recalled by the listener with no prior training:

Piano: piano, harp, guitar, celesta, and xylophone.

Organ: organ and harmonica.

Wind: trumpet, French horn, tuba, trombone, and saxophone.

Woodwind: clarinet, English horn, pan pipes, piccolo, oboe, bassoon, and flute.

Strings: violin, cello, and bass.

Drums: drums.

The above families were derived from the recall experiment — see Section 3.2. This experiment shown that only a limited number of instruments were successfully recalled by name in the absence of training. Most of the recall confusion was with instruments belonging to the same family.

When more than two instruments are needed, the designer must be very careful in allocating appropriate timbres. Some principles need to be followed. These principles have been observed in other experiments (Rigas & Alty, 1997; Rigas et al., 1997), the design of which was partly based upon the experiments documented in Sections 3.1–3.3. These are:

1. The musical messages must be grouped into task domain categories and the designer must avoid using similar timbre instruments in the same categories.

2. The usage of musical instruments must be consistent across the application user interface.

3. At critical points of user perception, very dissimilar musical instruments must be used to avoid user confusion.

4. Other distinguishing properties (such as stereo and rhythm) should be used where possible in parallel, to enhance disambiguation.

The recognition experiment demonstrated that users were more confident in recognizing instruments than recalling them. However, there are difficulties. These difficulties apply when listeners cannot properly recognize some names of the instruments which are utilized to communicate information. It was observed (in experiments discussed in Sections 3.3 & 3.4) that subjects had to hear all the instruments before allocating names to unknown or vaguely known instruments.

For instance, when five instruments are heard and listeners can recall only two, they attempt to associate names and sounds for the remaining three unknown instruments using their general knowledge. At this stage, these associations are provisional. In the next cycle**, listeners try to form further associations until all instruments have been correctly or wrongly associated with names. However, it is important to note that up to now listeners have been busy trying to form associations. Thus, they may not have processed the information which is being communicated by the musical stimuli. If the period of time in which the musical instruments introduce themselves (i.e. the first cycle) is short then listeners will be able to follow the process perhaps from cycle two onwards. Problems will be more evident when the introductory cycle is long because listeners may have lost crucial interactions as a result of having formed either the wrong associations or having not established any at all. This is more problematic when no clues are offered with regard to the identity of the instrument by the musical interaction. This was observed in other experimental programmes using structured music and various musical voices (Rigas, 1996; Rigas & Alty, 1997; Rigas et al., 1997).

Thus, we suggest that the following approach is taken:

1. One must use musical instruments from the list we have shown to be successfully identifiable by the recall process (e.g. piano, guitar, drums, organ) when it is critical for the listener to immediately identify the instrument.

2. Musical instruments shown to be capable of being identified by recognition can be used when the instruments have time to introduce themselves at the start of the interaction, and there is no critical significance if the user misses some communicated information.

3. The first cycle should ideally be used as a recognition cycle (e.g. as the listeners hear the different timbres, they are in a position to provisionally assign names to each timbre used and by the end of the cycle to finalize the provisional assignments of names).

**Cycle is defined as the time required for all instruments to be heard.

	PIANO	HARP	GUITAR	CELESTA	XYLOPHONE	ORGAN	HARMONICA	TRUMPET	TUBA	SAXOPHONE	CLARINET	PAN PIPES	PICOLO	FLUTE	VIOLIN	CELLO	DRUMS
Survey	94	53	96	3	30	35	37	42	20	76	34	27	16	55	82	37	83
Recall Exp. No training	50	62.5	12.5	0	100	87.5	6.2	25	0	6.2	50	50	0	18.7	25	25	93.7
Recall Exp. Training	-	-	-	100	-	-	60	70	80	-	100	100	70	60	90	60	-
Recognition	81.2	31.2	87.5	-	-	-	-	-	-	93.7	-	-	-	87.5	87.5	-	100

All values are in percentages

Table 3: Comparison of successful rates (shown in percentages) for some instruments from survey, recall experiment with no training, recall experiment with training and recognition experiment.

It is better to train users when many instruments are involved. It was shown that an introductory demonstration — i.e. musical dictionary, see Section 3.4 — of the timbres assists in successful recall of the subsequent musical instruments tested. As it can be seen in Table 3, the dictionary of musical instruments was found to be an important aid in assisting listeners to make correct recalls. In addition, there are also a number of other advantages when one uses a dictionary of instruments:

1. The listeners uses the dictionary of the musical instruments as a reference basis for comparison and recall as opposed to using their memory of previous experience with timbres.

2. The dictionary of the instruments uses the same synthesizer (internal or external) and, thus, any distortion in the musical instrument is reflected uniformly in the dictionary as well as in the musical output.

3. The need for the instruments dictionary, although necessary at the beginning, gradually diminishes as the listener becomes more experienced. This was observed in experimental trials.

The use of a dictionary is suggested for the circumstances where a large number of instruments need to be used or when instruments belong to the same family and may sound alike in an untrained ear.

4 Conclusion

These results show that multimedia interface designers can use different musical voices to communicate different types of information. The recall experiment — see Section 3.2 — demonstrated that listeners cannot successfully recall a number of instruments. Recall is poor particularly when many instruments (say 10 or more) are involved. This happens regardless of how distinctive the timbre may be. For example, if 10 instruments are used to communicate 10 different types of information, the risk that users will confuse the names of instruments is very high. When using fewer numbers of instruments (say 5 or fewer), the success rate in listeners' successful recognition is greatly improved — see Section 3.3. It was found that if instruments were chosen from the six families created from this experimental data then recognition or recall was higher. Instruments from the same family (the ones introduced earlier) must be avoided but if training is offered to the listener then some instruments (from the same family) may be recognized.

The introduction of an on-line dictionary of musical voices — see Section 3.4 — was shown to assist listeners in overcoming problems with poor quality audio cards or external synthesizers, which produce different levels of distortion. Users can be given the opportunity of hearing the sound of the instruments through their own synthesizers or audio card, and thus store appropriate labels of the instruments used into their memory. Thus, because the user is conditioned, the possibility of recalling the name of the instrument is higher.

A number of problems were also observed in listeners' recall and recognition for some instruments (e.g. harp and piano) which are under further investigation.

References

Alty, J. (1995), Can we use Music in Human–Computer Interaction?, *in* M. A. R. Kirby, A. J. Dix & J. E. Finlay (eds.), *People and Computers X (Proceedings of HCI'95)*, Cambridge University Press, pp.409–23.

Blattner, M., Sumikawa, D. & Greenberg, R. (1989), "Earcons and Icons: Their Structure and Common Design Principles", *Human–Computer Interaction* 4(1), 11–44.

Brewster, S. A. (1994), Providing a Structured Method for Integrating Non-speech Audio into Human–Computer Interfaces, PhD thesis, University of York, England, UK.

Brewster, S. A., Raty, V. & Kortekangas, A. (1996), Earcons as a Method of Providing Navigational Cues in a Menu Hierarchy, *in* A. Sasse, R. J. Cunningham & R. Winder (eds.), *People and Computers XI (Proceedings of HCI'96)*, Springer-Verlag, pp.167–83.

Brewster, S. A., Wright, P. C. & Edwards, A. D. N. (1995a), Experimentally Derived Guidelines for the Creation of Earcons, *in* G. Allen, J. Wilkinson & P. Wright (eds.), *Adjunct Proceedings of HCI'95: People and Computers X*, British Computer Society, pp.155–9.

Brewster, S. A., Wright, P. C., Dix, C. & Edwards, A. D. N. (1995b), The Sonic Enhancement of graphical buttons, *in* K. Nordby, P. H. Helmersen, D. J. Gilmore & S. A. Arnessen (eds.), *Human–Computer Interaction — INTERACT'95: Proceedings of the Fifth IFIP Conference on Human–Computer Interaction*, Chapman & Hall, pp.43–8.

Brown, M. H. & Hershberger, J. (1992), "Color and Sound in Algorithm Animation", *IEEE Computer* 12(25), 52–63.

Edwards, A. D. N. (1987), Adapting User Interfaces for Visually Disabled Users, PhD thesis, Open University, Milton Keynes, UK.

Edwards, A. D. N. (ed.) (1995), *Extra-Ordinary Human–Computer Interaction*, Cambridge University Press.

Grey, J. M. (1982), "Multidimensional perceptual scaling of musical timbres", *Journal of the Acoustical Society of America,* **61**(5), 1270–7.

Rigas, D. I. (1996), Guidelines for Auditory Interface Design: An Empirical Investigation, PhD thesis, Loughborough University, Leicestershire, UK.

Rigas, D. I. & Alty, J. L. (1997), The Use of Music in a Graphical Interface for the Visually Impaired, *in* S. Howard, J. Hammond & G. K. Lindgaard (eds.), *Human–Computer Interaction — INTERACT'97: Proceedings of the Fifth IFIP Conference on Human–Computer Interaction*, Chapman & Hall, pp.228–35.

Rigas, D. I., Alty, J. L. & Long, F. W. (1997), Can Music Support Interfaces to Complex Databases?, *in EUROMICRO-97, New Frontiers of Information Technology*, IEEE Computer Society Press, pp.78–84.

Roederer, J. G. (1994), *The Physics and Psychophysics of Music: An Introduction*, third edition, Springer-Verlag.

Vickers, P. & Alty, J. L. (1996), CAITLIN: A Musical Program Auralization Tool to Assist Novice Programmers with Debugging, *in* S. Frysinger & G. Kramer (eds.), *Proceedings of ICAD'96*, pp.17–23.

Using Earcons to Improve the Usability of a Graphics Package

Stephen Brewster

Glasgow Interactive Systems Group, Department of Computing Science, University of Glasgow, Glasgow G12 8QQ, UK.

Tel: *+44 141 330 4966*
EMail: *stephen@dcs.gla.ac.uk*
URL: *http://www.dcs.gla.ac.uk/~stephen/*

This paper describes how non-speech sounds can be used to improve the usability of a graphics package. Sound was specifically used to aid problems with tool palettes and finding the current mouse coordinates when drawing. Tool palettes have usability problems because users need to see the information they present but they are often outside the area of visual focus. An experiment was conducted to investigate the effectiveness of adding sound to tool palettes. Earcons were used to indicate the current tool and when tool changes occurred. Results showed a significant reduction in the number of tasks performed with the wrong tool. Therefore users knew what the current tool was and did not try to perform tasks with the wrong tool. All of this was not at the expense of making the interface any more annoying to use.

Keywords: earcons, sonically-enhanced widgets, sound, interface sonification.

1 Introduction

This paper describes how the usability of a graphics package can be improved by the addition of non-speech sound. It might not be immediately obvious how sounds could be used in a graphics package which is, of course, highly visual by its nature. One problem with modern graphical displays is that they are very visually demanding; all information is presented graphically. As has been demonstrated, this can cause users to become overloaded and to miss important information (Brewster, 1997). One reason is that our eyes cannot do everything. Our visual sense has a small area of high acuity. In highly complex graphical displays users must concentrate on one part of the display to perceive the graphical feedback, so that feedback from another part may be missed as it is outside the area of visual focus (Brewster & Crease, 1997). This problem is worse for partially sighted users whose area of acuity may be reduced by problems such as tunnel vision. Sound also does not take up any screen space and so does not obscure parts of the display, it is good at getting our attention whilst we are looking at something else and it does not disrupt our visual focus.

As an example, imagine you are working on your computer creating a drawing and are also monitoring several on-going tasks such as a compilation, a print job and downloading files over the Internet. The drawing task will take up all of your visual attention because you must concentrate on what you are doing. In order to check when your printout is done, the compilation has finished or the files have downloaded you must move your visual attention away from your picture and look at these other tasks. This causes the interface to intrude into the task you are trying to perform. It is suggested here that some information should be presented in sound. This would allow you to continue looking at your drawing but to hear information on the other tasks that would otherwise not be seen (or would not be seen unless you moved your visual attention away from the area of interest, so interrupting the task you are trying to perform). Sound and graphics can be used together to exploit the advantages of each. In the above example, you could be looking at the drawing you are creating but hear progress information on the other tasks in sound. To find out how the file download was progressing you could just listen to the download sound without moving your visual attention from the drawing task.

In this paper the use of non-speech sound, and not speech, is suggested. Speech is slow and serial (Slowiaczek & Nusbaum, 1985); to get information the user must hear it from beginning to end. Speech is similar to text, whereas non-speech sounds are similar to graphical icons. An icon, or non-speech sound, can concisely represent a concept whereas many words may be needed to describe it. The non-speech sounds described later in the paper are very short (the longest was less than 0.5s) and can communicate their meaning quickly, but speech sounds would take longer. Speech is also language dependent, whereas non-speech sound is universal. For these reasons this paper suggests the use of non-speech sound in this case.

Even though sound has benefits to offer it is not clear how best to use it in combination with graphical output. The use of sound in computer displays is still in its infancy, there is little research to show the best ways of combining these different media (Brewster et al., 1994; Alty, 1995). This means sounds are sometimes added in ad hoc and ineffective ways by individual designers (Barfield et al., 1991; Portigal, 1994). This paper describes the addition of sound to a graphics package (see Figure 1) as an example of how it can be used effectively. Such packages are visually demanding and users may become visually overloaded when they have to look at the drawing they are working on and the interface to the package. Sounds were added to tool palettes to stop tool mis-selection errors, and for indicating the cursor position when drawing.

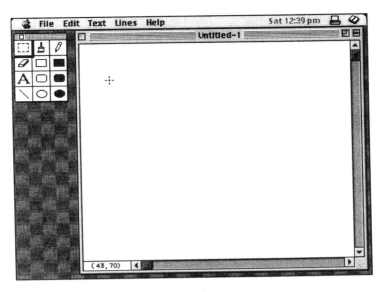

Figure 1: Screen-shot of the graphics package used.

2 Previous Uses of Sound

One of the first attempts to use sound in a graphical interface, in this case the Macintosh Finder, was Gaver with the *SonicFinder* (Gaver, 1986; Gaver, 1989). The SonicFinder added sounds for selecting different types of items, dragging and copying. The extra sonic feedback gave users information that they could not see, for example file size and type when selecting. The same approach was taken in sonifying the graphics package; sounds were to give users information that they could not see without taking their eyes off the task in which they were involved. However, one thing that Gaver did not do was formally experimentally test his sonic enhancements to see if they actually improved usability. His results were more anecdotal. The addition of sounds to the graphics package had to be fully tested to ensure they improved usability.

Brewster and colleagues have successfully improved the usability of buttons, scrollbars and menus with non-speech sound (Brewster et al., 1994; Brewster, 1997; Brewster & Crease, 1997). Sounds were added to help users in situations where they could not see graphical feedback they needed. For example, sounds were added to pull-down menus because users may slip off the item they want on to one above or below (Brewster & Crease, 1997). This is often not noticed as their visual attention is elsewhere. Sonic enhancements reduced time taken to recover from errors, time taken to complete tasks and workload without any increase in subjective annoyance. Beaudouin-Lafon & Conversy (1996) added sound to overcome usability problems in scrollbars. They used an auditory illusion called Shepard–Risset tones which increase (or decrease) in pitch indefinitely (similar to the Escher drawing of an endless staircase). When the user was scrolling down a continuously decreasing tone was used, when scrolling up an increasing one. If scrolling errors occurred then the user would hear tones moving in the wrong direction. Results from these earlier experiments suggested that sound would be effective in overcoming the problems in a graphics package. Therefore, the same approach was used here.

Rigas & Alty (1997) used non-speech, musical sounds in the interface to a graphics package for blind people. They were able to use sounds to present the layout and structure of simple graphical images. To represent coordinate locations they used a *note-sequence* technique: notes were used to represent each of the points between the origin and the current location; the sequence of notes was then played to indicate the location. Results were favourable within a small (40×40) grid. In the graphics package described in this paper there could be a very large grid (up to 1024×768). Therefore it would not be possible to play a sequence of notes as Rigas & Alty had done because this would take too long. However, Rigas & Alty showed that it was possible, suggesting that, with some adaptation, cursor location could be presented in sound.

The commercial graphics application KidPix by Brøderbund Software also uses sound to make it more engaging (Kramer, 1994) for its users (who are children). The sound effects it uses are generally added for amusement but do indicate the drawing tool that is currently being used. For example the pencil tool sounds similar to a real pencil when used (making a scratching sound). These sounds were not an attempt to improve usability but to make the interface more engaging. It is hoped that the graphics package described in this paper can take advantage of the added engagement provided by sound but also improve usability.

One of the problems with graphics packages is that they often have modes (see Section 4 for more details). In early work, Monk (1986) suggested that non-speech sounds could be used to overcome mode errors. In an experiment he tested the use of keying-contingent sounds to indicate different modes in a simple chemical plant simulation. Participants had to type in codes to transfer oxygen to reactors to keep the plant running. Errors occurred when switching between column-identifier mode and oxygen-addition mode. His results showed that with sounds one third less mode errors occurred, indicating that sound could provide valuable feedback on mode state. The research described in this paper builds on this earlier work.

3   Overall Structure of the Sounds Used

The sounds used were based around structured non-speech musical messages called *Earcons* (Blattner et al., 1989; Brewster et al., 1993). Earcons are abstract, musical sounds that can be used in structured combinations to create audio messages to represent parts of an interface. The earcons were created using the earcon guidelines proposed by Brewster et al. (1995)

The widgets in any application form a hierarchy. For example, a simple application might bring up a window as in Figure 2. This window is made up from a frame which contains a menu bar, a listbox and a scrollbar. The menu bar contains two menus and, in turn, these menus will contain menu items. The windowing system will represent this as a hierarchy of widgets. This hierarchical structure was used to define the sounds for the graphics package.

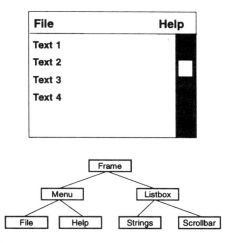

Figure 2: A simple window with several widgets and the hierarchy used to represent them.

The overall structure of the sounds was as follows: The application had its own spatial location (via stereo position) as a base for all of its sounds (just as an application has a base frame for all of its widgets). All widgets within the application used this and added to it by changing timbre, rhythm, pitch, etc.

This approach to allocating sounds is the same as for graphical widgets: A graphical application has a base frame for its widgets. This frame has a spatial location and any widget drawn within the frame uses the base spatial location to position itself. If the frame is moved then all of the widgets move accordingly. In terms of the sounds, if the application is moved all of the sounds play from a new stereo location.

Each of the main components was given a different timbre, as suggested by the earcon construction guidelines (Brewster et al., 1995). For example, the selection tool was given a marimba timbre and the other drawing tools a trumpet (for more detail on this see below). For drawing or selecting horizontally a higher pitched sound was used than for drawing/selecting vertically (see below).

The overall structure of the sounds has now been described. In the next sections the specific uses of sound and the usability problems to be addressed will be dealt with. In particular, the use of earcons to correct problems with tool palettes and drawing will be discussed.

4 Problems with Tool Palettes

Tool (or button) palettes are a common feature of most graphical interfaces and especially graphics packages. One reason for this is that they allow the user easy access to a set of tools and indicate which tool is currently active (see Figure 3(a)). Put another way, palettes are mode indicators; they allow the user to set the mode and then indicate what the current mode is (Dix et al., 1993). Figure 3(a) shows a set of

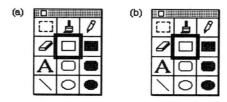

Figure 3: Rectangle tool selection by (a) single click, and (b) double click.

standard tools from a graphics package (shown in Figure 1). The currently selected tool (in this case the rectangle drawing tool) is highlighted by changing its border.

In some systems (for example the Microsoft Word drawing package) after one rectangle has been drawn the system will change back to the default tool, often the selection tool (the dotted square at the top left of Figure 3(a)). In other systems (for example Adobe Illustrator) the tool will remain selected until the user changes it (the tools in some packages use a mixture of both of these methods). There is a hybrid of these two (for example ClarisDraw) where the user can single-click a tool for it to be selected once or double-click for it to remain permanently selected. This method has the advantage that users can choose whether they want to stay in a drawing tool or revert back to the selection tool — it is more flexible. Figure 3(a) shows an example of the different feedback indicating a single click and Figure 3(b) shows a double click on a tool icon.

Interaction problems occur because users may not notice the currently active tool. In a graphics package users will be occupied with the drawing task they are doing (perhaps drawing a series of rectangles) which will require their full visual attention. This means that they will not be looking at the palette to see the current tool. If the system switches back to a default tool users may try to draw another rectangle but end up using the selection tool by mistake. If, on the other hand, the system remains in the current tool they may draw another rectangle by mistake when they really wanted to position the rectangle just drawn. These problems are exacerbated by the hybrid system because it is less predictable as the user may not remember if the current tool was single or double clicked.

4.1   Overcoming the Problems of Tool Palettes

In order to solve the problems of tool mis-selection users must get the right feedback to ensure that they know what is going on (Reason, 1990). This paper suggests using auditory feedback to solve the problems. Why use sound, why not just use extra graphical feedback? It is difficult to solve these problems with extra graphics. Graphics displayed on the palette will not be seen by users because their visual attention will be on the drawing task they are engaged in. The visual system has a narrow area of focus which means that users cannot look at the palette as well as their main task. Information could be displayed at the mouse location — often the shape of the cursor is changed to reflect the current tool. This has some effect but if the different cursors are too big they will obscure the drawing underneath or if they are too small they will be too subtle to be noticed by users who are concentrating on the drawing they are creating and not the cursor. Sellen et al. (1992) have also demonstrated that the use of even gross graphical feedback (changing the colour of the entire screen) can be ineffective at indicating modes. Therefore, a different approach was needed. If we give tool information in sound then it will not obscure the display, it will be noticeable and we do not need to know where users are looking in order for them to perceive it. If users must look at the palette then it forces them to stop what they are doing for their main task and causes the interface to intrude; sound does not have such drawbacks.

4.2 Earcons for the Tool Palette

Earcons were needed to indicate the currently active tool (the hybrid system of single and double clicking of tools will be used as an example). The main problems with the tool palette occur when switching from one tool to another. If the user does not know a switch has occurred (or conversely does not know that the same tool is still active) then errors will result as the wrong tool will be used.

An earcon was played when a tool was chosen. This occurred when (a) the user clicked on a new tool or (b) after he/she had finished drawing. In (a) this could be a single or double-click sound. In (b) if no tool change occurred (i.e. the user had doubled-clicked a tool) the same tool earcon was played again to reinforce that the tool had not changed, otherwise a sound indicating a switch back to the default tool was played.

The earcons were created using the earcon guidelines proposed by Brewster et al. (1995). The default selection tool was given a marimba timbre and the other tools a trumpet timbre. Only two instruments were needed because any automatic tool changes would always be from a drawing tool to the default tool. This situation was where errors were likely to occur so these changes had to be made salient to the user. The difference between these instruments when the earcons were played would grab the users' attention (Brewster et al., 1995).

For a single-click selection one 100ms note at pitch C_3 (261Hz) was played. When a tool was selected by a double click the user heard the single-click earcon, to indicate a change in tool, and then two 100ms notes at a higher pitch, C_2 (523Hz), to indicate a double-click selection. These sounds were played in the timbre of the tool selected.

The intensity of sound was not used to make the earcons grab the users' attention to alert them to a tool change. Instead, a change in the earcon's instrument and pitch were used. In general, intensity changes should be saved for the most important events that must be communicated (for example, serious errors) because intensity has the most potential for annoyance (Berglund et al., 1990; Brewster et al., 1995).

The advantage of earcons used in this way is that they can stop errors happening. In previous experiments Brewster et al. used sound to help users recover from errors more quickly (Brewster et al., 1994; Brewster & Crease, 1997) but did not stop the errors from occurring in the first place. In this case, the sounds alert users to the next tool that will be used and therefore if that is the wrong tool they can choose the correct one before beginning to draw, so avoiding the error in the first place.

5   Problems when Drawing

The other (related) problem is that of coordinate display when drawing. Many graphics packages give cursor coordinates to the user in the form of a small box at the bottom edge of the drawing area (see Figure 1) or by rulers around the edge of the drawing area. When users are drawing they can look across at the ruler and see where they are, but this means they must take their eyes off the drawing as the ruler is outside the area of visual focus.

When precisely drawing or positioning objects it is common to see users with their noses up close to the screen concentrating hard so that they can position an object exactly where they want it. In this situation they cannot easily look at the coordinates or the ruler — they have to take their eyes off the drawing area and the task they are performing to get the information they need (this is a similar problem to the tool palettes above — the interface is intruding into the task the user is trying to perform).

If users must look at the ruler then they must take their eyes off the objects being positioned. By the time users have moved their eyes from the object to the ruler, or back from the ruler to the object, they may inadvertently move their hand slightly on the mouse and so move the object being positioned. They may not notice this movement (and so position the object incorrectly) or may then have to look back to the ruler again to check if the position is correct (with the potential of the same error happening again).

For example, suppose you wanted to position a label five pixels to the left of the top of a rectangle. You would move to the approximate location and then have to look at the ruler or coordinates to check if you were in right location. You would then move and check until the position was correct. When doing this your hand may move slightly so moving the label. This is particularly important when doing very fine positioning tasks.

One way to solve the problem is to make the position information easier to get at. The coordinates could be presented graphically at the mouse location so that users would not have to move their visual attention away from their drawing task, but then the coordinates would obscure the drawing underneath (in a similar way to the tool palette described above). An alternative solution is to use sound. This would not require users to take their eyes off their drawings, so making it less likely that they would accidentally move the mouse when positioning items (also the drawing will not be obscured by extra graphics).

5.1   Earcons for Drawing

Earcons were needed to indicate the coordinate location. An earcon was played if the mouse was moved one pixel with the mouse button down. This meant that if a user wanted to move five pixels he/she could listen to five sounds, making the task simpler as he/she would not have to look away from the drawing at the ruler or coordinates.

In the example just described, if the user moved to the approximate location, he/she could look once at the coordinates to find out the current location and then move to the correct location by listening to the sounds. If he/she had moved to within five pixels of the correct location of the label he/she could move the five by listening to the sounds without needing to look away from the drawing task. The chance of

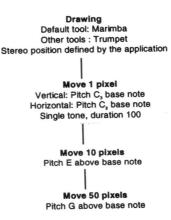

Figure 4: Hierarchy of earcons used for drawing.

moving the mouse inadvertently would be removed as the user would be looking at the object being positioned all of the time.

The hierarchy of earcons used is shown in Figure 4. The timbre of the earcon played depended on which tool was being used. This also acted to reinforce the current tool in the users mind, helping with the problems described for the tool palette. For drawing horizontally the earcons were played at pitch C_2 and for vertically at C_3, the timbre was based on the current tool.

It was decided that the sounds could be made to emulate a ruler more closely by providing different earcons to represent 1, 10 and 50 pixels. On a ruler it is common to see the units represent by small tick marks, the tens represented by longer marks and the fifties by the longest marks. The same was done with earcons.

When users moved 1 pixel the 1 pixel earcon was played. When the mouse was moved over a 10 pixel boundary (as would be shown by a longer tick mark on a graphical ruler) the 10 pixel earcon was played in addition (see Figure 4). This made a chord of C and E (the pitch was defined by whether the movement was horizontal or vertical, the timbre was defined by the current tool). When the user moved over a 50 pixel boundary the 50 pixel earcon was played. This added another note (G) into the chord. By doing this users could drag objects around and get much of the information in sound that was given visually by the ruler without having to take their eyes off their drawing.

However, if a sound was heard for every pixel all of the time then it could become annoying. To avoid this problem the speed of movement of the mouse was used to determine when earcons should be played. If the user was moving fast ($X > 90$ pixels/s) then only the 50 pixel earcon was played. If the user was moving more slowly (15 pixels/s $< X < 90$ pixels/s) then the 10 pixel earcon was played. Finally, if the user was moving very slowly ($X < 15$ pixels/s) then the one pixel earcon was played (as described in the previous paragraph). Slow movements usually mean that fine positioning tasks are being undertaken whereas fast movements mean

Figure 5: Examples of the cursor shapes used in the graphics package. The first is for the selection tool, the second for the line/rectangle tools and the final one for the eraser.

positioning is more general. When making fast movements users do not need to know about each pixel they move over. The values for the speeds of movement were defined by some simple trials with users.

6 Experiment

An experiment was needed to investigate if the addition of sound to the graphics package would increase the usability. Due to time constraints it was only possible to test the tool palette to investigate if sound could solve the problems of tool mis-selection. Twelve participants were used. They were undergraduate students from the University of Glasgow with three years of experience with graphical interfaces and tool palettes. Participants had to be familiar with graphics packages so that they could concentrate on the drawing tasks they were given and use the tool palette as they would in their everyday interactions.

6.1 Hypotheses

The extra auditory feedback heard by participants should make the task easier because they will be able to tell they have made errors and recover from them more readily. This should result in an overall reduction in subjective workload.

There should be no increase in annoyance due to the sounds as they will be providing information that the participants need to overcome usability problems.

The number of tasks performed with the wrong tool should be reduced when sound is present as users will know which tool is currently active; sonic presentation of the current tool is the most effective method. This will be indicated by a decrease in the number of tasks performed with the wrong tool.

6.2 Task

Participants were required to perform drawing tasks set by the experimenter in a simple graphics package. Figure 1 shows a screen-shot of the graphics package, the tool palette used is shown in Figure 3. The package was a standard one with standard tools. It was based on ArtClass, a demonstration program supplied with Symantec Think Pascal for the Macintosh. The hybrid method for tool selections was added to the package as this has the potential for the most usability problems. However, the results would also show how errors with the other types of palettes could be solved.

Participants	Condition 1		Condition 2	
Six Participants ➡	Sonically- Enhanced Palette Train & Test	Workload Test	Visual Palette Train & Test	Workload Test
Six Participants ➡	Visual Palette Train & Test		Sonically- Enhanced Palette Train & Test	

Table 1: Format of the Experiment.

In the standard ArtClass package different tools were indicated graphically by a change in cursor shape. Some of the cursor shapes are shown in Figure 5 (these are similar to the ones used in the Microsoft Word drawing editor and are standard shapes used on the Macintosh). These were left in for the experiment as many packages do use cursor shape to indicate the tools. The hypothesis here is that these are not salient enough to indicate the current tool to the user.

The drawing tasks performed involved users drawing a simple car, tree and sun. The eight car-drawing tasks were described step-by-step, the final two tasks were left more open (so that the users could do them as they liked). The tasks were designed to mimic the standard drawing tasks a user might perform. The tasks also gave participants the opportunity of double and single clicking the tools in the palette.

6.3 Experimental Design and Procedure

The experiment was a two-condition, within-groups design. The order of presentation was counterbalanced to avoid any learning effects. One group of six participants performed the auditory tool palette condition first and the other used the standard visual palette first (see Table 1). Ten minutes of training was given before each condition to enable the participants to become familiar with the system, the sounds and the types of drawing tasks they would be required to perform. Each condition lasted approximately 20–25 minutes. During each condition the participants had to perform the standard drawing tasks set by the experimenter. Instructions were read from a prepared script.

To get a full measurement of usability combined measures of error rates and subjective workload were used. Such qualitative and quantitative tests give a good measure of usability (Bevan & Macleod, 1994). The standard six-factor NASA Task Load Index (TLX) was used for estimating workload (Hart & Staveland, 1988). To this was added a seventh factor: annoyance. One of the concerns of potential users of auditory interfaces is annoyance due to sound pollution. In the experiment described here the annoyance was measured to find out if it was indeed a problem. It is important when evaluating systems that use sound to test a full

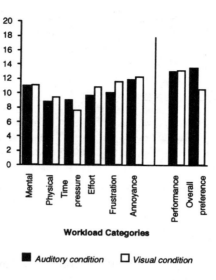

Figure 6: Average workload scores for the two conditions. In the first six categories higher scores mean higher workload. The final two categories are separated as higher scores mean lower workload.

range of subjective factors, including annoyance. The area is still in its infancy and it is not yet clear how to design sonically-enhanced interfaces that work well. Just evaluating performance time or errors may not be enough to bring up all of the potential problems. Participants were also asked to indicate overall preference, i.e. which of the two interfaces they felt made the task easiest.

7 Workload Results

The average TLX workload scores for each category were calculated and are shown in Figure 6. They were scored in the range 0-20. The average raw workload was 9.29 in the auditory condition and 9.61 in the visual. There was no significant difference in the workload between conditions ($T_{11} = 0.26$, $p = 0.79$).

There was no significant difference in terms of annoyance between the conditions ($T_{11} = 0.24$, $p = 0.81$). Six of the participants felt the visual condition was more annoying, five felt the auditory more annoying and one felt them equal.

The average scores for overall preference was 13.67 for the auditory condition and 10.67 for the visual condition. Again, this was not significantly different ($T_{11} = 1.70$, $p = 0.12$). Nine participants preferred the tool palette with sounds, and three participants preferred it without.

8 Error Results

Figure 7 shows the number of tasks performed with the wrong tool (i.e. the participant used the wrong tool and then had to change to the correct one. This could happen

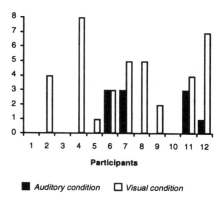

Figure 7: Number of tasks performed with the wrong tool.

either because an automatic tool change occurred and was not noticed or the tool did not change). There was a significant reduction in the number of such tasks in the auditory condition ($T_{11} = 3.08$, $p = 0.01$). The average number of tasks performed with the wrong tool fell from 3.25 in the visual condition to 0.83 in the auditory. This indicated that the earcons did help participants remember the tool they were using. In total, eight participants never used a wrong tool in the auditory condition with only three not making such errors in the visual.

8.1 Discussion

The workload analysis showed no significant differences in terms of workload. Even though the error results showed that sound reduced the number of times the wrong tools were used, workload was not reduced (as had been hypothesized). One explanation for this is that users were asked to rate the workload of the task as a whole rather than for the tool palette specifically. They may have considered the selection of tools a small part of the whole task so any differences in the workload attributable to tool selection were lost amongst the data for the whole task.

The results show no difference in the annoyance experienced by users. This indicates that if care is taken in the design of the earcons, and they solve specific usability problems, users will find them useful and not annoying.

Analysis of the errors made by participants showed that there were significantly fewer tasks performed with the wrong tool in the auditory condition (as hypothesized). This meant that the earcons were successfully indicating to the participants what tool, or mode, they were in. In fact only four of the twelve participants tried to perform any of the tasks with the wrong tools in the auditory condition. When tool errors did occur there were two possibilities: The user could try to draw another object but end up using the selection tool (as a tool change occurred and was not noticed) or the user could try and position an object but end up drawing another (as the tool did not change). Analysis showed that 86% of all of the errors that occurred in both conditions were of the former type. Even though the earcons were effective at reducing the number of errors, further development of this work should concentrate on making such tool changes as salient as possible to users.

The tool palette evaluated in the experiment was the hybrid type. However, the sounds needed for the other types mentioned above would be very similar. For the type in which the system changed back to the default tool after every use the changes must be made salient to the user. This could be done, as here, by playing a sound that indicated a change had occurred.

For the type where the current tool stays selected until the user changes it, the system must make it clear to the user that the tool has not changed. This could be done, as in this experiment, by playing the same earcon again.

9   Conclusions

Results from the experiment described here showed that sonic-enhancement of a tool palette could significantly increase the usability, and therefore productivity, of a graphics package without making it more annoying to use. The package used here was very simple, with only one tool palette. In more complex applications (for example, large CAD packages) there may be many tool palettes conveying many different types of information to the user. Users are likely to miss information displayed in palettes, and the more palettes there are the worse this problem will be. The results given in this paper show that with the simple enhancement of the existing interface many of these problems can be removed. Designers of graphics packages can use this work to enhance their products and allow their users to increase their productivity.

Acknowledgements

Thanks to Catherine Clarke who helped in this research as part of her undergraduate project. Thanks also to Michel Beaudoin-Lafon for discussions on this work. Part of this work was supported by EPSRC Grant GR/L79212.

References

Alty, J. (1995), Can we use Music in Human–Computer Interaction?, *in* M. A. R. Kirby, A. J. Dix & J. E. Finlay (eds.), *People and Computers X (Proceedings of HCI'95)*, Cambridge University Press, pp.409–23.

Barfield, W., Rosenberg, C. & Levasseur, G. (1991), "The use of Icons, Earcons and Commands in the Design of an Online Hierarchical Menu", *IEEE Transactions on Professional Communication* **34**(2), 101–8.

Beaudouin-Lafon, M. & Conversy, S. (1996), Auditory Illusions for Audio Feedback, *in* Tauber (ed.), *ACM CHI'96 Conference Companion*, ACM Press, pp.299–300.

Berglund, B., Preis, A. & Rankin, K. (1990), "Relationship between Loudness and Annoyance for Ten Community Sounds", *Environment International* **16**, 523–31.

Bevan, N. & Macleod, M. (1994), "Usability Measurement in Context", *Behaviour & Information Technology* **13**(1-2), 132–45.

Blattner, M., Sumikawa, D. & Greenberg, R. (1989), "Earcons and Icons: Their Structure and Common Design Principles", *Human–Computer Interaction* **4**(1), 11–44.

Brewster, S. (1997), "Using Non-Speech Sound to Overcome Information Overload", *Displays* **17**, 179–89.

Brewster, S. & Crease, M. (1997), Making Menus Musical, *in* S. Howard, J. Hammond & G. K. Lindgaard (eds.), *Human–Computer Interaction — INTERACT'97: Proceedings of the Fifth IFIP Conference on Human–Computer Interaction*, Chapman & Hall, pp.389–96.

Brewster, S., Wright, P. & Edwards, A. (1993), An Evaluation of Earcons for use in Auditory Human–Computer Interfaces, *in* S. Ashlund, K. Mullet, A. Henderson, E. Hollnagel & T. White (eds.), *Proceedings of INTERCHI'93*, ACM Press, pp.222–7.

Brewster, S., Wright, P. & Edwards, A. (1994), The Design and Evaluation of an Auditory-enhanced Scrollbar, *in* B. Adelson, S. Dumais & J. Olson (eds.), *Proceedings of CHI'94: Human Factors in Computing Systems*, ACM Press, pp.173–9.

Brewster, S., Wright, P. & Edwards, A. (1995), Experimentally Derived Guidelines for the Creation of Earcons, *in* M. A. R. Kirby, A. J. Dix & J. E. Finlay (eds.), *Adjunct Proceedings of BCS HCI'95*, Cambridge University Press, pp.155–9.

Dix, A., Finlay, J., Abowd, G. & Beale, R. (1993), *Human–Computer Interaction*, Prentice–Hall.

Gaver, W. (1986), "Auditory Icons: Using Sound in Computer Interfaces", *Human–Computer Interaction* **2**(2), 167–77.

Gaver, W. (1989), "The SonicFinder: An Interface that uses Auditory Icons", *Human–Computer Interaction* **4**(1), 67–94.

Hart, S. & Staveland, L. (1988), Development of NASA-TLX (Task Load Index): Results of Empirical and Theoretical Research, *in* P. Hancock & N. Meshkati (eds.), *Human Mental Workload*, North-Holland, pp.139–83.

Kramer, G. (1994), An Introduction to Auditory Display, *in* G. Kramer (ed.), *Auditory Display*, Addison–Wesley.

Monk, A. (1986), "Mode Errors: A User-centered Analysis and Some Preventative Measures using Keying-contingent Sound", *International Journal of Man–Machine Studies* **24**, 313–27.

Portigal, S. (1994), Auralization of Document Structure, Master's thesis, The University of Guelph, Canada.

Reason, J. (1990), *Human Error*, Cambridge University Press.

Rigas, D. & Alty, J. (1997), The use of Music in a Graphical Interface for the Visually Impaired, *in* S. Howard, J. Hammond & G. K. Lindgaard (eds.), *Human–Computer Interaction — INTERACT'97: Proceedings of the Fifth IFIP Conference on Human–Computer Interaction*, Chapman & Hall, pp.228–35.

Sellen, A., Kurtenbach, G. & Buxton, W. (1992), "The Prevention of Mode Errors through Sensory Feedback", *Human–Computer Interaction* **7**, 141–64.

Slowiaczek, L. & Nusbaum, H. (1985), "Effects of Speech Rate and Pitch Contour on the Perception of Synthetic Speech", *Human Factors* **27**(6), 701–12.

A New Concept Touch-Sensitive Display Enabling Vibro-Tactile Feedback

Masahiko Kawakami, Masaru Mamiya,
Tomonori Nishiki, Yoshitaka Tsuji , Akito Okamoto
& Toshihiro Fujita

IDEC IZUMI Corporation, 1-7-31 Nishimiyahara, Yodogawa-ku,
Osaka 532-8550, Japan.

Tel: *+81 6 398 2518*
Fax: *+81 6 398 2545*
EMail: *mkawakam@izm.idec.co.jp*
URL: *http://www.izumi.com/*

This paper describes the concept and the characteristics of a newly developed touch-sensitive display which supports vibro-tactile feedback. This new touch-sensitive display named 'Vibration Touch' was developed to improve the uneasy operation of touch-sensitive displays due to lack of tactile feedback. Vibro-tactile feedback is realized by a combination of solenoid and spring which is directly attached to touch-sensitive panel. Vibration Touch is operated by a two-step input operation which enables certain operations and prevents mis-operation.

Keywords: touch-sensitive display, vibro-tactile feedback, GUI, LCD, HMI.

1 Introduction

Recently, touch-sensitive displays are frequently being used where many and a variety of persons utilize input devices such as ticket vending machines, ATMs (Automated Teller Machine) and also in applications of FA (Factory Automation). Among those touch-sensitive displays, FPDs (Flat Panel Displays) are preferred and LCDs (Liquid Crystal Displays) are the popular display device utilized. Touch-sensitive displays are attractive because they are easy to learn, directly operated and

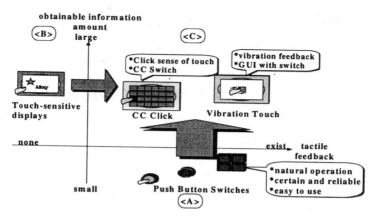

Figure 1: Concept of vibration touch.

have a high degree of freedom in application designs by utilizing a GUI (Graphical User Interface) (Shneiderman, 1997).

Thinking of touch-sensitive displays from the standpoint of HMI (Human–Machine Interface), they satisfy the information displaying ability performed by a GUI environment. However, as we asked 120 users of touch-sensitive displays whether they have ever mis-operated the device, 66% of them have answered they have. Popular reasons for mis-operation were that they fall into confusion when displayed information changes and touch the undesired button, and uncertain operation due to lack of tactile feedback as indicated in the earlier studies (Ostroff & Shneiderman, 1988; Sears et al., 1992). Visual and audible feedback may be used to supplement the absence of tactile feedback, however, tactile feedback is essential to touch-sensitive display applications since visual feedback is not effective when performing button presses without watching the display, and audible feedback is not effective in noisy circumstances such as in a factory.

To improve the operating environment of touch-sensitive displays, we have developed a device named 'CC Click' that enables tactile feedback on a touch-sensitive display (Hasegawa et al., 1996; Mamiya et al., 1997; Miwa et al., 1997).

We have been continuously researching to improve the operating environment of touch-sensitive displays and have now developed a new touch-sensitive display with vibro-tactile feedback named 'Vibration Touch' (Kawakami et al., 1997). Vibration Touch enables two-step input operation which prevents mis-operation of touch-sensitive displays and realizes finger tracing of buttons on touch-sensitive displays.

2   Concept of Vibration Touch

Figure 1 shows the concept of Vibration Touch. The horizontal axis shows the existence of tactile feedback of the input device and the vertical axis shows the amount of information obtainable from the device.

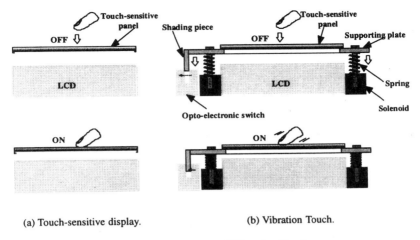

(a) Touch-sensitive display.   (b) Vibration Touch.

Figure 2: Structure of Vibration Touch.

Push button switches are classified in area <A> where sufficient tactile feedback is obtained but the amount of information obtainable is small. Touch-sensitive displays are classified in area <B> where large amounts of information are obtained, however, tactile feedback does not exist.

CC Click classified in area <C> is a device which has transparent buttons above the touch-sensitive display and it has similar switching characteristics compared to conventional push button switches as explained later in Section 4. CC Click enables tactile feedback in touch-sensitive displays while allowing mass-information display as well. With transparent buttons on a touch-sensitive display, the operator can feel the boundaries of buttons which enables recognition of the buttons. On the other hand, with CC Click having physical buttons, button layout on the display is fixed. Therefore, we propose for the first time a device named 'Vibration Touch' which has the following characteristics:

1. Three types of vibro-tactile feedback.

2. Finger tracing of buttons on touch-sensitive display.

3. Free layout of the buttons on the display.

3 Structure and Operation Principle of Vibration Touch

Figure 2(a) & (b) show the structure of conventional touch-sensitive displays and Vibration Touch, respectively. With conventional touch-sensitive displays, the touch-sensitive panel located above the LCD is not designed to give tactile feedback. On the other hand, with Vibration Touch, the touch-sensitive panel is designed to move in vertical direction with respect to the LCD and it will give the operator vibro-tactile feedback. Vibration Touch consists of a resistive type touch-sensitive panel, LCD, combination of solenoid and spring, and an opto-electronic switch which detects the

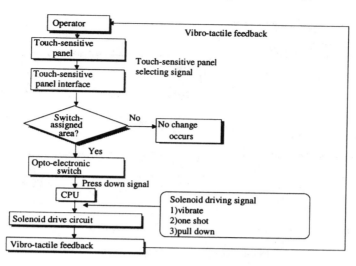

Figure 3: Operation flowchart of Vibration Touch.

touch-sensitive panel being depressed. The touch-sensitive panel is attached to a supporting plate which is attached to the solenoid and shading piece of the opto-electronic switch.

The operation flowchart of Vibration Touch is shown in Figure 3. The touch-sensitive panel of Vibration Touch functions as the touch-sensitive panel of a conventional touch-sensitive display. Therefore, by touching the switch-assigned area of the touch-sensitive panel, a touch-sensitive panel selecting signal is passed on to the CPU making the shape, size and the colour of the displayed button change. This is to show that the operator is selecting a certain button and to inquire the operator whether it is the desired selection. If the operator is satisfied with the selected button and wishes to make a successful input, the operator must further press down the touch-sensitive panel. When the touch-sensitive panel is pressed down enough that the shading piece blocks the light path of the opto-electronic switch, a press down signal is passed on to the CPU. If both touch-sensitive panel selecting signal and press down signal are detected, a solenoid driving current is applied to the solenoid. Then the touch-sensitive panel attached to the solenoid vibrates according to the driving mode assigned to the selected button. Thus, the operator will feel this vibration through their finger as vibro-tactile feedback.

Three types of vibro-tactile feedback can be obtained in Vibration Touch as shown in Table 1. The first mode is 'vibrate', in which the touch-sensitive panel vibrates at a certain frequency as long as the operator is pressing the touch-sensitive panel. The second mode is 'one shot' in which the touch-sensitive panel is pulled down for a certain period of time and then released to its initial position. The last mode is 'pull down' in which the touch-sensitive panel is pulled down as long as the operator is pressing the touch-sensitive panel.

	Vibrate	One shot	Pull down
State of opto-electronic switch	ON / OFF	ON / OFF	ON / OFF
Solenoid driving signal	ON / OFF	ON / OFF	ON / OFF
Explanation of operation modes	Touch-sensitive panel vibrates as long as opto-electronic switch is turned on.	Touch-sensitive panel is pulled down and released after a while as opto-electronic switch is turned on.	Touch-sensitive panel is pulled down as long as opto-electronic switch is turned on.

Table 1: Types of operation mode enabled in Vibration Touch.

Each operation mode can be assigned to any part of the touch-sensitive panel of Vibration Touch and a combination of the three different types of vibro-tactile feedback in one touch-sensitive display can be obtained.

With Vibration Touch, touching the touch-sensitive panel means selecting buttons and is not an input. Therefore, the operator can trace the buttons with their finger until satisfied and may further press down to complete the input or even raise their hands after selecting a button to cancel the input. In this way, mis-input by careless touch can be prevented.

4 Characteristics of Vibration Touch

To understand the characteristics of Vibration Touch, we measured the switching characteristics of Vibration Touch and those of various switches as well. Switching characteristics are expressed by stroke vs. load.   Stroke means how much the switch can be pressed down and load means how much force is needed to press down the switch. Figure 4 shows the switching characteristics of various switches. The horizontal and the vertical axis of each figure correspond to stroke and load, respectively.

Figure 4(a) shows the switching characteristics of a push button switch. This switch has maximum and minimum point in its characteristics curve which the operator feels as a 'click' sense of touch when the curve passes over the maximum point and the switch input will be 'ON' at the minimum point. Figure 4(b) shows the switching characteristics of a touch-sensitive panel. It is clear from the figure that a touch-sensitive panel has little switching stroke which yields no tactile feedback and it is operated with light load which will easily be mis-operated by careless touch. As mentioned earlier in this paper, by implementing the transparent CC Switch on the LCD, switching characteristics similar to those of a push button switch are obtained as shown in Figure 4(c).

Figure 4(d), (e) & (f) show the switching characteristics of Vibration Touch. The static characteristics of Vibration Touch are shown in Figure 4(d).   The turn

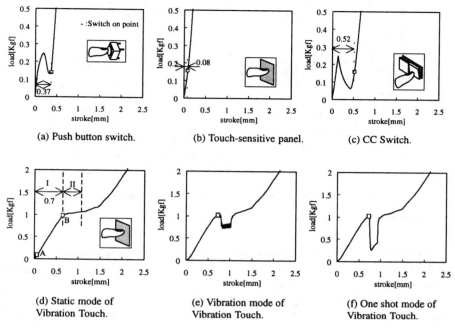

Figure 4: Switching characteristics of switches.

on point marked 'A' at 0.08mm stroke is where the touch-sensitive panel turns on and at this point the operator can select any other button without making a final input. The slope between 0 to 0.7mm stroke marked with 'I' indicates that the spring is being compressed. At point marked 'B', the shading piece blocks the light path of the opto-electronic switch which is the switch on point of Vibration Touch and the solenoid operates in stroke range marked with 'II'. Thus, Vibration Touch is an input device which has two-step input. Figure 4(e) shows the switching characteristics of Vibration Touch in vibration mode, and Figure 4(f) shows the switching characteristics of Vibration Touch in one shot mode.

5 User Research

Today there are devices that offer vibro-tactile feedback such as joystick of a computer game, cellular phone and pager. However, the vibro-tactile feedback are not the same and are unique to each device. Therefore, we performed a user research to evaluate Vibration Touch and to obtain the optimum vibro-tactile feedback for Vibration Touch.

5.1 Experimental Procedure

The vibration frequency of Vibration Touch was made to vary continuously within 20–1000Hz. Participants were given an introduction to Vibration Touch and after that

User specification	90 male, 31 female
Operation method	Press touch-sensitive panel with pointing finger
Vibration frequency	Variable from 20–1000Hz
Setup condition of Vibration Touch	90cm above the floor and 30 degrees tilt to the operator
User position	Standing position
Size of display	111.3mm × 83.5mm (5.5" diagonal)
Displayed button size	16mm × 16mm

Table 2: Conditions for user research.

Vibration Touch

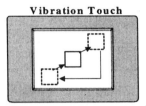

Figure 5: Button layout of Vibration Touch in user research.

they were given time to practice the operation of the device. In the mean time, they were asked to vary the vibration frequency themselves to the optimum frequency that they would like to operate. After setting the vibration frequency to the participants' choice, they were asked to operate the device again to fill out the evaluation sheets. The evaluation sheets had a scale of 1 to 7 for each attribute: certainty of operation, ease of learning, ease of use, and interest. Desirable attributes were given the value of 7 while undesirable attributes were given the value of 1.

The conditions of the experiment are shown in Table 2. There were a total of 121 participants, 90 were male, 31 female, age from 20 to 60. As shown in Figure 5, a 16mm × 16mm rectangular button was programmed to jump from centre to upper right and to lower left of the display as each input operation is complete.

5.2   Results and Discussion

5.2.1   Evaluation Results

Figure 6(a), (b), (c) & (d) show user evaluation results of (a) certainty of operation, (b) ease of learning, (c) ease of use, and (d) interest, respectively.

Since the concept of Vibration Touch is to enable certain operation and prevent mis-operation of a touch-sensitive display, high ratings of 'certainty of operation' were expected, and from Figure 6(a), a 5 or higher value rating by 62% of participants was obtained. This value is thought to rise if comparisons to conventional touch-sensitive displays are performed. We are planning to perform this evaluation in the next version of Vibration Touch.

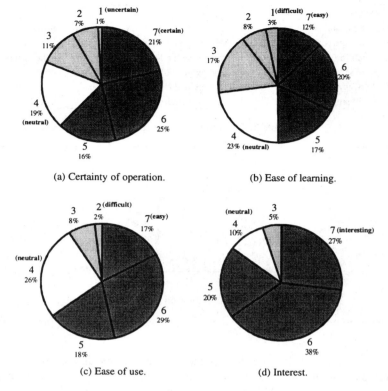

(a) Certainty of operation.   (b) Ease of learning.

(c) Ease of use.   (d) Interest.

Figure 6: User research results.

From Figure 6(b), half of the participants rated 'ease of learning' with a 5 or higher value. Although participants were given introduction to Vibration Touch before they operated the device, most of them were surprised with the vibro-tactile feedback. Moreover, because most of the participants were familiar with touch-sensitive displays which operate with single touch, they needed practice to learn the two-step input operation of Vibration Touch. On the other hand, as shown in Figure 6(c), 64% of participants rated 'ease of use' with a 5 or higher value.

Most of the participants evaluated Vibration Touch as 'interesting' as shown in Figure 6(d). Comments were obtained to use this device in barrier free applications, such as "This device should be used for visually handicapped people if used with audible feedback".

In making a prototype of Vibration Touch, we first assumed use in industrial FA applications and therefore set the necessary force to press down the touch-sensitive panel of Vibration Touch relatively high, as shown in Figure 4(d), (e) & (f). By assuming the various applications that Vibration Touch will be used, and from participants' comment such as: "it is hard to press down the touch-sensitive panel", the press down force is desired to be adjustable by the user.

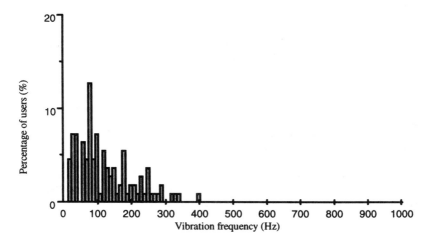

Figure 7: User preference of vibration frequency.

5.2.2 Results on Vibration Frequency

Participants' preferences on vibration frequency seems to scatter as shown in Figure 7. However, there can be seen a peak preference of vibration frequency at around 80Hz. From the study of skin's mechanical properties against vibration (Lundström, 1984), it is found that the skin is comparatively easy to be vibrated within the frequency range of 80–200Hz. The optimum vibration frequency is thought to vary in what application the device is to be used and therefore, from this research, we found that it is better to have the vibration frequency variable by the user rather than to set a fixed vibration frequency.

6   Conclusion

In our modern, highly informationalized society where multimedia is the keyword, having interactiveness in devices such as computers is becoming common sense (Kurosu, 1997).

   In these multimedia circumstances, input/output devices must be utilized in order to send or receive information. As input devices are so important in multimedia situations, their usability must be considered carefully. Input devices which have no tactile feedback to their input operation are inconvenient even for able bodied people to use, but much harder for handicapped people. We believe that the Vibration Touch that we propose offers certain operation not only usable in public facilities and FA, but also in multimedia and barrier free applications.

   We will continue our research for an input device which will be more naturally operated and is useful for everyone.

Acknowledgements

The authors would like to thank Dr. M. Kurosu of Shizuoka University and people in IDEC IZUMI Corp. for valuable discussion and help in research.

References

Hasegawa, H., Sekino, Y., Kawakami, M., Nishiki, T., Tsuji, Y., Okamoto, A. & Fujita, T. (1996), Development of Multimedia Objective Terminal Incorporating Click Mechanism, *in* M. Onoe (ed.), *Proceedings of the 12th Symposium on Human Interface*, Technical Committee for Human Interface, pp.477–82. in Japanese.

Kawakami, M., Nishiki, T., Tsuji, Y., Okamoto, A. & Fujita, T. (1997), Development of Touch-sensitive Displays with Unique Tactile Feedback, *in* K. Horii (ed.), *Proceedings of the 13th Symposium on Human Interface*, Technical Committee for Human Interface, pp.299–304. in Japanese.

Kurosu, M. (1997), Human Interface and Input/Output as its Origin, *in IDEC Review 1997*, IDEC IZUMI Corp, pp.2–13. in Japanese.

Lundström, R. (1984), "Local Vibrations-Mechanical Impedance of the Human Hand's Glabrous Skin", *Journal of Biomechanics* 17(2), 133–44.

Mamiya, M., Hasegawa, H., Sekino, Y., Kawakami, M., Nishiki, T., Tsuji, Y., Okamoto, A. & Fujita, T. (1997), A New Way to Overcome the Uneasy Operation of Touch-Sensitive Displays by Incorporating 'Click' Mechanism CC Switch, *in* G. Salvendy, M. J. Smith & R. Koubek (eds.), *Proceedings of the 7th International Conference on Human–Computer Interaction (HCI International '97)*, Elsevier Science, pp.619–22.

Miwa, T., Inada, K., Okamoto, A., Matsumoto, Y. & Fujita, T. (1997), Progress in Comfortable Operation of Programmable Display Incorporating Click Mechanism 'CC Switch', *in* K. Horii (ed.), *Proceedings of the 13th Symposium on Human Interface*, Technical Committee for Human Interface, pp.293–8. in Japanese.

Ostroff, D. & Shneiderman, B. (1988), "Selection Devices for User of an Electronic Encyclopedia: An Empirical Comparison of Four Possibilities", *Information Processing & Management* 24(6), 665–80.

Sears, A., Plaisant, C. & Shneiderman, B. (1992), A New Era for High-precision Touchscreens, *in Advances in Human–Computer Interaction*, Vol. 3, Ablex, pp.1–33.

Shneiderman, B. (1997), *Designing the User Interface: Strategies for Effective Human–Computer Interaction*, third edition, Addison–Wesley.

Preliminary Investigations into the Use of Wearable Computers

Chris Baber, David Haniff, Lee Cooper, James Knight & Brian Mellor[†]

School of Manufacturing & Mechanical Engineering, The University of Birmingham, Birmingham B15 2TT, UK.

Tel: *+44 121 414 4273*
EMail: *c.baber@bham.ac.uk*

[†] *Speech Research Unit, DERA, Malvern, Worcestershire, UK.*

In this paper, we investigate human factors which could have a bearing on the use of wearable computers. The first study examines performance on a reaction time task using a head-mounted display in comparison with performance on a sVGA visual display unit. While the number of missed targets was not significantly different, there were significant differences in reaction time to displays. The second study shows performance time of participants using a wearable computer to be superior to those using paper-based manual and recording, but there is a trend for more errors to be made when using the wearable computer.

Keywords: wearable computers, head-mounted displays, speech technology.

1   Introduction

There is an increasing range of computer products which fall under the heading of portable computers, e.g. from laptops to palmtops to Personal Digital Assistants. The intention behind these products is to allow users access to computer functions while they are away from offices. Consequently, having computers which are small enough to be worn could be seen as an extension of the portable computer concept. From a different perspective, work could be improved (both in terms of efficiency and effectiveness) if a person could have access to the computing power

Speech Technology	Wearable Computers
Hands free	One or both hands free
Eyes free	Can switch attention between task and display
Ease of use	Good fit with task
Mobility of user via radio microphone	Mobility of user via body worn computer
Limited requirements in training	?
Reduce eyestrain during data entry	?
Naturalness of interaction	?
Direct data capture	Direct data capture
Rapid data entry	?
Flexible vocabulary	?
Easily edited command set	?
Reduced desk space requirements	No desk space needed

Table 1: Comparison of claimed benefits of speech technology and wearable computers.

of a conventional personal computer whilst working; and an obvious, and popular, application of wearable computers lies in the domain of maintenance work, where a technician could have access to manuals and procedures via a wearable computer while carrying out maintenance tasks (Smith et al., 1995; Bass et al., 1997; Esposito, 1997). We should distinguish between computers which are worn and those which are merely carried as this has implications for design and development of computers, and selection of appropriate application domains. Wearable computers, by definition, become part of the wearer's personal space, in much the same way as clothing (Mann, 1996). This means that a wearable computer will be continually present (unless the person takes it off). We need to distinguish computers which are worn from other worn technologies, such as wristwatches, pace-makers, hearing-aids, etc., and from technologies which can be put into pockets, such as pagers, calculators, etc. The main factor is that a wearable computer supports continuous interaction, i.e. it is "… a computer system that is body worn, lightweight, and enables hands free access to pertinent … information." [Smith et al., 1995, p.119]. This means that the user can interact with the device by changing parameters, modifying the displayed information, entering new information, etc. without breaking the flow of ongoing actions. Thus, hearing-aids and pace-makers would be deemed to support passive interaction on the part of the user/wearer, and use of a pager requires specific actions which interrupt ongoing actions.

It is interesting to compare the proposed benefits of wearable computers with those of speech technology in the last decade. Baber (1991) reviewed studies of speech technology and summarized benefits which were claimed by speech technology marketing into the points shown in table one. Comparing the points with wearable computers indicates obvious parallels and differences.

In Table 1, the underlined items in the speech technology column have been demonstrated to be more complicated than originally imagined; the items marked ? in the wearable computers column have yet to be established, and the items in italics in the wearable computers column are considered in the studies reported in this paper. Of course, wearable computer systems often utilize a speech recognizer for hands-free interaction. However, they are not simply vehicles to allow mobile speech recognition as a brief review of the technical considerations, below, demonstrates. Finally, human factors research issues for speech recognition have been handling recognition error, and integrating speech with other media into multi-modal systems. These topics are equally important for wearable computers.

Ongoing research into wearable computers for use by the emergency services, i.e. Police, Fire and Ambulance, suggest the following generic types of application:

1. Situation awareness, e.g. position and location of the wearer.

2. Access to specialist knowledge, e.g. procedures for handling chemicals, maps or floor plans.

3. Data entry, i.e. allowing information to be entered in real time.

4. Zero-dialogue interaction, e.g. physiological monitoring of wearer to measure oxygen consumption or heart rate.

While this list is not exhaustive, it allows us to consider design issues in terms of requirements engineering, with particular reference to the domains of the emergency services. In the studies reported in this paper, we consider human factors implications of the first three of these application types — readers interested in the fourth type are advised to consult Picard (1998).

1.1 Technical Considerations

Wearable computers are body worn devices which support continuous interaction (by allowing the user to interact without stopping ongoing tasks, by being always on and by updating information for the user). The range of possible applications for such technology is only just beginning to be defined let alone explored: popular examples concern maintenance aids (see below), but this could be extended to industrial inspection tasks or to surveillance tasks performed by military, police, customs officers, etc.; ongoing research in a number of centres has identified potential uses of wearable computers for paramedics; moving away from industrial/military/services applications, there is some interest in the use of wearables are consumer products, with go-anywhere computing being of possible.

1.1.1 Processors

Two commercially available products package the equivalent of a desktop personal computer into a wearable product: InterVision's ManuMax 2000 offers a 486 (at 50MHz with 16MB RAM and 170MB memory on pcimca card), packaged in a case 11.5cm×12cm×7cm (weight 2.7lbs). An updated version has a Pentium processor in a smaller package. Computing Devices International's (CDI) Wearable has a 486 processor with 8MB RAM, with up to 510MB hard disk, is packaged in a case 40cm×12.5cm×3cm (weight 2lbs).

1.1.2   Displays

Both ManuMax 2000 and CDI's Wearable use head-mounted, monocular displays, e.g. ManuMax 2000 uses a Seattle Sight display which has a resolution of 640×480 pixels. The display is suspended from a head-mounted frame (e.g. from a head-strap, a spectacles frame, or a hat) approximately 2cm from the wearer's eye and project a display about 1 metre from the viewer. A popular (and cheaper alternative) is to use Reflection Technology's PrivateEye display, which is approximately 1 ounce in weight, and has a scanning mirror and a row of LEDs which give the wearer the impression that they are viewing a 15" monitor. It has a resolution of 360×280 pixels. A recent development has been MicroOptical's eyeglasses which uses light reflected from a tiny mirror mounted in the lens of the eyepiece of a pair of glasses to give a 320×240 pixel display. While visual displays may be desirable for many applications, it is important to realize that there will be situations where visual displays are not appropriate; the obvious example comes from visually-impaired wearers. In this instance, auditory display can be used with headphones worn by the user. Headphones could block out environmental sounds, but work at Hatfield University has led to the suggestion that a simple remedy to the potential problem will be to wear the headphones in front of the ears, to allow auditory information from both headphones and the external environment to be presented to the wearer. Audible displays could have a public display of information, but this will have several negative consequences, e.g. distraction, annoyance of other people, unwanted sharing of information. The notion of tactile displays for wearable computers seems intuitively appealing but there has been little work done on this topic.

1.1.3   Interaction Devices

One of the avowed aims of wearable computers is to allow hands-free access to computer functionality. Baber (1997) discusses the notion of interaction devices as clothing, and notes that current research appears to be directed at the use of speech for mobile computing, at the mounting of pointing devices and keyboards to the person, or on the use of limb and muscle movement as input to the computer, e.g. via gloves, finger-mounted or face-mounted devices. Commercially available devices tend to rely on speech recognition as their primary means of input. Presumably one of the reasons for this is the avowed aim to allow hands free interaction with the product.

Products developed at MIT are currently using hand-held chord keyboards ('Twiddlers') to allow one-handed typing. In this approach, data entry is a prime activity in the use of wearable computers, e.g. the MIT wearables community can use their computers to browse the Web, manage email and take notes during presentations. The use of a chord keyboard requires considerable practice to allow typing without looking at the keyboard and could interrupt primary task performance. The Navigator and VuMan2 from CMU use a rotary control switch to select menu items (Bass et al., 1997; Bass, 1995; Smith et al., 1995). In this design, data entry is less important than information selection and manipulation. The advantage of this approach is that it does not require continuous interaction, with the wearer being able to select information and then return to the primary task. This work raises interesting questions concerning the relationship between the design of the display and the operation of the interaction device. Both examples require at least

Task Dependency	Modality	
	Same	Different
Dependent	Exclusive	Synergistic
Independent	Alternate	Concurrent

Table 2: Task–modality relationships.

one handed operation, which could defeat the requirement that operation should not interfere with the primary task.

1.1.4   Multi-modal Computing for Multi-modal Work

The idea of having direct access to a computer, through hands free capabilities, raises questions concerning how work activity and use of the computer will interact with each other.   In current work into multi-modal systems, we have found it useful to relate the variable of modality, i.e. whether tasks employ the same or different modality, to that of task dependency, i.e. whether performance of one task is dependent upon that of a second task (see Table 2). This produces the following simple framework:

Exclusive: in an inspection task, a set of measurements are made which are recorded at the end of the inspection, i.e. attention is exclusively devoted to the inspection task and then to recording.

Alternate: while the computer information will be permanently available, the wearer will alternate attention between computer and work object, e.g. take one measurement and then record it before taking the next measurement.

Synergistic: this will allow task performance on the work object to be performed at the same time as use of the computer. For instance, using speech recognition to record data while taking measurements.

Concurrent: this will allow data entry or information retrieval to be performed at the same time as performing other tasks, but not necessarily in relation to those other tasks.

1.2   Wearable Computers and Maintenance Work

Vehicle maintenance is a major application for wearable computers. The increasing complexity of vehicles means that engineers no longer encounter enough failures of the same type to develop shortcut diagnoses of problems. Instead, it is necessary to individually diagnose maintenance problems from first principles (Bass, 1995). This means that engineers require access to detailed information about the vehicle and specialist knowledge about how to find and repair faults. Additionally, accessing the information required to diagnose such problems entails the engineer searching through maintenance manuals and catalogues on site, with at best only a hand-held UHF radio as a means of communication with colleagues (Smith et al., 1995). Vehicle maintenance, therefore, is a particularly time-consuming and demanding process. In an attempt to enhance the maintenance process wearable computer systems are now being used. Wearable computers allow maintenance personnel to bring highly structured and specialized knowledge in the form of databases, diagnostic software and documentation to the worksite as well as accommodating a full communications capability. In addition, speech technology combined with head-mounted communication and display capabilities allow users to carry out necessary manual operations while recording, retrieving or viewing information (Esposito, 1997). In addition to maintenance work, such systems have obvious benefits for quality control and inspection (Najjar et al., 1997) or for supervisory control of production systems (Schlick et al., 1997).

1.3 Comparison Studies

Najjar et al. (1997) compared performance of a head-mounted display with a paper-manual as an aid in performing an origami task. They found that the time taken to find specific information was similar across conditions (21.7s vs. 18.3s). However, the paper-based system led to faster performance on the task (241.9s vs. 384.7s). This was probably due to the fact that they presented video information over the computer display, which would, by definition, slow the interaction. Of particular interest is the error data they recorded, with the paper condition leading to more 'fixed errors', i.e. errors which were spotted and corrected, than the head-mounted display condition (2.5s vs. 1.8s).

Field studies comparing wearable computers with paper-based manuals have reached inconclusive results. On the one hand, trials at a military maintenance depot found a 40% reduction in time required to inspect vehicles (Bass et al., 1997). On the other hand, a wearable system was found to be 50% slower than a paper-based system (Siegel & Bauer, 1997). The authors of the second paper suggest that the main reason for the differences in performance time arose from engineers following procedures more carefully in the wearable computer condition. Thus, the nature of the work which a person is performing while using a wearable computer could have significant impact on how well the system works.

2 Study 1: Signal Detection Task

The first study addresses the ease with which visual attention can be switched between a head-mounted display and other visual stimuli. It is proposed that this would have a bearing on applications related to situational awareness. Wickens (1997), in his discussion of attentional issues in head-up displays, suggests that we need to consider four factors in evaluating display design:

Degree of scanning: the requirement to scan either the display or the external world when searching for information;

Clutter: ISO 9241 recommends that 40% or less of the screen should be covered with information. The percentage of information on the screen can be reduced accordingly to meet this recommendation and minimize problems of clutter;

Object fusion: this could lead to information in the display being inappropriately aligned with the environment, or to information in the environment being ignored;

Allocation of attention: in order to handle the stream of information presented to them, wearers of head-mounted displays might attempt to fuse information sources or they might decide to focus their attention exclusively on a single source.

A wearable computer could offer a means of improving or enhancing the wearer's situational awareness by providing more information than can be directly perceived from the environment. Endsley (1995) proposed that situation awareness can be local, i.e. related to specific aspects of the immediate environment, or global, i.e. related to general appreciation of the persons relationship with the environment. For firefighters, local situation awareness could be given by the level of air in breathing apparatus (BA) which allows the wearer to determine how long they can safely spend in the environment, and global situation awareness would include the orders communicated by the Officer in Charge (currently using radio communications), and memory of landmarks and features in the environment to aid navigation (which is often made impossible by the presence of smoke). NRC (1997) discusses potential problems which can arise from head-mounted displays, namely a reduction in awareness of immediate environment, perhaps through limitation on field of view or through obscuration of real-world features by display features. To date, there is little published evidence to indicate how much of the visual field is blocked by monocular displays and anecdotal reports suggest that, while the wearer is conscious of the display in peripheral vision, the display does not interfere with visual perception. In study one, we were concerned with the use of the Seattle Sight monocular, head-mounted display and wished to use a experimental design that allowed comparison with conventional display technology. It was decided to use a simple reaction time task for this study. The task required participants to respond to targets presented on the head-mounted display; this was felt to be analogous to inspection of complex systems. By using reaction time, we circumvented problems relating to visual search strategy or inspection skill.

2.1 Method

Eleven postgraduate students participated in this study (7 male, 4 female). All participants had normal or corrected to normal vision. None of the participants had previous experience of using head-mounted displays nor with the experimental task. The experiment employed a within subjects design, with order of presentation counter-balanced across participants.

2.2 Equipment and Procedure

A 14" sVGA monitor was used as the visual display for comparison with the Seattle Sight head-mounted display. This display was VGA resolution and projects an image some 1m in front of the viewer. The task required participants to view a display and press the space bar when four targets appeared on the screen (one in each corner of the display). The targets were approximately 15mm tall and participants were placed in front of the visual display terminal such that the target subtended a similar angle of arc to those using the head-mounted display. In order to minimize visual distraction for the head-up display, participants were seated facing a large white screen.

2.3 Results

Two measures were taken: reaction time to signals and number of misses. A t-test showed a significant difference between conditions for reaction time (mean reaction time = 0.709s for head-mounted display vs. 0.45s for visual display unit; t(21) = 4.52, p < 0.01). A similar test on the misses data showed no difference (mean number of misses = 1.5 for head-mounted display vs. 0.9 for visual display unit, t(21) = 0.46, ns).

2.4 Conclusions

Discussion with participants suggested two possible explanations for the results. Firstly, the head-mounted display was perceived as uncomfortable. This criticism was also found by Esposito (1997). Some participants felt that the fit of the display affected visibility of the targets; while there were more misses, on average for the head-mounted display, the lack of significant difference in miss rates questions this assumption. However, one might anticipate that reaction time could be affected by uncertainty if participants had difficulties viewing the display. Secondly, viewing of the monocular display was reported to 'feel peculiar'. NRC (1997) suggest that a particular problem of monocular displays is binocular rivalry, i.e. information to one eye competes for attention with information to the other. Reports from the participants suggested that this may have been a non-trivial factor in this study, despite the use of a white screen. The effort to focus on a display using one eye may have affected reaction time, e.g. one or two participants closed their non-display eye to make the task 'easier' (although this had no apparent affect on performance time).

Taking Wickens' (1997) four factors we can review the results to consider possible confounding variables. As both displays employed the same information, there would not be any difference in display clutter between conditions. As far as possible the conditions were made comparable in terms of scanning required of the display: participants viewing distance was comparable, the size of targets was similar, the possibility of extraneous visual stimuli was reduced. While, binocular scanning of a display is clearly different from monocular scanning, this is not a sufficient explanation (preliminary studies conducted recently have found little affect on reaction time when viewing the visual display unit using one eye against using two eyes). This suggests that:

1. display quality had an adverse effect; or

2. 'noise' to the non-display eye was a sufficient distracter to impair performance.

In terms of (1), while there have been reports of performance variation between types of display (Dillon, 1994), these have typically compared VDU with paper rather than different graphic displays. In terms of (2), this could relate to the concepts of attention of allocation or object fusion; we presented a white screen to participants in an effort to reduce the possibility of object fusion. NRC (1997) considered the issue of situational awareness for helmet-mounted displays and suggested that there might be a reduced awareness of the immediate environment, through occlusion or binocular rivalry. As the display used in this study was transparent, it is unlikely that occlusion is the main factor although mounting and positioning could influence field of view. This leaves binocular rivalry, and there was a feeling that the display eye was

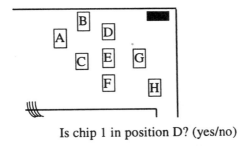

Is chip 1 in position D? (yes/no)

Figure 1: Page of manual for a checking task.

having to work hard to view the display but we have insufficient evidence to support this from the experiment.

3 Study 2: Inspection Support

In this study, we wished to compare a wearable computer with a paper-based version of a simple inspection task. This would provide comparison between the exclusive and synergistic task x modality relationships defined in table two. Of particular interest in this study are the requirements to allow hands/eyes free interaction, good task fit, direct data capture (as outlined in table one). The application type combines access to specialist knowledge and reporting of information. The data collection took place at the Speech Research Unit, DERA, Malvern and involved participants working at this centre. Thus, the population was familiar with speech recognition and with the concept of wearable computers.

3.1 Method

The experiment used a between subjects design, with 10 participants (9 male, 1 female). Participants were first trained in the use of the equipment and the fault finding tasks. Each participant completed two tasks for a series of three trials. Each trail took approximately 30 minutes, including setting up equipment, briefing and debriefing participants. In Task 1, checking, participants were required to identify marked microchips and ensure that they were in the correct position. Figure 1 shows the prompt used for one of these checks. In Task 2, troubleshooting, participants were required to check the wiring of the loudspeaker.

3.2 Equipment

A 19 page manual was produced which covered some basic aspects of a BBC Model B Microcomputer. This computer was to be used for the inspection task. The manual was printed onto paper and also used as a hypertext document (produced using VisualBasic v3.1). The computer condition used a monocular Virtual Vision Sport PAL display and an AURIX speaker independent, connected word recognizer. As the screen dimensions were approximately 1.5cm×1cm, it was necessary to ensure that the information presented was legible. We chose 24 and 32 point Times New

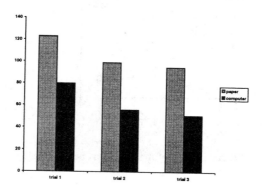

Figure 2: Average transaction times across trials for each condition.

Roman font for the display as this provided both a legible display and sufficient space to present all the information. Diagrams and figures were scaled accordingly (see Figure 1).

Given the fact that the head-mounted display was a CRT mounted on a headband, it was decided to position the display above the line of sight; this meant that the display was positioned just above the right eyebrow and required the wearer to glance up to read the display. Consequently, the wearer needs to switch attention between the head-mounted display and the workpiece.

3.3   Results

Three measures were taken for this study. The first measure concerned the number of pages checked for each condition. It was assumed that any difference in number of pages checked could have affected task difficulty. The data show no difference between conditions, with an average of 11 pages checked. The second measure was the time taken to complete the inspection tasks. This is shown in Figure 2.

For the paper-based condition, performance improved from a mean of 123s to 95s, while for the wearable computer condition, performance improved from 80s to 51s. Comparison of total transaction times between groups was found to be significant ($p < 0.0001$). Comparison of performance over the three sets of trials indicated no significant change in performance for the computer condition, but a small effect of trial on performance for the paper-based condition ($p < 0.01$). Consequently, we used the data from the last two trials (over which there was no learning effect), and found mean transaction times of 54s for the computer and 97s for the paper-based version. This difference was significant ($p < 0.0001$).

The third measure concerned the number of errors made in completing the reports. It was found that while none of the trials using the paper-based system produced errors, in the computer conditions, errors were apparent on all trials. Figure 3 shows recognition and user errors. Substitution errors occur when the users

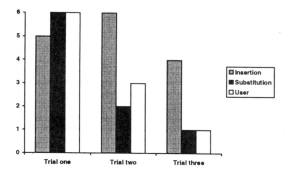

Figure 3: Errors produced in the computer condition.

speaks a word and the computer recognizes another word; insertion errors occur when background noise leads to a false recognition. The majority of substitution errors occurred in the first trial. Following the analysis of transaction times, we will only consider errors in Trials 2 and 3. In the trials, most of the background noise problems were attributable to parts or tools being dropped onto the table. There does not appear to be any link between insertion errors and trial. Finally, user errors occur when the user speaks the wrong command word, e.g. either due to mistaking the current state or failing to notice that a previous recognition error has led to a change in state and issuing a word not relevant to the current state. Considering errors in Trials 2 and 3, notice that the number of substitution and user errors in Trials 2 and 3 are similar (these are not simply the consequence of one error leading to the other).

3.4 Conclusions

Use of the computer led to faster performance and it is proposed that this is due to the following factors: direct data capture minimized task intrusion between inspection and reporting; hands-free and eyes-free interaction allowed simultaneous performance of inspection tasks, data capture and use of tools and the manual. Hands/eyes free benefits are often claimed for speech technology systems (see Table 1) and the head-mounted display seemed to further support such benefits. Participants did not report any complaints about wearing the head-mounted display during debriefing, and only one participant said that the display quality was unsatisfactory. However, the error data suggest a note of caution. In previous work, we have noted that users of speech technology do not necessarily notice or correct mis-recognitions (Baber et al., 1992), and this led us to propose the display was not attended to fully; in other words, the mere presence of the information in the display is treated as indication to proceed rather than as a cue to check the information. Consequently, it is proposed that user errors in the computer condition arose from users not reading the display in sufficient detail to determine which command word to use. This assumption is further supported by the findings of Najjar et al. (1997), discussed above, who found that the computer condition led to fewer 'fixed errors' than a paper-based condition.

4   Discussion

In this paper we have examined two issues relating to the use of wearable displays. The first study was aimed at defining possible variables which could affect situation awareness. We were surprised at the differences which were found. To some extent these results will be influenced by the difficulty participants reported when using the head-mounted display. While the study does not provide any information as to why problems arose, it does suggest that the design and use of monocular displays could prove problematic. Anecdotal evidence from other researchers suggests that the problems are reduced when the wearer is concentrating on the display, e.g. for object selection or data entry tasks. It might be the case that the display is sufficient for single task activity, but that when distractions occur performance could be affected. A further study is underway investigating the impact of dual-task performance, with the reaction time study being combined with a problem solving task on a separate display.

Comparison of a wearable rig with paper-based versions of an inspection manual suggests that head-mounted displays with speech interface lead to faster performance time. However, the task requirements in the two conditions differ to such an extent that direct comparison is not necessarily possible. For example, the time taken to retrieve information in the computer condition was influenced by the recognition accuracy of the speech recognition system, while for the paper-condition it was influenced by the speed with which the participant could move from the workpiece and turn the page. Furthermore, having hands free interaction means that the time taken to manipulate tools will be affected by use of the manual, i.e. for the computer condition, tool use could be performed concurrently with reading the manual, while for the paper-based condition, these activities tended to be separated. Having pointed out these differences, it should be noted that published work from other researchers suffers from similar problems. Current work is underway to compare a computer manual presented on head-mounted displays and visual display units for performance on a problem solving task.

The studies reported in this paper are early attempts to scope the human factors problems which could be anticipated with the use of wearable computers. Our results do not permit us to offer guidance to people developing the technology but do indicate specific issues relating to the use of the technology, i.e. the relationship between computer use and task performance, and the use information presented on head-mounted displays. We are currently relating this work to the development of wearable computers for paramedics, fire fighters and police officers.

Acknowledgements

This work has been partly supported by EPSRC grant GR/L48508 (Human Factors of Wearable Computers). We are grateful to Neil MacLean for his assistance in running study two.

References

Baber, C. (1991), *Speech Technology in Control Room Systems: A Human Factors Perspective*, Ellis Horwood.

Baber, C. (1997), *Beyond the Desktop: Designing and Using Interaction Devices*, Academic Press.

Baber, C., Usher, D., Stammers, R. & Taylor, R. (1992), "Feedback Requirements for Automatic Speech Recognition in the Process Control Room", *International Journal of Man–Machine Studies* **37**(6), 703–19.

Bass, L. (1995), Is There a Wearable Computer in your Future?, *in* L. Bass & C. Unger (eds.), *Human–Computer Interaction*, Chapman & Hall, pp.1–16.

Bass, L., Kasabach, C., Martin, R., Siewiork, D., Smailagic, A. & Stivoric, J. (1997), The Design of a Wearable Computer, *in* S. Pemberton (ed.), *Proceedings of CHI'97: Human Factors in Computing Systems*, ACM Press, pp.139–46.

Dillon, A. (1994), *Designing Usable Electronic Text*, Taylor & Francis.

Endsley, M. R. (1995), "Toward a Theory of Situational Awareness", *Human Factors* **37**(1), 32–64.

Esposito, C. (1997), "Wearable Computers: Field-test Observations and System Design Guidelines", *Personal Technologies* **1**(2), 81–8.

Mann, S. (1996), "SmartClothing: The Shift to Wearable Computing", *Communications of the ACM* **39**, 23–34.

Najjar, L., Thompson, J. C. & Ockerman, J. J. (1997), A Wearable Computer for Quality Assurance Inspectors in a Food Processing Plant, *in* L. Bass, D. Siewiorek & A. Pentland (eds.), *Digest of Papers for First International Symposium on Wearable Computers*, IEEE Computer Society Press, pp.163–4.

NRC (1997), *Tactical Display for Soldiers*, National Academy Press.

Picard, R. (1998), *Affective Computing*, MIT Press.

Schlick, C., Daude, R., Luczek, H., Weck, M. & Springer, J. (1997), "Head-mounted Display for Supervisory Control in Autonomous Production Cells", *Displays* **17**(3-4), 199–206.

Siegel, J. & Bauer, M. (1997), A Field Usability Evaluation of a Wearable System, *in* L. Bass, D. Siewiorek & A. Pentland (eds.), *Digest of Papers for First International Symposium on Wearable Computers*, IEEE Computer Society Press, pp.18–22.

Smith, B., Bass, L. & Siegel, J. (1995), On Site Maintenance Using a Wearable Computer System, *in* I. Katz, R. Mack, L. Marks, M. B. Rosson & J. Nielsen (eds.), *Proceedings of CHI'95: Human Factors in Computing Systems*, ACM Press, pp.119–20.

Wickens, C. D. (1997), Attentional Issues in Head-up Displays, *in* D. Harris (ed.), *Engineering Psychology and Cognitive Ergonomics*, Vol. I, Avebury, pp.3–21.

On the Problems of Validating DesktopVR

Chris Johnson

Glasgow Interactive Systems Group (GIST), Department of Computing Science, University of Glasgow, Glasgow G12 8QQ, UK.

Tel: *+44 141 330 6053*
Fax: *+44 141 330 4913*
EMail: *johnson@dcs.glasgow.ac.uk*
URL: *http://www.dcs.gla.ac.uk/~johnson/*

For the last twenty years, human–computer interfaces have been dominated by two-dimensional interaction techniques. Things are changing. Techniques that were previously restricted to specialized CAD/CAM tools and immersive VR systems are now being extended to the mass market. The photo-realistic facilities offered by QuicktimeVR and the model based renderings of VRML (Virtual Reality Mark-up Language) provide sophisticated tools for interface design. As a result, three dimensional visualization techniques are being widely exploited in the financial services industry, airports and even off-shore oil production. In January 1997, there were some 2,000 VRML models on the web. By January 1998, this number had grown to over 20,000. Research in human–computer interaction has, however, lagged behind these developments. Few guidelines can be applied to support the design of desktopVR. This paper, therefore, describes three criteria that can be applied to assess the usability of these interfaces. We then go on to validate these criteria against a number of case studies. Unfortunately, it is concluded that standard measures of task performance, successful navigation and subjective satisfaction cannot easily be applied to assess the utility of 3D systems.

Keywords: desktopVR, 3D interfaces, VRML, QuicktimeVR.

Figure 1: VRML Architectural Model of the Hunterian Museum, Glasgow.

1   Introduction

A number of authors have developed a range of effective 3D presentation techniques
(Mackinlay et al., 1991; van Teylingen et al., 1995). Unfortunately, relatively
little work has been done to support the evaluation of these interfaces (Sutcliffe &
Patel, 1993; Duke, 1998). There are some notable exceptions. Tweedie (1995)
has developed techniques that support the validation of 3D visualizations in general.
Others have focused upon the evaluation of immersive 3D systems (Benford et al.,
1993). Unfortunately, these results cannot easily be applied to support the validation
of desktopVR. The findings of immersive evaluations provide few insights into the
usability of more 'conventional' interfaces that rely upon standard input and output
devices. Similarly, general findings about the usability of model-based visualizations
cannot easily be used to inform the development of photo-realistic interfaces, such as
those supported by QuicktimeVR. As Sutcliffe & Patel argue:

"... little is known about the cognitive functioning of these interfaces. Indeed,
there is relatively little data and few criteria for assessing the cost effectiveness and
usability of 3D over 2D interfaces. With a growth in virtual reality, understanding the
usability of 3D representations will be critical for design" (Sutcliffe & Patel, 1996).

1.1   DesktopVR

The last three years have seen the development of a range of tools that enable
interface designers to go beyond the flatlands of a conventional desktop. It is
possible to distinguish at least two radically different approaches. The first has
much in common with traditional 3D modelling techniques. The second offers
photo-realistic presentations of real-world objects.

The Virtual Reality Mark-up Language (VRML) is a platform independent
language for composing 3D models from cones, spheres and cubes. These primitives
are combined to create more complex scenes such as those shown in Figure 1. One
of the reasons for the rapid rise in the popularity of this medium is that it provides

Figure 2: QuicktimeVR model of the Macintosh House, Glasgow.

interface designers with a means of delivering 3D interfaces over the web (Johnson, 1997a). With the advent of VRML 2.0 it is possible to generate and animate scenes that contain links to a wide variety of other information sources including videos, databases and other web pages.

In contrast to VRML, QuicktimeVR enables interface designers to rapidly generating three dimensional resources without the costs of model building. Rather than painstakingly transforming and translating primitive objects, this approach works by shooting a large number of photographs. QuicktimeVR software is then used to 'stitch' the images together so that users can pan or zoom into a 3D scene. The photographs are taken using a motorized tripod and a digital camera so that large buildings and complex objects can be recorded in a relatively short period of time. This offers some advantages over the VRML approach which requires considerable time and skill in order to construct relatively simple worlds. Figure 2 shows an excerpt from a QuicktimeVR tour of the Macintosh House in Glasgow. As with VRML, the visualization facilities supported by QuicktimeVR have recently been extended to support more complex forms of interaction through the introduction of embedded links to other resources.

2 Criteria for the Evaluation of 3D Interfaces

It is difficult to identify criteria that can be applied to evaluate the 'usability' of desktopVR systems. Some requirements such as 'task fit' can be extended from the general literature. Other criteria are less straightforward and relate to the navigation problems of using 'conventional' input devices to traverse three dimensional space. This section, therefore, proposes three requirements that must be satisfied by desktop, virtual reality systems. These criteria are heuristic. However, unless we begin to identify such constraints then designers will continue to lack constructive requirements for the development of future interfaces to desktopVR.

2.1 Task Fit

The images in Figure 2 help people to visualize the layout and contents of the Macintosh House. The three dimensional navigation facilities offered by QuicktimeVR support this visualization process. Users can direct their browsing in a manner that reflects the physical layout of the building itself. It is important

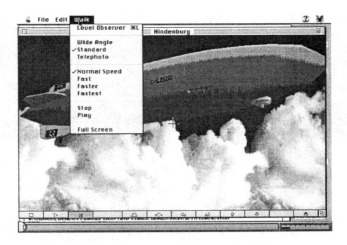

Figure 3: The Virtus VRML Viewer.

to emphasize, however, that the visualization benefits of desktopVR may not be significant for all tasks (Sutcliffe & Patel, 1996). For example, Figure 2 provides little support for users who are trying to find out when Macintosh's Rose Boudoir was first completed. *DesktopVR must, therefore, make a clear contribution to the users' tasks or information needs.*

2.2 Subjective Satisfaction

DesktopVR cannot simply be assessed in terms of the support it offers for particular tasks. Subjective satisfaction and 'enjoyment' are also significant considerations. Commercial motivations for adopting VRML and QuicktimeVR often include their impact upon user motivation. Arguably the best analysis of motivational factors in human computer interfaces comes from Lisa Neal's pioneering study into the implications of game playing. She concluded that:

"Games and other forms of software provide incremental learning situations, in which learning certain rules or elements is necessary for successful use. Learning a game is accomplished through the use of prior knowledge and analogies and through exploration" (Neal, 1990).

There are strong parallels between the use of analogy in computer games and the virtual or photo-realistic worlds of desktopVR. Both games and 3D interfaces rely upon users learning by exploration. A second criteria is that *users should exhibit strong subjective satisfaction ratings in support of the application of desktopVR systems.*

2.3 Navigational Support

A critical difference between new generations of 3D interfaces and more conventional interaction techniques is that many users have little experience with using two dimensional input devices to navigate through three dimensional information spaces.

Figure 4: Excerpts from the Hunterian's Video on Roman Armour.

Figure 3 illustrates this point by providing a screen shot of the Virtus VRML player. Here the user must select perspective constraints, including wide angle and telephoto options. They must also select the speed with which they will travel through a scene. These are not common aspects of 'conventional' user interfaces. *3D interfaces must, therefore, enable their users to quickly traverse and manipulate the scenes and objects that the new technology provides.*

3   The Problems in Applying Criteria

The previous section has identified three criteria against which designers might assess the utility of desktopVR: there must be a clear contribution from the 3D model or visualization to the user's task; users should exhibit strong subjective satisfaction ratings in support of desktopVR and the interface's browsing facilities must enable users to quickly traverse and manipulate scenes and objects. This section goes on to describe the problems that arise when designers attempt to apply these criteria during the evaluation of desktopVR systems.

3.1   *The Problems of Task Fit*

The previous section argued that desktopVR systems must provide a clear contribution to users' tasks. Unfortunately, it can be hard for designers to satisfy such a requirement. Many of these interfaces are characterized both by the diversity of their user population and by the heterogeneous nature of their tasks. For example, the VRML gallery shown in Figure 1 was designed to house a collection of multimedia exhibits for the Hunterian Museum in Glasgow. The prototype was intended to support groups ranging from schoolchildren to curators, from historians and archaeologists to casual browsers, from computing scientists to graphic designers. Each group had their own 'agenda', each had their own set of distinct tasks. In consequence, each had a different sets of requirements against which to measure the success or failure of those tasks.

It can be difficult to evaluate 'task fit' even when designers can identify a characteristic set of user tasks. For instance, Figure 4 presents a movie clip that was used in conjunction with QuicktimeVR object models. The intention was to provide primary school children with an idea of how particular artefacts were used within the daily lives of the Romans in Scotland. In conjunction with teachers and

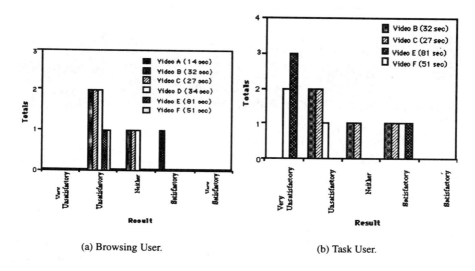

(a) Browsing User.

(b) Task User.

Figure 5: Attitudes to retrieval delays for task-directed users and casual browsers.

museum curators, we identified two different classes of task. The first was directed search where teachers asked their students to find particular items of information. The second was free browsing. We, therefore, conducted an evaluation to determine whether the new media offered different degrees of support for the students' tasks. In particular, we predicted that the rich, three dimensional information in QuicktimeVR and other video resources might hinder active search tasks. In contrast, browsing users would be more attracted to the mass of contextual information that is available from desktopVR. Figure 5 presents the results from two classes of primary level schoolchildren. One group were given a set of comprehension questions to complete. The other group were allowed to browse at will. We felt sure that the task 'directed' group would exhibit more negative attitudes towards the delays associated with finding and accessing the material. However, the children had broadly the same reaction to the interface whether or not they had to answer their teacher's questions (Johnson, 1997b). These findings came as a considerable surprise. They challenged our assumption about the effects of task motivation. They also reflect some of the difficulties that other authors have had in anticipating the results of their evaluations with desktopVR systems (Sutcliffe & Patel, 1996).

Further problems complicate the application of task measures to evaluate the 'usability' of VRML and QuicktimeVR systems. For example, our experience with the 'Romans in Scotland' exhibition questioned the value of traditional comprehension tests. Such performance measures often ignore the longer term learning effects that are a principle motivation for the application of Information Technology in the class room. Simple comprehension tests may also fail to capture the motivational

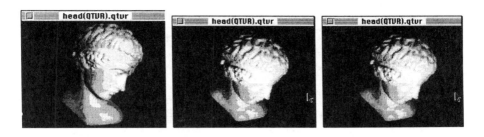

Figure 6: A QuicktimeVR Object Being Rotated Forward to View Upper Surface.

---

effects that are an important, and even necessary, justification for the application of desktopVR. Conventional measures of task performance are inappropriate in contexts where motivation and long-term learning are more important than short-term comprehension scores.

3.2 The Problems of Evaluating Subjective Satisfaction

Subjective satisfaction and 'fun' can be more important for the suppliers and users of desktopVR than task performance. Many of the commercial and industrial contracts that have driven the work described in this paper were originally offered because users abandoned the standard text and pictures of more 'conventional' CAL tools. Again, however, true measures of satisfaction, or performance, can only really be assessed through longitudinal studies (Neal, 1990). The earliest of our VRML and QuicktimeVR systems has only been 'live' for eight months. It continues to be used by a wide range of visitors (see http://www.gla.ac.uk/Museum/MacHouse/) but it is still too early to see whether teachers in schools, colleges and Universities will return to the site in future years.

Figure 6 provides shots from a QuicktimeVR movie of a Greek head from the Hunterian Museum. It was hypothesized that this resource would help to capture the users' attention in a way that would not have been possible using a more static image. In anticipation of the results of longitudinal studies, it is important that designers have some means of validating such intuitions about the subjective appeal of a desktopVR interface.

Visitors to the Hunterian Museum were shown a series of Web pages that contained QuicktimeVR movies such as that shown in Figure 6. They were asked whether or not the three dimensional models actually 'improved' the pages. Figure 7 presents our results. The graph on the right presents the reasons given by those who said that the QuicktimeVR exhibitions did add something to the Museum's web pages. These initial observations again challenged our assumptions. The motivational impetus of keeping attention for longer was less important than providing a greater "feel for the object". If this is true then there are important consequences for the development of future desktopVR systems. Designers must focus more on finding the value added by the introduction of this technology, in this case the 'feel' for the

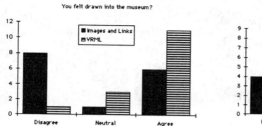
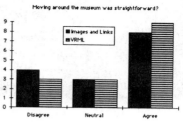

Figure 7: Subjective Evaluations of QuicktimeVR Objects.

sculptor's work, and less upon the superficial attractions of innovative interaction techniques.

3.3   The Problems of Evaluating Navigational Support

DesktopVR systems must *enable users to quickly traverse and manipulate the scenes and objects that the new technology provides*. A number of measures might be used to validate this criteria. For example, users could be timed as they move between specified areas of a VRML model. The same could be done for the scenes in a QuicktimeVR clip. Alternatively, designers might monitor the differences between actual user performance and an optimal set of actions when manipulating three dimensional objects. We have, however, argued that user-directed exploration is a key strength of desktopVR systems. Such activities cannot easily be assessed by measures that force users to follow a pre-determined path.

Rather than focus upon the timings for users traversing through three dimensional scenes, designers can evaluate desktopVR in terms of subjective satisfaction ratings for the navigational facilities offered by a particular interface. For example, we wanted to establish that the VRML interface shown in Figure 1 was easier to navigate than a previous system which used image maps. The existing interface is shown in Figure 8.

Figure 9 presents the results of a comparison. using a broad cross-section of users from the different categories mentioned in Section 3.1. Perhaps the most striking feature is the similarity between the two sets of results. Users reported few difficulties in navigating both the VRML model and the image-mapped interface. Again, this came as a considerable surprise. Many aspects of the VRML browsers are counter-intuitive. Museum visitors had little or no experience of navigating through complex three dimensional spaces using keyboards and mice. More surprising is that many users expressed considerable frustration when navigating our systems even though they stated that the desktopVR systems were 'straightforward' in post hoc questionnaires. This apparent contradiction is illustrated by the following excerpt from a 'think aloud' conducted with the VRML model shown in Figure 1:

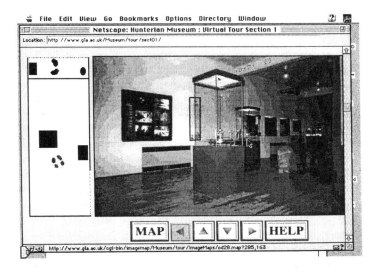

Figure 8: Two Dimensional Navigation Using Pictures and Links.

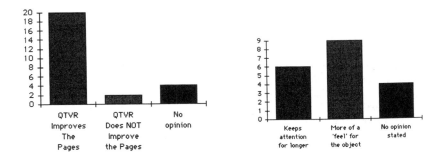

Figure 9: Further Comparisons between Conventional HTML and VRML Access Techniques.

Evaluator: How are you trying to find the exhibit?

User 1:   I'm looking for the exhibit from the picture and trying to move
              towards the area that seems most relevant ... this area bears no
              relation to where I wanted to go ...

One partial explanation for our findings is that people find it difficult to
explain what does and what does not contribute to a successful three dimensional
interface. For example, the following excerpt is taken from a session in which
the user had browsed through both conventional web pages and VRML models:

Evaluator: Do you prefer pictures or the models?

User 2:   The models are great.

Evaluator: Why?

User 2:   Um, ... it just feels different.

Such findings have profound implications for designers. If users cannot explain
exactly what they do or don't like about desktopVR then it will be extremely difficult
to exploit iterative design techniques. User feedback is effectively blocked by the
problems that people face when trying to verbalize their experiences in virtual worlds.
This observation should not be surprising.

"Not only do we perceive in terms of visual information, we can also think in
those terms. Making and looking at pictures helps us to fix these terms. We can also
think in terms of verbal information, as is obvious, and words enable us to fix, classify
and consolidate our ideas. But the difference is that visual thinking is freer and less
stereotyped than verbal thinking: there is no vocabulary of picturing as there is of
saying." (Gibson, 1971)

4   Further Work and Conclusions

Many VRML and QuicktimeVR applications have a strong initial appeal but provide
few long term benefits to their users. This problem is partly due to the gratuitous
application of 3D technology. However, we also believe that some of these problems
stem from the lack of design principles that can be applied to guide the development
of 3D interfaces (Sutcliffe & Patel, 1996). We have, therefore, identified criteria that
might be used to assess the utility of desktopVR:

- There must be a clear contribution from the 3D model or visualization to the
  user's task.

- The interface's browsing facilities must enable users to quickly traverse and
  manipulate the scenes and objects that the new technology provides.

- Users should exhibit strong subjective satisfaction ratings in support of the
  application of desktopVR systems.

Unfortunately, our attempts to apply these criteria during the development
of VRML and QuicktimeVR resources has been less than successful. We found
great difficulty in clearly defining the intended user population for many of
these applications. Our clients often cited the accessibility of desktopVR as a
key motivation for their use of the technology. Similar problems arose when we

attempted to evaluate our users' subjective experience with desktopVR. Many of our findings contradicted our initial hypotheses. This is particularly worrying because many desktopVR systems have not been available long enough for designers to obtain longitudinal data about satisfaction and usage levels for both medium and long term usage. We also found great difficulty in assessing the navigation problems that users experience when using 'conventional' keyboards and mice to traverse three dimensional space. In particular, it is surprising that users report relatively few problems in navigating VRML models and yet exhibit clear frustration during observational studies. People find it extremely difficult to describe the features that contribute to successful and unsuccessful interfaces to desktopVR applications.

Although interface designers have relatively little direct guidance about the development of desktopVR, there is a considerable body of results from the Psychological literature that might be applied in this context (Gordon, 1990). Previous work has considered the perception of movement, pattern recognition in complex scenes, even interaction with objects in three dimensional space. Unfortunately, hardly any of these findings have been applied to support design. This omission must be addressed if we are to improve the usability of QuicktimeVR and VRML interfaces.

Acknowledgements

Thanks go to members of the Glasgow Interactive Systems Group. In particular, I would like to thank James Birrell; Karen Howie; Anthony McGill; James Macphie; Bryan Mathers; Pete Snowden and Mike Waters. I am very grateful to the staff of the Hunterian Museum and Art Gallery, Glasgow for providing technical advice during the development of the VRML and QuicktimeVR resources that are mentioned in this paper. Thanks are due to Steve Draper and Paddy O'Donell of the Psychology Department, University of Glasgow for their advice about psychological theories of perception. Finally, I would like to thank Mary Czerwinski and Kevin Larson of Microsoft Research for pointing out areas in which this work needs to be developed.

References

Benford, S., Bullock, A., Cook, N., Harvey, P., Ingram, R. & Lee, O. (1993), "From Rooms to Cyberspace: Models of Interaction in Large Virtual Computer Spaces", *Interacting with Computers* **5**(2), 217–37.

Duke, D. (1998), "INQUISITIVE Project". EPSRC award 12/97, See http://www.cs.york.ac.uk/~duke/inqu.html.

Gibson, J. (1971), "The Information Available in Pictures", *Leonardo* **4**, 27–35.

Gordon, I. (1990), *Theories of Visual Perception*, John Wiley & Sons.

Johnson, C. (1997a), Electronic Gridlock, Information Saturation and the Unpredictability of Information Retrieval Over the World Wide Web, *in* F. Paterno' & P. Palanque (eds.), *Formal Methods in Human Computer Interaction: Comparisons, Benefits, Open Questions*, Springer-Verlag, pp.261–82.

Johnson, C. (1997b), Ten Golden Rules for Video over the Web, *in* J. Ratner, E. Grosse & C. Forsythe (eds.), *Human Factors for World Wide Web Development*, Lawrence Erlbaum Associates, pp.207–24.

Mackinlay, J., Robertson, G. & Card, S. (1991), The Perspective Wall, *in* S. P. Robertson, G. M. Olson & J. S. Olson (eds.), *Proceedings of CHI'91: Human Factors in Computing Systems (Reaching through Technology)*, ACM Press, pp.173–9.

Neal, L. (1990), The Implications of Computer Games for System Design, *in* D. Diaper, D. Gilmore, G. Cockton & B. Shackel (eds.), *Proceedings of INTERACT'90 — Third IFIP Conference on Human–Computer Interaction*, Elsevier Science, pp.93–9.

Sutcliffe, A. & Patel, U. (1993), The Three Dimensional Graphical User Interface Evaluation for Design Evolution, *in* J. Alty, D. Diaper & S. Guest (eds.), *People and Computers VIII (Proceedings of HCI'93)*, Cambridge University Press, pp.311–34.

Sutcliffe, A. G. & Patel, U. (1996), 3D or not 3D: Is it Nobler in the Mind?, *in* A. Sasse, R. J. Cunningham & R. Winder (eds.), *People and Computers XI (Proceedings of HCI'96)*, Springer-Verlag, pp.79–94.

Tweedie, L. (1995), Interactive Visual Artefacts: How can Abstractions inform Design?, *in* M. A. R. Kirby, A. J. Dix & J. E. Finlay (eds.), *People and Computers X (Proceedings of HCI'95)*, Cambridge University Press, pp.247–65.

van Teylingen, R., Ribarsky, W. & van der Mast, C. (1995), Virtual Data Visualizer, Technical Report 95-16, Georgia Tech.

Author Index

Keyword Index